Other books in the *Astrol*
[call 1.800.7⋮

Volume I -

"What it comes down to is that Bla⋮ different levels—practical, theore information in it ... I have a feeling t treatment of the subject, c⋮
- *Kenneth Irving, American Astrology*

Volume II - Sabian Aspect Orbs

"What the author has uncovered for us is an underlying energy between any two degrees in the Zodiac - no matter what planets may be tenanting them. This precision enables clear distinctions to be drawn between - say - an applying trine of one degree and a separating trine of one degree (or any other combination of aspect and orb). And such precision, which before may have appealed more to the mathematically-minded than the intuitive, is brought out of the abstract realm of measurement and into the colourful realm of meaning by the inclusion of the Sabian Symbols. What a wonderful world this opens up. Pictures to explain technical measurements. Right brain married to left. A remarkable achievement, a fascinating book, and an invaluable reference."
- *Paul F. Newman, The Astrological Journal (UK)*

"Robert has an ingenious mind, with which he examines the Sabian Symbols in a unique context, that of relating every aspect to a degree meaning. With his usual thorough and clear explanation, he examines the difference between waxing and waning aspects together with their applying and separating pattern."
- *Lois M. Rodden, Data News*

Volume III - A Handbook for the Self-Employed Astrologer

"This book is a subtle one. On the surface it is a manual for solid business techniques, innovative ideas and grass roots common sense. It is so well constructed that it could be followed step-by-step by anyone starting out in the profession. A 'no bull' manual for success. Underpinning this is a very emotive personal story, illustrating the subjectivity of this profession, its anxieties, emotional content and lack of guarantees. He shows how there is no separating the person from the business nor the business from the person and does so in a very ingenious way ... Robert explores and advises on many of the opportunities that are available to achieve a decent living. There are some excellent chapters dealing with the logistics of setting up an office, right down to a shopping list of office supplies, bulk-mailing, telephone services, licensing, marketing techniques, setting up a school, writing, publishing, lecturing, breaking into the lecture circuit and associations with other astrologers. He examines the legal aspects of the profession along with tax liabilities etc. Throughout the book the story of his own journey from corporate security to soulful insecurity, his anecdotal successes and failures encourage the reader to learn from his experience, laugh with him and share his moments of despair. For someone yet to take this journey there is a heartening message that success can be achieved as he tells us of his journey with great humility. Robert is totally realistic about the occupational hazards but never once gives the impression he regrets one moment of his decision to become a professional astrologer. His writing style is conversational - reading the book is like having a chat with a well-informed businessman but making a personal connection with a sensitive human being. He makes it clear that one does not have to be coy about earning a decent living and does so by spelling out exactly his own income and expenses. One of my criteria is that a book should have no padding. Every word should count. There is no padding here. Every page has something to offer. There are not many books I call *'Highly Recommended'* but this one is."
- *Linda Reid, FAA Journal (Australia)*

...dedicated with love and respect to:
astrologers helping clients to understand relationship from a spiritual perspective...

cover art from a commissioned original water color painting
by Michelle Glennon   August 2004

Scorpio 5°
A massive rocky shore presents its unchanging face of the
centuries to the furies and coaxing calms of the sea.
[Marc Edmund Jones; Lecture~Lessons; 1931]

Astrology
A Language of Life

Volume IV - Relationship Analysis

Robert P. Blaschke

Edited by Patricia Laferriere

Earthwalk School of Astrology Publishing
Port Townsend, Washington USA

First edition published in 2004 by

Earthwalk School of Astrology
PO Box 1623
Port Townsend WA 98368 USA

1.800.778.8490

www.earthwalkastrology.com

First printing: October 2004 - 1000 copies
Second printing: May 2007 - 1000 copies

Copyright © 2004 Robert P. Blaschke

All rights reserved. No part of this publication may be reproduced or transmitted in any form or by any means, electronic or mechanical, including photocopy, without permission in writing from Earthwalk School of Astrology. Reviewers may quote brief passages, as may scholars writing astrological journal articles.

Library of Congress Control Number: 2004096800

International Standard Book Number (ISBN): 0-9668978-3-8

Printed in the United States of America

in loving memory of my mother
Clarine Marie Blaschke

born 10 September 1922
died 7 September 2004

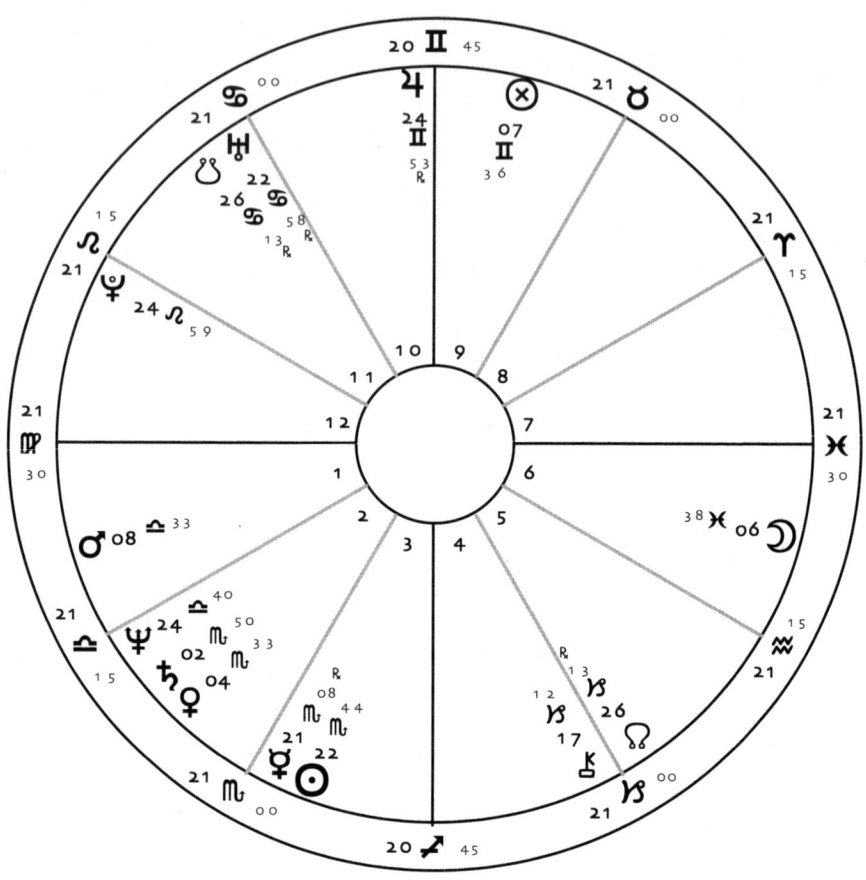

Nativity of the Author

15 November 1953
1:37 AM PST
Santa Monica, California
33N50   118W29
Porphyry Houses
True Node
[from birth certificate]

Table of Contents

Acknowledgments xi

Introduction 1

Chapter One

Astrological Relationship Theory . . . 3
    Tripartite Love: Eros, Philos and Agape   3
    The Fixed Cross and Succedent Houses   4
    The Hemispheres and Quadrants of the Horoscope   7
    The Continuum of Consciousness: Fear Versus Love   9
    The Age Factor and Seven-Year Life Cycles   10
    Exaltations of Venus and Mars   11
    The Arabic Part of Marriage   13

Chapter Two

Preparing for a Relationship Analysis Consultation . 17
    How to Prepare for a Relationship Analysis Consultation   18
    Case Study: Mia Farrow and Woody Allen   20
    Relationship Analysis Preparation Worksheet   23
    Evaluation of the Nativities   28
    Comparison by Element   30
    Balance and Compensation   32
    The House Overlay Technique   33

Chapter Three

Synastry and the Composite Chart . . . 39
    Synastry: Interchart Aspects   39
    Attraction-Endurability-Mental Agreement-Karmic Lessons   46
    The Composite Chart   54

Chapter Four

Davison Charts, Past Lives, Midpoints & Configurations . 61
    The Davison Time-Space Chart   61
    Past Life Connections: The IC, South Node and Vertex   65
    Synastry, Composite and Davison Midpoints   70
    Synastric Aspect Configurations   78

Chapter Five

Additional Interpretive Considerations . . .	**83**
Mutual Reception and Sole Dispositors in Davison Charts	84
The Sun/Moon Midpoint	87
The Effect of Astro*Carto*Graphy® on Relationships	88
Using Draconic, Heliocentric or Sidereal Zodiacs in Synastry	91
Sabian Aspect Orbs in Synastry and Relationship Charts	99
Unaspected Planets in the Composite or Davison Charts	101
Second or Third Marriages and the Derivative House System	104
The Problems with Computerized Relationship Analysis	105
Holographic Links from Synastry to Progressions or Transits	107

Chapter Six

Analyzing Relationships Moving Through Time . .	**111**
Transits and Progressions to the Natal Chart	111
Progressed Composite Charts	116
Progressed Davison Time-Space Relationship Charts	119
Transits to Composite or Davison Charts	123
Transits to Progressed Composite or Davison Charts	125
Synastric Progressions	127
The Condition of the Solar Return Venus	132
Annual Progression of the Solar Return Horizon	138
The Solar Return Sun-Venus Eight Year Cycle	141

Chapter Seven

Electing A Wedding Chart	**145**
Obtaining Date and Time Parameters From Your Clients	145
Elimination of Personal Planets in Fall or Detriment	146
Elimination of Retrograde Personal Planets	147
Finding Sign-Strength for the Moon and Venus	148
Planetary Aspects and the Luminaries' Relationship	149
Using Decanates and Dwadashâmshas in Electional Work	149
The Lunar Degree and Her Applying Aspect to a Benefic	152
Selecting an Ascendant and Fortifying the Ruler on an Angle	153
Fine-Tuning the Ascendant Using Sabian Symbols	153
Linking the Wedding Part of Fortune with the Nativities	157
The Diurnal Moon and Her Connection to the Nativities	157

Chapter Eight

Partners Who Activate Our Shadow . . . 159
    The Shadow Defined in Astrological Terms   160
    Some Examples of Natal Shadow Content   162
    The Shadow in Synastry and Composite Charts   175
    Transit Saturn Aspecting the Secondary Progressed Moon   179
    The Astrology of Anger and Transformational Relationships   182
    The Midpoint Vector of Natal or Composite Squares   189

Chapter Nine

Mirror Degree Synastry 193
    Solstice Points (Antiscia)   194
    Equinox Points (Contrascia)   196
    The Astrological Double Helix and DNA Theory   197
    Existing Theory and Applications of Antiscia and Contrascia   201
    Revealing Invisible Synastry from Behind the Veil   204
    Using Sabian Symbols with Mirror Degree Synastry   206
    Research Statistics   208

Chapter Ten

Social, Cultural and Historical Perspectives . . 209
    The Transits of Uranus, Neptune and Pluto Through Libra   209
    Progressed Venus and Mars in the USA Sibly Chart   211
    Chiron and Homosexuality   215

Chapter Eleven

Epilogue 225
    The Sun-Venus Synodic Cycle   225
    Soul Groups and the Astrology of Families   231
    Friendship   233
    Widowhood, Divorce and Being Single   234
    Preparing One's Heart for Love   236

Appendix I

Sun-Venus Inferior and Superior Conjunctions 1900 to 2020   237

Appendix II

Lecture, Class and Workshop Tapes by the Author . 241

Appendix III

Astrology Software Programs 242

Appendix IV
Computer Chart Services 243

Appendix V
The Sacred Heart of Astrology Correspondence Course . 244

Appendix VI
Contacting The Author 245

Bibliography 246

Footnotes 247

Acknowledgments

I want to give special thanks to my longtime editor, Patty Laferriere, for the superb job she has done in editing this book. As in earlier volumes, she has improved my manuscript with her editorial skills and insight. How fortunate am I to have an editor whose Mercury-Saturn-Neptune conjunction in Libra trines my Jupiter in Gemini on the Midheaven.

I want to sincerely thank my artist, Michelle Glennon of Atlanta, for her beautiful watercolor painting that graces this book's cover. As in my previous books, I gave her the Sabian Symbol for one of my natal planets, and she painted that symbolism with such beautiful colors. With her Neptune in Scorpio 5 (degree of my Venus), which is the Sabian Symbol used for the cover, it is no small coincidence that she attended my lecture at the Metropolitan Atlanta Astrological Society in 2003 and offered her services as an artist for my new book cover.

I also wish to thank Sally Dishong for her work in 2002 on initial research into Mirror Degree synastry, and for helping to compile the statistics found in Chapter Nine. She also created the tables of Antiscion and Contrascion degrees.

To my big brother, Jim, and to my sister-in-law, Ana, I wish to thank you both for your loving strength in holding the family together as mom was dying.

And, to Deborah Bouvier, my constant companion for the last year, thank you for sharing your tree house in the woods with me while I wrote this book. Our paths crossed for a short time, and then parted after my mother passed away and I moved home to care for my father. I will always be grateful for how you held my mother's hand and read to her from the Bible as she lay dying. Whatever merit this book may have, it is largely due to your love and kindness holding me together during a very difficult year. May the angels guide you always, my dear Scorpio sister.

Introduction

This most complex branch of astrology is the greatest professional challenge for a consulting astrologer. Fraught with not only the raw emotions, sensitive feelings, childlike aspirations, and memories of the past pain of one's clients, the astrologer is also drawing upon his own relational successes or failures while navigating the waters of these personal consultations. Attempting to articulate the planetary patterns at work inside any kind of human relationship requires an inner Light.

The intention of this, my fourth volume in the *Astrology: A Language of Life* series is to further assist my fellow astrologers in their relationship analysis work with individuals, couples and families. Astrological relationship theory is included, as are detailed methods for preparing for a relationship consultation. An analysis of relationships moving through time, and how to elect a wedding chart are covered.

Additionally, partners who activate our shadow are examined, as is the astrology of anger and transformational relationships. A rarely used method of relationship analysis—Mirror Degree synastry—involving antiscion and contrascion degrees, is presented in Chapter Nine. Some social, cultural and historical perspectives are offered about changes in the institution of marriage since the 1940s, and the book concludes with an appraisal of the prenatal Sun-Venus synodic cycle.

This has been the most difficult book yet in my planned series of seven volumes to write. As would be anticipated for any fourth book out of seven, which lies at the middle of this series and represents its heart and soul, it has taken me over two years to research and complete. And, as also would have been expected, to write an authentic book about relationships requires an author to have some personal experience with the ups and downs of life. Despite his personal shortcomings in love and marriage, this astrologer has taken the liberty to presume that being born with Venus and Saturn conjunct in Scorpio, and Venus in mutual reception with Mars in Libra, he might qualify for the task. It is my hope that this book makes a small contribution to the existing astrological literature on relationships.

I wrote this book with progressed Mercury and Venus in square to my Mars, and Uranus in stationary conjunction with my natal Moon. Pluto stationed on my IC after a progressed New Moon solar eclipse landed on my Sun/Moon midpoint in late July, and my mother passed away suddenly in September. The new progressed lunation cycle ends a long and winding road for me begun in December 1974.

Robert P. Blaschke
Woodside, California
27 September 2004

Chapter One
Astrological Relationship Theory

When a soul incarnates, it carries with it a pattern of the heavens that existed at the moment of birth. The first breath of a newborn baby sets into motion an astral growth matrix that parallels the physical growth and the accumulation of earthly experience by the soul.

Just as an astrological nativity can be used to understand personality, character, temperament and individual life purpose, birthcharts can be compared to determine compatibility, past life connections, and joint purpose. Additionally, a third chart can be calculated to symbolize the energy and life force of the relationship itself. How can astrology do this?

When two souls are brought together, whether they are husband and wife, parent and child, lifelong friends, fleeting lovers, siblings, or rivals, there is a deeper purpose for the relationship. A chart comparison can reveal the purpose for these relationships at the soul level.

The same patterns that show up in individual charts also exist in compared and combined charts. Astrological techniques of relationship analysis assume that these patterns are just as relevant in relationships as they are in individual lives.

All of us experience difficult endings. Our parents die, we divorce, our children leave home, lovers leave us or we initiate the partings. Endings can be predicted by the astrologer and along with them, a context and meaning for the relationship and why it came undone. In our roles as astrologers, we can provide comfort and reassurance to our clients during times of crisis and pain. Potentials for these are revealed in natal or progressed charts and transits to these charts. The consulting astrologer is often called upon to help clients understand the purpose for their connections to others.

In this chapter, I will discuss how concepts of love and human relationship are woven into the astrological language. Greek philosophy, the fixed cross, succedent houses, and horoscope hemispheres and quadrants will be discussed. The polarity of love and fear, age factors, exaltations of Venus and Mars, and the Arabic Part of Marriage will be explained.

Tripartite Love: Eros, Philos and Agape

The ancient Greeks described three distinct aspects of love: *Eros, Philos,* and *Agape. Eros* is sexual, romantic and erotic love. It involves physical attraction, desire and attachment, and sometimes ownership and possession. This type of love exists for the propagation of the species.

Philos refers to brotherly love. It is the abiding affection of friends that most often outlasts *Eros*, the heated love of sexual passion. In *Philos*, there is little of the attachment found in *Eros*. *Philos* is the feeling of wishing only the best for the other soul.

The third aspect of love is *Agape*—the spiritual love for God and for His heavenly realms. It is the purest of all and devoid of ego. Surrender, sacrifice and devotion are the hallmarks of *Agape*; one of the most poignant ironies in life is that loss, sorrow, physical pain or death precede the final attainment of *Agape*. In esoteric traditions, this love is described as being *washed by the blood of the heart*.

Meditating on this Trinity, consider the possibility of a fourth condition as being necessary to these three manifestations of love. This would be the human body, known esoterically as the temple of the Living God. Described by spiritual teachers of all religions as a rare gift, this body is only granted to the soul after lifetimes in the lower levels of creation. It is animated by the essence of the Creator with an unbroken silver cord connecting it to God.[1]

The divine science of astrology also explains a threefold manifestation. There are the cardinal signs and angular houses of physical action; the fixed signs and succedent houses of the feelings; and the mutable signs and cadent houses of the mental spheres. Which of the three astrological crosses illustrate the tripartite love of *Eros*, *Philos* and *Agape*? The trinity of love can be found in the fixed cross.

The Fixed Cross and Succedent Houses

Astrologers Alan Leo and Charles E.O. Carter wrote about how the life force flows through the three quadruplicities sequentially. After movement is initiated in the cardinal signs of Aries, Cancer, Libra or Capricorn, it becomes concentrated and transitions into non-movement in the fixed signs of Taurus, Leo, Scorpio or Aquarius. The fixed signs generate power. The common or mutable signs of Gemini, Virgo, Sagittarius and Pisces alternate between movement and non-movement. This threefold manifestation of energy is likened to linear, circular and vibratory motion. It is also characterized as the centrifugal, centripetal and helical forces.

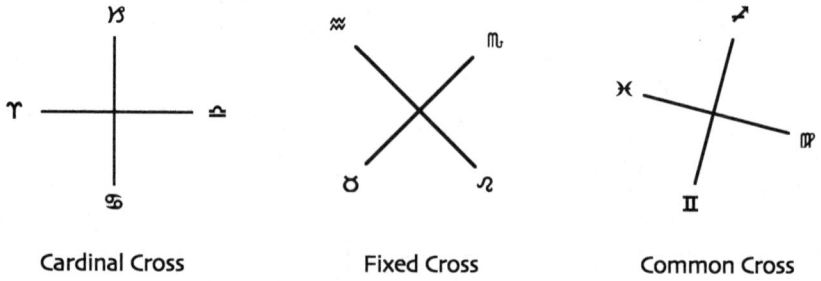

Cardinal Cross   Fixed Cross   Common Cross

Where is love found in the horoscope? Much has been written about the 7th house of marriage, its association with Libra, the sign of marriage, and the Descendant. Yet, this is just the outer shell of relationship because Saturn, exalted ruler of Libra and the 7th house, has domain over form and structure.

If love is hidden in the chart, where might it be found?

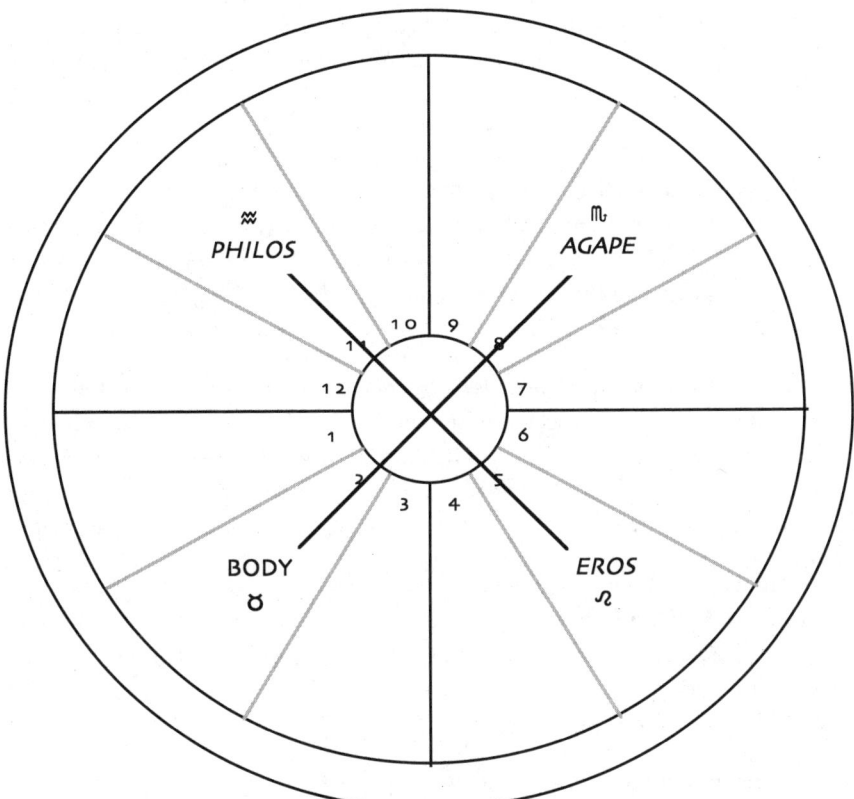

This illustration shows the natural association of the fixed cross with succedent houses. Our physical body, *the temple of the Living God*, stands at the base of the cross which contains the three forms of love, and is symbolized by Taurus and the 2nd house. *Eros*, sexual love, is found in the 5th house of physical love-making, and is associated with the sign of romance and children, Leo.

Non-sexual love, *Philos*, is found opposite *Eros* in the 11th house of friendship, and is affiliated with the sign of brotherly love, Aquarius. Lastly, opposing the body temple is *Agape*, the spiritual temple, found in the 8th house of loss, which is analogous with Scorpio. The 8th house is often referred to as the house of ego-death, the dark night of the soul, and of the mystic adept. From this diagram showing the fixed cross placed within the succedent houses, one clearly sees how love, in each of its threefold expressions, is experienced by human consciousness.

To understand how a client experiences love in general, look to the quadruplicity found on the cusps of the succedent houses. Cardinal signs often denote an active relational life, where the soul is continually initiating connection with others. Even after painful heartbreaks and losses, these souls will again and again create new relationships in their lives.

Fixed signs on the cusps of the 2nd, 5th, 8th and 11th houses commonly produce the fortunate souls who remain steadfastly married for over thirty years to the same spouse. With the fixed signs here, the reverse is also sometimes true, people remain celibate for years and years, choosing not to be in sexual relationship.

Mutable signs found on the succedent houses often are souls mentally preoccupied with the concept of partnership, but not necessarily always ready to enter into a committed sexual relationship, such as marriage. Just as often, more than one lover at a time is found, resulting in substantial juggling acts being necessary within their minds as they attempt to keep each of the different relational facts separate.

How do interceptions affect this cross? Where there is not an even distribution of the quadruplicities on the wheel, I recommend using the Equal House system. The mode that follows the Ascendant will then be found on the cusps of houses 2-5-8-11. Cardinal signs rising would have fixed signs on the succedent houses, the fixed signs rising would have mutable, and mutable signs rising would have cardinal.

To determine how a client experiences a specific form of love, look to the ruler of the particular succedent house in question. For example, the ruler of the 5th house of *Eros* in trine with the ruler of the 11th house of *Philos* suggests that former lovers will remain friends. A square involving malefics between the two rulers suggests that love affairs end harshly.

When clients have gone through personal loss, such as a divorce or the death of a spouse, the astrologer finds himself in the position of discussing the spiritual side of love during the consultation. It has been common in my practice to talk about the contact from the Spirit plane that clients have had with their departed loved ones.

The deepest dimension of love is *Agape*, which cannot be terminated, not even by death. When love for the departed human form has been released to God's care, and that love still remains active in the heart, look to the 8th house ruler.

The ruling planet of the 8th house (using Mars as the ruler of Scorpio, Jupiter as the ruler of Pisces, or Saturn as the ruler of Aquarius) holds the key to the innermost love of a soul, its *Agape*. It literally symbolizes the Light at the end of the tunnel of loss or death. If this planet falls, for example, at the midpoint of a square to Pluto, the client will find *Agape* through painful endings in his own life.

But if this ruling planet of the 8th is in favorable aspect with the ruler of the 11th house of *Philos*, then the client will find *Agape* love through the losses occurring in the lives of those around him, such as friends or colleagues.

These interconnections between the rulers of the succedent houses, along with the quadruplicity found on the cusps of these houses show how people experience the different kinds of love *(Eros, Philos, Agape)*.

The Hemispheres and Quadrants of the Horoscope

Another theoretical dimension of relationship analysis is in the hemispheric preponderance or deficiency of planets. Houses that lie to the right of the vertical meridian (4 through 9) symbolize awareness of others. Conversely, houses 10 through 12 and 1 through 3, left of the meridian, symbolize an awareness of self.

Houses below the horizon, 1 through 6, signify one's inner and private life. Houses above the horizon, 7 to 12, represent the outer and public life of an individual. Combining the left or right halves of the wheel with the upper or lower halves produces the four astrological quadrants.

The first quadrant, made up of houses 1 through 3, symbolizes an awareness of self and is the least relationally oriented. A certain amount of self-centeredness is found in individuals whose nativities contain five or more planets in these houses. Outstanding athletes, especially those not in team sports, gifted artists and talented writers are often found with a first quadrant emphasis. When no planets are placed in houses 1 to 3, self-motivation is rarely found. A strong case may be made for the Sun, exalted in Aries, as ruler of the first quadrant.

The second quadrant, consisting of houses 4 through 6, represents an inner awareness of others that is much more acclimated to relationship than its northern counterpart. Individuals with a preponderance of planets here have lives centered around the home or family, such as housewives or those employed as domestics working with children or cleaning other's homes. Think of Jupiter having domain over this quadrant since its exaltation in Cancer speaks of a concern for other's well-being.

Teachers, coaches or social workers specializing in child welfare are often found having five or more planets in the second quadrant, and especially when the Midheaven ruler is in houses 4, 5 or 6. Physicians, nurses, massage therapists and other health care providers who cater to the physical needs of others in their work commonly have several planets in houses 4 through 6. The relationship orientation of this quadrant is more of an impersonal nature with service, care and love given to others as an expression of one's spiritual values. Nativities found without planets in houses 4 to 6 indicate a lack of sensitivity to others.

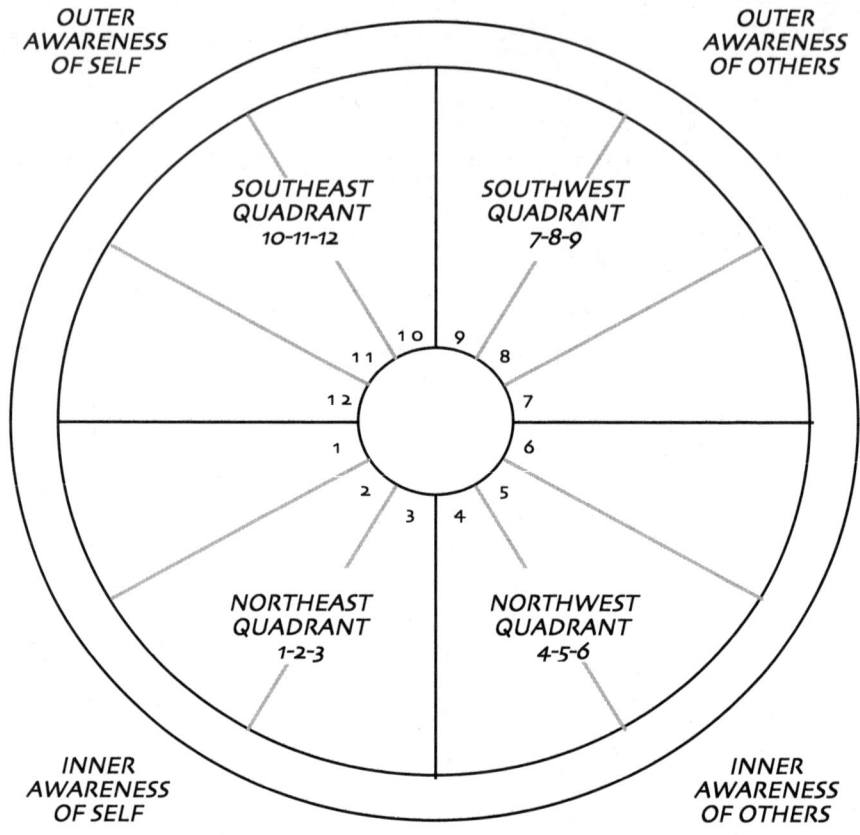

The third quadrant, comprised of houses 7 through 9, symbolizes an outer awareness of others and is the most relationally oriented of the four. A preponderance of planets in this quadrant results in souls who work very closely with others in a highly personalized way. Attorneys, psychotherapists, pastors, accountants, college professors and other professionals involved in working one-on-one with people often have five or more planets in these houses. Saturn, exalted ruler of Libra, governs this quadrant. I have observed that souls with a preponderance of planets here often have lives that are adversely affected by the spouse. An absence of planets in this quadrant is strikingly similar to a nativity devoid of oppositions and usually produces a person who prefers to work alone.

Lastly, the fourth quadrant, houses 10 through 12, represents an outer awareness of self. With five or more planets here, an individual is chiefly concerned with finding his identity through groups. You find these people working in the corporate world or in non-profit agencies. They are involved in professional associations, social activities with colleagues, spiritual communities, and dream or meditation groups. For these people, group activities serve to create relationships within social structures and to build confidence. Mars, exalted in Capricorn, is the ruler of this quadrant, and illustrates how the individual rises in social stature through his self-disciplined accomplishments. Souls without planets in these houses often struggle to find fulfilling work in life.

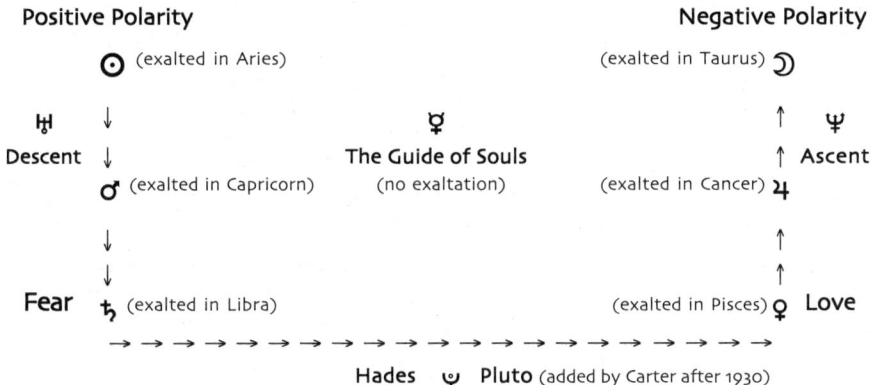

The Zodiac and the Soul by Charles E.O. Carter; L. N. Fowler & Co., Ltd.; London; 1928

A spiritual model of the solar system was put forward 75 years ago by the eminent British astrologer, C.E.O. Carter. Using the exaltations of the planets handed down to modern astrologers by the ancient Chaldeans, Carter postulated an elegant metaphysical theory for the descent of Spirit into matter and the heavenly ascent of matter back into Spirit. The above diagram details this spiritual journey.

Starting with the Sun, the quintessential masculine force, symbolizing separation of the soul from the Father into egoism and the Sun's path into physical creation, the first descent is to the lesser malefic, Mars, ruler of the Sun's exaltation, Aries. As the soul further descends, it arrives at the greater malefic, Saturn, ruler of Mars' exaltation, Capricorn. Uranus, in this model, is the Oversoul of the Descent.

The soul is overwhelmed by fear, utterly lost, a stranger in a strange land. An earthly ordeal then ensues—the long journey of lifetimes to travel from fear to love. Ever present are the hot coals of Hades symbolized by the lord of the underworld, Pluto, which lies in wait for a soul who fails his earthly test to love and forgive.

Peering across this chasm, the soul finds the lesser benefic, Venus, ruler of Saturn's exaltation, Libra. This part of the journey is a *continuum of consciousness*, through which all souls must pass to reach the home of the Divine Mother. A few fortunates will arrive at the spiritual understanding that only love can heal fear.

When a soul embraces love, it is transported upward to the greater benefic,

Jupiter, ruler of Venus' exaltation, Pisces. Upon receiving the spiritual blessing of wisdom, a soul further ascends into the bosom of the Divine Mother, the Moon, ruler of the exaltation of Jupiter, Cancer. Neptune is the Oversoul of the Ascent.

According to the Chaldeans, Mercury was the only planet with no exaltation. In this metaphysical model of the solar system, Mercury is seen as the Guide of Souls. This most misunderstood spiritual planet, the Winged Messenger, travels with the soul both on its journey downward into physical creation and with its ascent heavenward. It is no small coincidence that Mercury is nearest to the Sun.

The Age Factor and Seven-Year Life Cycles

Astrological relationship analysis is more beneficial to clients when it is presented within the context of the age at which each person entered into the union. For example, a relationship between a man who was 43, and a woman who was 37 when they married is experienced by both individuals differently as they each progress through subsequent life cycles.

The most comprehensive analysis of this age factor, consisting of the generic seven-year life cycles that we all pass through, was written by the Swiss astrologer and osteopath, Alexander Ruperti (1913-1998), in *Cycles of Becoming*. As a young man, Dr. Ruperti studied with C.E.O. Carter in London during the 1930s at the Astrological Lodge. He first read Dane Rudhyar in 1936 when *The Astrology of Personality* was published. Ruperti was the first astrologer in Europe who actively promoted the pioneering work of Rudhyar.

Rudhyar had formulated a humanistic approach to astrology which acknowledges that human consciousness grows in definable seven-year cycles and that these life periods can be measured by the astrological cycles of Jupiter, Saturn, Uranus, the secondary progressed Moon, and the lunar nodes. Unfortunately, Rudhyar not only had a loquacious Sagittarius Ascendant, with its ruler in diffuse Gemini, but also a natal Mercury in detriment in Pisces, and was not capable in his rambling books of concisely summarizing his theoretical models of humanistic astrology.

However, Dr. Ruperti, born with a North Node in Aries conjunct Rudhyar's Sun, became the student who better articulated his mentor through his own writing. Ruperti's Sun-Saturn conjunction in Gemini, synastrically conjoined with Rudhyar's Mars-Neptune-Pluto triple conjunction, and in square to Rudhyar's Mercury, along with a Pluto in late Gemini conjunct Rudhyar's Jupiter, allowed Ruperti to go further with Rudhyar's work.

How can today's astrologers use and apply analyses of the seven-year life cycles in relationship analysis work? Alas, *Cycles of Becoming* has gone out of print. Rather than allowing these ideas to die, they deserve our attention.

The gist of the age factor model is that a 70-year life cycle can be divided into 10 seven-year subcycles. A waxing growth arc passes through five levels of development between birth and age 35, and a waning arc ensues from age 35 to age 70. The five levels—organic, power, psychological, social and individual—have seven-year counterparts in the opposite half of the cycle.

This model equates birth to age 7 with age 63-70; age 7-14 with age 56-63; age 14-21 with age 49-56; age 21-28 with age 42-49; and age 28-35 with age 35-42. The universal life process (physical, emotional, psychological, social and individual) during an ascending arc of growth from birth to age 35, while the soul is extrovertedly meeting life, has an introverted counterpart during the descending arc of growth from age 35 until age 70, where the soul revisits the corresponding previous era of life, synthesizing its meaning.

What does the age factor have to do with relationship analysis? It gives a context in which to frame the developmental issues that will confront couples. Whether the individuals are close in age and cycling through similar periods or several years apart and in different cycles, an astrologer can give perspective on various developmental processes that they will experience throughout the relationship.

Within these seven-year cycles, Rudhyar and Ruperti detailed patterns of growth found in each of the individual years. They used a waxing and waning hemicycle, with a critical turning point at 3 1/2 years into the cycle. Spiritual levels were assigned to years 1 and 7; mental levels to years 2 and 6; physical levels to years 3 and 5. The 4th year stood alone as the linchpin.

Exaltations of Venus and Mars

This opening chapter has been chiefly concerned with different theoretical models in astrology that place human relationship in context with all of life's varied experiences. This has been done through an examination of the Zodiac where we saw the fixed cross having relevance to the threefold love of the Greeks; through an understanding of the succedent houses and their meaning as the central realities in life; by a study of the horoscopic hemispheres and quadrants; and through the solar system model of the planetary exaltations expounded by C.E.O. Carter. But, what about Venus and Mars specifically, the two planets most identified with love?

Bounding the earth on either side, with Venus inside Earth's orbit and Mars beyond it, these two planets symbolize the duality of inner feminine and outer masculine forces. The Sun and Moon, exalted in signs that are ruled by Mars and Venus, metaphysically symbolize the origins of life itself. The Sun is the Heavenly Father, while the Moon is Mother Nature. Venus and Mars, however, are exalted in Pisces and Capricorn respectively, the dignities of Jupiter and Saturn, and suggest that love is an intricate part of the design that binds societies and cultures.

How can an astrologer perceive the meaning of love through these exaltations of Venus and Mars? Capricorn, the exaltation of Mars, is the culminating sign of the Zodiac and esoterically is the gate through which a soul must pass to be judged for its earthly deeds. Pisces, the exaltation of Venus, is the final sign of the Zodiac, ruling earthly contact with the Spirit world through universal love and devotion. Is there a pattern in the Zodiac illuminating the esoteric role of Venus and Mars?

Consider the aspect configuration known as the *Yod*. This Y-shaped figure, called by spiritual astrologers *The Finger of God* or *The Celestial Pointer*, is comprised of an isosceles triangle with a 60° sextile as its base and two equal legs made up of 150° inconjuncts as its sides. A contemplative astrologer may wonder, just what is God pointing at? If He were pointing at Himself and beckoning the earthly soul to remember his Divine Origins, it would be reasonable to presume that this configuration would then be pointing at the Sun.

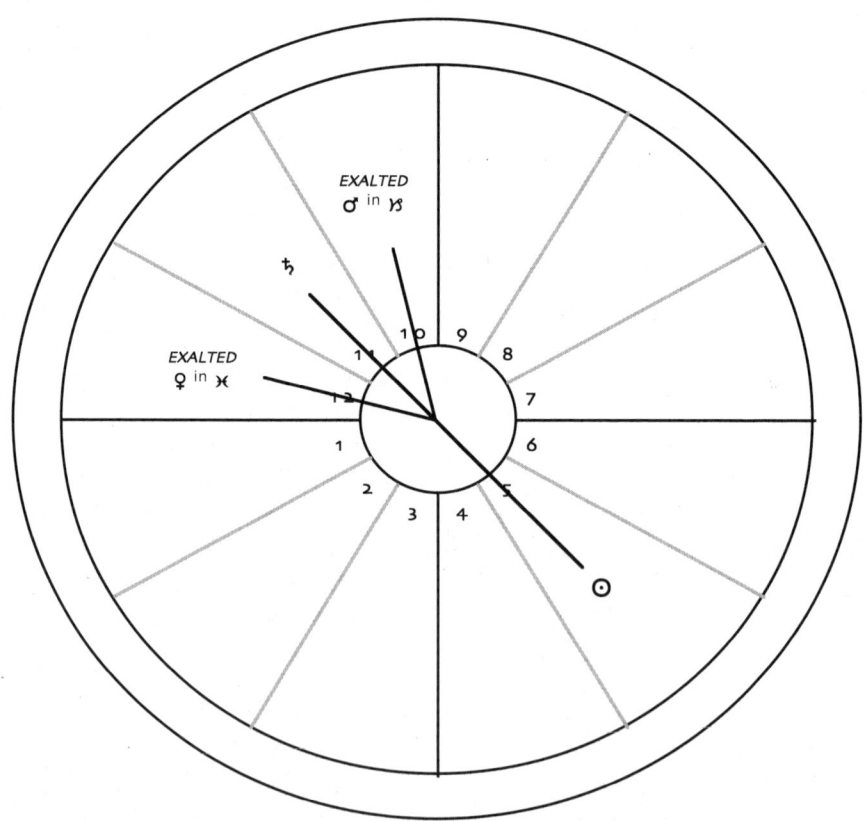

Converting this theoretical metaphor from the Zodiac to the horoscopic wheel creates a configuration that is pointing at the 5th house, which has the Sun as its natural significator. A most special type of the *Finger of God* is called a *Tetradic Yod*, wherein a fourth planet is located at the near midpoint of the sextile, and which opposes the apex planet. A compelling case can be made then for this planet to be Saturn, the natural significator of Aquarius and the 11th house.

Contemplating this esoteric design, behold opposing forces of Light and Darkness, symbolized by the Sun and Saturn. At the base of the isosceles triangle are Venus and Mars in their exaltations of Pisces and Capricorn, with the spiritual implication that Universal Love (Venus in Pisces) and Individual Character (Mars in Capricorn) are containing and overcoming Darkness, and pointing to the Light of God's radiance. An uplifting homily, indeed.

The Arabic Part of Marriage

One question that consulting astrologers are often asked is, *"When will I get married?"* This is a significantly different inquiry than *"what are the chances for relationship this year,"* as it indicates that the client has already set the intention for marriage. Can astrologers answer this query with any certainty?

There is a sensitive degree in each nativity that is known as the *Part of Marriage*. This degree is found by adding the Ascendant to the Descendant, and from this sum subtracting the natal position of Venus. This formula, as well as dozens of other Parts, or 'lots,' have been handed down to modern day practitioners by the Arabic master astrologer, Al-Biruni, from the 11th century. Theoretically, the Part of Marriage degree would have to be activated for a wedding to occur. Is this always the case and is this degree also relevant to subsequent marriages?

This author has had ample experience to test this theory as he has married six times between 1973 and 2002, with the 3rd and 4th marriages being to the same woman. It would be pertinent here to state that he is not aiming for a page in the Guinness Book of World Records nor trying to overtake Larry King or Zsa Zsa Gabor, both of whom have been married nine times (so far). Rather, he perhaps has been paying off a massive load of karma, being as he was born with Venus conjunct Saturn in Scorpio. However, back to the point, it has only been on the day of his first wedding that his Part of Marriage was activated. Let us now review these calculations together, using the nativity of your author.[2]

The Part of Marriage formula, again, is ASC + DSC - Venus. One must convert any degree of the Zodiac into a number value from 1 to 360. The following table shows the numerical value of each of the twelve signs, starting at their beginning degree.

The Ascendant at 21° Virgo 30', converts to 150° + 21° 30 = 171° 30. To this add the Descendant, 21° Pisces 30', which converts to 330° + 21° 30' = 351° 30'. The sum of the two is 523° 00'. From this subtract the degree of natal Venus, 04° Scorpio 33', converted to 210° + 04° 33' = 214° 33'; 523° 00' less this amount equals 308° 27'. It becomes 08° Aquarius 27', the author's Part of Marriage.[3]

Aries = 0
Taurus = 30
Gemini = 60
Cancer = 90
Leo = 120
Virgo = 150
Libra = 180
Scorpio = 210
Sagittarius = 240
Capricorn = 270
Aquarius = 300
Pisces = 330

On the day of his first wedding, 1 December 1973, Jupiter, significator of his 7th house of marriage, was transiting the 9th degree of Aquarius, arriving at precise conjunction with the Part of Marriage as wedding vows were being exchanged!

First Wedding

Dec 1 1973   2:53:00 PM PST
San Ramon   California
37N36   121W59
Dec 1 1973   22:53:00 GMT
Tropical Porphyry True Node

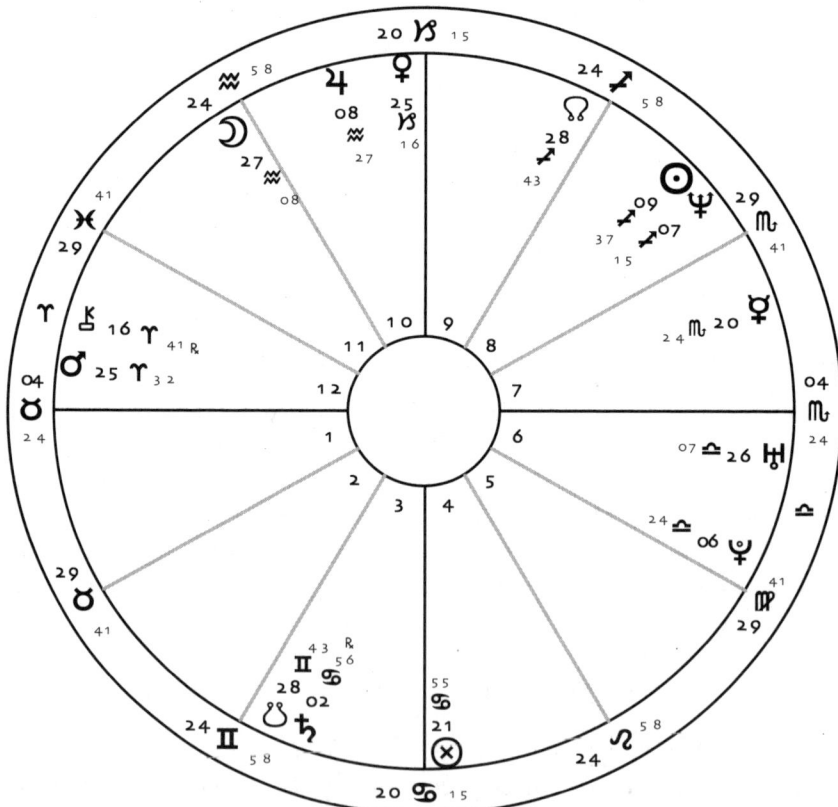

Note that the 5th degree of Scorpio was setting, the same degree as the natal Venus of the author. It should also be pointed out that this dreadful chart was not elected, as the author was barely 20 years old, and had been studying astrology for just two years at the time. Needless to say, with a Cardinal T-Cross absolutely eviscerating that elevated Venus, anchored by the Mars-Uranus opposition, this writer spent over a year dodging frying pans, even as the passion was wonderful! With the rising degree having the Sabian Symbol of the widow kneeling at an open grave, in hindsight it is probably best that the marriage was so short lived.

It is clear from this example that the Part of Marriage was indeed activated during the first marriage of your author, yet another question remains: *Is the degree of the Part of Marriage involved in any way with subsequent marriages?* It has been my experience that it is not. I have calculated the secondary progressed angles for the dates of subsequent marriages, adding the progressed ASC and DSC together, and from this sum subtracting the degree of the progressed Venus. In each case, this *progressed Part of Marriage* was not involved in any planetary activity.

Neither were there any progressions nor transits *in the degree of the natal Part of Marriage* at the time of subsequent marriages. I even went so far as to employ the derivative house system, wherein the 9th house rules second marriages, the 11th house rules 3rd marriages, and so on. In these cases, I added the ASC to cusp 9 or to cusp 11, and from these sums subtracted natal Venus. But, again, these degrees were not present in the progressions or transits.

It may be of interest to readers to explain how the 9th house was designated as the house of second marriages. In the *secondary house influence* technique, also known as the *derivative house system*, each house is related to every other. When one first marries, it falls under the domain of the 7th house. Divorcing, one must go to court, a 9th house matter. The 9th house from the 7th is therefore the 3rd house. Now divorced, and standing in this 3rd house, for an individual to marry for a second time, he must then find the 7th house from the 3rd—voilà, this is the 9th house.

The experienced astrologer may ask at this point if the Part of Marriage could be used for rectification. The nativity of Charles, Prince of Wales, as shown in the Clifford Data Compendium, was 14 November 1948 in Buckingham Palace at 9:14 PM GMT. On 29 July 1981 at 11:17:30 AM GMD in St Paul's Cathedral, London, as Charles and Diana were married, transit Uranus, co-significator of Charles' Aquarius Descendant, was at 26° Scorpio 04' in the Zodiac. By rectifying the Prince of Wales' birth time to 9:19:18 PM, a difference of just over five minutes, his Part of Marriage now becomes 26° Scorpio 04', and would have had Uranus, co-ruler of his 7th, precisely conjoined it as he exchanged vows with Princess Diana.[4]

In summary, an astrologer could predict with certainty a marriage for *a never-married person* using a Part of Marriage degree. If this degree was to be conjoined by the transit of the ruler of the 7th, or if the 7th ruler were to progress to a conjunction with this degree, an astrologer could predict this with confidence. If the client was divorced, however, and inquiring about the possibility of another marriage, then the ruler of the 9th house of second marriages, or the ruler of the 11th house of third marriages would be scrutinized to see if it were to receive a favorable progression or transit in the near future. In my own case, absurdly, I would be back to the 7th house ruler if I were to ever marry again!

Chapter Two
Preparing for a Relationship Analysis Consultation

Astrologers use numerous techniques to compare and contrast horoscopes for evidence of compatibility or antagonism. Chief among these are the *house overlays, synastry aspects* and the *composite chart*. In this chapter, I will review these and several other methods that I have used in my practice and taught in my school. Relationship astrology is the most demanding and time-consuming as preparation for this type of consultation, if done well, is extensive and highly detailed.

Between 1975 and 1979, just after the Uranus ingress into Scorpio, some excellent astrology books were published on this subject such as *Planets in Composite* (Robert Hand; 1975), *The Astrology of Human Relationships* (Frances Sakoian & Louis S. Acker; 1976), and *Relationships & Life Cycles* (Stephen Arroyo; 1979). Along with *How To Handle Your Human Relations* (Lois Haines Sargent; 1958) and the massive *Astrology, The Divine Science* (Marcia Moore & Mark Douglas; 1971), these five books were my original resources as I honed my relationship astrology skills.

A few years later in 1984, *Karmic Relationships*, by Martin Schulman appeared. It contains highly regarded synastry aspect delineations from a spiritual point of view. Then in 1989, *Skymates*, written by Jodie and Steven Forrest, became a beloved reference book for astrologers. It is not my intention to write about synastry or composite chart aspects in this volume, as so many of these fine texts are still in print. Rather, I will compile a summary of most of the methods and techniques currently in use, in addition to introducing some novel interpretive material.

The most challenging task when preparing for relationship analysis consultations is how to manage all of the details. Rather than scrutinizing a single nativity as is the case for a natal interpretation, relationship astrology involves looking at two birthcharts, all of the aspects occurring between two sets of planets, and a third chart that symbolizes the relationship itself. When I am preparing for these appointments, my desk is blanketed with many different charts. I take countless notes.

Using the best methods from the above-mentioned books, I have devised a form to help streamline the preparation process. This worksheet has made my work as an astrologer much more efficient.[5]

How to Prepare for a Relationship Analysis Consultation

Most professional astrologers have a system for preparing for a relationship analysis appointment. The following areas of pre-consultation research are necessary for assessing any personal relationship:

1. evaluation of the nativities
2. comparison by element
3. balance and compensation
4. house overlays
5. synastry aspects
6. composite chart
7. Davison time-space chart
8. past life connections
9. synastry & composite midpoints
10. synastric aspect configurations

Throughout the next three chapters, I will refer to the natal charts of Mia Farrow and Woody Allen. Each of the sections in these three chapters will examine the interpretive techniques listed above using their nativities:

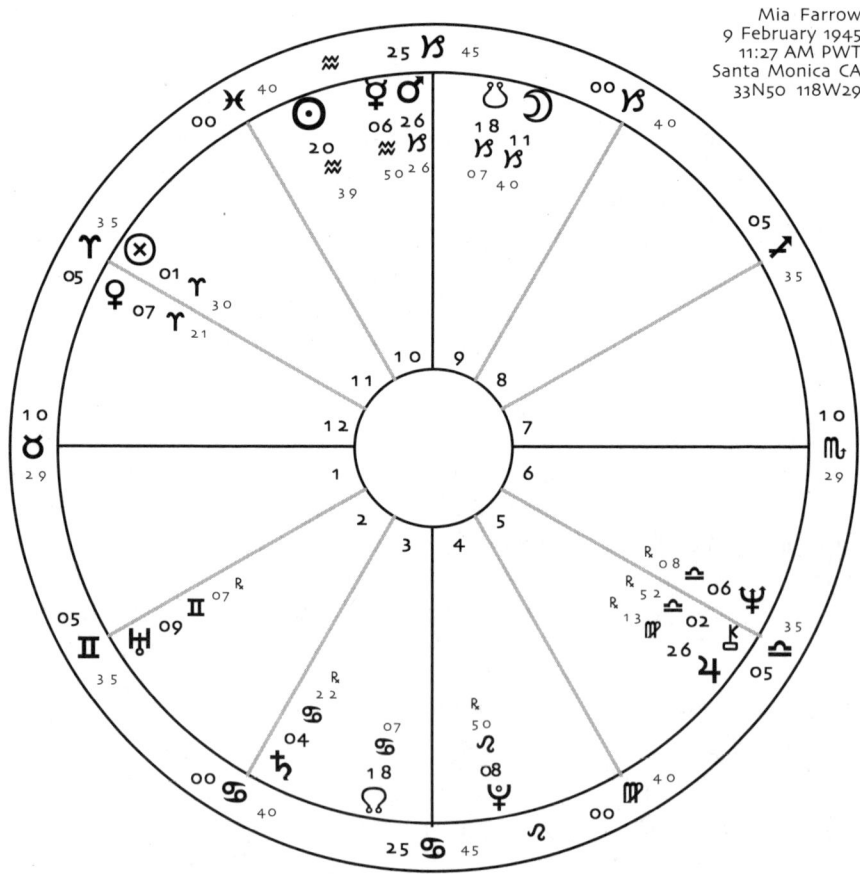

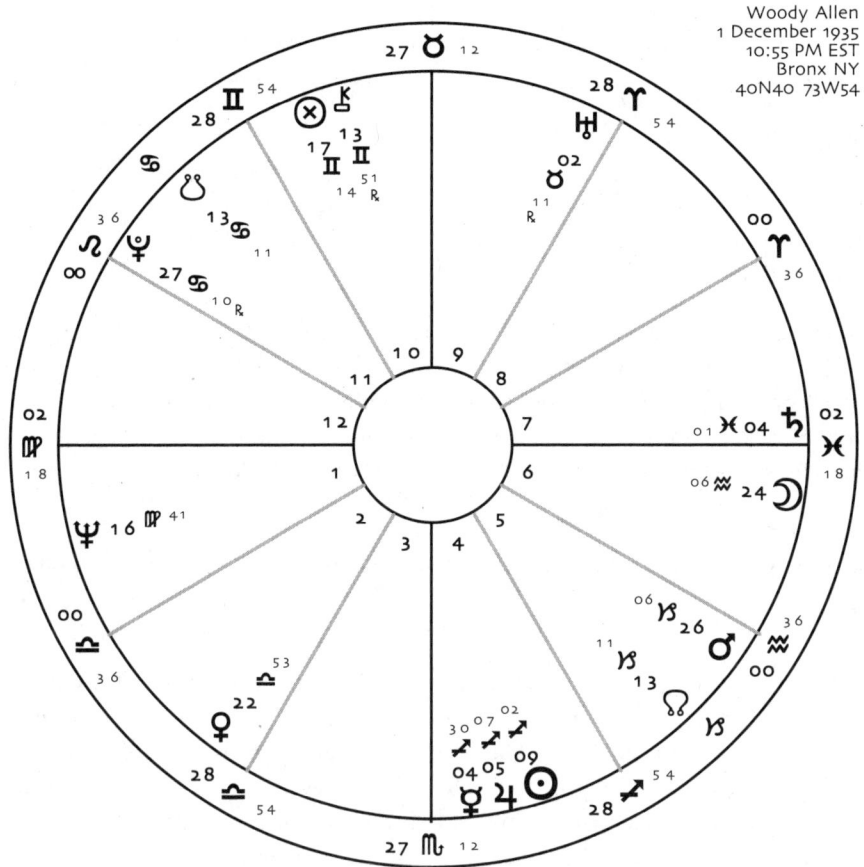

When preparing for a relationship consultation, the astrologer needs to calculate the following charts and tables:

1. natal chart for person A
2. natal chart for person B
3. composite chart
4. synastry table of interchart aspects between person A and person B
5. bi-wheel chart with person B's planets placed in person A's houses
6. bi-wheel chart with person A's planets placed in person B's houses
7. 360° midpoint sort for person A
8. 360° midpoint sort for person B
9. Davison time-space chart

As you can imagine, nine charts will completely cover your desk so it is imperative to organize a system that allows you to quickly extract only the most pertinent and relevant details. Early in their careers, most professional astrologers spend hours upon hours preparing for their clients only to find that during the sixty or ninety minute consultation, they refer to just 20% of the prepared notes. It is only through experience that each astrologer learns which of the prep work to continue and which to eliminate.

Case Study: Mia Farrow and Woody Allen

I presume that most of my readers are very familiar with the lives of Mia Farrow and Woody Allen. Each has been well known to the public since the early 1960s and an exact birthtime is available for each of them from their birth certificates. It has been a number of years since the break-up between these two, whose relationship as a famous couple spanned all of the 1980s. They made a total of thirteen films together.

I have chosen them as our case study because their natal charts, synastry and composite chart make for textbook astrological education. I have taught for many years on relationship analysis technique, both in classes at my school and at workshops for local astrology groups around the country. I have used these nativities as examples for many of these classes and workshops.

So that my readers may familiarize themselves with the details of their lives, I am including some biographical information about them from two Internet web sites.

About Mia Farrow [6]

Mia Farrow was born Maria de Lourdes Villiers Farrow on 9 February 1945 in Los Angeles, California. She was the daughter of hard-living director John Farrow and the actress Maureen O'Sullivan, best known as *Jane* in the *Tarzan* films of the 1930s. Despite his reputation as one of the most notorious womanizers in Hollywood, John Farrow was a devout Catholic and the author of several critically acclaimed books on the Church.

Farrow's childhood was interrupted by a bout with polio, from which she fully recovered. Her father died when she was a teenager and she suddenly felt financially responsible for her large family. Her money problems were solved when she landed the role of heroine *Alison MacKenzie* on the prime-time soap opera *Peyton Place,* co-starring Ryan O'Neal. She moved on to film, and was cast by director Roman Polanski in *Rosemary's Baby*, a horror film about a woman who gives birth to the child of Satan.

In the mid-1960s, Farrow met Frank Sinatra who was thirty years her senior. Despite their age difference, they married in 1966 causing a scandal and becoming the butt of many jokes. Problems soon arose when Sinatra wanted Farrow to give up her career and devote her life to travelling with him. Farrow also had difficulty relating to his middle-aged, Las Vegas entourage. Like many people her age, she preferred marijuana to martinis. The marriage was over in a few years.

She met and fell in love with conductor Andre Previn while he was still married to his wife, Dory. Dory resisted divorce and Farrow gave birth to several of Previn's children before they were finally able to wed. They also adopted several children, most fatefully, a Korean orphan named Soon-Yi. The honeymoon didn't last long. Farrow was bored living at Previn's country estate in England and suspected him of infidelity when he traveled, which was almost constantly. They parted amicably in the late Seventies.

In 1982, Woody Allen cast Farrow in a film, *A Midsummer's Night Sex Comedy*. The two fell in love and began a very successful creative partnership. Allen tailored roles to fit Farrow's ethereal beauty and quirky personality. She starred in *The Purple Rose of Cairo*, a film many critics consider to be his masterpiece. Others, such as *Hannah and Her Sisters* and *Crimes and Misdemeanors* were box office hits.

However, there were always problems in the Allen-Farrow relationship. Farrow felt that Allen exploited her family for material, a charge that seems undeniable in the case of *Hannah and Her Sisters*. Allen cast Farrow's mother in the film, shot it in Farrow's apartment, and even used her children to play Hannah's children. The movie got raves from both critics and audiences, but the portrait was not flattering. O'Sullivan was caricatured as a washed-up show-biz floozy, and Mia was portrayed as an overbearing martyr.

In 1992, the situation exploded when Farrow found nude photographs of her twenty year-old daughter, Soon-Yi, in Allen's apartment. She sent Soon-Yi off to school, but, amazingly, continued to work with Allen on their latest film, *Husbands and Wives*. Her hopes of a reconciliation were shattered when she found out that Allen and Soon-Yi were still in communication and planning a future together. In the huge scandal and legal battle that followed, Allen lost custody of two adopted children and a biological son he shared with Farrow. Allen and Soon-Yi married in December 1997 and eventually adopted two daughters of their own.

Farrow continues to work in film and television. She wrote a best-selling memoir, *What Falls Away*. Farrow devotes most of her time to her thirteen children, many of whom are physically handicapped. A fourteenth child, Tam, died at the age of 19 in 2000.

About Woody Allen [7]

A pale, bespectacled, 120-pound neurotic, Woody Allen polished his misfit persona in Greenwich Village cafés before recording three hit comedy albums in the 1960s. In his early twenties, he was already joking about his divorce from Harlene Rosen (they had spent four years together), and earning six thousand dollars a month as a television gag writer. In 1965, Allen wrote and acted in *What's New, Pussycat?* with Louise Lasser, whom he married the following year. In 1969, he made his directorial debut with *Take the Money and Run*, a spoof on crime documentaries. From his idiosyncratic, urban-Jewish shtick, Allen also mined two Broadway hits, many New Yorker pieces, and several books.

As Allen's career and neuroses blossomed apace, he tethered himself to a ritualized life of tennis, clarinet and shrink sessions, film making, and dinner at Elaine's. He is reclusive and anti-Hollywood and he rarely leaves Manhattan. "I don't want to live in a city where the only cultural advantage is that you can make a right turn on a red light," he said in *Annie Hall*.

Allen drove the point home by not showing up to collect his three Oscars for that 1977 film (he chose instead to keep his regular Monday-night gig with his jazz band). Around that time, Allen lost his leading lady and lover, Diane Keaton, who took up with Warren Beatty. In 1982, he embarked on a live-out relationship with actress Mia Farrow and her brood of children. With Farrow he adopted two more children (Moses and Dylan) and had a son of his own (Satchel), bringing Mia's total to twelve. Also with Farrow, he made thirteen films and became the subject of shocking headlines. Accused of incest with Dylan and infamy with young Soon-Yi Previn (whom Mia had adopted during her marriage to conductor Andre Previn), the auteur of angst waged a losing custody and publicity battle in 1993. The sexual-abuse accusations were found to be unsubstantiated, but the infamy he readily admitted (he and Soon-Yi would marry in late 1997). Allen was later permitted to resume visitation with Satchel (now called Seamus), but was barred from spending time with Dylan (now called Eliza).

In 1994, Allen made a film, *Bullets Over Broadway*, with an unmistakable message: all's fair in love and art. His next, *Mighty Aphrodite*, dealt with adoption and infidelity, two topics he is intimately familiar with. He plumbed the light-hearted side of neurosis in his first feature musical, 1996's *Everyone Says I Love You*, but the following year's *Deconstructing Harry* witnessed his return to familiar dark exploration and self-loathing.

In 1998, Allen voiced the regular-Joe insect hero of *Antz*, and delivered the goods with *Celebrity*, which follows the lives of two New Yorkers following their divorce. He married two of his weaknesses—music and nostalgia—in the 1999 release *Sweet and Lowdown*, which showcased Sean Penn in the role of a 1930s-era drunken scamp of a jazz guitarist.

Relationship Analysis Preparation Worksheet

A blank relationship analysis worksheet is included here. Some of the content on the form comes from the books, *How To Handle Your Human Relations* and *Relationships & Life Cycles*. In the next few chapters, each section of the worksheet is filled in with the particulars from our two case study birthcharts. All of the interpretive techniques will be subsequently explained in detail.

RELATIONSHIP ANALYSIS WORKSHEET

1) INDIVIDUAL CAPACITY FOR RELATIONSHIP:
KNOW THE INDIVIDUALS BEFORE EVALUATING THEIR RELATIONSHIP

person A

DESCENDANT _____ 7th HOUSE RULER _____ SIGN/HOUSE _____

SUN SIGN/HOUSE/ASPECTS _____

MOON SIGN/HOUSE/ASPECTS _____

ASC/CHART RULER BY SIGN/HOUSE _____

MERCURY SIGN/HOUSE/ASPECTS _____

VENUS SIGN/HOUSE/ASPECTS _____

MARS SIGN/HOUSE/ASPECTS _____

ANGULAR PLANETS (only in same sign) _____

ASPECT CONFIGURATIONS _____

CURRENT PROGRESSIONS AND TRANSITS _____

SOLAR RETURN VENUS/7th HOUSE _____

AGE _____ MARRIAGE(S) _____ CHILDREN _____ PARENTS _____

person B

DESCENDANT _____ 7th HOUSE RULER _____ SIGN/HOUSE _____

SUN SIGN/HOUSE/ASPECTS _____

MOON SIGN/HOUSE/ASPECTS _____

ASC/CHART RULER BY SIGN/HOUSE _____

MERCURY SIGN/HOUSE/ASPECTS _____

VENUS SIGN/HOUSE/ASPECTS _____

MARS SIGN / HOUSE / ASPECTS _____

ANGULAR PLANETS (only in same sign) _____

ASPECT CONFIGURATIONS _____

CURRENT PROGRESSIONS AND TRANSITS _____

SOLAR RETURN VENUS / 7th HOUSE _____

AGE _____ MARRIAGE(S) _____ CHILDREN _____ PARENTS _____

2) COMPARISON BY ELEMENT: SIMPLE COMPATIBILITY EVALUATION

	person A	person B	ELEMENTS
SUN			
MOON			
ASCENDANT			
MERCURY			
VENUS			
MARS			
JUPITER			
SATURN			

3) BALANCE: DOES THE COUPLE COMPENSATE FOR EACH OTHER?

	person A	person B	COMBINED
FIRE			
EARTH			
AIR			
WATER			
CARDINAL			
FIXED			
MUTABLE			

Sun, Moon, ASC, Mercury, Venus, Mars, Jupiter and Saturn only

Individual element total = 8 ~ Average = 2.0
Combined element total = 16 ~ Average = 4.0

Individual mode total = 8 ~ Average = 2 2/3
Combined mode total = 16 ~ Average = 5 1/3

4) HOUSE OVERLAYS ~ THE BI-WHEEL CHARTS:
HOW EACH PERSON EXPERIENCES THE OTHER

_____ Planets in _____ Houses		_____ Planets in _____ Houses	
person A	person B	person B	person A
A's Sun in B's	_____ house	B's Sun in A's	_____ house
A's Moon in B's	_____ house	B's Moon in A's	_____ house
A's ASC in B's	_____ house	B's ASC in A's	_____ house
A's Mercury in B's	_____ house	B's Mercury in A's	_____ house
A's Venus in B's	_____ house	B's Venus in A's	_____ house
A's Mars in B's	_____ house	B's Mars in A's	_____ house
A's Jupiter in B's	_____ house	B's Jupiter in A's	_____ house
A's Saturn in B's	_____ house	B's Saturn in A's	_____ house
A's Uranus in B's	_____ house	B's Uranus in A's	_____ house
A's Neptune in B's	_____ house	B's Neptune in A's	_____ house
A's Pluto in B's	_____ house	B's Pluto in A's	_____ house
A's MC in B's	_____ house	B's MC in A's	_____ house

SUBTOTALS BY HOUSE TYPE   12 = TOTAL   3 = AVERAGE

A's Planets in B's Houses   B's Planets in A's Houses

____ FIRE (1-5-9)	IDENTITY	____ FIRE (1-5-9)
____ EARTH (2-6-10)	USEFULNESS	____ EARTH (2-6-10)
____ AIR (3-7-11)	RELATING	____ AIR (3-7-11)
____ WATER (4-8-12)	FEELING	____ WATER (4-8-12)
____ YANG (Fire & Air Houses)		____ YANG (Fire & Air Houses)
____ YIN (Earth & Water Houses)		____ YIN (Earth & Water Houses)

SUBTOTALS BY HOUSE TYPE   12 = TOTAL   4 = AVERAGE

____ ANGULAR (1-4-7-10)	ACTIVATING	____ ANGULAR (1-4-7-10)
____ SUCCEDENT (2-5-8-11)	STABILIZING	____ SUCCEDENT (2-5-8-11)
____ CADENT (3-6-9-12)	COMMUNICATING	____ CADENT (3-6-9-12)

5) SYNASTRY ~ INTERCHART ASPECTS:
HARMONY OR STRIFE BETWEEN TWO SOULS

KEYWORDS FOR PLANETARY INFLUENCES

SUN	POWER; AUTHORITY; ENERGY
MOON	FAMILY; CHANGE; NURTURING
ASCENDANT	APPEARANCE; ATTRACTION; PERSONA
MERCURY	COMMUNICATION; REASON; INTELLECT
VENUS	SHARING; AFFECTION; HARMONY
MARS	SEXUALITY; INITIATIVE; COMPETITION
JUPITER	GENEROSITY; GROWTH; UNDERSTANDING
SATURN	COMMITMENT; CRITICISM; LIMITATION
URANUS	UPHEAVAL; INDEPENDENCE; FREEDOM
NEPTUNE	SPIRITUALITY; PLATONIC; ESCAPISM
PLUTO	DESTRUCTION; REGENERATION; CONTROL
MIDHEAVEN	CAREER; REPUTATION; AMBITION
LUNAR NODES	PAST LIVES; SOUL PURPOSE; DESTINY

	☌	☍	△	□	✶	⊼
person A SUN						
MOON						
MERCURY						
VENUS						
MARS						
JUPITER						
SATURN						
ASCENDANT						

aspects to person B planets

	☌	☍	△	□	✶	⊼
person B SUN						
MOON						
MERCURY						
VENUS						
MARS						
JUPITER						
SATURN						
ASCENDANT						

aspects to person A planets

SYNASTRY ASPECT SUBTOTALS

CONJUNCTIONS _____

HARMONIOUS - SEXTILES / TRINES _____

INHARMONIOUS - SQUARES / OPPOSITIONS _____

INCONJUNCTS (quincunx or semisextile) _____

SEMISQUARES & SESQUIQUADRATES _____

QUINTILES, SEPTILES & NOVILES _____

OUTER PLANETS / ANGLES / LUNAR NODES _____

TOTAL SYNASTRY ASPECTS _____

6) THE COMPOSITE CHART ~ THE MYSTIC THIRD: THE LIFE FORCE OF THE RELATIONSHIP ITSELF

SUN HOUSE/ASPECTS _____

MOON HOUSE/ASPECTS _____

SABIAN SYMBOL OF ASC _____

MERCURY HOUSE/ASPECTS _____

VENUS HOUSE/ASPECTS _____

MARS HOUSE/ASPECTS _____

JUPITER HOUSE/ASPECTS _____

SATURN HOUSE/ASPECTS _____

ASPECT CONFIGURATIONS _____

UNASPECTED PLANETS _____

7) THE DAVISON TIME-SPACE CHART: FORCES WORKING ON A COUPLE FROM OUTSIDE THE RELATIONSHIP

SUN SIGN/HOUSE/ASPECTS _____

MOON SIGN/HOUSE/ASPECTS _____

SABIAN SYMBOL OF ASC _____

MERCURY SIGN/HOUSE/ASPECTS _____

VENUS SIGN/HOUSE/ASPECTS _____

MARS SIGN/HOUSE/ASPECTS _____

JUPITER SIGN/HOUSE/ASPECTS _____

SATURN SIGN/HOUSE/ASPECTS _____

DIGNITY/EXALTATION/DETRIMENT/FALL + HOUSES RULED _____

CONFIGURATIONS/STATIONS/MUTUAL RECEPTION _____

8) PAST LIFE CONNECTIONS: THE KARMIC HISTORY OF THE RELATIONSHIP

CONJUNCTIONS TO THE IC _____

CONJUNCTIONS TO THE SOUTH NODE _____

CONJUNCTIONS TO THE VERTEX _____

12th HOUSE OVERLAY (Note if on 12th cusp) _____

ACTIVATION OF NATAL VERTEX _____

ACTIVATION OF PROGRESSED VERTEX _____

9) SYNASTRY, COMPOSITE AND DAVISON MIDPOINTS:
HOW THE RELATIONSHIP CREATES INDIVIDUAL INTEGRATION

PERSON A NATAL CONJUNCT PERSON B MIDPOINTS _____

PERSON B NATAL CONJUNCT PERSON A MIDPOINTS _____

PERSON A NATAL CONJUNCT COMPOSITE MIDPOINTS _____

PERSON B NATAL CONJUNCT COMPOSITE MIDPOINTS _____

PERSON A NATAL CONJUNCT DAVISON MIDPOINTS _____

PERSON B NATAL CONJUNCT DAVISON MIDPOINTS _____

10) SYNASTRIC ASPECT CONFIGURATIONS:
HOW YOUR PURPOSE AND MY PURPOSE BECOME OUR KARMA

SYNASTRIC STELLIUMS _____

SYNASTRIC T-SQUARES _____

SYNASTRIC YODS _____

SYNASTRIC GRAND TRINES _____

SYNASTRIC KITES _____

SYNASTRIC GRAND CROSSES _____

SYNASTRIC MYSTIC RECTANGLES _____

SYNASTRIC GRAND SEXTILES _____

Evaluation of the Nativities

At least four different categories of people schedule relationship analysis consultations. The first category is a client who has just met someone and is keen to know if they are compatible. Here the astrologer must request permission from the second party to compare that horoscope with the nativity of his client.

The second class of client is one who has been dating someone for several months and the relationship is becoming more serious and committed. These individuals sometimes come to the astrologer to *get the green light* for engagement or marriage. It is quite likely that both parties will show up for the appointment as opposed to only one of the individuals.

A third category of client is the long-term married couple. Often they are undergoing crisis, a separation or infidelity. In these cases, the astrologer is at times put on the spot to render a judgment about the marriage either remaining together or ending in divorce. This is most difficult to navigate as ethically, the astrologer cannot make their decisions.

The fourth type that I encounter is the couple who is getting along well but wishes for a deeper understanding of the dynamics and spiritual purpose of the marriage. In my experience, these clients are the most satisfying. It can be quite a relief to consult with couples who are not going through crisis or feeling enmity toward each other.

In some of these four categories, the astrologer is familiar with the nativities of the client or clients. In these cases, begin preparation for the relationship analysis with the comparisons of the two horoscopes. In other cases, however, it's a first time appointment for both clients and the astrologer is not familiar with either nativity. This is why the worksheet begins with an *evaluation of the individual capacity for relationship.*

I recommend first looking at the Descendant and the condition of its ruler by sign and house. Remember to use Mars as a 7th ruler for a Taurus rising person, Jupiter for Virgo Ascendants, or Saturn for the Leo rising individuals. The house position of a Descendant ruler shows how relationship most directly affects an individual. For example, if the ruler of the 7th is in the 2nd, financial gain may occur through marriage. If the Descendant ruler is in the 10th, career enhancement is likely, as is one's marital experience, for better or worse, becoming public knowledge.

Here is section (1) of the worksheet for Mia Farrow:

<u>Mia Farrow</u>
person A

DESCENDANT ♏   7th HOUSE RULER ♂   SIGN/HOUSE ♑ in 10th

SUN SIGN/HOUSE/ASPECTS ☉ intercepted in ♒ in 10th; unaspected (Ptolemaic)

MOON SIGN/HOUSE/ASPECTS ☽ in ♑ in 9th; □♀ ☍♄ ⚻♅ □♆ ⚻♇ △AS
                                                                           apex of Yod

ASC/CHART RULER BY SIGN/HOUSE ♉ Rising AS □♇; ♀ in ♈ in 12th

MERCURY SIGN/HOUSE/ASPECTS ☿ in ♒ in 10; ⚹♀ ⚻♄ △♅ △♆ ☌♇ □AS

VENUS SIGN/HOUSE/ASPECTS ♀ in ♈ in 12th; □♄ ⚹♅ ☍♆ △♇ ⚼MC

MARS SIGN/HOUSE/ASPECTS ♂ in ♑ in 10th; △♃ ☌MC

ANGULAR PLANETS (only in same sign) ♂ ☌ MC

ASPECT CONFIGURATIONS Cardinal Cross; Yod; Grand Trine; 2 Kites; Mystic Rectangle

CURRENT PROGRESSIONS AND TRANSITS Calculate for date of consultation

SOLAR RETURN VENUS/7th HOUSE From birthday prior to consultation

AGE 37 (1982)   MARRIAGE(S) 2   CHILDREN 7   PARENTS father deceased

After examining the Descendant, proceed to a summary of the Lights and personal planets, noting their sign, house position and aspects. The Ascendant and its ruler should also be included, and any aspect configurations involving the five personal planets (Sun-Moon-Mercury-Venus-Mars). When taking birth data, inquire also as to the number of marriages and children, and if parents are living or deceased.

To place relationship dynamics in context with what each client is experiencing at the time of the consultation, use a summary of current progressions and transits for the clients. Limit these to conjunctions, oppositions, trines and squares. In addition, examine the current solar return for the condition of Venus and the state of any planets found in its 7th house.

Here is section (1) of the worksheet for Woody Allen:

Woody Allen
person B

DESCENDANT ♓   7th HOUSE RULER ♃   SIGN/HOUSE ♐ in 4th

SUN SIGN/HOUSE/ASPECTS ☉ in ♐ in 4th; ☌ ☿ ☌ ♃ □ ♄ □ ♆ □ AS ☉ = ♀/♂

MOON SIGN/HOUSE/ASPECTS ☽ in ♒ in 6th; △ ♀ ⚻ ♆ □ MC

ASC/CHART RULER BY SIGN/HOUSE ♍ Rising AS □ ♃ AS ☍ ♄ AS △ ♅ ; ☿ in ♐ in 4th

MERCURY SIGN/HOUSE/ASPECTS ☿ in ♐ in 4th; ☌ ♃ □ ♄ ⚻ ♅ □ AS

VENUS SIGN/HOUSE/ASPECTS ♀ in ♎ in 2nd; □ ♂ □ ♆ apex of T-Square

MARS SIGN/HOUSE/ASPECTS ♂ in ♑ in 5th; □ ♅ ☍ ♆ △ MC ☌ Vertex

ANGULAR PLANETS (only in same sign) ♄ ☌ DSC ♆ in 1st

ASPECT CONFIGURATIONS Cardinal T-Square

CURRENT PROGRESSIONS AND TRANSITS Calculate for date of consultation

SOLAR RETURN VENUS/7th HOUSE From birthday prior to consultation

AGE 46 (1982)   MARRIAGE(S) 2   CHILDREN 0   PARENTS deceased

Completing section (1) for both individuals gives a feeling for the two nativities. Proceed to comparing and combining the charts to assess the relational dynamics.

Comparison by Element

In the last thirty-five years, psychological principles combined with insight from Oriental religious thought and Jungian ideas have penetrated the astrological language. Beginning at the ingress of Uranus into Capricorn in February 1988 (precisely conjunct Saturn), top astrologers began to more extensively research and translate Greek, Latin and Arabic manuscripts from our predecessors. This journey through the historical evolution of astrology has reintroduced traditional techniques and ancient terminologies into the astrological language.

For the most part, this has been beneficial for the profession. Yet one relatively recent period of astrology has unfortunately been squeezed out of a reformulation of the astrological language. In my opinion, the writings of both Alan Leo and C.E.O. Carter, from the 1890s to the 1950s, are no longer given the prominence that they deserve. What does their work have to do with relationship analysis technique? And have modern rulerships of planets obscured valuable perception?

Consider prevailing astrological wisdom regarding the harmony or dissonance between the four elements of fire, earth, air and water. Psychological astrology in modern times has placed the fire and air elements together in a *Yang* category, and the earth and water elements into a *Yin* grouping. Hijacked eastern philosophy now underpins much of western astrological thinking when it comes to assessing relational compatibility. Are these classifications always accurate?

Writing in *The Zodiac and the Soul*, published in London in 1928, C.E.O. Carter postulated a grouping for the four elements based on signs that share traditional planetary rulerships. For relational compatibility, this model can be used as an alternate to the standard grouping of the four elements into *Yang*, extroverted fire and air, or *Yin*, introverted earth and water, categories.

FIRE AND WATER SIGNS

♋ AND ♌ RULED BY THE LUMINARIES

♈ AND ♏ RULED BY MARS

♐ AND ♓ RULED BY JUPITER

FIRE OR WATER = EMOTIONAL AND INSTINCTUAL

EARTH AND AIR SIGNS

♊ AND ♍ RULED BY MERCURY

♉ AND ♎ RULED BY VENUS

♑ AND ♒ RULED BY SATURN

EARTH OR AIR = MENTAL AND DELIBERATIVE

Using these groupings, a strong case can be made for a water Moon being more compatible with a fire Moon, rather than with a Moon in earth (if out of orb of the fire-water square). Likewise, an argument is made for an air Moon as more suitable in relationship with that earth Moon, rather than with a fire Moon, as is traditionally thought (if also out of orb of the earth-air square). It is quite common to find spouses with the Luminaries interchanged in, say, Cancer and Sagittarius; whether this compatibility is based on shared emotionality and both having instinctual natures, or if it comes from these two signs being each other's contrascia (Equinox Points), is unclear.

Section (2) of the worksheet:

	Mia Farrow person A	Woody Allen person B	ELEMENTS
SUN	♒	♐	AIR/FIRE
MOON	♑	♒	EARTH/AIR
ASCENDANT	♉	♍	EARTH
MERCURY	♒	♐	AIR/FIRE
VENUS	♈	♎	FIRE/AIR
MARS	♑	♑	EARTH
JUPITER	♍	♐	EARTH/FIRE
SATURN	♋	♓	WATER

From this very basic and simple compatibility evaluation, the astrologer can see at a glance whether the same planet in one chart is compatible with its counterpart in the second horoscope. Applying the two different pairings of the elements, which denote compatibility or the lack of it, one can make the following assessment:[8]

> Fire signs are more compatible with air or water; less so with earth.
> Earth signs are more compatible with water or air; less so with fire.
> Air signs are more compatible with fire or earth; less so with water.
> Water signs are more compatible with earth or fire; less so with air.

Fire signs:	Aries	Leo	Sagittarius
Earth signs:	Taurus	Virgo	Capricorn
Air signs:	Gemini	Libra	Aquarius
Water signs:	Cancer	Scorpio	Pisces

Between Farrow and Allen, the two Jupiters are the least compatible pairing. Considering that Jupiter rules Farrow's 8th house of sexuality, and Allen's 5th house of children, it is no surprise that his sexual relationship with her adopted daughter would be the ruin of it all.

Balance and Compensation

One ideal is finding a mate who can compensate for what you lack, and who is in turn compensated by what you can bring to the relationship. When assessing a relationship, can this be found by astrologers? Yes, because people are created from differing combinations of energy, denoted by triplicities and quadruplicities. A simple matter of adding up the number of planets that each person has in the four elements, and in the three modalities, and then comparing the combined sums against an average, reveals much about any couple.

Taking only the Sun, Moon, Ascendant, Mercury, Venus, Mars, Jupiter and Saturn from each nativity, now consider section (3) of the worksheet:

	Mia Farrow person A	Woody Allen person B	COMBINED
FIRE	1	3	4
EARTH	4	2	6
AIR	2	2	4
WATER	1	1	2
CARDINAL	4	2	6
FIXED	3	1	4
MUTABLE	1	5	6

Individual element total = 8 ~ Average = 2.0
Combined element total = 16 ~ Average = 4.0
Individual mode total = 8 ~ Average = 2 2/3
Combined mode total = 16 ~ Average = 5 1/3

From this we find that the combined earth element is the strongest, fire and air are average, and water is the weakest. In the modes, there is a fairly even distribution. This couple made a lot of money together with the films that Allen directed and Farrow starred in, as shown by the high score in earth. However, with only the Saturns in water, the pair was likely sorely lacking in emotional closeness, as evidenced by the separate residences on either side of Central Park in Manhattan.

The lack of mutability in Farrow's nativity, (only Jupiter in Virgo), was compensated for by the high score in mutable that Allen brought to the relationship with his triple conjunction in Sagittarius, a Virgo Ascendant, and a Saturn in Pisces. When scrutinizing the balance and compensation scores for any couple, make a note of any extreme highs or lows.

The House Overlay Technique

When two souls meet and become partners, they are not only putting their lives together but also experiencing each other as individuals. A relationship analysis technique, *the house overlay system,* is used to see how and where each individual most directly experiences the distinct peculiarities of the other.

In addition, this method allows the astrologer to see which of the two individuals' identity is more impacted by the other, who finds the partner more useful, who feels more able to relate to the other, or who becomes the more dependent and attached of the two.

As the name implies, the analysis is accomplished by simply overlaying the planets of the one horoscope into the houses of the second. These combined horoscopes are also known as *bi-wheel charts* and are found in all of today's software programs. The most significant houses activated by this overlay method are the ones into which the other's Luminaries fall. Let us now again refer to our case study.

Woody Allen

Dec 1 1935 10:55 PM EST
Bronx New York
40N40 73W54
Dec 2 1935 03:55:00 GMT
Tropical Porphyry True Node

Second Chart Natal Chart
Mia Farrow
Feb 9 1945 18:27:00 GMT

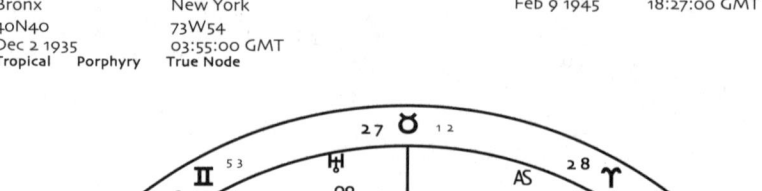

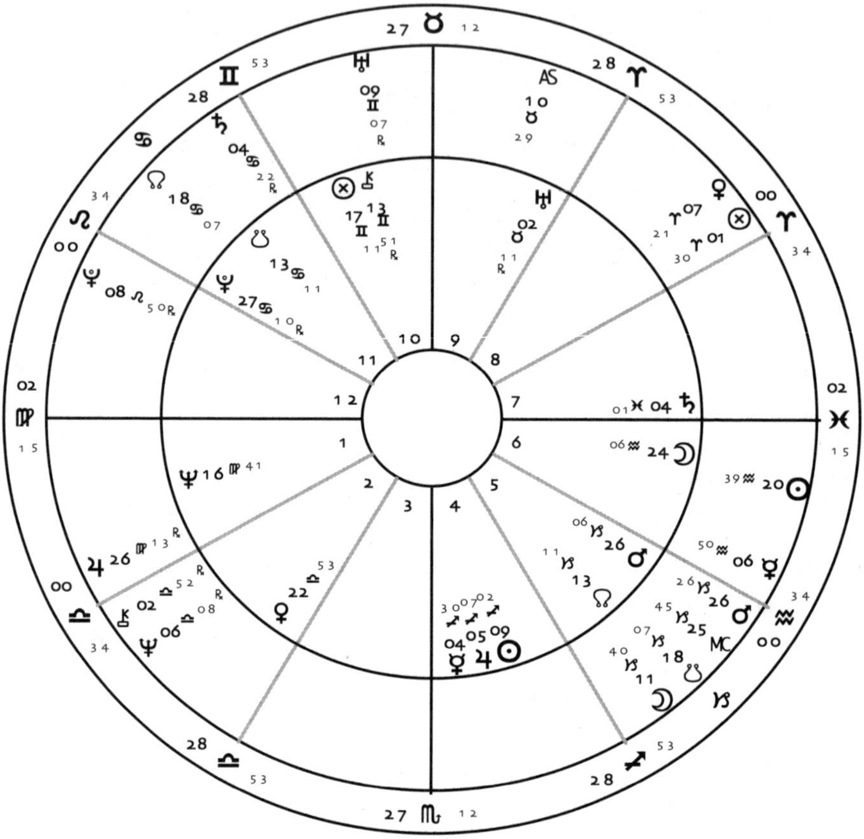

In this first overlay chart, we have placed Farrow's planets into the houses of Allen's chart. His Ascendant, Midheaven and other house cusps are the ones found around the outer circumference of the wheel. Notice that the 5th and 6th houses of his are activated by her Lights. From this one can see her impact on his life since she brought no fewer than seven children with her when they became a couple in 1982.

Her Venus overlaid in his 8th house, along with her Mars in his 5th house, are both indications of strong sexual attraction. Ultimately, with her Uranus in his 10th house, his reputation was to be damaged by her accusations of sexual incest. One also suspects that their break-up was very costly for Allen, as her Neptune is in his 2nd house. This overlay also symbolizes money made making films together.

Mia Farrow
Feb 9 1945   11:27 AM PWT
Santa Monica   California
33N50   118W29
Feb 9 1945   18:27:00 GMT
Tropical   Porphyry   True Node

Second Chart   Natal Chart
Woody Allen
Dec 2 1935   03:55:00 GMT

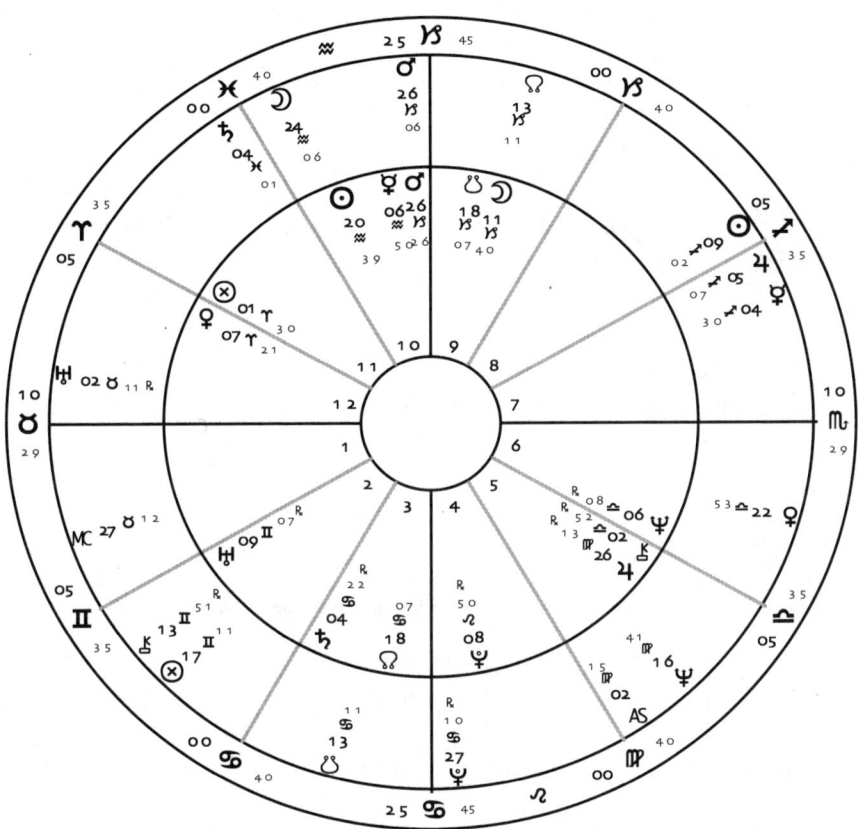

In this second overlay chart, Allen's planets are in the houses of Farrow's horoscope. Her Ascendant, Midheaven and other house cusps are found on the circumference of the wheel. Note his Luminaries in her 8th and 10th houses, attesting to the joint income earned by the films they made together and the public visibility they shared as a couple.

Section (4) of the relationship analysis worksheet refers to these two bi-wheel charts, for a tally of which houses in the first horoscope the planets of the second person fall into. The reverse is then done. Following this, you are ready to *work the numbers*. The resultant subtotals of planets that fall in each other's fiery, earthy, airy or watery houses, or in the angular, succedent or cadent houses of the partner, shed further light on the relationship.

Mia's Planets in Woody's Houses			Woody's Planets in Mia's Houses	
person A	person B		person B	person A
A's Sun in B's	6th house		B's Sun in A's	8th house
A's Moon in B's	5th house		B's Moon in A's	10th house
A's ASC in B's	9th house		B's ASC in A's	5th house
A's Mercury in B's	6th house	(on 8th cusp)	B's Mercury in A's	8th house
A's Venus in B's	8th house		B's Venus in A's	6th house
A's Mars in B's	5th house		B's Mars in A's	10th house
A's Jupiter in B's	1st house	(on 8th cusp)	B's Jupiter in A's	8th house
A's Saturn in B's	11th house		B's Saturn in A's	11th house
A's Uranus in B's	10th house		B's Uranus in A's	12th house
A's Neptune in B's	2nd house		B's Neptune in A's	5th house
A's Pluto in B's	12th house		B's Pluto in A's	4th house
A's MC in B's	5th house		B's MC in A's	1st house

SUBTOTALS BY HOUSE TYPE   12 = TOTAL   3 = AVERAGE

A's Planets in B's Houses			B's Planets in A's Houses	
5	FIRE (1-5-9)	IDENTITY	3	FIRE (1-5-9)
4	EARTH (2-6-10)	USEFULNESS	3	EARTH (2-6-10)
1	AIR (3-7-11)	RELATING	1	AIR (3-7-11)
2	WATER (4-8-12)	FEELING	5	WATER (4-8-12)
6	YANG (Fire & Air Houses)		4	YANG (Fire & Air Houses)
6	YIN (Earth & Water Houses)		8	YIN (Earth & Water Houses)

SUBTOTALS BY HOUSE TYPE   12 = TOTAL   4 = AVERAGE

2	ANGULAR (1-4-7-10)	ACTIVATING	4	ANGULAR (1-4-7-10)
6	SUCCEDENT (2-5-8-11)	STABILIZING	6	SUCCEDENT (2-5-8-11)
4	CADENT (3-6-9-12)	COMMUNICATING	2	CADENT (3-6-9-12)

From the results, astrologers can see how and where each individual experiences the other person. Does the planet person or the house person have the greater effect? It is the house person who receives the planetary energy from the other in that area of their life. For example, if person A's Moon falls in person B's 6th house, then person A supports diet, nutrition and exercise habits of person B.

As a general rule, if the fiery 1st, 5th and 9th houses are heavily tenanted by the planets of the partner, *the planet person has a strong impact on the identity of the house person.* This can result in transformation of the house person's religious identity, or the planet person may influence the house person to change his or her appearance, such as clothing and hair style. If the earthy 2nd, 6th and 10th houses contain several of the partner's planets, *the house person finds the planet person materially useful.* I have seen many cases where the house person was financially supported by the planet person as the house person returned to school to pursue a new career.

When the airy 3rd, 7th and 11th houses are occupied by several planets of the partner, *the house person feels that the planet person can relate to, and understand him or her, well.* It is quite common with this overlay for the couple to enjoy an active social life together, joining each other's existing circle of friends. Lastly, when the watery 4th, 8th and 12th houses have many overlay planets, *the planet person can enter deeply into the soul and feelings of the house person, and, should their relationship terminate, grievously wound the feelings of the house person.*

An absence of planets in one house type in both of the overlays, such as Allen and Farrow each having only one planet in the airy houses of the other (both of the Saturns), shows a lack of flow in that dimension of the relationship. In this case, one presumes that there was little mutual understanding and poor communication between them.

Since 1979, when I first read *Relationships & Life Cycles,* by Stephen Arroyo, and began to apply some of his house overlay methods in my practice, one in particular has stood the test of time and has been useful to my clients during consultations.

If an astrologer calculates which of the two persons has more planets of the partner falling into their *Yin* houses (earthy 2nd, 6th and 10th plus watery 4th, 8th and 12th), he can determine who in the relationship is more attached and dependent on the other. In some cases, it seems obvious on the surface, such as where one is the breadwinner, and the other is at home with the children. Yet, beneath the outward appearances, the truth often lies.

Most individuals have sensitive areas where they feel vulnerable. For some, it is sexual. For others, it is financial. Still others struggle with career, vocation or life purpose concerns. Appearance issues, such as being overweight, too short, or not pretty or handsome enough, can also plague the self worth. Relationship will eventually expose any and all of these fears, as two souls become closer and drop their guard around each other. When fear is objectified, it loses much of its grip.

The astrologer can help by objectively naming any fears. By pointing out to the couple who has more of the other's planets occupying their *Yin* houses, and who therefore usually feels more needy and more dependent, the astrologer can bring to awareness which party needs to be reassured more, and who needs to avoid exploiting any vulnerability in the other.

While employing this technique, in addition to paying particular attention to the overlay houses containing the Luminaries, an astrologer can also discuss overlay placements of the other planets. For example, the Uranus of one in the house of the other will likely bring some upheaval in that area of life, as well as serving as an awakener and liberator should the person have any repression issues there.

Referring to our case study, Allen has his 10th house of reputation overlaid with the Uranus of Farrow. As we will discuss later in the chapter, in 1992, when she found the pictures of her adopted daughter, Soon-Yi, in his apartment, it began a long and painful ending of the ten-year relationship, winding up in court amidst allegations of sexual abuse of their children, which most certainly caused upheaval and damage to his public image (10th house).

How the astrologer perceives an overlay is crucial. Rather than articulating only negative potential to clients, one should look for positive manifestation. Person A having their Saturn, for example, falling into person B's 4th house, does not mean that person A will only be critical of person B's family; on the contrary, person A might become a loyal and beloved son or daughter-in-law to the spouse's parents. Or it could simply mean that the couple lives in a small home originally occupied by person A, with the house person having moved in to share the cozy space.

It is also of value for the astrologer to tally up the count of Lights and planets in the *angular, succedent* or *cadent houses.* A mutual overlay of planets in the angular houses makes for a very active relationship, such as where there is much effort involved in visiting one another, or where the couple places great emphasis on doing things together. A strong overlay emphasis in the succedent houses produces a relationship that can stabilize the lives of both individuals. Previously, they might not have felt like they had any roots, but since becoming a couple, they feel more secure. When a couple has good communication, sharing ideas with one another, as well as enjoying the company of each other's relatives, it is likely that there will be a mutual cadent house overlay involving several planets.

Many times in class my students have asked which of the charts are most relevant to a new relationship: the composite chart, the synastry, or the house overlays. A new couple, in my opinion, should be presented primarily with house overlays. The astrologer can verbalize *how each can enter into the life of the other* by delineating each overlay planet in each house and leaving it there.

He can recommend that the couple check back in six months, when the relational patterns have become more apparent. Synastry aspect interpretations can then be given. Only after a relationship has lasted for over a year should the composite chart be used. The reasoning is that astrologers can unintentionally prejudice a couple into forming attitudes and beliefs about their relationship when chart patterns are discussed before the two individuals have developed a natural feel for one another. There are ethical issues involved here, such as the culpability of the astrologer who advises a couple to split up because of difficult synastry or composite aspects when persevering together through hard times would be appropriate.

Chapter Three
Synastry and the Composite Chart

Synastry: Interchart Aspects

At the heart of any relationship analysis for an established couple is the technique of synastry. The aspects formed between the Sun, Moon, planets and angles in one chart, and their counterparts in the second chart, are also called the *interchart aspects*. These show where couples will clash or where they will be compatible. This analytical technique knows no generalities, for, as each individual is different, so, too, are his relational needs and aversions.

One self-evident fact in astrology is the obvious impact of the astrologer's personal philosophy on how he reads and compares horoscopes. The Sun, Moon, planets and angles symbolize, for any individual, layers of consciousness that make up the soul, character and personality. Entering into a relationship brings into play forces coming from a second person that are designed to draw out and build upon one's latent potential. How the astrologer has integrated his own relational experience is, without exaggeration, 50% of the interpretation.

A hidden trade secret of synastry analysis is this subjectivity factor, and an admission of the unscientific nature of relationship analysis will actually make one a better counseling astrologer. The reason for this is that consultations with couples are most effective when the astrologer uses personal anecdotes to explain and articulate the various chart dynamics. In this most intimate of all of the types of astrological consultations, the personal connection between the astrologer and his client, and the astrologer's *bedside manner*, are as important as technical competence in reading birthcharts. Love will always remain a mystery, and there are areas within any relationship that can never be explained by astrology.

That said, synastry aspects open up a vast window into the world of any couple. Attraction between a man and a woman, the likelihood of a relationship enduring, how well two people communicate, and how they teach each other lessons—all this and so much more can be seen by the experienced astrologer. In section (5) of the relationship analysis worksheet are keywords for planetary influences, followed by two synastry grids where aspects forming between the two nativities can be tabulated, sorted and organized. From there, the interpretation can proceed.

While valuable insight can be gained from astrology books that contain *cookbook interpretations* for all the various combinations of aspects, house overlay positions, and the composite chart, there is also a major drawback in using these books. *They keep the astrologer from thinking for himself and reasoning through his understanding of the energies interacting for the couple.* It is safe to say that early in one's career, these books will be needed as a resource, but the goal should be to free oneself from reliance on other's interpretations and to develop one's own.

A key determinant of the quantity of synastry aspects in a relationship is the orb that is set for the different aspects. To illustrate this, two Synastry Tables are shown below. The first table uses standard natal orbs of 8-10° for conjunctions and oppositions, 6-8° for trines and squares, 4-5° for sextiles, 3-4° for quincunxes, 2-3° for semisextiles, semisquares and sesquiquadrates, and 1-2° for quintiles, septiles and noviles.

Mia Farrow
Woody Allen
Tropical   Porphyry

Synastry Table

	☉	☽	☿	♀	♂	♃	♄	♅	♆	♇	MC	AS	☊
☉	000 S Q 22	002 S ⚼ 38	002 A ✱ 12	001 S △ 41	002 A ∠ 23	000 S Q 49		000 A ☍ 04	002 S ✱ 54	000 S △ 12	001 ∠ 43	001 ⚻ 26	
☽	003 S ☌ 26	002 A ∠ 34		001 S ∠ 44	002 A ⚼ 19	002 ⚻ 07		002 S ⚼ 57		001 ⚼ 39			
☿			002 S ✱ 19	002 A △ 50	000 A ⚼ 29		000 S ⚻ 08	004 A ☍ 36	001 A ✱ 37	004 A △ 19	000 ✱ 10		001 S ⚼ 23
♀	002 S △ 14				003 A □ 32		001 A ⚼ 13			002 □ 51			004 S □ 46
♂				000 A Q 45	000 A ☌ 19	000 A △ 06	001 S ⚼ 59			000 ☌ 20			007 S ☍ 58
♃		001 S ✱ 43	002 S △ 13	000 A ☌ 06		000 S ⚻ 45	003 A ☍ 59	001 A ⚼ 00	003 A △ 43	000 ✱ 47			001 S ⚼ 59
♄							000 A △ 21	005 A □ 06	002 A ⚻ 07				000 S ⚼ 53
♅	000 S Q 28		004 S □ 39		005 A □ 45	002 A ✱ 10							
♆	003 S ⚻ 58	005 A △ 00				000 S Q 19							001 A ✱ 26
♇				000 A ☍ 44	000 S ✱ 57						001 ☍ 24		
MC	006 □ 32	000 ⚼ 31			000 △ 46	000 △ 58				000 Q 21	001 △ 26		000 ✱ 30
AS						002 ✱ 06							000 ∠ 52
☊		001 A ☌ 30		005 A □ 50							002 △ 41	004 S ☍ 56	

The second Synastry Table uses my *recommended relationship analysis orbs* of 4-5° for conjunctions and oppositions, 3-4° for trines and squares, 2-3° for sextiles, 1-2° for quincunxes, semisquares and sesquiquadrates, and 1° for semisextiles, quintiles, septiles and noviles. As you can see, there is a significant reduction in synastry aspects. In both tables, the higher orb is for the Lights, and the lower orb is for the planets.

Mia Farrow
Woody Allen
Tropical   Porphyry

Synastry Table

	☉	☽	☿	♀	♂	♃	♄	♅	♆	♇	MC	AS	☊
☉	0°00 S Q 22		0°02 A ✶ 12	0°01 S △ 41		0°00 S Q 49		0°00 A ☍ 04	0°02 S ✶ 54	0°00 S △ 12	0°01 ∠ 43	0°01 ⊼ 26	
☽	0°03 S ☌ 26		0°01 S ∠ 44										
☿			0°02 A △ 50	0°00 A ✶ 29		0°00 S ⊼ 08		0°01 A ✶ 37		0°00 ✶ 10			
♀	0°02 S △ 14										0°02 □ 51		
♂			0°00 A Q 45	0°00 A ☌ 19	0°00 A △ 06					0°00 ☌ 20			
♃			0°01 S ✶ 43	0°02 S △ 13	0°00 A ✶ 06	0°00 S ⊼ 45	0°03 A ☍ 59	0°01 A ✶ 00		0°00 ✶ 47			
♄					0°00 A △ 21							0°00 S Q 53	
♅	0°00 S Q 28												
♆					0°00 S Q 19							0°01 A ✶ 26	
♇			0°00 A ☍ 44	0°00 S ✶ 57							0°01 ☍ 24		
MC		0°00 Q 31		0°00 △ 46	0°00 △ 58				0°00 Q 21	0°01 △ 26			0°00 ✶ 30
AS													0°00 ∠ 52
☊		0°01 A ☌ 30										0°02 A △ 41	

The practical result of this reduction in orb allowance is a Synastry Table that drops from 74 total aspects to 46, a difference of about one third. Is this important, and why would it be? Yes, it is a crucial difference for the astrologer who has limited time to prepare for a consultation. It is far better to *focus attention on just the close synastry aspects,* as these will always be central to the relationship issues. Wider orb aspects are of much less value and relevance. The only exception to this would be if an orb is widened to allow for a synastric aspect configuration. For example, a quincunx with a 2-4° orb between the Sun in one chart and a planet in the other chart should not be overlooked if it was the second inconjunct of a synastric Yod.

In considering synastry aspects, the following ranking system may be employed:

1. The closest orb conjunctions or oppositions involving the Lights.
2. Planets exactly conjunct the other's angles (exclude cadent house positions).
3. Near to exact planet-to-planet conjunctions or oppositions.
4. The closest trines or squares involving the Lights.
5. The closest trines or squares between mutual planets.
6. Lights or planets exactly conjunct an intermediate house cusp.
7. All other aspects, or cadent house conjunctions to the other's angles.

From this list, presume that an exact to-the-degree conjunction of the Sun and Saturn would be the most powerful aspect between a couple. But, an exact trine of the Moon and Neptune, for example, is a stronger aspect than a conjunction of Sun and Saturn with a 7° orb. The gist of the ranking system is that conjunctions and oppositions are the primary aspects in synastry, aspects to the Lights are the most significant, the closest orb aspects are the most powerful, and conjunctions to the angles, as in natal astrology, are always paramount.

In the 1970s, prior to the arrival of personal computers and astrology software, the astrologer would have to manually tabulate all of the synastry aspects between two birth charts. In so doing, he would *get a feel* for the energy of the relationship by noticing, for example, that one person had five aspects to his Moon from the partner, while the other only received one aspect.

These subtle nuances of relationship analysis have, to some degree, been obscured and compromised by astrology software programs, which do all of the synastry aspect calculations for the astrologer and somewhat remove him from the scrutiny of the two nativities. I recommend filling in section (5) of the relationship analysis worksheet by hand, even if you calculate all of the synastry aspects by computer.

<u>Mia Farrow</u> person A

	☌	☍	△	□	✱	⚻
SUN	☽		♀			
MOON	☊					
MERCURY						♃
VENUS			♃			
MARS	♂	♆	MC			
JUPITER			MC		♆	
SATURN			♄			
ASCENDANT			☊			

aspects to <u>Woody Allen's</u> planets

Woody Allen person B	☌	☍	△	□	✶	⚻
SUN		♅	♀ ♆		☿ ♆	AS
MOON						
MERCURY			♀		♆	♄
VENUS				♂ MC		
MARS	MC		♃			
JUPITER		♅			♆	♄
SATURN						
ASCENDANT						

aspects to <u>Mia Farrow's</u> planets

At a glance, these two synastry grids give the astrologer *a summary of the major interchart aspects sorted by aspect type,* rather than displaying them in a grid with the planets of person A across the top, and planets of person B along the left vertical edge. In my experience, this has been easier to work with during my consult preparations. If astrologers first computer-calculate a standard Synastry Table, the relationship of each planet to the entire chart of a second person can easily be seen. If astrologers also enter by hand the specific aspect types into these worksheet grids, they will have the best layouts for both analytical perceptions.

Astute astrologers scrutinizing the second Synastry Table may have noticed that a total of six artistic quintiles exist between the nativities of Farrow and Allen, all within a one degree orb. Most significant of these are quintiles from his Sun to both her Sun and Jupiter, and from her Sun to both his Sun and Uranus.

Finding two of the same aspect alerts one to either the existence of a synastric aspect configuration, or, as in this case, a planet in one nativity at the midpoint of a pair of planets in the second horoscope. Farrow has a close biquintile between her Sun and Jupiter, with Allen's Sun at the midpoint, forming synastric quintiles to each body. Allen has a natal biquintile between his Sun and Uranus, with Farrow's Sun at the midpoint, quintile to both planets. In Chapter Four, I will discuss these synastric midpoints and configurations.[9]

Exceptionally alert astrologers will have also noticed five synastric septiles in that second Synastry Table; a group of four forming between Allen's Mercury-Jupiter conjunction and Farrow's Mars-Midheaven conjunction, and perhaps more importantly considering the outcome of the relationship, a septile from her North Node to his MC. Given the fated nature of this seventh harmonic aspect and the artistic connotations of the quintile, if the astrologer spots three or more of these esoteric aspects in a Synastry Table, he should make a note of it.[10]

For an astrologer to see a ratio of the harmonious and inharmonious synastry aspects, he can tabulate subtotals of each aspect type from the Synastry Table. The various astrology software programs normally show conjunctions to the IC or to the Descendant as oppositions to the MC or Ascendant, respectively. I recommend adjusting your subtotals to reflect this, as in the case of Allen's Pluto being conjunct Farrow's IC, yet shown in the Table as an opposition to her Midheaven.

SYNASTRY ASPECT SUBTOTALS

CONJUNCTIONS	5
HARMONIOUS - SEXTILES / TRINES	17
INHARMONIOUS - SQUARES / OPPOSITIONS	3
INCONJUNCTS (quincunx or semisextile)	3
SEMISQUARES & SESQUIQUADRATES	5
QUINTILES, SEPTILES & NOVILES	11
OUTER PLANETS / ANGLES / LUNAR NODES	2
TOTAL SYNASTRY ASPECTS	46

It is common with my *recommended relationship analysis orbs* to see approximately 35 to 50 interchart aspects between any couple. Relationships having key synastric conjunctions possess stronger bonds, especially so if the Luminaries are conjoined as is the case for Allen and Farrow. A Sun conjunct Saturn or with the Ascendant of the other may also hold a couple together for many years.

I have tabulated many hundreds of these synastry subtotals during my career and have observed that there can quite often be an almost even distribution of harmonious and inharmonious interchart aspects. It is not uncommon to find couples with just as many sextiles and trines between them as oppositions and squares. These relationships may be the strongest for longevity considerations, as having a number of stressful aspects, primarily oppositions, requires a couple to thrash out their differences, eventually creating a healthy respect for each other.

Too many synastric sextiles and trines, without the balance of enough squares or oppositions, can lead to boredom because of the lack of conflict. Perhaps this is what ebbed the sexual tension between Farrow and Allen, leading to the sexual affair with her daughter. A little sparring and jostling never hurt anybody, yet the moody and sensitive types who are composed of mostly water and little or no fire, may at first wince from these interactions until they learn how to take it lightly.

A number of my students have asked about the relevance of synastric semisquares, sesquiquadrates, and inconjuncts. It should be stated here that both the semisextile and quincunx are considered to be inconjuncts; the former symbolizing unification of the inner and outer selves, while the latter represents the necessary internal resolution of conflict in reaction to external stressors.

In synastry, the 45° semisquare (octile) appears to show how stress release occurs between a couple; symbolically, it is the midpoint of a tension-producing square. For example, a Mercury semisquare to Mars in a relationship shows that a good argument now and then *is essential to clear the air.* Mercury square to Mars, on the other hand, will produce *almost constant quarrels, with little relief in sight.*

In a similar vein, I have observed the 135° sesquiquadrate (trioctile) to be where a couple learns self-restraint, as in biting their tongues and saying nothing to upset the other's *sacred cows*. This does not necessarily result in repression, rather it produces awareness of how one's behaviors interfere with the other's priorities in daily life. If, for example, a partner's planet is in sesquiquadrate to the other's MC, certain behaviors of the partner will interfere with the other's work in some way. Once this pattern is explained by the astrologer, the partner can choose to avoid unnecessary interaction when the other is trying to concentrate on work.

As regards the inconjuncts, either the 30° semisextile or 150° quincunx, it has been my experience that physical discomfort results. It is not uncommon to hear a man or a woman yelling at their spouse, *"you make me sick!"* When an astrologer looks closely at the couple's synastry, he will find quincunxes to the Moon, which usually result in indigestion when around the other person. In this case, perhaps the astrologer could advise the couple to have meals separately, or if this is not practical, then to avoid controversial subjects while dining.

A close orb quincunx in synastry is likely to be where the couple has their biggest disconnect. For example, a couple with Mercury in quincunx to Jupiter may have such different politics and religious beliefs as to view world events from a different perspective. Each may also see personal responsibilities from a different moral position. This will not render a couple incompatible; rather, with the right attitude, each can benefit from the other's point of view.

When there is an exact semisextile between a couple's planets, a process of inner and outer unification appears to be taking place. For example, if a woman's Mercury is 30° from her man's Neptune, he may tune into her private thoughts in such a way so as to help her unite her reason with her spiritual understanding. This is her cognitive process, yet he, simply through his presence, is part of it.

These minor and esoteric aspects were defined in *Volume II - Sabian Aspect Orbs.*

Attraction ~ Endurability ~ Mental Agreement ~ Karmic Lessons

In the world of astrology, synastry technique is used as much by professional astrologers and astrology students to comprehend their personal relationships as it is used with clients during a paid consultation. What actually gets discussed during a relationship analysis appointment? Can an astrologer actually help couples to better understand love and partnership?

As I wrote in Chapter Two, I have seen at least four different categories of clients for relationship analysis consultation. A person who had just met someone new; a couple asking about a *green light* for marriage; a husband and wife in crisis; or a happily married pair wishing to deepen their love. In each of these consultations, I used very specific synastry techniques.

I first learned this targeted synastry when I read Lois Sargent's *How To Handle Your Human Relations* in the late 1970s. This little yellow book contained a gold mine of practical delineations and methods with which to analyze relationship. I especially appreciated her way of dividing specific aspects into categories such as *Attraction, Endurability, Mental Agreement* and *Life Lessons*. After twenty-five years of using these techniques, they are still my favorite approach to synastry.

When I think back as to why so many astrology books were published in the 1970s on relationship analysis, besides the obvious assumption of Uranus being first in Libra, then Scorpio, it occurs to me now that it was also because divorce became so prevalent then. In addition, couples began living together without any formal commitment, and a rapidly growing number of adults had to periodically look for new love each time they ended relationships. This wasn't always so.

Compare this to the generation of my parents who had been married for 58 years and were still together at the ages of 80 and 81. Astrological relationship analysis is largely an irrelevant concern for them and others their age, simply because they have stayed with one spouse all of their lives. With my experience in marriage, I can sure see how *astrological laws of supply and demand* have opened up this branch of astrology.

Perhaps this is why in his classic book, *The Principles of Astrology*, published in 1925, C.E.O. Carter devoted a scant seven pages to marriage in his chapter on *The Judgment of the Horoscope: Destiny*. I can remember the first time I meticulously studied *the general circumstances of the marriage being shown by the application of the appropriate Luminary*. Carter wrote that the Sun stood for the husband in a woman's nativity, and the Moon for the female in a man's horoscope, and that the first applying aspect of these bodies to a natal planet *denoted the kind of marriage partner and the conditions of marriage*. Subsequent applying aspects, in theory, would denote successive attachments. In my life, this rule has borne out.

I also remember feeling somewhat relieved reading this, which was around the time of my first divorce in 1975. Knowing that my Moon was in a relatively low degree (6° Pisces), I felt that there might be prospects for marriage again, as I had several planets between 21° and 24° degrees the Moon would continue to apply to (Ptolemaic aspects - 0°-60°-90°-120°-180°). But, by the time I read his last page on marriage, and about 8° of Aries-Libra being indicative of matrimonial troubles if occupied by the malefics or involved in afflictions, and with my natal Mars in that degree of Libra, my initial relief then was quite short lived.

However, I do recall thinking that there would be hope for me to marry again as my Moon would next apply to a trine with my Sun. My brief initial marriage, shown by the Moon applying to her first aspect (trine Mercury—married young), had resulted in a wife with Virgo rising. Five years later, unexpectedly becoming a father,[11] I married the mother to give the child my last name. The ceremony was performed in Seattle by a New Age preacher with a mail order ministry license. I don't believe that he ever filed the legal papers with the local county offices.

That unlawful marriage turned out to be a *loveless debt of honor,* ending in a year. With my Moon's second application being a trine to my Sun, I married again in 1983 to a woman who had Scorpio rising conjunct my Sun. We divorced in 1988, but remarried a second time from 1991 to 1994. After all of these personal ups and downs, however, I was not much interested in this astrological rule any longer.

Of course, it did cross my mind that my Moon would then apply to a trine with Uranus, and sure enough my next wife had Aquarius rising. After the demise of that union, which took me to South Carolina in 1995, I was now down to my last applying aspect, a square with Jupiter, before the Moon would mercifully go void-of-course. Lo and behold, my last marriage took me to Florida in 2002, where my new wife had Jupiter in 18° of Virgo, conjunct my Ascendant. Now divorced once more, and out of aspects, I truly don't really care if I ever marry again. It appears that I have fully exhausted my Venus-Saturn conjunction and its love of formality.

The reason I am offering up my tattered trail of marital history for the good of astrology is to illustrate C.E.O. Carter's *Law of Marriage Being Shown by the Application of the Appropriate Luminary.* This astrological rule simply states that a woman's natal Sun, in its first, and then successive, applying aspects will *denote the kind of marriage partner and the conditions of marriage.* For a man, this rule regards his natal Moon and the first, and then successive, applying aspects after birth. From my personal history, one can see that the Ascendant of the spouse, or a planet in the spouse's chart conjunct my Ascendant, precisely followed the pattern (Virgo and Aquarius rising wives with Moon applying to Mercury or Uranus; Moon applied to Sun with Scorpio rising wife with her Ascendant conjunct my Sun; and Moon applied to Jupiter—wife's Jupiter conjunct my ASC).

A personal testimony can be given here to the quality of the work of the eminent C.E.O. Carter, who first published these correspondences to specific Zodiac degree areas in 1924 in *An Encyclopædia of Psychological Astrology*. His research showed that 8° Aries-Libra, 25° Virgo, 19° Leo-Aquarius, and 27° Leo-Aquarius indicated problems in marriage. I have found again and again that clients with Mars or Saturn in these degrees, or other planets in these degrees and in bad aspect to the malefics, have indeed suffered ill fortune in love.

I believe that the dynamics of an aspect being formed, such as precise angular separation, is more important than the two planets involved. However, when certain planets are in synastric aspect, they will nearly always produce a predictable result in relationships.

Regarding *Attraction*, a conjunction of the Sun, Moon, Venus or Mars with the Ascendant of the other results in a strong enticement toward the opposite sex. Aspects between the masculine and feminine bodies, such as Sun-Moon, Sun-Venus, Mars-Moon or Mars-Venus, will also be of a highly sexual nature. Of these four, Mars-Moon appears most passionate, and Sun-Venus is more on the affectionate and sensual side of the spectrum. Sun-Moon conjunctions are *the Cadillac of all synastry aspects for marriage*, with the trine between the Luminaries, or a Sun-Ascendant conjunction, tying for second place.

Also producing instant attraction, although not necessarily a lasting relationship, are aspects between Sun, Venus or Mars and another's Uranus. I have known clients who met in a tavern, were smitten immediately, flew to Las Vegas and got married within 48 hours of meeting one another! Venus and Uranus were conjunct in one synastry aspect; the other Uranus was conjunct the spouse's Ascendant.

Sun-Mars aspects can also be placed in this category of immediate allure, yet it must be said that disastrous results may follow. I am not the one to provide sound, objective analysis about this aspect, as I have married two Librans born on the 2nd and 3rd of October and both with Suns conjunct my Mars. After starting out as *the hero*, by the end of these marriages, I had metamorphosed into *a poophead*.

Putting these *attraction* synastry aspects to the test in our case study, we find:

1. Farrow's Sun conjunct Allen's Moon.
2. Sun trine Venus both ways (what Stephen Arroyo calls a *double whammy*).
3. Allen's Venus square Farrow's Mars (3-4° orb).
4. Allen's Venus-Mars midpoint exactly opposite Farrow's Uranus.
5. Allen's Venus and Mars sesquiquadrate Farrow's Uranus (1-2° orb).
6. Allen's Sun opposite Farrow's Uranus.
7. Farrow's Venus-Mars midpoint conjunct Allen's Descendant.

Regarding *Endurability*, clients may ask if a relationship looks like it will last and result in marriage. Can astrologers answer this question with certainty? Yes, and particular aspects are targeted in pre-consultation research. C.E.O. Carter, in *The Principles of Astrology*, said Suns in square were undesirable in marriage, and I concur, but only if in orb. Former President Clinton is a Leo and his wife is a Scorpio. Square by sign, yes, but 26° Leo and 02° Scorpio are well out of orb.

Aspects to Saturn must be present for a marriage to endure; conjunctions of Sun to Saturn will weather all tempests, as will Saturn-Ascendant conjunctions and Saturn overlays in the partner's 7th house. I must say here that the orb of this conjunction will not hold much beyond 4-5°, as I had a wife with Saturn in 29° of Scorpio, 7° away from my Sun. The harmony of the Moons tends more to the daily flow of a marriage, but disharmony need not be a *backbreaker*. If a Venus-Saturn synastry aspect is to be the glue, one body will have to rule either a Descendant or an Ascendant in the nativities. Moon-Saturn aspects will keep a couple together for the sake of children, but the marriage may waver when they leave home.

Elemental harmony between the Suns is also a key ingredient here, and this would include Suns conjunct, sextile or trine each other *by sign,* even if out of allowable orb of these aspects. Fire Suns with fire or air are best, but also a water Sun out of orb of the square is commonly seen. Earthy Suns with earth or water is preferred, but again, one finds many a Taurus wed to a Libra, so earth with air is also OK.

Air sign Suns will be happiest with fire or another air sign, yet many are seen in relationship with earth signs. In the artistic circles of actors, novelists, musicians and film makers, one finds many air signs wedded to water signs. Perhaps one can say that this element (air) is the most versatile when it comes to partnering.

Water sign Suns are likely best off with their own kind, as even with an earthy Sun, who can contain their moodiness and remain steady when they go bipolar, they will bore easily without occasional drama. This Scorpio has been married to two Libras, a Gemini, a Scorpio and a Capricorn, and would pass on future union with air signs. After being drawn out of his cave, licking his wounds after his last divorce, the author was found by a fellow Scorpio with her Sun in the same degree as his Saturn. They were two peas in a pod, and she, never married at 44, joked that between them, they had the societal average of divorces.

As regards the astrologer stating with certainty that a new relationship will result in marriage, a very specific rule applies here. Having first read about this in Lois Sargent's book in the late 1970s, I have observed this three-part rule time and again holding up to the test of practical application: *The ruler of one Ascendant or Descendant must be conjunct the horizon in the other nativity; or, two of the four rulers of both horizons must be conjunct, in any combination; or, either ruler, from the other nativity, of one's horizon must be conjunct one's Ascendant or Descendant.*

Let us now consider some examples of the three variations of our marriage rule:

1. Paul Newman and Joanne Woodward: Both have Capricorn rising; her Saturn is conjunct his Ascendant.
2. Prince Charles and Princess Diana: Diana had Sagittarius rising; her Jupiter was exactly conjunct his 5° Aquarius Descendant.
3. Bill and Hillary Clinton: Bill has Aries setting; Hillary has Gemini rising; his Mercury is conjunct her Mars. (With all of the storms that this couple has endured, you guessed it—a Sun-Saturn conjunction with a 4-5° orb).[12]
4. Dwight and Mamie Eisenhower: He had Virgo rising and Pisces setting; her Jupiter, ruler of his Descendant, was conjunct his Virgo Ascendant.
5. John and Jacqueline Kennedy: She had Scorpio rising and Taurus setting; he had Libra rising and Aries setting; his Mars conjoined her Descendant.

A case can be made that if one of these conditions is met, marriage will result. Seasoned astrologers might ask, *"what is the orb allowance here?"* If you will forgive me yet another personal testimonial, I have intimately known two women born ten days apart in 1956, both with Jupiter (my DSC ruler) on my Ascendant.

With one, born in late September of that year, I had a child. We were engaged to be married but marriage did not occur. The other, born in early October, I married. The mother of my child had Jupiter at 15° Virgo 56', over 5.5° of an orb away from conjoining my Ascendant. The wife, born ten days later, had Jupiter at 18° Virgo 01', conjunct my Ascendant by 03° 29'. With these results, I would state that the 5° orb is the maximum allowable for conjunctions to the angle.

Putting these *endurability* synastry aspects and the marriage rule to the test in our case study, we find only a weak sextile from Farrow's Saturn to Allen's Ascendant. None of the three variations of the Marriage Rule are found. Despite having one biological child together and adopting two others, the couple neither married nor shared a home.

Turning now to our third category of *Mental Agreement,* to assess communication potential in a relationship, an astrologer would look for synastric aspects involving the Moon, Mercury and Jupiter, the heavenly bodies associated with *responsiveness, discourse* and *understanding.* It is essential in relationship to be able to communicate with the partner. Problems in marriage are inevitable and the ability of a couple to talk out their differences is crucial to a lasting union.

Among the most fortunate synastry aspects for excellent communication are conjunctions, sextiles or trines between the Moon and Mercury, the Moon and Jupiter, or Mercury and Jupiter. Conjunct Mercuries are also a blessing, as couples will think alike and understand one another's reasoning on an issue.

A most capacious predicament in relationship is *communication breakdown:* a partner whose feelings are hurt becomes defensive and refuses to talk about the upset. Synastric squares or oppositions to the Moon or Mercury are notorious for this condition, and astrologers need interpretive proficiency to be able to help couples cope with these types of communication problems.

One of the these skills is the ability to identify and inform clients about mitigating trines or sextiles to a synastric square or opposition. When this is explained, couples can improve their capacity to understand one another and grow together as a result. If the astrologer finds an aspect such as a Moon-Mars opposition, a Mercury-Uranus square, or a Mercury-Mars opposition between a couple, it is certain that arguing and quarreling will be part of the couple's reality.

It is rare that he will not also find a third planet sextile and trine to the opposing pair. This third planet is an *alleviation source,* a way out of any impasse. Putting this type of chart pattern into words that clients can use will take some time. Not all couples are comfortable admitting that they argue furiously in private at home. The astrologer needs to be diplomatic when pointing out these synastry dynamics.

One way that I have approached this is to identify which respective houses are ruled by the two planets in opposition. If, for example, a couple has a Moon-Mars opposition, with the Moon ruling the 5th house in one chart and Mars ruling the 9th house in the second nativity, it is likely that a major source of disagreement will be the way each wants to bring the children up religiously. I have also observed this aspect in synastry with couples from differing cultures.

If the couple acknowledges that they are at an impasse over an issue similar to this and ask the astrologer for guidance, he can look to see if a mitigating sextile and trine are also present in the synastry. If this third planet is Saturn, he would advise the younger individual to defer to the older. If the mitigating planet was the Moon or Venus, he would suggest that the wife has the better perspective about it.

Apply these *mental agreement* synastry aspects to our case study:

1. Allen's Moon quincunx Farrow's Jupiter (2-3° orb).
2. Mercury sextile Mercury (2-3° orb).
3. Farrow's Mercury sextile Allen's Jupiter.
4. Farrow's Mercury square Allen's Uranus (4-5° orb).
5. Allen's Mercury opposite Farrow's Uranus (4-5° orb).

One would presume that 4 and 5 were argumentative, with 2 and 3 the congenial communication. As children were involved in this relationship, 1 turned out to be a crucial aspect as it formed one leg of a synastric Yod, also involving the natal Pluto of Allen. More on these aspect configurations will be discussed later.

Other evidence of exemplary communication in relationship is found when a well-aspected Moon, Mercury or Jupiter falls into the partner's 3rd or 9th house. If this occurs both ways, for example, partner A's Jupiter falling into partner B's 9th, and partner B's Mercury falling into partner A's 3rd, then not only will verbal interaction be excellent, but opportunity also exists for extensive travel together.

One of the more intriguing categories of synastry analysis is of *Karmic Lessons*. The water element houses are associated with karma in the horoscope; ancestral and family karma is found in the 4th house, the karma of loss in the 8th house, and spiritual emancipation in the 12th house. Overlay planets found in these houses show how individuals learn karmic lessons in relationship.

Intrinsically, any astrological nativity contains a framework of karmic potential. When two souls join together in relationship, this latent capacity evolves into more of an active state. Can the astrologer see this type of activation in synastry? Yes, and he would see this most clearly when the Luminaries or Saturn overlay in the watery houses, in combination with synastry aspects to those same bodies.

An example of positive karma would be an overlay Saturn found in the 4th house, and in sextile or trine to the second person's Lights or Saturn. Here, both families would welcome the two individuals with open hearts and be very happy for them having found each other. For one or both of the individuals, the relationship might be a fulfillment of years of hopes and wishes to find the right mate, perhaps after years of personal effort to repair damage from a troubled childhood.

On the other hand, negative karma could be seen by the astrologer if that same overlay Saturn was also found in the 4th house, but in opposition or square to the Lights or Saturn in the second nativity. In that case, the challenging karma would be experienced as criticism or rejection coming from the families, perhaps because the couple was behaving immaturely or being irresponsible with their finances.

These examples illustrate an important rule in relationship analysis: *no synastry aspect acts alone without consideration of its overlay position, nor does any house overlay act separately without consideration of the synastry aspects to that planet.* This is exactly why computerized relationship analysis is limited and ineffective.

The deepest karmic lessons are usually accompanied by pain and suffering. How else can wisdom touch one on a soul level? Can the astrologer see this type of karmic lesson between a couple? Yes, it would be found with an overlay Sun, Moon or Saturn in the 8th house, with the planets also in synastric square or opposition. It is no small coincidence that sexuality and painful loss are both symbolized by this succedent water house.

For some souls, the deepest sexual experience is with a partner whom they cannot have. A fertile combination of passion, surrender, merging, and then ultimate loss, is what ushers the soul into the land of grief, wherein all true knowledge is found. It is thought that this state of consciousness cannot be attained on one's own and is only reachable through intimate union with another. When an overlay Light or Saturn is in the 8th house, and it also opposes or squares planets in that nativity, what should be said about this to the couple?

There is an ethical dimension in astrological relationship analysis, one that each astrologer must navigate for himself. If he sees this karma of loss in a combination of an 8th house overlay Luminary or Saturn that is also in bad synastry aspect, does he remain silent? To frighten a client who is deeply in love with discussion of a hypothetical loss would not be morally right. However, it has been my experience that a Light or Saturn overlay in the 8th house, which also opposes Uranus, Neptune or Pluto, or is in conjunction or square to the nodal axis, shows a relationship that will result in deep loss and sorrow, either through a painful ending or a death.

It is sometimes the nature of the 8th house to bring the deepest pleasure followed by the deepest pain. The astrologer can be of spiritual service to his clients by discussing this concept *after* a deeply sexual relationship has been terminated, when the client is seeking comfort and understanding to achieve closure on that love. By talking about that overlay planet of the former partner that was in their 8th house and in hard aspect to one of their transpersonal planets, the astrologer can provide perspective to the client about the purpose of the loss.

The presence of a Luminary or Saturn in a 12th house overlay, especially when conjunct the 12th cusp, and which also forms synastric conjunction or opposition with a planet in that nativity, shows the astrologer a relationship that is reforming again from past lives. This configuration is serving spiritual liberation.

Since the 12th house is one's personal prison, where fears and distortions lie deep within the innermost mind, another's Sun, Moon or Saturn falling into this house and conjoined a 12th house outer planet, is evidence for the astrologer that the planet person has arrived to help the house person free himself of a karmic pattern from which he could not extricate himself on his own.

Positive karma can be found, for example, when a Moon overlay in the 12th house conjoins a 12th house transpersonal planet. The Moon person has come to free the other from spiritual isolation, simply through love and emotional support. When Saturn is in a 12th house overlay and conjunct an outer planet therein, the Saturn person repays a karmic debt by helping to stabilize the other soul by being an example of personal emotional strength and strong character.

The overlays that involve the Lights or Saturn in the partner's 4th, 8th or 12th houses, and that are also in synastric aspect to outer planets in that chart, appear to illustrate *Karmic Lessons* that alter and transform the direction of a person's life. When sextile or trine, positive karma reaches fruition. Squares or oppositions bring negative karmic results, with life lessons from past incarnations repeating.

Investigating the *karmic lesson* house overlays and aspects in our case study:

1. Allen's Pluto falls into Farrow's 4th house and opposes her Mars.
2. His Sun falls into her 8th house and opposes her Uranus.
3. His Uranus falls into her 12th house and quintiles her Sun.
4. Her Venus falls into his 8th house and quintiles his Mars.
5. Her Pluto falls into his 12th house and quintiles his Midheaven.

In summary, this section of the chapter has shown how specific synastry aspects can be examined to find evidence of physical attraction, of the likelihood for relationship to endure and/or result in marriage, of the quality of communication, and of serious and transforming karmic life lessons for the benefit of either party.

The Composite Chart

In addition to comparing two horoscopes to analyze relationship, a third chart can be calculated, which is called the *Composite*. It symbolizes the life force energy of any partnership and is known as the *Mystic Third*. The composite consists of the near midpoints of the two Suns, the two Moons, and all of the other planets. Composite planets are placed into a third chartwheel, derived by first finding the midpoint of the two Midheavens and next determining a midpoint Ascendant.

As I wrote in Chapter Two, it is not recommended to use a composite chart until a couple has been together for at least a year, which is when they will have become familiar with patterns in the relationship. If the astrologer interprets this chart for his clients too soon after they have first met, it may predispose the couple to form a bias about the potential, or lack of potential, of their love.

This chart is read similarly to an individual nativity, with the exception of the sign placement of the Lights and planets, which I do not consider relevant. Because this horoscope does not exist in time or space, one will not find the positions of the planets in an ephemeris. The chart is quite simply just a mathematical construct, and I recommend limiting your interpretation of it to house position and aspects.

For any two individuals, the exact positions of their pairs of natal planets can be visualized as two points on the Zodiac circle. A vector intersects the Zodiac at the midpoint of these two degrees; one intersection at the near midpoint, another at the far midpoint. The near midpoint composite chart symbolizes how a couple *meets in the middle* and tries to form a relationship based on compromise, mutual agreement, common purpose, and shared goals. Two persons becoming one.

As in an individual nativity, the condition of a composite Sun is paramount, and is crucial to the long-term success of any relationship. Some aspects are somewhat tragic in the composite chart, for despite the love that any two souls may have for one another, certain aspects to the Sun can render a relationship unstable, full of strife, or make it nearly impossible to grow and flourish because of hindrances.

On the other hand, favorable solar aspects in the composite chart can keep two souls together despite challenging interplanetary or lunar aspects. It appears that the aspects to the Sun are *the heart and soul of any partnership,* and, *as a composite Sun goes, so goes a relationship.* Earlier in my career, I began to keep a scorecard of what I called *the backbreakers,* which were aspects that just killed a relationship, no matter how much the two people loved each other. I have since retired that list out of fear of it becoming a self-fulfilling prophesy for any couple I worked with.

There are certain peculiarities about the composite chart. It never has retrograde planets, and sometimes calculations of Mercury or Venus position them in opposition to the Sun, an astronomical impossibility. Some astrology software programs give an option to force the composite Mercury and Venus to be near to the Sun (using the far midpoint), which is what I advise to do.

Another idiosyncratic feature of a composite chart is found in its mathematical underpinnings. For example, if one person in relationship has a natal Moon trine Saturn, and the other has natal Moon sextile Saturn, the composite will contain a Moon square Saturn ($120° + 60° = 180° \div 2 = 90°$).[13] How could two individuals with favorable natal aspects between the same two planets then be castigated with a malefic aspect just by entering into the partnership? This is a mystery to me.

In other cases, I have seen individuals with natal quincunxes between the same two planets, where one was waxing, and the other was waning. In the composite, it became an opposition between the same two planets ($150° + 210° = 360° \div 2 = 180°$). In addition, I have also seen two individuals with natal squares between the same planets, but where one was first quarter, or waxing, and the other was a waning, or last quarter square. In the composite chart, it became a conjunction.

These examples illustrate how composite charts sometimes replicate pairs of natal planets that are in aspect, but with a rearranged geometry. My understanding of this phenomenon is that it symbolizes the transformation that one experiences by being in relationship. One's circuits become, in a sense, completely rewired. I recommend treating these replicated composite aspects as the most significant.

The spiritual dimension of any relationship can also be perceived with composite charts. I refer to this as the *Mystic Third*. It is similar to how marriage, in its ideal state, becomes sanctified when the couple is blessed by the Catholic *Sacrament,* or other religious ceremonies. In modern times, with so many divorces, it makes one wonder if the efficacy of the *Sacrament* is held together by a critical mass of souls believing in its power. Once collective belief fails, it is torn asunder.

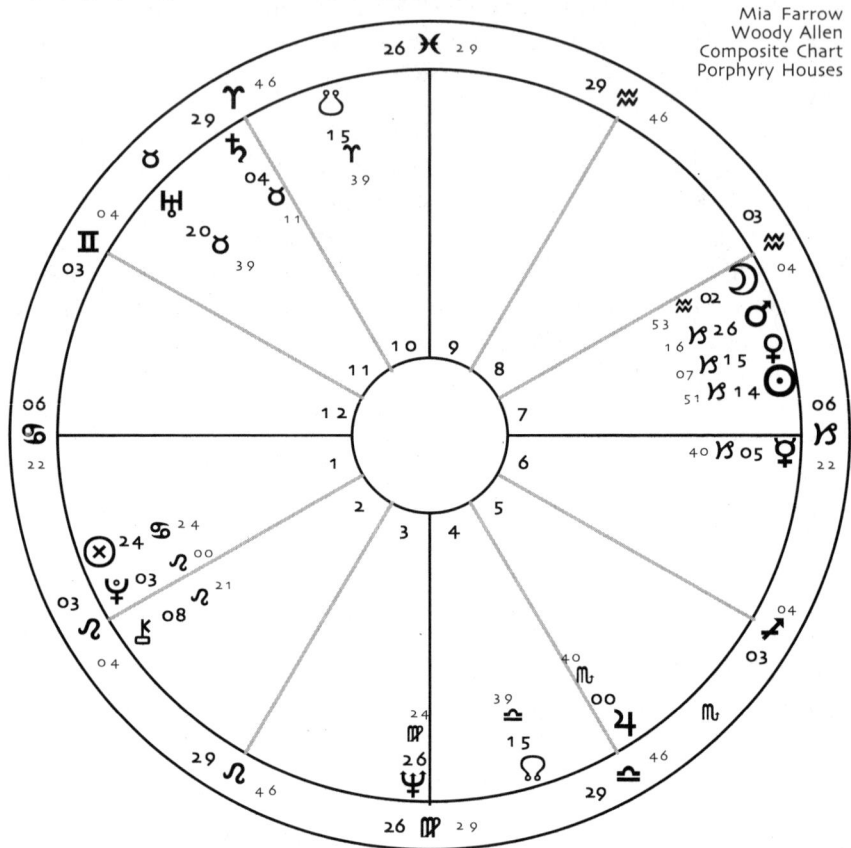

Mia Farrow
Woody Allen
Composite Chart
Porphyry Houses

Here are the near midpoint calculations for our case study couple:[14]

	Mia	Woody	<180° Arc	÷ 2	Add/Subtract	= Composite
Sun	320° 39'	249° 02'	71° 37'	35° 48.5'	284° 50.5'	14° ♑ 51'
Moon	281° 40'	324° 06'	42° 26'	21° 13'	302° 53'	02° ♒ 53'
Mercury	306° 50'	244° 30'	62° 20'	31° 10'	275° 40'	05° ♑ 40'
Venus	07° 21'	202° 53'	164° 28'	82° 14'	285° 07'	15° ♑ 07'
Mars	296° 26'	296° 06	00° 20'	00° 10'	296° 16'	26° ♑ 16'
Jupiter	176° 13'	245° 07'	68° 54'	34° 27'	210° 40'	00° ♏ 40'
Saturn	94° 22'	334° 01'	120° 21'	60° 10.5'	34° 11.5'	04° ♉ 11'
Chiron	182° 52'	73°51'	109° 01'	54° 30.5'	128° 21.5'	08° ♌ 21'
Uranus	69° 07'	32° 11'	36° 56'	18° 28'	50° 39'	20° ♉ 39'
Neptune	186° 08'	166° 41'	19° 27'	09° 43.5'	176° 24.5'	26° ♍ 24'
Pluto	128° 50'	117° 10'	11° 40'	05° 50'	123° 00'	03° ♌ 00'
MC	295° 45'	57° 12'	121° 27'	60° 43.5'	356° 28.5'	26° ♓ 29'
ASC	40° 29'	152° 18'	111° 49'	55° 54.5'	96° 23.5'	06° ♋ 22'

Here is section (6) of the worksheet for Farrow and Allen:

SUN HOUSE/ASPECTS ☉ in 7th; ☉☌♀ ☉△♅ ☉□☋

MOON HOUSE/ASPECTS ☽ in 8th; ☽□♃ ☽□♄ ☽☍♆

SABIAN SYMBOL OF ASC ♋7   In a fairy glade, in a quiet circle of moonlight, two of the little people are executing a fanciful dance.

MERCURY HOUSE/ASPECTS ☿ in 6th; ☿△♄ ☿⚼♅ ☿⚻♆ ☿☍AS

VENUS HOUSE/ASPECTS ♀ in 7th; ♀△♅ ♀□☋

MARS HOUSE/ASPECTS ♂ in 7th; ♂△♅ ♂△♆ ♂⚹MC

JUPITER HOUSE/ASPECTS ♃ intercepted in 5th; ♃☍♄ ♃□♆ ♃△AS

SATURN HOUSE/ASPECTS ♄ in 11th; ♄□♆ ♄⚹AS

ASPECT CONFIGURATIONS   Fixed Grand Cross; Earth Grand Trine

UNASPECTED PLANETS   None

With a powerful Sun-Venus conjunction in the 7th house, there is no question that this couple originally loved each other very much. Yet, they also experienced, through a betrayal (Neptune angular on the IC), how love can turn into hate. As a general rule, it is thought that the more desirable houses for the composite Sun are the 2nd or 7th (Venus ruled), in addition to the *love axis houses,* the 5th or 11th. A case can also be made for angular 1st or 4th house Suns being beneficial in the composite chart, but I would not place them in the same category as the other four.

However, this angular 7th house Sun-Venus conjunction was also square to the composite nodal axis, itself angular in the 10th house of public visibility and 4th house of private home life. One of the hallmarks of this relationship was Allen making movies based on her family, shooting some of these films in her apartment, such as *Hannah and Her Sisters* (1986; also symbolized by Neptune on the IC).

By far, the most fateful determinant in their composite chart was a Fixed Grand Cross involving the Moon in hard aspect to Jupiter, Saturn, Chiron and Pluto. This aspect configuration is shown here on the right. With a tragic end befalling this relationship, as Allen was discovered having sexual relations with her adopted daughter, Soon-Yi, a mythological scenario came to fruition. A female child abducted into the underworld has the signature of Moon opposition Pluto all over it. For my readers who also work with asteroids, Ceres, at 2° Scorpio, is conjunct Jupiter in the composite chart and an integral part of this Grand Cross.

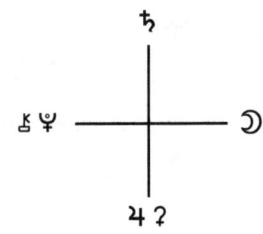

Composite charts can replicate aspects between the same pairs of planets that are in aspect in two nativities. These aspects then become quite significant in any relationship and can be placed at the top of a priority list, next to the close aspects to the composite Sun. Let us now examine the composite chart for Farrow and Allen to see if indeed these aspects exist.

In the nativity for Farrow, we find a waxing quincunx between her Moon and Pluto with a separating orb of 02° 50'. The angular separation of these two bodies is thus 152° 50'. Turning to the nativity for Allen, we also find the Moon and Pluto in quincunx aspect, however this one is waning, with a 03° 04' applying orb. The angular separation of his Moon and Pluto is therefore 206° 56'. Adding these two arcs of angular separation together, we arrive at the sum of 359° 46'. Dividing this sum by 2 we then get an arc of 179° 53', the nearly exact composite opposition of their Moon and Pluto, with its applying orb of 00° 07'.

One way astrologers can understand Moon quincunx Pluto in the nativity is as a symbol of broken emotional trust, which became deeply internalized and was not ever confronted openly with the parent who perpetrated the original wounding. If both individuals in a relationship have this childhood dynamic operative, as did Allen and Farrow, one can then see how there was a high probability in their life together for questionable behaviors being observed in the periphery of the vision (as is the nature of the 150° quincunx). But, by never being openly confronted and held compulsively within, these unrevealed internal tensions remained bottled up.

But, with the Moon and Pluto in opposition in their composite chart, geometrically being the near midpoint of her waxing quincunx and his waning identical aspect, the astrologer can see how this ultimately became an aspect of confrontational suspicion, yet only after several years of unexpressed concern about sexual trust. The karma for both Farrow and Allen was apparently to bring to full awareness (180° opposition) a deeply internalized (150° quincunx) pathology of feeling emotionally unsafe (Moon-Pluto) with the other, yet afraid to confront it.

Other instances of replicated natal aspects can also be found in their composite chart, such as the Mercury-Saturn and Mercury-Uranus relationships. In the case of the former, she has a waning quincunx (210°) between Mercury and Saturn, while he has a waning square (270°) between these two bodies. The near midpoint then becomes a 240° waning trine, which is the aspect you find in the composite.

Regards the latter, Farrow has a waning trine (240°) of Mercury and Uranus, while he possesses Mercury in waning quincunx (210°) to Uranus. The midpoint of the two calculates to 225°, the exact waning sesquiquadrate found in their composite. Besides these replicated natal aspects, are other aspects also found?

Yes, and these occur when a pair of planets that are not technically in aspect in either nativity, are in aspect in the composite chart. Consider the Moon-Jupiter square in the Allen-Farrow composite. Her Moon and Jupiter have an angular separation of 105° 27', midway between a biseptile and tridecile.

His angular separation between these two bodies is 78° 59', an applying waxing binovile. The sum of these arcs is 184° 26', and dividing by two we have 92° 13', the angular separation of the composite Moon square Jupiter, with its separating orb of 02° 13'. As the couple wound up in court in dispute over child custody issues, in addition to allegations of the sexual abuse of a young adopted daughter, this aspect certainly was operational (Moon = children; Jupiter = courts).

In summary, when investigating the composite chart, in addition to making notes of any aspect configurations, such as the Fixed Grand Cross and Earth Grand Trine which Farrow and Allen have, the astrologer should also note which of the composite aspects replicate natal aspects and which do not. As a general rule, the ones that exist in both nativities and in the composite will represent the issues a couple has to work on psychologically in relationship. Aspects occurring in the composite, but which do not occur in the nativities, seem to be circumstances arising within relationship that have not been dealt with before by either party.

Chapter Four

Davison Charts, Past Lives, Midpoints & Configurations

The Davison Time-Space Chart

In 1977, at the time several excellent astrology books on relationship were being published, the British astrologer, Ronald Davison wrote a book called *Synastry: Understanding Human Relations Through Astrology*. At this time, the composite chart had been in use in the United States for a few years, having been imported from Europe by the American astrologer, John Townley in the early 1970s. Davison first introduced the *Time-Space Relationship Chart,* which calculates the date, time and place midway between the two birthdays and two birth locations.

With this new Davison calculation, astrologers now had a relationship chart that did exist in both time and space, and its planetary positions could indeed be found in an ephemeris. It was not just a mathematical construct, as is the composite chart. The Davison chart also included retrograde planets, stationary planets, and other significant factors that could shed new light on partnership. However, a rift opened within astrology as to which of the two charts was the more accurate. This author believes that both are relevant, yet each indicates a different reality.

Your astrological software has two different ways to calculate Davison charts. From the *Io Relationship* program,[15] we learn: *"Great Circle Coordinates computes a median chart location by bisecting the great circle arc, the shortest possible path lying between the two chart locations. Average Coordinates computes a median chart location by averaging the latitudes and longitudes of the two chart locations."* Great Circle Coordinates are the method that I recommend for calculating these charts.

One of the bizarre things about this chart is how the length of time between births will affect its similarity to, or difference from, the composite chart. For example, a Sun in a composite chart may be opposite from the Sun in a Davison chart, such as with Allen and Farrow who were born nine years and two months apart, Allen in December 1935, and Farrow in February 1945. Let us now examine their Davison time-space chart.

Whereas in the composite chart for Farrow and Allen, there is a 14° Capricorn Sun, the Davison chart has an opposite position of the Sun at 14° Cancer. In the near midpoint composite calculation, halfway from her Sun at 20° Aquarius to his Sun at 09° Sagittarius is the composite Sun at 14° Capricorn. However, the date midway between their two births is 6 July 1940, which is 55 months after his birth, and equally 55 months before hers. This Davison date thus produces a Sun in Cancer. The MC/IC axis is reversed as well.

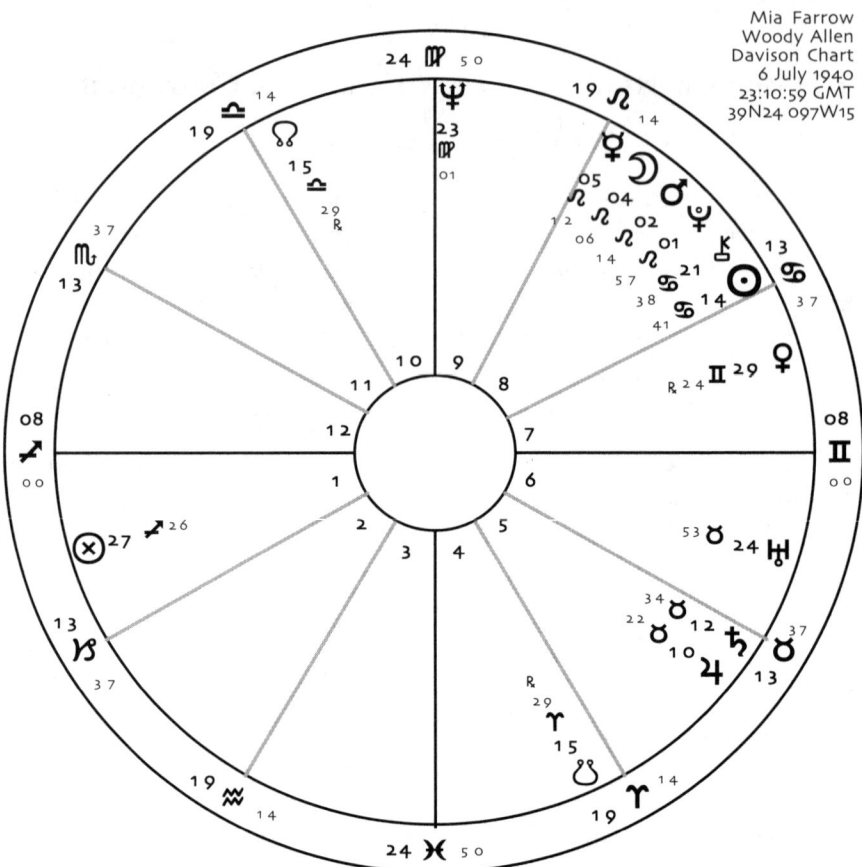

One difference between a Davison chart and a composite chart is that births that are an even number of years apart often have close to identical Suns in both charts. But, if the births are an odd number of years apart, it is likely that a Davison Sun will be opposite from the composite Sun.

For example, if a Cancer and a Scorpio are in relationship, the astrologer would know that halfway between the 4th sign and the 8th sign of the Zodiac would be Virgo, the 6th sign, and he could then see at a glance that this would be the near midpoint position of the composite Sun. But if that Scorpio was born in November 1955, for example, and the Cancer in July 1958, the date midway between the two births is in March 1957, and would therefore produce a Davison Sun in Pisces.

The author believes that differences between composite and Davison charts can be understood in this way: *a composite chart symbolizes the life force energy of a couple as if it were a third personality, a separate relationship entity; whereas the Davison chart, because it exists in both time and space, symbolizes forces working on a couple from outside of their relationship, be they from the family, from children, from financial pressures, or from past life factors that are creating present karma.*

Here is section (7) of the worksheet for Mia Farrow and Woody Allen:

SUN SIGN / HOUSE / ASPECTS ☉ in ♋ in 8th; ☉☌⚷ ☉⚹♃ ☉⚹♄ ☉□☊☋

MOON SIGN / HOUSE / ASPECTS ☽ in ♌ in 8th; ☽☌☿ ☽☌♂ ☽☌♇ ☽△AS

SABIAN SYMBOL OF ASC ♐ 8 In the caldron of the universe the rocks and world stuff are in process of formation; the metals glint within.

MERCURY SIGN / HOUSE / ASPECTS ☿ in ♌ in 8th; ☿☌♂ ☿□♃ ☿☌♇ ☿△AS

VENUS SIGN / HOUSE / ASPECTS ♀℞ in ♊ in 7th; ♀□♆

MARS SIGN / HOUSE / ASPECTS ♂ in ♌ in 8th; ♂☌♇ ♂△AS

JUPITER SIGN / HOUSE / ASPECTS ♃ in ♉ in 5th; ♃☌♄ ♃⚻AS

SATURN SIGN / HOUSE / ASPECTS ♄ in ♉ in 5th/6th; ♄⚻☊

DIGNITY / EXALTATION / DETRIMENT / FALL + HOUSES RULED none

CONFIGURATIONS / STATIONS / RECEPTION Stellium; ☿ Stationary; ☉☽ in MR

It is also my belief that a date and location midway between two births functions like a karmic vortex similar to a mass of fluid whirling about an axis—creating a time-space force field that affects the lives of any two souls who are born at equal measures of time and space before and after it. The metaphysics of this theory also implies that there can be other pairs of souls born equidistant from a same moment in time and space, yet at different measures, who would experience a very similar karma to the other couples who were older or younger than they are.

This is why astrologers should investigate the celestial dynamics on the date of a Davison chart for stations, retrograde planets, major conjunctions or eclipses. These forces affect the two souls born an equal measure of time before and after this date. A notable major conjunction in the Davison chart, such as the Jupiter-Saturn grand conjunction that occurred in the Allen and Farrow time-space chart from 1940, would be significant.

In Farrow and Allen's Davison chart we also find a retrograde Venus in the anaretic 30th degree of the dual sign, Gemini, symbolizing the fated and illicit second relationship of Allen with Soon-Yi. Mercury, ruling the Descendant and MC, is stationary retrograde. Neptune (films) is angular on the MC, instead of on the IC as in the composite, symbolizing the highly public scandal that followed the painful sexual betrayal. The 8th house of sexuality has a tight stellium in the sign of children, Leo, containing the Moon, Mercury, Mars and Pluto all within less than 4° of total orb from one another. Jupiter and Saturn are also parallel.

I consider sign placements of the Lights and planets in the Davison chart as important, whereas I ignore them in the composite chart. Planets in dignity or exaltation in the Davison chart can further a relationship's strength. In contrast, Davison Luminaries or planets in detriment or fall can weaken a relationship, including the houses that debilitated planets rule.

An intriguing example of this interpretive technique is found in the Davison chart for former U.S. president Clinton, and his wife, Hillary.[16] Highly embarrassing and very public sexual affairs have plagued this marriage, yet they have remained together despite these unfaithful transgressions. Mrs. Clinton has likened her husband to *a dog that you couldn't keep on the front porch.* One presumes that these dynamics could be seen in the time-space chart, with the assumption that Davison charts symbolize outside forces acting on a relationship.

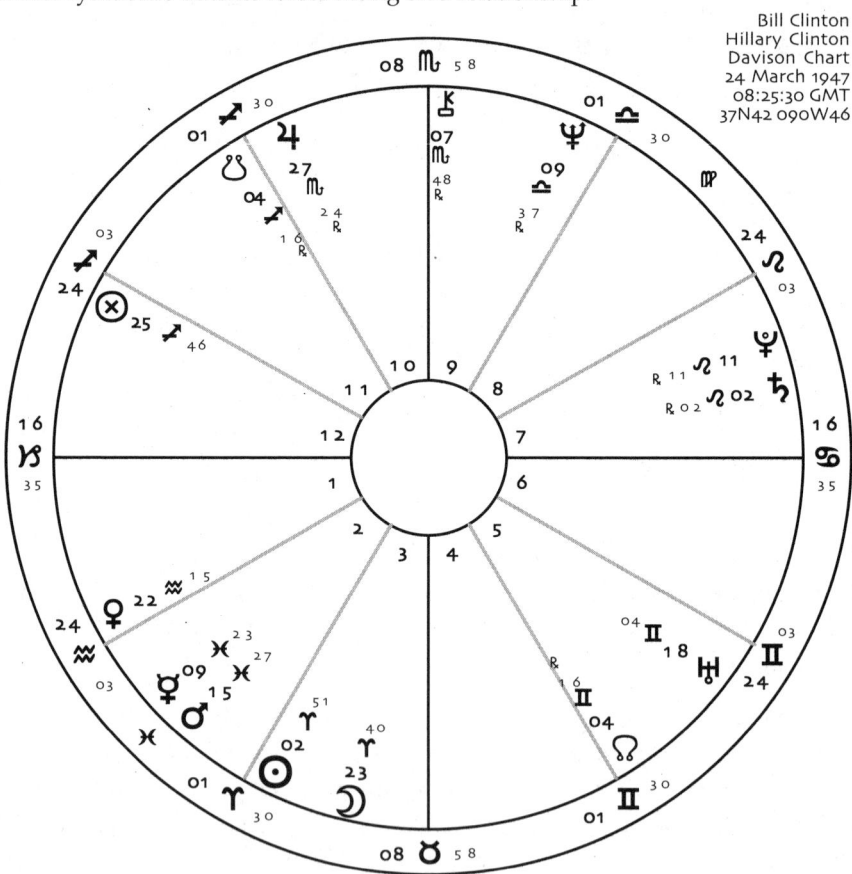

With an exalted Sun exactly trine to the chart ruler, a retrograde Saturn in detriment, an astrologer can see how this marriage, although highly flawed, has held together. A case could be made for Mercury being the most debilitated planet in this chart, as it is intercepted and in detriment in Pisces, at the finger of a Yod, and conjunct a malefic. Mercury rules the 5th house of affairs, and an intercepted Virgo in the 8th house, symbolizing concealed sexual relationships. The Moon is void-of-course, and an elevated retrograde Chiron on the Midheaven in the sexual sign of Scorpio certainly appears to accurately symbolize the public wounds of this marriage.

The Sabian Symbol for the rising degree, Capricorn 17, is highly relevant: *A young woman, mature but long repressed, is surreptitiously bathing in the nude, finding a new release in spirit.* I leave it to my erudite readers to draw whatever conclusion they wish from this symbolism. In summary, I recommend using the sign placements of planets only in the Davison chart and to ignore them in composites. Planets in dignity or exaltation will help a relationship through the houses that they rule, while Davison planets in detriment or fall weaken a marriage with forces from the outside, through the houses ruled by these debilitated Luminaries or planets.

Past Life Connections: The IC, South Node and Vertex

Many times in my career, clients have asked me if a certain soul whom they loved dearly could be seen in the charts as a past life connection or as a soul mate. Could the astrologer answer this question with any certainty or would the rejoinder be unscientific, a bit of metaphysical baloney doled out to the client to feed their esoteric fantasies? Consider my professional experiences.

Without inquiring, I have had clients volunteer information that they received during a psychic reading with a clairvoyant, through their dreams, or during a past life regression with a psychotherapist. I began to compare these stories through the years with three specific horoscopic factors to see if correspondences existed. I was looking at the IC, South Node or Vertex.

I noticed a pattern. When the progressed IC conjoined a natal planet, or with outer planets in transit over a natal or progressed IC, clients reported dreams of dead and departed relatives contacting them from the Spirit plane and becoming spirit guides for them. If the progressed IC conjoined natal Mercury, for example, the visitation would be from a deceased sibling who had died in childhood, or in some cases, who had committed suicide as a young adult.

In one case, when a progressed IC conjoined Venus, the client, who had given birth to a stillborn daughter many years earlier, was contacted in her dreams by the spirit of the deceased child. Another client had transit Neptune conjoin his progressed IC at the same time he began contact from the other side with ancestors from the 19th century. With reports of these experiences, I began to view the natal or progressed IC as a very sensitive degree, connecting the client with his ancestral blood lines and to his family and racial lineage.

I also heard of frightening experiences from some of my clients, such as a transit of Pluto over the progressed IC corresponding with a dark entity attempting to take possession of a client's thoughts. In her past life regression, this woman learned that the spirit had been her father in a past life who had murdered her.

When clients ask about these troubling visitations, I discuss with them spiritual techniques that are used for protection. The most powerful method is to ask the entity three times if it is from the Light in the name of Jesus Christ. If it remains, it is safe to communicate with it. If the entity dissipates at the first or second inquiry, it is from the dark side and is to be spurned. Methods of testing spirits are elucidated in the New Testament letter, 1 John 4:1-6.

A logical next step is to apply these sensitive points to relationship analysis. When I see a synastric conjunction from one person's Light or planet to the partner's natal IC, I interpret it as a past life family connection. The key assumption is that the two individuals had been family members in a past life. The accuracy of this became somewhat confirmed for me when I had couples as clients who both underwent past life regression and reported the findings to me.

On a personal note, the only other astrologer with whom I have formed a deep friendship that felt like a family bond, has been Mary Plumb, the book review editor for *The Mountain Astrologer,* and a dear friend and colleague. Her natal Chiron is 20° Sagittarius 48', and conjunct my natal IC within 03' of arc. My natal Moon is 06° Pisces 38'—the exact degree of her natal IC.

I have been asked by several clients to do comprehensive family analysis, using data for three or four generations of births. In some of these cases, I find an inordinate percentage, such as nine out of thirteen in the group having composite or Davison planets exactly conjunct the IC. Past life therapists believe that previously related souls often reunite in present family systems.

I feel it is professional and ethical for an astrologer to state these findings to his clients when they specifically ask about past life connections with a family member. If an astrologer sees dual or triple indications of this, such as Allen's Pluto conjoined Farrow's natal IC, and Neptune on their composite IC, he can express this with certainty. It is also common to see a mother's progressed Moon on her infant's IC at the time of birth.

In addition to the natal or progressed IC being an indicator of past life family connections, the astrologer will also find Luminaries or planets in one chart in conjunction with a South Node in the second chart. This is, in my opinion, a clear indication of a soul connection spanning many lifetimes.

The 12th house symbolizes the most recent past life and a synastric conjunction with the 12th cusp is an indicator of two souls having been together in their most immediate past lives. However, the South Node represents the ongoing spiritual growth for as many as seven past incarnations. If the astrologer sees a synastric conjunction to the South Node, he knows that two souls have had a long history.

During the secondary progressed lunation cycle's fourth quarter, and particularly during the balsamic phase, it is quite common for past life connections to arrive in a person's life. If a client inquires if a new love looks like an old soul coming back into her life again and the astrologer sees a Light or planet of the client's conjunct the other's South Node and the client is in the progressed lunar balsamic phase, the astrologer can confirm this.

It must be said here that many of the synastric conjunctions to the South Node are not pleasant. Sometimes karma involves ending a connection with another soul with whom one has experienced animosity, hostility or hatred. The only way that the astrologer can render a judgment about the nature of this type of karma is to examine the horoscopes to see if there are also conjunctions to the North Node. If for example, a man and a woman have a composite Moon on the South Node, and this Luminary is also opposite a composite Saturn conjunct the North Node, the astrologer would know that they had been family members in many past lives, and have reunited again to support each other's accomplishments in this life.

However, if the astrologer sees a synastric conjunction of Mars to the South Node, but with no mitigating conjunction to the North Node, he should inform his client of the past life link, and also explain that there is a strong likelihood of residual aversion, and perhaps even hatred, due to an abrupt separation during a past life. Of my clients with this synastric aspect, and who had also been regressed, it was a usually a death of one during war which had so devastated the other's core.

Many students in my classes have asked for case histories from my practice or for personal stories to help illustrate these synastric or composite chart dynamics involving the South Node. One of the jokes that I told is how one, when seeing that another soul has planets on their South Node, instinctively reaches for their wallet and asks, *"how much do I owe you?"* Karmic debts are one way to view conjunctions to the Dragon's Tail, even when there are just synastric planets *in the same sign* as one's South Node. In my life, after my elder daughter was born in 1980, I paid child support to her mother every month for 18 years; the mother had five planets in Cancer, plus Cancer rising, all in the sign of my South Node.

One other story involves a period in my life when I was divorced and dating, hoping to establish a lasting relationship again. For a few years, Neptune was in transit square first to my natal Venus, then to my progressed Ascendant and Mars, and every woman I met had natal Venus-Neptune aspects. I laugh about it now, but back then it felt like I was chasing an impossible dream, and nothing became solid and lasting. Four of the women I met in a row were Cancer Suns who had planets conjunct my South Node, and each was definitely an old connection from past lives. They were all loving souls for whom I felt much affection, but it became clear that we would not be part of each other's future. During this chapter of my life, I was in the fourth quarter of my progressed lunation cycle.

In contrast to this, when astrologers see synastric or composite conjunctions to a North Node, they can view this as a karmic credit. In the case of synastry, however, the planet person will repay the Node person in some positive way. When found in the composite chart, couples will have positive karma. A favorite story about this is of an astrologer in Vancouver, British Columbia, Canada, who was a 1961 Pisces with a Jupiter-Saturn conjunction right on my Capricorn North Node. She purchased a lecture tape of mine in April 1996 and enjoyed it so much that she invited me to speak at a regional conference in Vancouver two years in a row, assiduously promoting my work there. She was very kind and supportive to me and I am still grateful for her efforts. The North Node connection was visceral.

As a general rule, the astrologer can interpret synastry conjunctions to the South Node that are not also accompanied by a conjunction to the North Node, as the karma of conscious completion. The two souls may accomplish this over many years, even remaining together until death, but a series of lifetimes together has reached its fulfillment. If there is also a North Node conjunction, astrologers can view this as an ongoing soul connection, continuing into the next life together.

Regarding questions as to whether a new love will turn out to be a soul mate, can the astrologer answer with any certainty? Yes, and to assess this possibility he must examine both the natal and secondary progressed Vertex. This sensitive degree in the horoscope has been associated with fated love, and appears to symbolize relationship brought into one's life for karmic purposes, such as for the birth of a child, or a life-changing transformative journey together.

To calculate the Vertex, follow these steps:

1. Subtract the birth latitude from 90° (this is the *co-latitude*).
2. Take the degree of the IC, find it in a Tables of Houses (as if it were an MC).
3. Go down the Ascendant column in the Tables of Houses to the co-latitude.
4. The Ascendant for that co-latitude is the Vertex (with the IC as the MC).
5. A Vertex has to be located on the right side of a chart (western hemisphere).
6. The opposite degree is called the Antivertex; together, a very sensitive axis.

To calculate the secondary progressed Vertex: in 2, substitute the current degree of the progressed IC, while retaining the *co-latitude* in 1 (derived from the place of birth; not relocated). As to how to determine the progressed IC, I recommend using the *MC by Solar Arc* method of progressing a vertical axis. This is where one takes the angular separation between the natal Sun and the secondary progressed Sun, and then adds this number of degrees and minutes to the natal Midheaven and IC.

It is fairly common to find synastry, composite or Davison planets conjunct the IC. It is also not too rare to find synastry, composite or Davison planets conjunct the South Node. But, what allows the astrologer to definitively say that one soul is truly fated to be with another is when there are progressed or transit conjunctions to the natal Vertex, or to the progressed Vertex, or if a progressed Vertex conjoins a natal or progressed planet in either nativity as the relationship is beginning.

I have known clients with a secondary progressed Moon conjunct a natal Vertex when they met their soul mate. I know of a couple who both had progressed Vertex in the same degree when they first met (and conjunct Jupiter in the man's chart). I have seen female clients who had natal Venus in the exact degree of the Vertex of the man to whom they felt irresistibly drawn. Additionally, I watched marriages break up when transit Uranus, or progressed Mars, conjoined a natal Vertex.

It is reasonable to predict, if an astrologer sees that his client is about to have the Vertex-Antivertex axis conjoined by the progressed Moon, or by transit from the Descendant ruler, that his client is now *in the fated love zone*, and he should advise his client to prepare the heart, and be ready to welcome love into their life. If the astrologer sees that a progressed Vertex is about to conjoin a Light or planet, and that body rules the Descendant, he can predict the arrival of love.

How long does the progressed Vertex remain in the same degree, and what would be the allowable orb here? The rate of progressed degree movement for the Vertex can exceed three degrees a year. At other times, it can be closer to one degree per year. This variation is caused by the 23.5° axial tilt of the Earth, which produces signs of short or long ascension. Because the Vertex is calculated as if it were the *co-latitude Ascendant of the IC,* it is affected by the variability of the rising degrees found in Tables of Houses.

Regarding the allowable orb, I have only seen the arrival of the fated love into the life of the client when the orb was exact, e.g., in the same degree, and not during the one degree applying nor the one degree separating orb. Will the particular planet that the progressed Vertex is conjoining or opposing (where the Antivertex progresses into a conjunction) define the karma in a fated love relationship? Yes, and realism is called for here.

It is obvious that a progressed Vertex conjunct natal Saturn at the time of entering into relationship could signify ultimate sorrow or failure in love. But is it ethical for astrologers to steer clients away from meaningful relationships when those soul connections have likely pain in their scripts? This is a hard call to make. I do not feel qualified to advise fellow astrologers on whether to do this. Based on my own experiences, I have learned some valuable lessons about life and love while experiencing deep sorrow. Sounds like a guy with Venus conjunct Saturn, eh?

The concept of a soul mate is not limited to only happiness and joy. Souls may have a fated connection and exquisite love may exist between them, but the karma that they must go through may contain loss as well as gain. The mother of my younger daughter had a progressed Vertex in 29° Taurus exactly conjunct her progressed South Node when we met up again after a hiatus of over twelve years with no contact. I saw her Vertex progressing onto that South Node but I went willingly into personal relationship with her and we had a child together. True, I got massacred emotionally before all was said and done, but that's a Scorpio's life and I'd do it again tomorrow.

Here is section (8) of the worksheet for Allen and Farrow:

CONJUNCTIONS TO THE IC Allen ♆ ☌ Farrow IC; ♆ ☌ Composite IC

CONJUNCTIONS TO THE SOUTH NODE Synastric Nodal Opposition

CONJUNCTIONS TO THE VERTEX Farrow ♂ ☌ Allen Vertex

12th HOUSE OVERLAY (Note if on 12th cusp) Farrow ♆ in Allen 12th; Allen ♅ in Farrow 12th

ACTIVATION OF NATAL VERTEX 1982: Allen progressed ☉ = natal Vertex

ACTIVATION OF PROGRESSED VERTEX 1982: Allen SP Vertex = natal ♅ + Farrow SP ♀

The exact date that Farrow and Allen entered into relationship is not known but it appears to have been in 1982, when they made their first film together, *A Midsummer Night's Sex Comedy*. At that time, Allen's progressed Sun conjoined his natal Vertex of 26° Capricorn 34', which is also the degree of his Mars, and the degree of her Mars. Also during that year, the Vertex in Allen's chart had progressed to 2° Taurus, conjoining his natal Uranus in the exact degree of Farrow's progressed Venus. Vertex activation for certain.

This section of the chapter has been an analysis of past life dynamics that can be seen in synastry, composite or Davison chart factors involving the IC, South Node, 12th house, or the Vertex. My experience in practice corroborates what most astrologers know: we regularly get asked spiritual questions about soul mates, fated love, and past life connections. Often people ask about these things so that they can find peace concerning a lost love that held deep purpose for them. The astrologer needs to know what he is looking for when trying to explain a karmic history and he should take these questions seriously.

Synastry, Composite and Davison Midpoints

Love between two souls ideally exists to transform each into a fully integrated individual. The gestalt of a nativity is a celestial pattern of interconnected forces (Luminaries and planets) that are seeking to find unified expression and purpose through a human personality.

The soul who inherits this moment in time as his birthright is the crucible in which these patterns seek to find cohesion. That personal relationship contributes to this process is rarely disputed, but in an astrological synastry analysis, where would one look to see this spiritual mechanism at work? Can astrology perceive this?

This astrologer has seen how formidable natal aspects can condemn individuals to battle with internal conflict during the first half of life. Gradually, healing takes place due to the help of other souls, who, through their love, can understand and accept the inner turmoil with which the person is struggling. Real love is thus a bridge for two souls to build between their hearts, with both being made whole.

The astrologer can look inside this process for any couple by examining midpoints between pairs of planets in one nativity which are in synastric conjunction with a Luminary or planet in the second horoscope. This technique is principally useful when examining midpoints of any two planets that are natally semisquare (45°), square (90°), sesquiquadrate (135°), quincunx (150°), or opposite (180°), as these five aspects are notorious for causing turmoil, discomfort and psychic imbalance.

After listing midpoints for pairs of planets in one nativity that are in stressful aspect, the astrologer then looks to see if there are Lights, planets or angles in the second horoscope that are in synastric conjunction with those midpoint degrees. When this occurs, astrologers know that the planet person is helping the midpoint person to integrate parts of his character. This unifying force is the energy of one person's planet acting on both of the other's stressed planets.

From our case study, a recap of Allen's stressful natal aspects and his midpoints:

1. Sun semisquare Venus; 1° 09' applying; midpoint = 15° Scorpio 58'.
2. Sun semisquare Mars; 2° 04' applying; midpoint = 02° Capricorn 34'.
3. Sun square Saturn; 5° 01' separating; midpoint = 21° Capricorn 31'.
4. Moon quincunx Pluto; 3° 04' applying; midpoint = 10° Taurus 38'.
5. Mercury square Saturn; 0° 29' separating; midpoint = 19° Capricorn 16'.
6. Mercury quincunx Uranus; 2° 19' separating; midpoint = 18° Aquarius 21'.
7. Venus square Mars; 3° 13' applying; midpoint = 09° Sagittarius 30'.
8. Venus square Pluto; 4° 17' applying; midpoint = 10° Virgo 02'.
9. Mars opposite Pluto; 1° 04' applying; midpoint = 26° Libra 38'.

Then we examine Farrow's nativity to see if she has any Lights, planets or angles in the exact degree (no orb allowed) of any of Allen's midpoints. We find:

1. His Sun/Uranus midpoint = her Sun (20° Aquarius).
2. His Moon/Pluto midpoint = her Ascendant (10° Taurus).

Woody Allen

Dec 1 1935 10:55 PM EST
Bronx New York
40N40 73W54
Dec 2 1935 03:55:00 GMT
Tropical Porphyry True Node

360° Midpoint Sort

♄/♅	03 ♈ 06	♆/♇	21 ♌ 56	☊/AS	07 ♏ 43	☿/☊	23 ♐ 51	♂/♄	15 ♒ 03
☽/MC	10 ♈ 39	AS	02 ♍ 15	☿/♀	13 ♏ 42	♃/☊	24 ♐ 09	☿/♅	18 ♒ 21
♄/MC	15 ♈ 36	♆/AS	09 ♍ 28	♀/♃	14 ♏ 00	☉/☊	26 ♐ 06	♃/♅	18 ♒ 39
♅	02 ♉ 11	♀/♇	10 ♍ 02	♂/AS	14 ♏ 10	♀/♄	28 ♐ 27	☉/♅	20 ♒ 36
☽/♇	10 ♉ 38	♆	16 ♍ 41	♆/☊	14 ♏ 56	☿/♂	00 ♑ 18	☽	24 ♒ 06
♅/MC	14 ♉ 41	♀/AS	27 ♍ 34	☉/♀	15 ♏ 58	♂/♃	00 ♑ 36	☽/♄	29 ♒ 03
♄/♇	15 ♉ 35	☿/♇	00 ♎ 50	♂/♆	21 ♏ 23	☉/♂	02 ♑ 34	☿/MC	00 ♓ 51
MC	27 ♉ 12	♃/♇	01 ♎ 09	☽/AS	28 ♏ 10	☊	13 ♑ 11	♃/MC	01 ♓ 09
♄/AS	03 ♊ 08	☉/♇	03 ♎ 06	♀/☊	03 ♐ 02	☽/☿	14 ♑ 18	☉/MC	03 ♓ 07
♅/♇	14 ♊ 40	♀/♆	04 ♎ 47	☿	04 ♐ 30	☽/♃	14 ♑ 36	♄	04 ♓ 01
♇/MC	27 ♊ 11	☿/AS	18 ♎ 23	☿/♃	04 ♐ 49	☉/☽	16 ♑ 34	♅/☊	07 ♓ 41
♅/AS	02 ♋ 13	♃/AS	18 ♎ 41	♃	05 ♐ 07	☿/♄	19 ♑ 16	♂/♅	14 ♓ 08
♅/♆	09 ♋ 26	♇/☊	20 ♎ 11	☽/♆	05 ♐ 23	♃/♄	19 ♑ 34	☊/MC	20 ♓ 11
AS/MC	14 ♋ 43	☉/AS	20 ♎ 38	☉/☿	06 ♐ 46	♂/☊	19 ♑ 38	♂/MC	26 ♓ 39
♆/MC	21 ♋ 56	♀	22 ♎ 53	☉/♃	07 ♐ 05	☉/♄	21 ♑ 31	☽/♅	28 ♓ 08
♇	27 ♋ 10	☿/♆	25 ♎ 36	☉	09 ♐ 02	♂	26 ♑ 06		
♀/♅	27 ♋ 32	♃/♆	25 ♎ 54	♀/♂	09 ♐ 30	☽/☊	03 ♒ 38		
♀/MC	10 ♌ 03	♂/♇	26 ♎ 38	♄/♆	10 ♐ 21	♄/☊	08 ♒ 36		
♇/AS	14 ♌ 42	☉/♆	27 ♎ 51	☽/♀	23 ♐ 30	☽/♂	10 ♒ 06		

One synastrically conjoined midpoint involves two bodies that are in stressful aspect (Moon quincunx Pluto); the other is of two planets that are in creative aspect (Sun biquintile Uranus). I would interpret the synastry of her Ascendant conjoining his Moon/Pluto as how Farrow, a mother of seven children when they entered into relationship, helped Allen to overcome a compulsive fear of children. He and Farrow then had a son together and adopted two more children.

As to the synastry of her Sun conjunct the midpoint of an artistic biquintile between his Sun and Uranus, the couple made thirteen unique films together with Farrow starring as the leading actress; the scripts, written by Allen, showcased different facets of her character and personality. They were a very creative pair.

Mia Farrow

Feb 9 1945 11:27 AM PWT
Santa Monica California
33N50 118W29
Feb 9 1945 18:27:00 GMT
Tropical Porphyry True Node

360° Midpoint Sort

☉/AS	00 ♈ 34	♀/♄	20 ♉ 51	♇/☊	28 ♋ 29	☽/♆	23 ♏ 54	☿	06 ♒ 50
♅/MC	02 ♈ 26	♅/AS	24 ♉ 48	♃/♅	02 ♌ 40	♃/MC	25 ♏ 59	☉/MC	08 ♒ 12
♂/♅	02 ♈ 46	♀/☊	27 ♉ 44	♅/♆	07 ♌ 37	♂/♃	26 ♏ 19	☉/♂	08 ♒ 32
♀	07 ♈ 21	♄/AS	07 ♊ 25	♇	08 ♌ 50	♆/MC	00 ♐ 56	☉/☿	13 ♒ 45
☿/♅	07 ♈ 58	♀/♇	08 ♊ 05	♃/♄	15 ♌ 17	♂/♆	01 ♐ 17	☉	20 ♒ 39
☽/♄	08 ♈ 01	♅	09 ♊ 07	♄/♆	20 ♌ 15	☿/♃	01 ♐ 31	☽/♀	24 ♒ 30
☉/♅	14 ♈ 53	☊/AS	14 ♊ 18	♃/☊	22 ♌ 10	☿/♆	06 ♐ 29	♀/MC	01 ♓ 33
♄/MC	15 ♈ 03	♄/♅	21 ♊ 44	♆/☊	27 ♌ 07	☉/♃	08 ♐ 26	♀/♂	01 ♓ 53
♂/♄	15 ♈ 24	♇/AS	24 ♊ 40	♃/♇	02 ♍ 31	☉/♆	13 ♐ 23	☿/♀	07 ♓ 05
☿/♄	20 ♈ 36	♅/☊	28 ♊ 37	♆/♇	07 ♍ 29	☽	11 ♑ 40	☽/AS	11 ♓ 05
☊/MC	21 ♈ 56	♀/♃	01 ♋ 47	♃	26 ♍ 13	☽/MC	18 ♑ 43	☉/♀	14 ♓ 00
♂/☊	22 ♈ 16	♄	04 ♋ 22	♃/♆	01 ♎ 10	☽/♂	19 ♑ 03	AS/MC	18 ♓ 07
♀/AS	23 ♈ 55	♀/♆	06 ♋ 44	♆	06 ♎ 08	☽/☿	24 ♑ 15	♂/AS	18 ♓ 27
☿/☊	27 ♈ 29	♅/♇	08 ♋ 58	☽/☊	14 ♎ 54	MC	25 ♑ 45	☿/AS	23 ♓ 40
☉/♄	27 ♈ 30	♄/☊	11 ♋ 14	☽/♇	25 ♎ 15	♂/MC	26 ♑ 05	☽/♅	25 ♓ 23
☉/☊	04 ♉ 23	☊	18 ♋ 07	♇/MC	02 ♏ 18	♂	26 ♑ 26		
♀/♅	08 ♉ 14	♃/AS	18 ♋ 21	♂/♇	02 ♏ 38	☉/☽	01 ♒ 10		
AS	10 ♉ 29	♄/♇	21 ♋ 36	☿/♇	07 ♏ 50	☿/MC	01 ♒ 18		
☉/♇	14 ♉ 45	♆/AS	23 ♋ 18	☽/♃	18 ♏ 57	☿/♂	01 ♒ 38		

Here is a recap of Farrow's difficult aspects and midpoints:

1. Sun semisquare Venus; 1° 42' separating; midpoint = 14° Pisces 00'.
2. Sun sesquiquadrate Saturn; 1° 17' separating; midpoint = 27° Aries 30'.
3. Sun sesquiquadrate Neptune; 0° 29' applying; midpoint = 13° Sagittary 23'.
4. Moon square Venus; 4° 19' separating; midpoint = 24° Aquarius 30'.
5. Moon opposite Saturn; 7° 18' separating; midpoint = 08° Aries 01'.
6. Moon quincunx Uranus; 2° 33' separating; midpoint = 25° Pisces 23'.
7. Moon square Neptune; 5° 32' separating; midpoint = 23° Scorpio 54'.
8. Moon quincunx Pluto; 2° 50' separating; midpoint = 25° Libra 15'.
9. Mercury quincunx Saturn; 2° 28' separating; midpoint = 20° Aries 36'.
10. Mercury opposite Pluto; 2° 00' applying; midpoint = 07° Scorpio 50'.

11. Venus square Saturn; 2° 59' separating; midpoint = 20° Taurus 51'.
12. Venus opposite Neptune; 1° 13' separating; midpoint = 06° Cancer 44'.

After examining Allen's nativity to see if he has any Lights, planets or angles in the exact degree (no orb allowed) of any of Farrow's midpoints, we find:

1. Her Moon/Venus midpoint = his Moon (24° Aquarius).
2. Her Venus/North Node midpoint = his Midheaven (27° Taurus).
3. Her Jupiter/Pluto midpoint = his Ascendant (02° Virgo).

The one synastrically conjoined midpoint involving planets in stressful aspect in Farrow's nativity is especially poignant, considering what happened between Allen and her adopted daughter. Farrow's Moon-Venus square has his Moon at its midpoint, and complex mother-daughter relationships are seen in these squares. Women with a Moon in hard aspect to Venus also struggle with conflict between their mothering instincts and their feminine expression as a lover, or as a wife.

With his Moon (symbolizing a wife) at the midpoint of this square in her chart, one can speculate that if Allen and Farrow would have married (they never did), he could have possibly helped her to integrate this internal conflict. She then could have lived less through her children (Moon), and learned to be more of an equal partner to her mate (Venus). That he wound up in a sexual relationship with her adopted daughter, then married Soon-Yi and had children with her, is quite ironic.

Allen's two other synastric conjunctions to her midpoints involved his angles. With his Midheaven at the midpoint of her Venus/North Node, the astrologer can see how his professional skills as a film maker and director helped her to live up to, and to further integrate, her life potential as an actress. Venus is also her ruler.

His Ascendant at the midpoint of her Jupiter/Pluto, unfortunately, seems to have played out primarily through a custody battle in court over their children, with allegations of sexual molestation of an adopted seven-year old daughter brought against him, yet never proven. It is clear from all that these two have gone through, that he had a transformational impact on her outlook on life.

When employing this technique, the astrologer can look for any conjunctions from a planet in one chart to a midpoint in the second chart. The gist of it is quite simple. The planet person has an innate ability to help the midpoint person to integrate the energy of those two planets. This is particularly meaningful if the two planets whose midpoint is conjoined are also involved in a stressful natal aspect.

In addition to examining any synastic conjunctions to midpoints for a couple, it is also informative to apply this technique to the composite and Davison charts. To do this, an astrologer looks to see if either individual has natal planets that occupy the exact degree of any composite or Davison midpoint. If so, this is where that individual can help the relationship to further integrate, grow and evolve.

If, for example, a man's Sun is conjunct the midpoint of the composite Sun/Saturn with his wife, he may be the one who sets long term goals for the two of them, and the one who reaffirms his commitment to the marriage on a regular basis. If she has her natal Uranus, for example, conjunct the Sun/Moon midpoint in the composite, her role in the marriage would be as the catalyst for change and experimentation, and the one who challenges any traditional expectations of spousal roles.

When scrutinizing a Davison chart for midpoints that are conjoined by planets in either nativity, astrologers need to recall that these time-space charts represent forces working on a couple from outside the relationship. *These forces may include painful life lessons or any emotional baggage carried over from the past.*

If a man has his Mars, for example, in the degree of a Davison Moon/Uranus midpoint, the relationship requires his courage and leadership to confront any forces that create emotional disconnection in the relationship. These energies could be from outside the marriage, or they may be influences from past relationships that are affecting the free flow of emotion.

If the woman has her natal Jupiter, for example, in the degree of the Moon/North Node midpoint in a Davison chart, she would be the one who preserves the belief that the two of them belong together as family. She could also help, through humor and tolerance, to overcome any forces acting on the relationship from the past.

The astrologer can use the techniques of synastric conjunctions between composite chart midpoints and either natal chart, or from Davison chart midpoints to either nativity, as a means of explaining to a couple how each individual can contribute to ongoing integration of their partnership. I recommend describing these midpoint patterns as what the relationship needs from each person to flourish and grow.

Here is section (9) of the worksheet for Farrow (A) and Allen (B):

PERSON A NATAL = PERSON B MIDPOINTS ☉ = ☉/♅; AS = ☽/♇

PERSON B NATAL = PERSON A MIDPOINTS ☽ = ☽/♀; AS = ♃/♇; MC = ♀/☊

PERSON A = COMPOSITE MIDPOINTS ♆ = ☿/AS; ♆ = ♆/☊; ☉ = ☉/MC; ☉ = ♀/MC

⚷ = ♅/AS; ♆ = ♃/♇; ♃ = ♂/☊; ☉ = ☽/☊

PERSON B = COMPOSITE MIDPOINTS ☊ = ♃/MC; ♄ = ☿/♄

PERSON A = DAVISON MIDPOINTS ☊ = ♄/MC; ♃ = ☉/AS; ♆ = ☽/AS; ♆ = ☿/AS

PERSON B = DAVISON MIDPOINTS ⚷ = ☉/♄; ♇ = ♃/☊; ☽ = ♃/AS

Mia Farrow
Woody Allen
Tropical Porphyry
Composite

360° Midpoint Sort

☉/AS	10♈36	♅/♆	23♋31	☉/♇	23♎55	☽/♃	16♐46	☉/MC	20♒40
♀/AS	10♈44	♄/☊	24♋55	♀/♇	24♎04	☿	05♑40	♀/MC	20♒48
♄/MC	15♈20	♃/♄	02♌25	♂/♇	29♎38	☊/MC	06♑04	♂/MC	26♒22
♂/AS	16♈19	♇	03♌00	♃	00♏40	☉/☿	10♑15	☽/MC	29♒41
☽/AS	19♈37	♅/☊	03♌09	☽/♇	02♏57	☿/♀	10♑24	☿/♄	04♓56
♅/MC	23♈34	♃/♅	10♌39	☿/♆	16♏02	♃/MC	13♑34	☉/♄	09♓31
♄	04♉11	♆/AS	16♌23	☉/♆	20♏37	☉	14♑51	♀/♄	09♓39
♄/♅	12♉25	☊/AS	26♌00	♀/♆	20♏46	☉/♀	14♑59	☿/♅	13♓09
AS/MC	16♉25	♆/♇	29♌42	☿/☊	25♏40	♀	15♑07	♂/♄	15♓13
♅	20♉39	♃/AS	03♍31	♂/♆	26♏20	☿/♂	15♑58	☉/♅	17♓45
♇/MC	29♉44	♇/☊	09♍20	☽/♆	29♏39	☽/☿	19♑17	♀/♅	17♓53
♄/AS	05♊17	♃/♇	16♍50	☉/☊	00♐15	☉/♂	20♑33	☽/♄	18♓32
♅/AS	13♊30	♆	26♍24	♀/☊	00♐23	♀/♂	20♑41	♂/♅	23♓27
♄/♇	18♊36	☿/AS	06♎01	☿/♃	03♐10	☉/☽	23♑52	MC	26♓29
♆/MC	26♊26	♆/☊	06♎02	♂/☊	05♐57	☽/♀	24♑00	☽/♅	26♓46
♅/♇	26♊49	♃/♆	13♎32	☉/♃	07♐45	♂	26♑16		
AS	06♋22	☊	15♎39	♀/♃	07♐53	☽/♂	29♑34		
♄/♆	15♋18	☿/♇	19♎20	☽/☊	09♐16	☽	02♒53		
♇/AS	19♋41	♃/☊	23♎09	♂/♃	13♐28	☿/MC	16♒04		

This 360° midpoint sort for the Farrow-Allen composite chart can also be used to check if there are any synastric conjunctions between either nativity and a composite Luminary, planet or angle (besides conjunctions with composite midpoints). Recalling that it was a sexual betrayal with her adopted daughter that ended their relationship, it is of note that Farrow's natal Jupiter at 26° Virgo, ruler of her 8th house of sexuality, was conjoined by composite Neptune, symbolizing a deception.

In the same way, the 360° midpoint sort for the Farrow-Allen Davison chart can be used to see if there are any synastric conjunctions between either nativity and a Davison Luminary, planet or angle (besides conjunctions to Davison midpoints). Notice, for example, that the Davison Jupiter at 10° Taurus was exactly conjunct Farrow's Ascendant, symbolizing both the abundant wealth that she earned while starring in thirteen films for Allen, and sadly, at the end, winding up in court over child custody and allegations of sexual molestation.

Mia Farrow
Woody Allen
Tropical Porphyry
Relationship
Jul 6 1940 23:10:59
39N24 097W15

360° Midpoint Sort

♃	10♉22	☿/♄	23♊53	☉/☽	24♋23	☉/MC	19♌45	☉/AS	26♍20
♃/♄	11♉28	♅/♇	28♊25	♅/MC	24♋52	♀/☊	22♌26	♆/☊	04♎15
♄	12♉34	♂/♅	28♊34	☉/☿	24♋56	♆/♇	27♌29	♇/AS	04♎59
♃/♅	17♉38	♀	29♊24	♃/☊	27♋56	♂/♆	27♌38	♂/AS	05♎07
♄/♅	18♉44	☽/♅	29♊30	♄/☊	29♋02	♇/MC	28♌24	☊/MC	05♎10
♅	24♉53	☿/♅	00♋02	♇	01♌57	♂/MC	28♌32	☽/AS	06♎03
♀/♃	04♊53	☉/♀	07♋02	♂/♇	02♌06	☽/♆	28♌34	☿/AS	06♎36
♀/♄	05♊59	☉	14♋41	♂	02♌14	☿/♆	29♌06	☊	15♎29
♀/♅	12♊08	♀/♇	15♋40	☽/♇	03♌02	☽/MC	29♌28	♆/AS	00♏31
☉/♃	12♊31	♀/♂	15♋49	☽/♂	03♌10	☿/MC	00♍01	AS/MC	01♏25
☉/♄	13♊37	♃/♆	16♋42	☿/♇	03♌34	☉/☊	00♍05	☊/AS	11♏45
☉/♅	19♊47	☽/♀	16♋45	☿/♂	03♌43	♇/☊	08♍43	AS	08♐00
♃/♇	21♊10	☿/♀	17♋18	☽	04♌06	♂/☊	08♍52	♃/AS	24♒11
♂/♃	21♊18	♃/MC	17♋36	☽/☿	04♌39	☽/☊	09♍48	♄/AS	25♒17
☽/♃	22♊14	♄/♆	17♋48	♅/☊	05♌11	☿/☊	10♍20	♅/AS	01♓27
♄/♇	22♊16	♄/MC	18♋42	☿	05♌12	♀/AS	18♍42		
♂/♄	22♊24	☉/♇	23♋19	♀/♆	11♌12	♆	23♍01		
☿/♃	22♊47	☉/♂	23♋27	♀/MC	12♌07	♆/MC	23♍56		
☽/♄	23♊20	♅/♆	23♋57	☉/♆	18♌51	MC	24♍50		

Synastric Aspect Configurations

One is occasionally struck by how profoundly two souls can change each other's lives. Before the relationship, neither may have led an especially eventful life, but after meeting one another, both individual destinies became transformed, for better or for worse. Can this seemingly fated synergy between two souls be seen by astrologers? Yes, it can, and these destiny dynamics are explained by any aspect configurations in synastry.

In natal horoscopic work, aspect configurations can be viewed as one of the more karmic dynamics affecting the lives of individuals. Souls born with a Grand Trine or a Yod, for example, usually feel as if their lives are being directed by forces that are beyond their conscious control. The apex planet of a Yod can especially wreak catastrophe upon a soul in the area of life shown by the natal house(s) that it rules. To this, I can personally attest, as your author was born with a natal Yod pointing at Jupiter, with quincunxes to the Sun and North Node. With Jupiter ruling my IC and Descendant, and at the finger of this Yod, it is no surprise that I have married or moved so many times in my life.

In a similar fashion, those born with either a Kite or a Mystic Rectangle possess much creative and spiritual ability. The contributions they can make are almost limitless if the personality can align itself with the soul and integrate into the Higher Self. Persons born with a T-Square or Grand Cross are motivated and driven, and these *type A* personalities accomplish much in life. Souls having a Stellium or a Grand Sextile in their nativities are extraordinary beings, and are likely to be seen as one of the most unique people that others have ever met.

When do aspect configurations occur in a relationship? They result when planets in one horoscope, being overlaid into the houses of the second nativity, complete a multi-planet configuration which neither of the individuals natally possess. If one has a natal sextile between two planets, and then enters into a relationship with another soul who has a planet in synastric quincunx to both of those bodies, then a synastric Yod has been formed, and it will now act to affect the destinies of both.

In the nativity of Farrow, the astrologer finds an Air Grand Trine, along with two Kites comprised of Fire-Air oppositions between Venus in Aries and Neptune in Libra, and between Mercury in Aquarius and Pluto in Leo. Only the Uranus in Gemini, which is the third airy planet making up the Grand Trine, does not have a planet in opposition to it. These five planets, Mercury, Venus, Uranus, Pluto and Neptune, are thus one short of a Grand Sextile, or Star of David, lacking only the third planet of a Fire Grand Trine. Woody Allen, with his natal triple conjunction of Sun-Mercury-Jupiter in Sagittarius, filled in this Grand Sextile for Farrow. As with any Star of David, three Mystic Rectangles are formed; Allen synastrically added two more to the one that she already had.

Mia Farrow
Feb 9 1945　　11:27 AM PWT
Santa Monica　California
33N50　　　　118W29
Feb 9 1945　　18:27:00 GMT
Tropical　Porphyry　True Node

Second Chart　　Natal Chart
Woody Allen
Dec 2 1935　　03:55:00 GMT

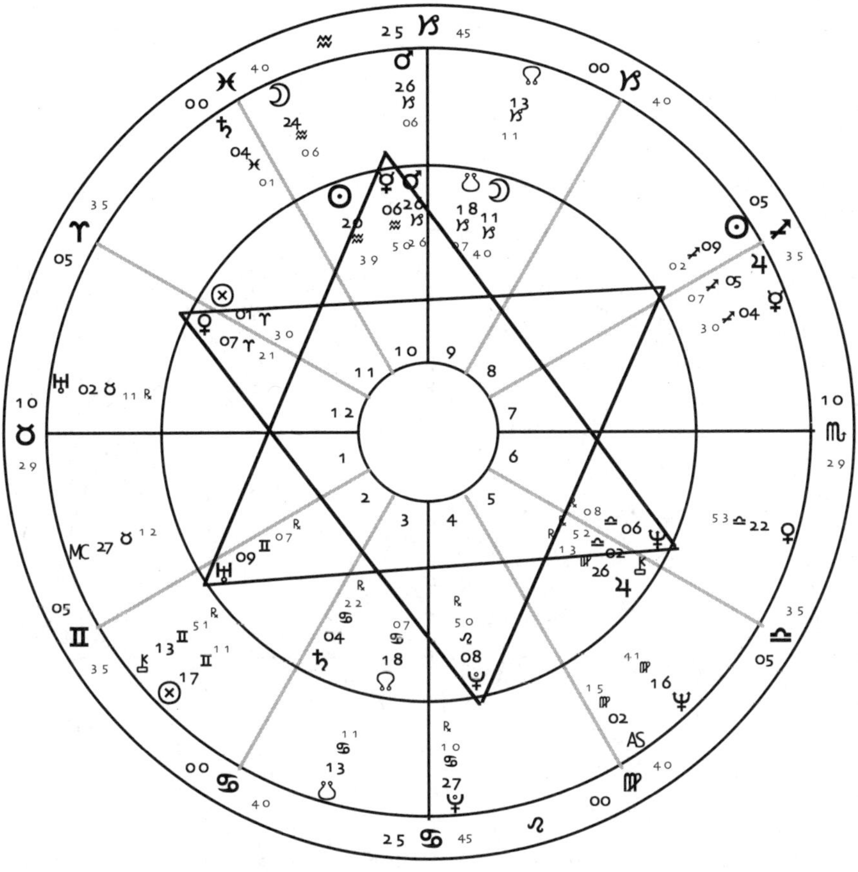

Here is the bi-wheel chart showing his planets in her houses. Note the Air Grand Trine and those two Kites. She was also born with a Cardinal Grand Cross, a Yod (apex Moon), a Fire/Air Mystic Rectangle, and an unaspected Sun (Ptolemaic). While it is quite rare to find this many aspect configurations in a single nativity, her life has been a remarkable journey, an attestation to this very unique natal chart. One can also see the three Sagittarius planets of his overlaying on her 8th cusp, synastrically creating the Fire Grand Trine, which in turn makes a synastric Star of David. Also forming are the two additional Mystic Rectangles.

The fated synergy between the two of them was not a one-way street. Astrologers can see that Allen was born with a natal Cardinal T-Square with Venus as the apex planet. He also possesses a Mutable T-Square with Neptune as the focal planet. However, the natal quincunx between his Aquarius Moon and Pluto in

Cancer is what dovetailed with Farrow. Her natal Jupiter in Virgo created a synastric Yod, as that Jupiter is sextile to his Pluto, and forms a second quincunx to his Moon. There is also a second synastric Yod formed between their two horoscopes, as Allen has Mercury and Jupiter in Sagittarius quincunx to Uranus in Taurus, and Farrow has Saturn in Cancer making the second quincunx.

Woody Allen
Dec 1 1935
Bronx
40N40
Dec 2 1935
Tropical Porphyry

10:55 PM EST
New York
73W54
03:55:00 GMT
True Node

Second Chart
Mia Farrow
Feb 9 1945

Natal Chart

18:27:00 GMT

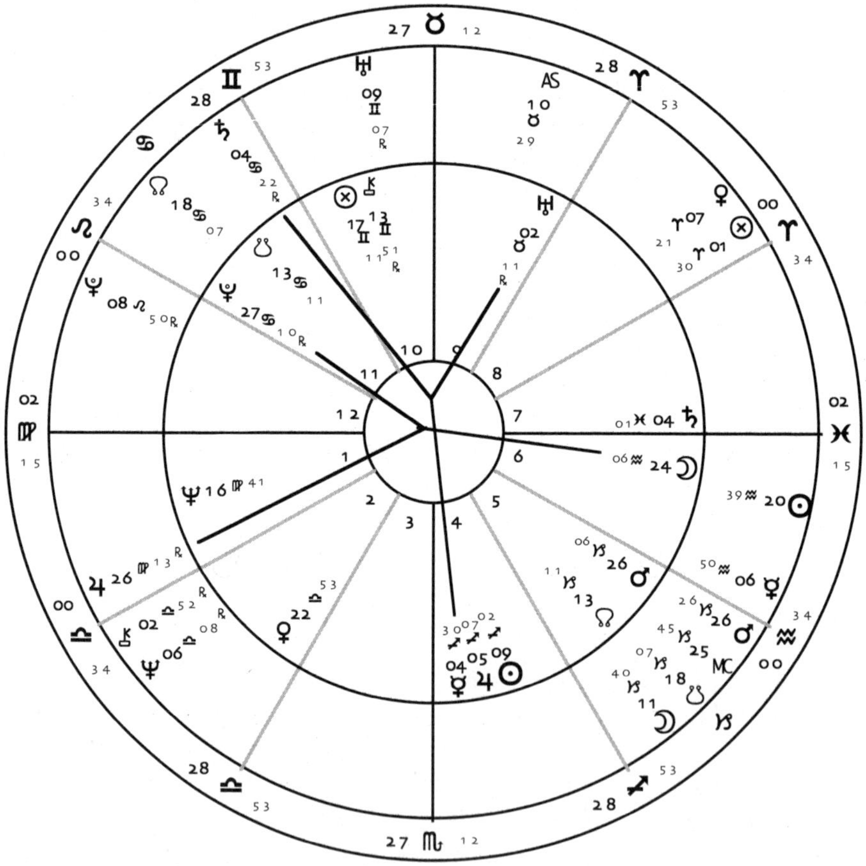

The astrologer should look for any synastric aspect configurations such as these when preparing for a relationship analysis consultation. Just as marriage vows being recited at a wedding ceremony state that both parties take each other as their spouse, *for better or for worse*, so, too, do shared configurations manifest in either a positive or negative fashion. How should the astrologer interpret them?

If a Grand Cross, T-Square or Yod are formed by synastry, then the couple, just by being together, will encounter unexpected stress factors in the relationship. This could be caused by problems with the in-laws, by one person losing their job, or by medical problems that arise after the wedding. What is odd in these cases is that most often neither individual has ever faced any of these dilemmas before.

If a Kite or Mystic Rectangle is synastrically formed, then couples can experience states of creative or spiritual consciousness not previously accessible or thought to be possible. For meditating couples on a spiritual path together, there is no finer aspect configuration other than the Mystic Rectangle. Because each opposition is balanced by sextiles and trines, interpersonal conflict evaporates and harmony is quickly restored. If mental equilibrium and deep concentration is desired, such as by couples who practice yoga, or who both write, synastric Rectangles are useful.

When a Grand Trine is produced by synastry, couples can appear to withdraw into a cocoon, a sort of private world that is not shared with others outside of the relationship. If in fire, a love of camping and being outdoors by themselves is common. In air, going to movies or reading books, and discussing them afterward is a joy. If in earth, making money and buying items for the home is a shared delight. In water, just being in love, cuddling on the couch and feeling close is quite enough.

A synastric Stellium is very powerful, especially when four or more Lights and planets are in the same sign and house, and all within a few degrees of each other. This will create many synastric conjunctions for the couple, this aspect being the strongest of any in a relationship analysis. Couples with synastry Stelliums live as if they are one unified being, made whole by their love.

The most rare of these eight synastry aspect configurations is the Grand Sextile, as our case study couple has. Opportunities for these infrequent patterns come in bunches, as during certain years, such as in 1945 when Mia Farrow was born, three slow moving outer planets comprised half of the six-pointed Star of David (Uranus trine Neptune, with Pluto at the near midpoint in sextile to each). With Farrow also possessing Mercury opposing Pluto and Venus opposite Neptune, she only required a first decanate Sagittarius planet to fill in that sixth position.

I have known clients, born in the middle 1960s, who also had this rare synastric Star of David. In early April of 1967, for example, a Water Grand Trine formed in the heavens between Jupiter in Cancer, Neptune in Scorpio and Mercury in Pisces. At the same time, a dignified Venus in Taurus was in trine with the Uranus-Pluto conjunction in Virgo, and all of the planets were between 18° and 24° of these earth and water signs. Three of these clients had married another soul who has a Luminary or planet in the third decanate of Capricorn (20° to 25°), thus creating a synastric Grand Sextile together. All of the couples were highly creative people.

Here is section (10) of the worksheet for Farrow and Allen:

SYNASTRIC STELLIUMS None

SYNASTRIC T-SQUARES Her ☿ ☍ ♇ □ His ♅

SYNASTRIC YODS Her ♃ His ☽ ⚻ ♇; Her ♄ His ☿ ♃ ⚻ ♅; Her ⚷♆ His ♄ ⚹ ♅

SYNASTRIC GRAND TRINES Her ♀ △ ♇ His ☉ ☿ ♃

SYNASTRIC KITES Her ☿ △ ♅ △ ♆ His ☉ ☿ ♃

SYNASTRIC GRAND CROSSES None

SYNASTRIC MYSTIC RECTANGLES Her ♀ ♅ ♆ His ☉ ☿ ♃; Her ☿ ♅ ♆ His ☉ ☿ ♃

SYNASTRIC GRAND SEXTILES Her ☿ ♀ ♅ ♆ ♇ His ☉ ☿ ♃

Chapter Five
Additional Interpretive Considerations

In the previous three chapters, I summarized common techniques used when preparing for a relationship analysis consultation. In addition to this routine preparation before an appointment, consulting astrologers will also make certain observations during the session, as they listen to clients talk about their life experience, and their issues in marriage.

In this way, you will build a mental database where each consultation is an ongoing educational experience. I have consistently observed several other forces that affect human relationships besides synastry aspects, house overlays and composite or Davison charts.

Around 1975, I found a delightfully unique astrology book in a used bookshop in Los Angeles. Entitled *Side Lights of Astrology,* by Thyrza Escobar, it was first published by the Golden Seal Research Headquarters in Hollywood in 1968. With my natal Jupiter in Gemini, this book was a real treat, as it contained a mélange of astrological techniques and interpretations. The author had been a professional astrologer since the 1930s and she shared generously her knowledge of Yods, Dwads, Dispositors, Stationary Planets and other miscellany.

Mrs. Escobar-Jones was born exactly at a Uranus-Neptune opposition in August 1909 and she died in 1993 at the conjunction of these two planets. With her Pluto conjunct my Jupiter, the little book left a deep impression on me, still in effect thirty years later. These so-called *Side Lights,* while not the main event in astrological delineation, were shown to be as necessary to understanding a nativity as the primary techniques. In a similar vein, considerations besides major relationship analysis methods can shed light on love.

These other techniques include using mutual reception and sole dispositorships in Davison charts, Sun/Moon midpoints and the effect of Astro*Carto*Graphy® on relationships. Besides these methods, this chapter will discuss using Draconic, Heliocentric and Sidereal Zodiacs in synastry, how to use my original Sabian Aspect Orb technique with the angular separation between synastric or composite planets, the role of unaspected planets in composite or Davison charts, and the importance of using the derivative house system when working with clients who have been married more than once.

At the conclusion of this chapter, I will discuss the inherent problems in using a computerized relationship analysis. For my fellow Virgo rising colleagues who wish to apply maximum discernment in their astrological consultations, I am introducing a new technique, *Holographic Links from Synastry to Progressions or*

Transits. This multi-dimensional approach to relationship analysis correlates current progressions or transits with their same-planet counterparts in synastry, allowing astrologers to discern which of these aspects are currently activated.

Mutual Reception and Sole Dispositors in Davison Charts

This author is of the opinion that the sign positions of the Luminaries and planets in composite charts are irrelevant. While I have found that the house position and aspects of the Sun, Moon and planets in these charts are legitimate, I view the signs of the composite bodies as only an artificial Zodiacal construct. Created by a near midpoint calculation of pairs of Lights or planets from two separate charts, these signs certainly cannot be used to determine planetary strength or debility.

I also believe that sign strength trumps aspect. Thus, a square from the Sun to a dignified Saturn in Aquarius is a better aspect for accomplishment than is a trine from the Sun to Saturn in detriment in Cancer. The underpinning of the rule first elucidated by C.E.O. Carter, is: *the two planets which are involved in the aspect relationship, and the sign strength or weakness of either or both bodies, is more important than the specific aspect being formed.* This law is consistently reliable and can be used with utmost confidence.

One of the more neglected dimensions of astrological relationship analysis is the application of dignity, detriment, exaltation or fall to the Luminaries and planets. With so much attention being given to the synastry aspects, house overlays and the composite chart, astrologers can be forgiven for overlooking this. The Davison chart, its planetary positions being true and real, would be the place to apply these principles.

Aspects in the Davison chart should be examined in context with sign positions of the two bodies involved. While most astrologers would consider Moon square Venus as an unfavorable aspect in a relationship, however, if the Davison Moon were dignified in Cancer and Venus dignified in Libra, this would actually be a very powerful aspect for owning a tastefully decorated home, and for the couple to enjoy socializing with and entertaining friends in their domicile.

In addition to assessing sign strength or weakness of planets in aspect in Davison charts, astrologers should also investigate these horoscopes for mutual reception or sole dispositorships, as these sign-based techniques are of critical importance. Just as in an individual nativity, when the astrologer finds a final dispositor, he takes this to mean that the person has a strong inner core, so, too, can the Davison chart with a dignified Light or planet that disposits every other body, show a relationship that can stand the test of time and a couple who will stay together.

A pertinent example of this can be seen in the Davison chart for Paul Newman and Joanne Woodward.[17] Married since January 1958, this couple certainly has one of the more enduring celebrity relationships in America.

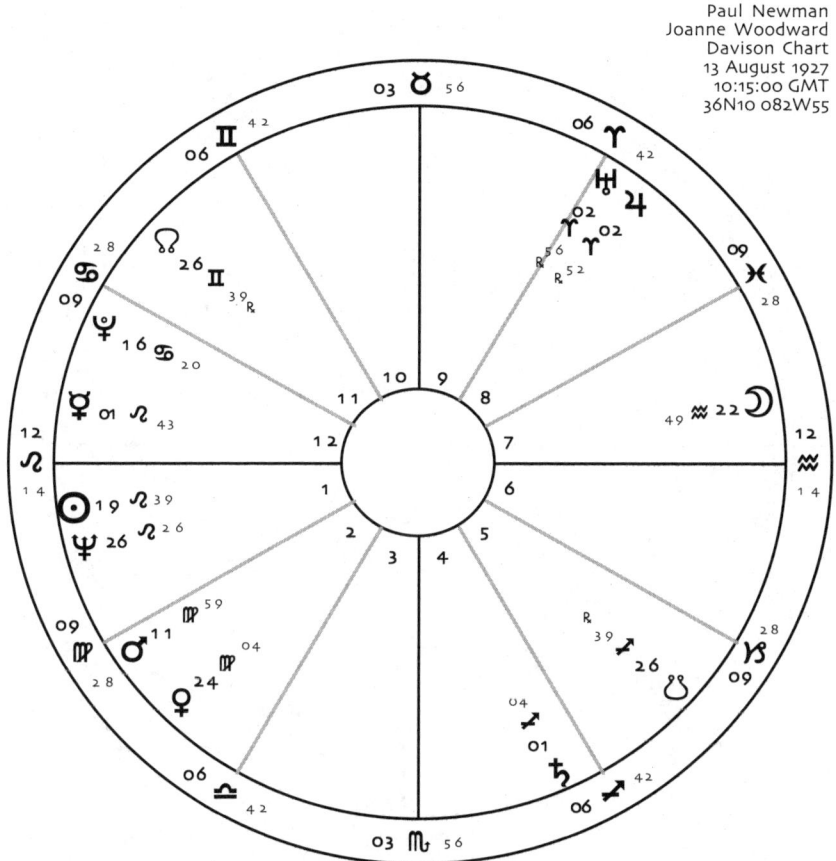

Paul Newman
Joanne Woodward
Davison Chart
13 August 1927
10:15:00 GMT
36N10 082W55

At first glance, most astrologers would notice a Fire Grand Trine and the angular Full Moon in aspect with Neptune, ruler of movie stars. One would then notice the sign strength or weakness of the Luminaries and planets. Finding a Sun in dignity and Venus in fall, we next trace the dispositors, limiting our consideration to the Lights and five classical planets only.

1. Aquarius Moon disposited by Saturn in Sagittarius.
2. Saturn disposited by Jupiter in Aries.
3. Jupiter disposited by Mars in Virgo.
4. Mars (and Venus) disposited by Mercury in Leo.
5. Mercury disposited by a dignified Sun in Leo.
6. The Sun is the sole and final dispositor (dignified planet has no dispositor).

A Davison sole dispositor which is also the ruler confers marital longevity. A second example of this can be seen in the Davison chart for the author's parents, who married in February 1946 (together 58 years until her passing away).[18]

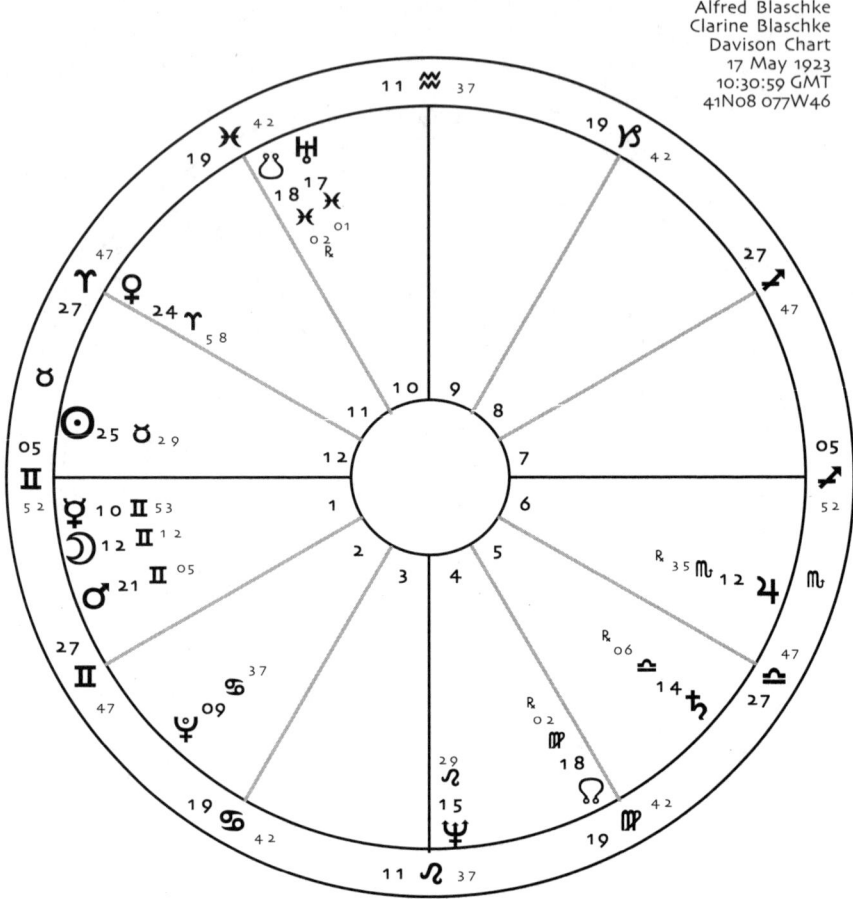

Examining the dispositorships, we find:

1. Sun in Taurus disposited by Venus in Aries.
2. Saturn in Libra disposited by Venus in Aries.
3. Venus disposited by Mars in Gemini.
4. Jupiter in Scorpio disposited by Mars in Gemini.
5. Mars (and Moon) disposited by Mercury dignified in Gemini.
6. Mercury is the chart ruler, and the sole and final dispositor.

A reasonable argument can be made for the Moon being most favorably aspected, with her conjunction to dignified Mercury, and trine to exalted Saturn. They lived in the same house since 1967, some 37 years as this book goes to press, and the marriage improved over time (ruler trine to Saturn). They owned a second home (Moon in Gemini) for a few years in the 1960s.

Just what would make these Davison charts exert influence over a couple? How can a point in time and space, midway between any two births, contain this power? As I wrote in Chapter Four, it is my belief that a *karmic vortex* exists at the time and place of any Davison chart. This vortex links to both individual birth times and places, which are in equal measure from that vortex. An analogy can be made likening the Davison chart to a radius vector that lies in the center of a circle and makes a line segment to any point on its circumference.

Another significant feature of Davison charts is a potential for mutual reception. This occurs when two planets occupy the other's sign. Recalling our case study of Mia Farrow and Woody Allen, an astrologer could see that in the Davison chart[19] there was mutual reception between the Luminaries, with the Sun in Cancer and the Moon in Leo. This phenomenon is as powerful as a conjunction. I consider just the Lights and the five classical planets for receptions, excluding the outer planets.

Regarding former President and Mrs. Clinton, whose Davison chart is also shown in Chapter Four,[20] recall that the exalted Sun in Aries, exactly trine retrograde Saturn in detriment in Leo, was put forward as the aspect that holds the couple together (there is also a synastric conjunction between these two bodies). But with the marriage having had a long history of sexual affairs, legal problems, and countless political enemies, astrologers would usually correlate these activities with Mars or Jupiter. While the two planets are found in sextile in their composite chart, in the Davison chart they are not in aspect, but rather in mutual reception.

In addition to examining Davison charts for sign strength or weakness, mutual reception, and sole dispositors, astrologers should also look closely into the exact date of the time-space calculation. Key factors would be any stationary planets, recent or upcoming eclipses, and any preponderance of retrograde planets. As I mentioned in Chapter Four, the case study Davison chart for Mia Farrow and Woody Allen had a time-space date of 6 July 1940, with a stationary retrograde Mercury at the bookend of a Stellium, and ruling the Descendant and Midheaven.

In conclusion, this segment of the chapter is intended to stress the importance of sign placements in Davison charts, while ignoring them in composite charts. When working with the sign-based techniques, I recommend using only the Luminaries and the five classical planets, with Mars ruling Scorpio, Jupiter ruling Pisces, and Saturn ruling Aquarius. The date of the Davison calculation should be checked against an ephemeris, as most software programs will not show planet stations.

The Sun/Moon Midpoint

Besides the Vertex (which is a sensitive degree associated with fated love) and the Arabic Part of Marriage (which is activated by the transit or progression of the

Descendant ruler at one's inaugural wedding), another distinctive degree exists in any nativity that symbolizes an integration of the masculine and feminine forces within the soul. This degree is the Sun/Moon midpoint, used by astrologers in relationship analysis as both a point of synastry contact and as a timing tool.

Similar to how a marriage partner enters the life of an individual at a progressed conjunction, sextile or trine between the Luminaries, or how a progressed conjunction of Venus to the natal Sun coincides with meeting the love of one's life, so, too, can the Sun/Moon midpoint be activated by progression when meeting one's spouse. In my practical experience, the activation of this midpoint is not the leading factor showing up in the charts, but rather plays a supporting role.

One often finds a composite Sun/Moon midpoint conjunct one of the Luminaries in either nativity; a natal planet progressing over a Davison Sun/Moon midpoint is commonly seen when two persons who later get married, first meet. It is my belief that this midpoint symbolizes the inner work that an individual has done, and therefore can be viewed as a synastric point that is ripe for contact when this interior spiritual journey has reached proper maturity. It does not appear to be as sensitive to transits as it is to secondary progressions.

On a personal note, this author's natal Sun/Moon midpoint is 14° Capricorn 41'. As this book was being written, a progressed New Moon Solar Eclipse occurred at 14° Capricorn 13' falling exactly conjunct this midpoint degree. I have seen this coming for well over twenty years now, and it feels a bit peculiar to have this materialization now at hand. Perhaps the timing for writing this book is ordained, as to write well about human relationship one must be balanced within.

If either of the clients' Sun/Moon midpoint degree is conjunct the rising or setting degree in the Davison or composite charts, or is conjunct a Luminary in either of these two charts, hearty assurance can be given to the couple that the relationship is a good one and effort should be made to preserve the love.

To recapitulate, a progressed Moon approaching conjunction or opposition with a Vertex, the Part of Marriage, or the Sun/Moon midpoint, is an indication that love is coming into one's life. If the client is already married and the Sun/Moon midpoint is about to be activated by the progressed Moon, or by an eclipse, it means that several years of internal spiritual work are now about to crystallize.

The Effect of Astro*Carto*Graphy® on Relationships

Many times in my career as a consulting astrologer, I have talked with clients who had been experiencing a repetitive pattern of painful, short-lived relationships. In some cases, these individuals did not have a natal Venus with bad aspects, nor were there abhorrent progressions or transits afflicting their Venus. Eventually, I came to a conclusion that the relational woes might be due to relocational factors that were tormenting their horizontal axis. After moving a sufficient distance from their previous homes, their love lives vastly improved.

The astrologer will find two variations of this condition. This first variation is a client who has moved from the place of birth and has, for example, a previously cadent or succedent Neptune now angular on the relocated Descendant. It is common for such a person to continually attract alcohol or substance abusers into personal relationship. A recommendation is to move to a different part of the country, either eastward or westward, or to move back home, to remove that relocated Neptune from the 7th house.

The second variation is a client who was born with Chiron, Uranus, Neptune or Pluto angular on the Descendant. This person may be in their 30s when coming to an astrologer for the first time and during the course of the consultation may ask why the choices for their personal relationships have been so unsuccessful. Many of these individuals have never heard of relocational astrology or how it works. These struggling souls may have never correlated moving with the ability to have a successful, long-term personal relationship.

If the astrologer also calculates the Astro*Carto*Graphy® map[21] for his client as a matter of routine before a consultation, he is better equipped to field these questions and to offer a recommendation for an alternate place to live. One must remember that east-west movement will have much more of an effect on the relocated chart than will north-south deviation. One client who was born in Oakland, California, with Chiron conjunct the Descendant, moved to Seattle when she was in her twenties. With both cities lying at 122° of west longitude, even as they are 10° of latitude apart, that Chiron didn't budge.

Over a six-year period, she scheduled twelve telephone consultations with me and during each appointment, she asked about the prospects for her love life. I always tried, at first, to offer hope by discussing an upcoming sextile of progressed Venus to Jupiter, or a transit of Jupiter through the fifth house. But year after year, her relationships continued to involve wounded men who were not emotionally capable of having equal partnership with her. She grew very sad.

About two years into our series of appointments, I brought up the concept of relocational astrology and explained to her that the angular Chiron on her Descendant was, in effect, overriding auspicious progressions or transits. She had Virgo rising, with Jupiter in Taurus ruling her Descendant and she was the kind of person who is very slow to embrace change. I tried to explain to her that, even though she had moved from Oakland to the Pacific Northwest, Chiron was, in fact, still angular in the 7th, and I sent her a Io Cartography™ map showing this.

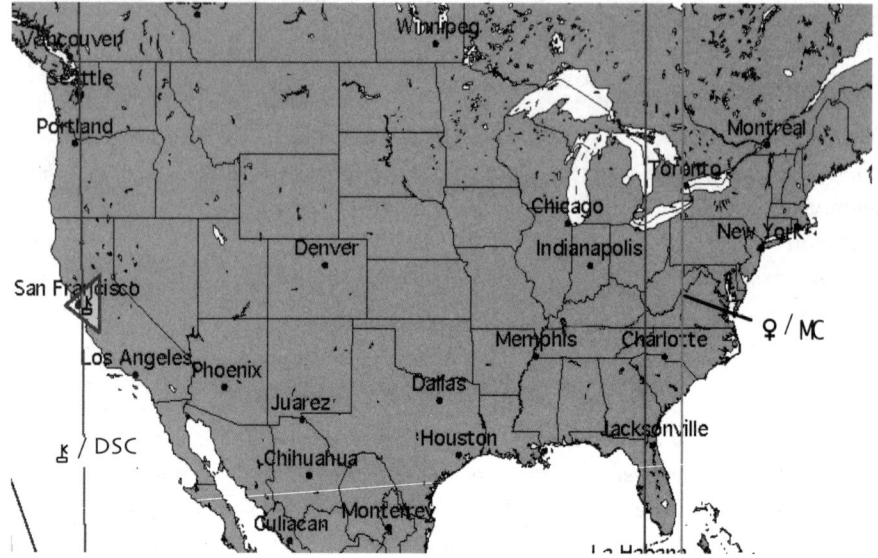

For the next two years, I encouraged her to consider moving away from the Chiron line, and, as she was in the fashion design business, I recommended that she move to North Carolina, where she would have Venus on the Midheaven. At first she resisted the idea, having never lived in that part of the country. Finally, when that Jupiter in Taurus had at last become convinced that patterns in relationship were not going to be any different unless she made changes, she decided to move when Uranus arrived at a transit opposition to her ruler, Mercury. She sent out résumés to a few companies in Raleigh and was hired immediately. Within a year, she had met a wonderful man and she got married shortly thereafter.

Most astrologers have stories of clients reporting improvement in relationships after moving away from locations where they had scurrilous planets angular on the Descendant, such as Chiron, Neptune or Pluto. There is another phenomenon to discuss with you regarding the effect of Astro*Carto*Graphy® on relationships. I have seen some startling results with *clients finding spouses without having physically moved to a location with favorable planets on the relocated Descendant.*

Several years ago, when more and more of my single or divorced clients began to tell me about their online dating experiences, I began to assess these stories with an eye to the progressions or transits that were in existence when they met a new lover, thinking at first that it was all a matter of correct timing. However, after I heard about some of my clients meeting a new love interest from another part of the country, when both of them had been involved in the same Internet mailing group, I began to investigate Astro*Carto*Graphy® maps to see if location was involved.

Lo and behold, what I found was that in a high percentage of cases, clients were meeting a new love on the Internet who lived where they had their benefics, or the Luminaries angular on the Descendant. I became convinced that *being physically present in the location of angularity was not required*. This revelation opened up a new interpretive strategy for my single clients who were willing to move for love.

After they had explained to me how one could simply enter a zip code on web sites such as Yahoo.com, or Match.com, and then a whole raft of single people looking for a husband or a wife who lived in that area would magically appear, I came up with the idea to inform these clients where in the country they had benefics or the appropriate Luminary (Sun = women looking for a husband; Moon = men looking for a wife) conjunct or trine the Descendant. I then suggested that they determine the zip codes for these areas and include these cities in their search for a partner.

After trying this, I am happy to report that some of these clients were able to find that someone special. In some cases, that person actually moved to join them where the client lived. In other cases, after the two met and became a couple, they moved to a third location. It is my belief that a favorable force field exists in the parts of the world where one has either Venus, Jupiter or the Lights on the relocated 7th cusp. One can find love through communication with other souls who live there. The phenomenon of Astro*Carto*Graphy® is not dependent on physical presence.

Using Draconic, Heliocentric or Sidereal Zodiacs in Synastry

Most astrological relationship analysis in the West employs the Tropical Zodiac. This geocentric model measures the orbits of the heavenly bodies as viewed from Earth. In traditional synastry, astrologers customarily use the signs and degrees of planets in this Zodiac to find aspects between two people. The Tropical Zodiac is ideal for understanding relationships at the personality level of consciousness.

However, three additional Zodiacs can be employed by an astrologer using synastry to see the soul contracts between family members, or to perceive the Higher Self of any individual, or to observe the completed karma with other souls. The Draconic, Heliocentric and Sidereal Zodiacs reflect additional layers of reality and can be used with spiritually oriented clients to great avail. It is best to limit comparison of charts derived from these Zodiacs to just the Tropical chart.

The Draconic chart transfers the North Node to 00° 00' Aries, then computes the differential arc between this Aries point and one's Tropical North Node, and adds this arc to the Luminaries, planets and angles in any nativity. The result is a chart that retains the identical *gestalt*, or pattern, of the Tropical horoscope, yet now has different Zodiac degrees for everything. How can astrologers use this chart?

It is common to find Draconic Luminaries or planets exactly conjunct the Tropical positions of the immediate family members: one's parents, siblings or children. The

Draconic Zodiac is derived from the Lunar Nodes, so these synastric conjunctions may symbolize past life contracts between family members. It is not unusual to find three or more souls from the same family all having planets in the identical degrees.

The spiritual astrologer may ask at this point whether or not the Draconic Zodiac can also show a soul contract between a husband and wife, or between lovers, or cast light on the interaction between one's soul and personality? I cannot say that I know the answer, as this realm of astrological delineation enters a *metaphysical speculation zone;* one is hard pressed to either prove or disprove the theory. However, it is an area of astrology that begs much more research.

Using the Draconic Zodiac in relationship analysis also raises another question: *What else, if anything, can be seen with cross-conjunctions between the Tropical and Draconic charts that cannot be perceived with just the Tropical charts alone?* Using our case study of Mia Farrow and Woody Allen, most astrologers would have presumed that a shocking betrayal such as these two experienced could have been seen with synastry involving Uranus. Whereas Farrow has a natal Uranus in almost partile opposition to Allen's Sun, exact within 05' of arc, one would presuppose that, since it was he who shocked her, his Uranus formed aspects to her nativity. Upon investigating, one only finds a synastric quintile to her Sun.

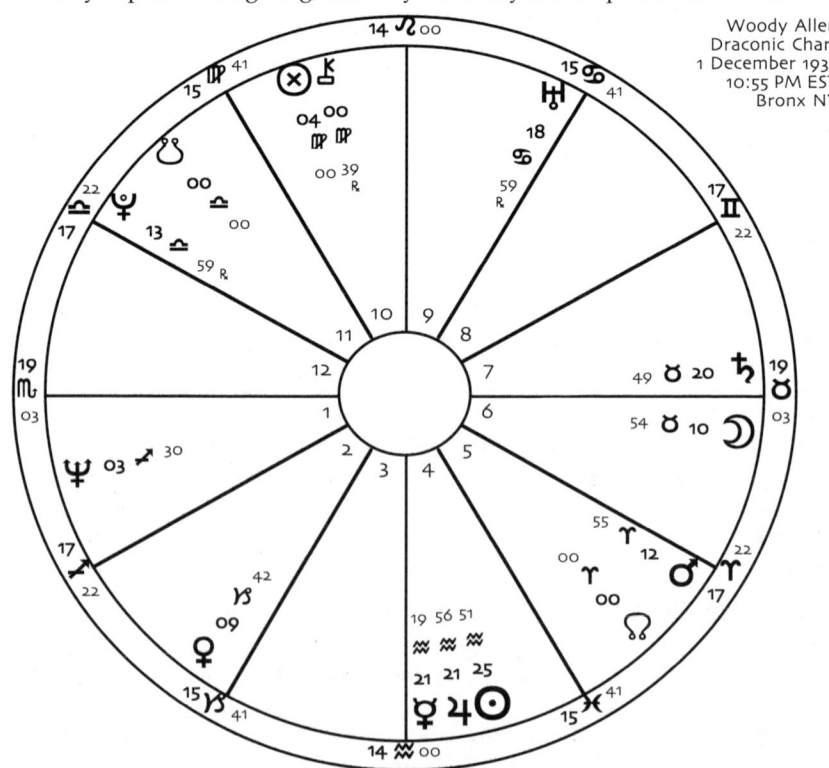

However, by comparing his Draconic chart to her Tropical chart, the astrologer finds his Draconic Uranus in the exact degree of her North Node. A spiritually speculative astrologer might, at this juncture, ruminate about how this shocking experience may have redirected her soul purpose in this lifetime. Eagle-eyed astrologers will also have detected his Draconic Moon in the exact degree of her Tropical Ascendant. For the technically minded astrologer, one finds the arc of difference between Allen's Tropical and Draconic charts to be 76° 49'; this arc is the distance from his Tropical North Node of 13° Capricorn 11' to 00° Aries 00'.

Some students have asked me, *"What is the relationship of one's own Tropical chart to one's Draconic chart?"* Is there a contract in existence between one's personality and one's soul? These are enchanting and intriguing questions, and I suspect they will have crossed the minds of astrologers who work with the Draconic Zodiac. It creates, for this author, a transcendent vision of parallel realities, with some kind of *wormhole* uniting the two planes of reality. This wormhole is the Draconic arc. Conjunctions from one's Draconic positions to one's Tropical Luminaries, planets, angles or Nodes may symbolize an attempt by the soul to illuminate a personality.

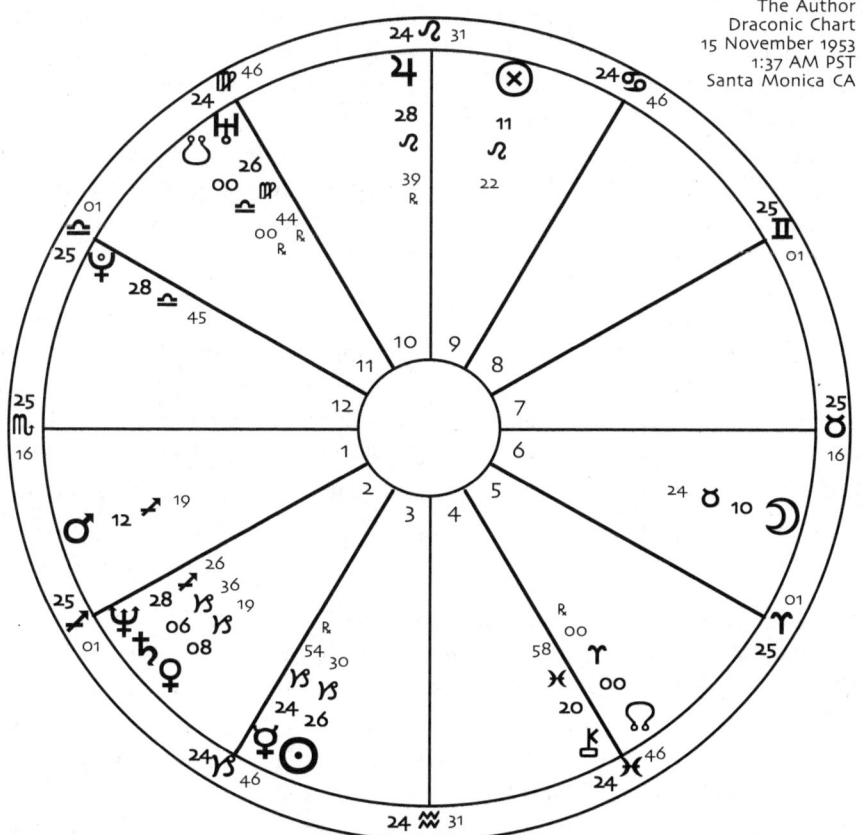

The Author
Draconic Chart
15 November 1953
1:37 AM PST
Santa Monica CA

In the author's Draconic chart, for example, the differential arc is 63° 47', which is the distance from his Tropical North Node of 26° Capricorn 13' to 00° Aries 00'. If any two positions in his Tropical chart are about 64° apart, then there will be a conjunction between the Draconic and Tropical charts. An example of this can be seen in the author's Draconic Sun being exactly conjunct his Tropical North Node; his natal Sun (22° Scorpio 44') is about 64° away from the North Node. A second occurrence of this can be seen in his Tropical MC at 20° Gemini 45' being 64° of arc away from his natal Pluto at 24° Leo 59'; thus, the Draconic MC = natal Pluto.

A technique exists for the astrologer to assist clients in aligning their personality with their soul. Taking the Draconic arc, convert it to its corresponding sign and degree, using a 360° Zodiac value, and then determine its relevant degree symbol. For example, the author's Draconic arc is 63° 47'. This equates to between 3-4° of Gemini. The Zodiac degree symbol for Gemini 4 is his key. I would recommend advising the client to meditate on the symbolism of this Draconic arc in order to encourage the personality to align itself more directly with the soul.

When contemplating degree symbolism for the Draconic arc it is as if one can hear his soul speak to his personality about the true essence from which he is made. For me, Gemini 4 from Charubel: *A profile, with only one eye in view.* "Great powers of perception. An active, sharp intellect; an exact or accurate observer of men and things. He would make a good detective; a practical mind; no mere theoriser." And from Sepharial's translation of *La Volasfera: A man dressed like a Minister of State, of venerable and kindly aspect.* "This degree will produce a person of kind and noble disposition; one who wilt occupy positions of trust, and, by his own merits, rise to eminence in his own sphere of work. It is a degree of DIGNITY."

It is almost universal for immediate family members to have Draconic planets conjunct the Tropical positions of parents, siblings or children. I believe that this synastry illuminates the family patterns and soul contracts. My Draconic Mars is exactly conjunct the natal Moon of my brother, and the Jupiter of our father. For me, this illustrates how brothers have a different soul contract with their father. My older brother followed in the educational and professional footsteps of our father (mechanical and aeronautical engineering), while I had a soul contract to separate from the father (Mars), and make my way in life independently of him.

My daughter has her Draconic Moon in the exact degree of my Tropical Mars. The soul contract appears to be one where the separation of her father from her mother took place, yet the love of the child for both parents remains intact. She also chose to forego a university scholarship in favor of becoming a musician, releasing two full length CDs by the age of 23, and following her father into the uncertainties of self-employment. A general rule for using this Draconic synastry with your family members is to limit aspects under consideration to exact degree conjunctions only.

The Heliocentric Zodiac is also infrequently used by astrologers in relationship analysis. This Sun-centered model measures the orbits of the celestial bodies from the Heart of our solar system and generates a horoscope that symbolizes one's Christ Consciousness, or Higher Self. Can the astrologer compare the Heliocentric chart of one individual against another's Tropical horoscope? Or does this chart, without a Sun position, operate at a level of reality where there are no individual egos, but only Higher Selves serving a larger purpose?

I recommend viewing the Heliocentric nativity as representing all that is virtuous within the individual, as if he were operating from pure Spirit. These horoscopes are calculated using Natural Houses, where 00° Aries is rising, and as such, house positions of the planets are transcendental in nature, as they are not bound by an earthly Ascendant or Midheaven. The position of the Earth in these charts is 180° opposite the position of the Sun in a Tropical nativity, as if a reflection of Spirit.

As there are no retrograde planets in a Heliocentric chart, its life force only goes forward into the future. Since there is no Moon in these charts, no memories from the past can affect the present. Because of their relative distance from the Sun, the superior planets of Jupiter, Saturn, Uranus, Neptune or Pluto are just a few degrees off from their counterparts in a Tropical nativity. However, the personal planets of Mercury, Venus and Mars can be found in different signs than in the Tropical chart; and in the case of the inferior planets, Mercury and Venus, these two can be opposite their Tropical positions, if geocentrically retrograde at birth.

It is a spiritual truth that to find God, one must know Love. It is also true that love exists deep within the human heart. If the Sun in astrology symbolizes this heart center, it therefore follows that an astrological nativity calculated from this Spiritual Source of the solar system would symbolize one's capacity for Love.

I have seen more exact-to-the-degree conjunctions between Heliocentric planets and Tropical Davison or composite charts than between Heliocentric and Tropical nativities. It appears that this synastry shows how the Higher Self connects with one's relationship, rather than how it connects one to another personality. I do not fully understand this phenomenon, but I will share my theory.

When one truly loves another soul, it sometimes feels as if Spirit is expressing love through you directly into your beloved's heart. There is an electrical sensation in one's chest when these sublime moments occur. One temporarily forgets his lower self and it is as if one floats inside the currents of a Love that does not originate with oneself. Perhaps it is so that watery souls are more aware of this merging of one's being with another, yet this kind of love is universal and is felt by all souls.

It is my belief that Heliocentric planets that are exactly conjunct the Davison or composite chart symbolize how spiritual love can flow through the Higher Self of one individual into the physical vessel of a relationship. If the Heliocentric Jupiter of a wife, for example, is in the same degree as the Davison chart Moon for her and her husband, Spirit is flowing through her higher mind, happiness and hopefulness into the home and family which she shares with her mate. If the Heliocentric Mars of a husband, for example, is in the same degree as the composite Jupiter for him and his wife, Spirit is flowing through his passion, drive and leadership into the hope, jubilation and happiness which he shares with his life partner.

It is, of course, discretionary for astrologers to even consider using Heliocentric charts when preparing for a synastry analysis. However, clients with spiritual or esoteric orientations will sometimes ask the astrologer how they can more readily access their Higher Self. If asked, the astrologer can then calculate the Heliocentric chart for his client, and compare it with the Tropical composite or Davison charts for the client's marriage. If there are conjunctions, the astrologer can explain how these planets show Spirit flowing through one's Higher Self into the marriage.

In Chapter Four, I wrote about past life connections and how these can be seen through contacts to the IC, South Node or Vertex. Two souls who meet up again in this lifetime and enter into a relationship, may then find themselves going through a parting of the ways and a painful completion and ending of the karma between them. Can this completed karma be seen in the astrology charts? Yes, and I have observed that the Sidereal Zodiac charts are often found to have exact synastric conjunctions with the other's Tropical chart when these karmic completions occur.

The Sidereal Zodiac is used primarily by Vedic and Hindu astrologers. Yet, even in the West, there has been a school of astrological thought promulgating the use of this Zodiac since the end of WWII. A practical problem is the perception by those outside of astrology that the one system appears to contradict the other. The Tropical Zodiac commences from the vernal equinox, and thus is a *point in time*, while the Sidereal Zodiac is measured from the star Spica (Virgo 30), or from Aldebaran and Antares (Taurus 15-Scorpio 15), which are *points in space*. It is my belief that karma can manifest only when incarnation into time and space occurs. Planetary conjunctions between these two Zodiacs show this phenomenon.

SOUL LEVEL	ZODIAC	ORIGIN	PLANE OF REALITY
4	HELIOCENTRIC	SOLAR	CHRIST CONSCIOUSNESS
3	SIDEREAL	SPACE	COMPLETION OF KARMA
2	TROPICAL	TIME	PRESENT INCARNATION
1	DRACONIC	LUNAR	ONGOING SOUL CONTRACT

This dual-Zodiac mechanism is similar to the relationship between the Draconic and Tropical Zodiacs. The difference is that the Sidereal-Tropical relationship is one of completion, whereas the relationship of the Draconic to Tropical Zodiacs symbolizes contracts of ongoing soul connection, such as family members reuniting again from lifetime to lifetime.[22] The preceding table shows the four Zodiac levels.

Turning to our case study of Farrow and Allen, the following bi-wheel chart shows his Tropical nativity in the inner wheel, and her Sidereal positions in the outer wheel. The *Ayanamsa* is Fagan/Bradley, which is computed from a baseline differential of 24° 44' 12" for the Sidereal Vernal Point as of 1 January 2000.

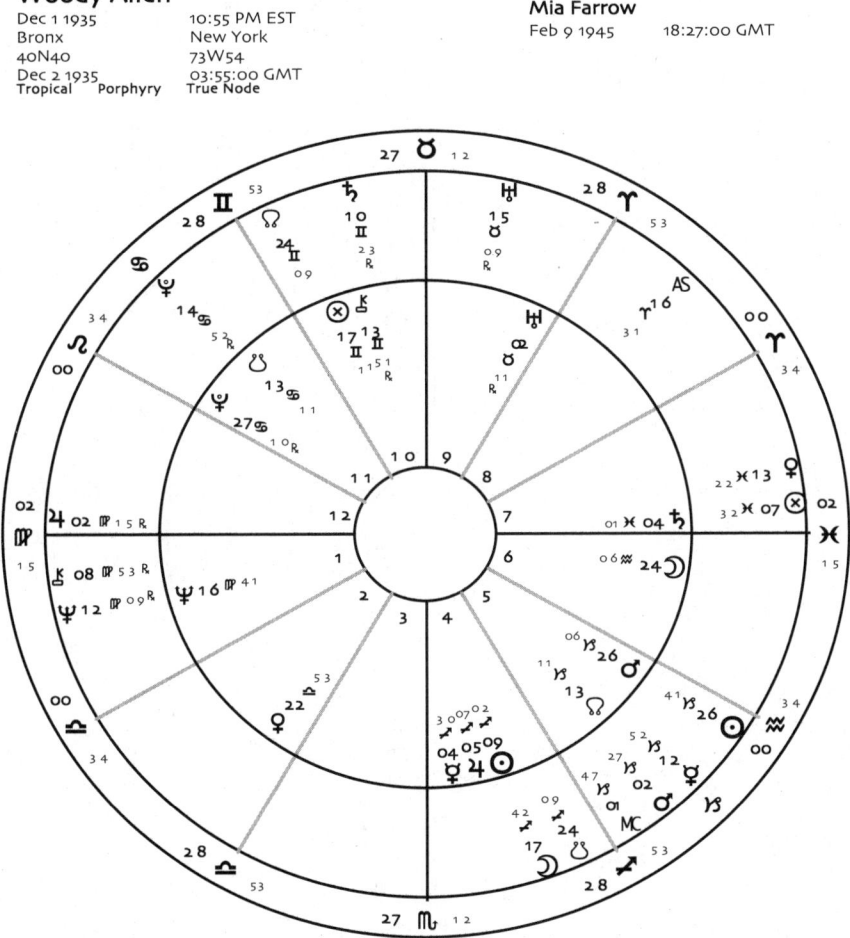

Just as conjunctions of the horizon rulers are involved in the *Marriage Rule*,[23] so, too, are these planetary rulers required when two souls end relational karma between themselves; in this case, it is the Sidereal ruler from one horoscope that is in conjunction with the Tropical horizon. The astrologer can see that Farrow's Sidereal Jupiter, ruler of Allen's Descendant, is in precise conjunction with his Tropical Ascendant. Astute astrologers will also note that Farrow's Sidereal Sun is exactly conjunct Allen's Mars, ruler of her Descendant. Although I only use exact-to-the-degree conjunctions in this type of karmic analysis, I realize that other astrologers may prefer to extend the orb to 1°-2° In this case, one would note Farrow's Sidereal Mercury-Pluto opposition conjunct Allen's Lunar Nodal axis.

This bi-wheel shows her Tropical nativity in the inner wheel, and his Sidereal positions in the outer wheel. As previously, the *Ayanamsa* used is Fagan/Bradley.

Mia Farrow
Feb 9 1945   11:27 AM PWT
Santa Monica   California
33N50   118W29
Feb 9 1945   18:27:00 GMT
Tropical   Porphyry   True Node

Second Chart   Natal Chart
Woody Allen
Dec 2 1935   03:55:00 GMT

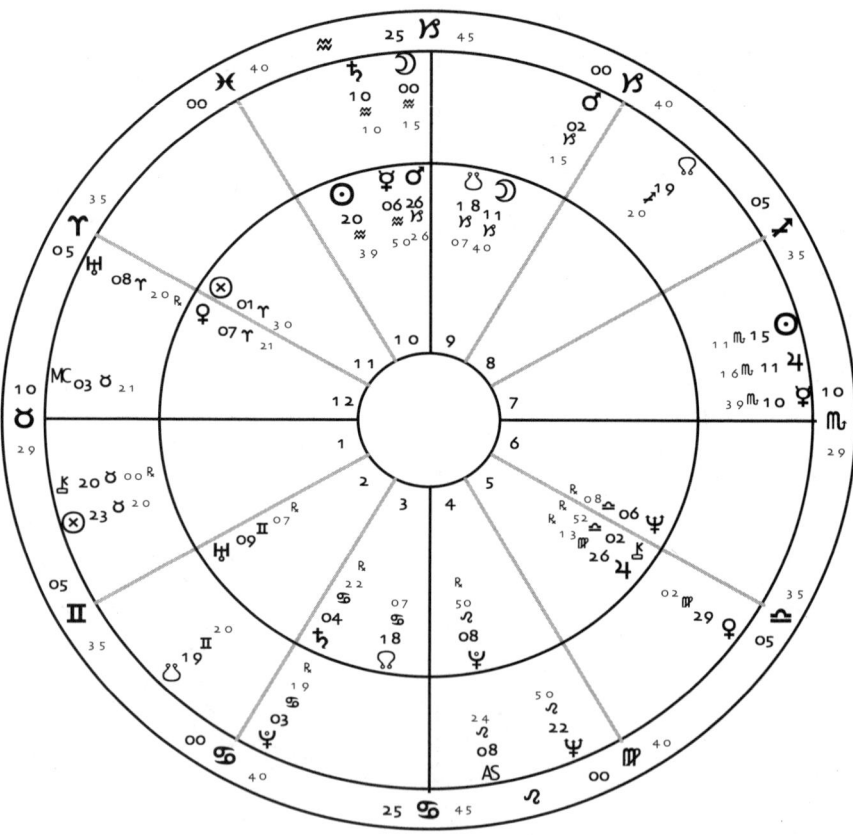

Here again we find the Sidereal ruler of one horizon conjunct the other horizon to the degree. Allen's Sidereal Mercury, ruler of his Tropical Ascendant, is in the exact degree of her Descendant. The astrologer also notes that Allen's Sidereal Ascendant is in the same degree as Farrow's Tropical Pluto. In the table showing a four-level model for the different planes of reality, the sequence goes from a lunar-based Zodiac to a time-derived one, then to a space-based level, and finally to one that is solar-derived.[24] It is this author's thesis that multi-dimensional synastry analysis, involving the Draconic, Tropical, Sidereal and Heliocentric Zodiacs, is not only accurate for determining past life soul contracts between family members, but also for ascertaining any completing relational karma between two souls.

In Chapter Six, analysis of relationships moving through time will be covered. I will show how progressed synastry can be used by astrologers to understand any of the current forces acting upon a couple. One of the prominent factors in our case study will be that of Farrow's secondary progressed Venus stationing retrograde in the 4th degree of Taurus while she was with Allen. Notice that this is also the degree of his Sidereal natal Midheaven.[25]

Sabian Aspect Orbs in Synastry and Relationship Charts

In my second book, *Volume II - Sabian Aspect Orbs,* I introduced a new technique for understanding aspects. The angular separation is measured between any two planets, whether or not the two are in conventional aspect, and then this x/360° value is equated to the Sabian Symbol for that point in the Zodiac circle. The slower body is positioned as if it were at 00° Aries 00', and one then measures to the faster body to determine the angular separation. In Chapter Thirteen of that book, there is a part on synastry and relationship charts.

The practical value of using the Sabian Aspect Orb technique is that it unites the left and right hemispheres of the brain. This method is a marriage of technique and symbolism, and, as such, it can help astrologers to further visualize any planetary relationship being explained to clients. This technique can be employed in natal astrology, in synastry, and with the Davison or composite charts.

Several astrologers have written me since the publication of *Volume II*, asking for my recommendation of which pairs of horoscope bodies are most valid to use with this system. Degree symbolism for the Sun-Moon angular separation in synastry or in relationship charts, in my experience, is foremost. In our case study of Allen and Farrow, the Luminaries are as follows:

A1. His natal Sun = 09° Sagittarius 02' = 249° 02'.
A2. Her natal Moon = 11° Capricorn 40' = 281° 40'.
A3. Angular separation = 32° 38' = 02° Taurus 38'.
A4. Taurus 3 symbol = *A double cross; two lines parallel in upright and two parallel in the horizontal.* (Charubel)
A5. RPB commentary: A double cross as in the sexual betrayal? Or as in her natal Cardinal Grand Cross and their composite Fixed Grand Cross?

B1. Her natal Sun = 20° Aquarius 39' = 320° 39'.
B2. His natal Moon = 24° Aquarius 06' = 324° 06'.
B3. Angular separation = 03° 27' = 03° Aries 27'.

B4. Aries 4 symbol = *Two lovers are strolling through a secluded walk. (MEJ)*[26]
B5. RPB commentary: Ironic how Allen and Farrow had separate apartments on either side of Central Park in Manhattan. One wonders if he and Soon-Yi took their clandestine walks together through the wooded paths of that park.

C1. Their composite Sun = 14° Capricorn 51' = 284° 51'.
C2. Their composite Moon = 02° Aquarius 53' = 302° 53'.
C3. Angular separation = 18° 02' = 18° Aries 02'.
C4. Aries 19 symbol = *A country site at the foot of a mountain, with many small dwellings thereon. There are coal-pits in the locality. A poor woman is nursing a baby; she is weeping, having just been made a widow. (Charubel)*
C5. RPB commentary: How sad life can be. One feels sympathy for Farrow and hopes that she is happier now in the current chapter of her life.

After determining the angular separation, and its corresponding degree symbol for the natal and composite Lights, the second most important pair of planets in a relationship analysis would be Venus and Mars. As before, one measures from the male Mars to the female Venus, from the female Mars to the male Venus, and from the composite or Davison Mars to Venus. Here is a summary for our case study:

D1. His natal Mars = 26° Capricorn 06' = 296° 06'.
D2. Her natal Venus = 07° Aries 21' = 07° 21'.
D3. Angular separation = 71° 15' = 11° Gemini 15'.[27]
D4. Gemini 12 symbol = *A little black slave-girl of ante-bellum days, with crinkly hair and saucy eyes, demands her rights of her mistress. (MEJ)*
D5. RPB commentary: I'd better not touch this one with a ten-foot pole!

E1. Her natal Mars = 26° Capricorn 26' = 296° 26'.
E2. His natal Venus = 22° Libra 53' = 202° 53'.
E3. Angular separation = 266° 47' = 26° Sagittarius 47'.
E4. Sagittarius 27 symbol = *A sculptor is at work in his studio, and under his skilled hands a lovely form slowly and surely takes shape. (MEJ)*
E5. RPB commentary: On 13 January 1992, Farrow finds nude pictures of Soon-Yi in Allen's studio.

F1. Their composite Mars = 26° Capricorn 16' = 296° 16'.
F2. Their composite Venus = 15° Capricorn 07' = 285° 07'.
F3. Angular separation = 348° 51' = 18° Pisces 51'.
F4. Pisces 19 symbol = *A man lying in a bed, a grey dark cloud hanging over him. His chamber is also dark and gloomy. Yet the horizon looks bright. (Charubel)*
F5. RPB commentary: One can charitably speculate that Allen's unhappiness with Farrow is perhaps what drove him to seek better days with Soon-Yi.

From these examples, astrologers can get a feel for how the degree symbols for the angular separation between the Lights, or Mars and Venus, bring the relationship between these bodies alive with symbolical meaning. I also recommend determining the angular separation for, and corresponding symbolism of, Jupiter and Mercury, Saturn and the Sun, and Saturn and the Moon. These planetary pairs rule signs in opposition to one another, and thus have relevance in relationship.

Unaspected Planets in the Composite or Davison Charts

Many of my students have asked me how to interpret unaspected planets in either the composite or Davison charts. As I wrote in *Volume II - Sabian Aspect Orbs*, I believe that all planets are in aspect with every other planet. *Volume II* proposed that all pairs of planets have angular separation between them, and this number of degrees correlates with a Sabian symbol, as was just evinced in our case study.

However, that said, I realize that many astrologers consider a planet unaspected if it either a) has no Ptolemaic aspects (0°-60°-90°-120°-180°) within reasonable orb, such as is the case of Farrow's natal Sun; or b) that planet is also beyond standard orbs for the minor aspects, such as the 30° semisextile, 45° octile, 135° trioctile, or the 150° quincunx. Astrologers usually do not regard esoteric aspects, such as the 72° quintile, 51 3/7° septile, 40° novile, 36° decile, or the 32 11/15° undecile,[28] as determinants for whether or not a planet is considered in aspect.[29]

As in individual charts, where it is somewhat unusual to find unaspected planets which are also not at the midpoint[30] of any two other bodies, so, too, is it rare to find a planet in the composite or Davison chart that also falls into this category. What may appear at first as an unaspected planet, after one examines midpoint structures it can be found to be very much integrated into the rest of the chart. At astrology conferences, I have overheard astrologers saying one thing or another about that so called unaspected planet in the composite or Davison chart for their marriage, sounding as if they had come to believe that something was missing.[31]

If an astrologer finds what seems to be an unaspected composite or Davison planet or Luminary, I recommend first checking to see if that body is either at the near, or the far midpoint of any two other planets. If this is the case, astrologers should not consider the planet unaspected and *being out of the loop* as regards the rest of the chart. Consider the Davison chart for our case study couple (page 62).

The Sun, at 14° Cancer, is in sextile with a Jupiter-Saturn conjunction. The Moon is part of a tight Stellium in the 8th house, along with Mercury, Mars and Pluto. Uranus is in trine with Neptune. One planet is missing from this summary—Venus. At first glance, she seems unaspected, sitting as she does just beyond the allowable orb of a square to Neptune, although she is accidentally dignified in the 7th house, retrograde, and in the fated 30th degree of Gemini. But, is Venus really *out of the loop* in this Davison chart? Remember, this is the ruling planet of daughters.[32]

Look more carefully and find that the Farrow-Allen Davison Venus also lies at the midpoint of the Moon and Uranus, exact within 06' of arc. If there were ever a planetary pair to be deemed a *homewrecker*, it would be Moon-Uranus. Venus, ruling planet of daughters (Soon-Yi), at the exact midpoint of the Moon and Uranus, induced the abrupt emotional upheaval of a discovered affair.

Recalling that the difference[33] between composite and Davison charts is that the latter symbolizes *forces working on a couple from outside of their relationship, be they from the family, from children, from financial pressures, or from past life factors which are creating present karma,* one can certainly understand how Soon-Yi was *a force from outside the relationship.* It is also of note that the angular separation between the Farrow-Allen Davison Moon and Uranus is 69° 13', analogous to Gemini 10. The La Volasfera symbol is: *A woman of pleasing appearance stands offering a glass of some fluid to a child.*

A composite chart from my client files for a couple who have an unaspected Moon:

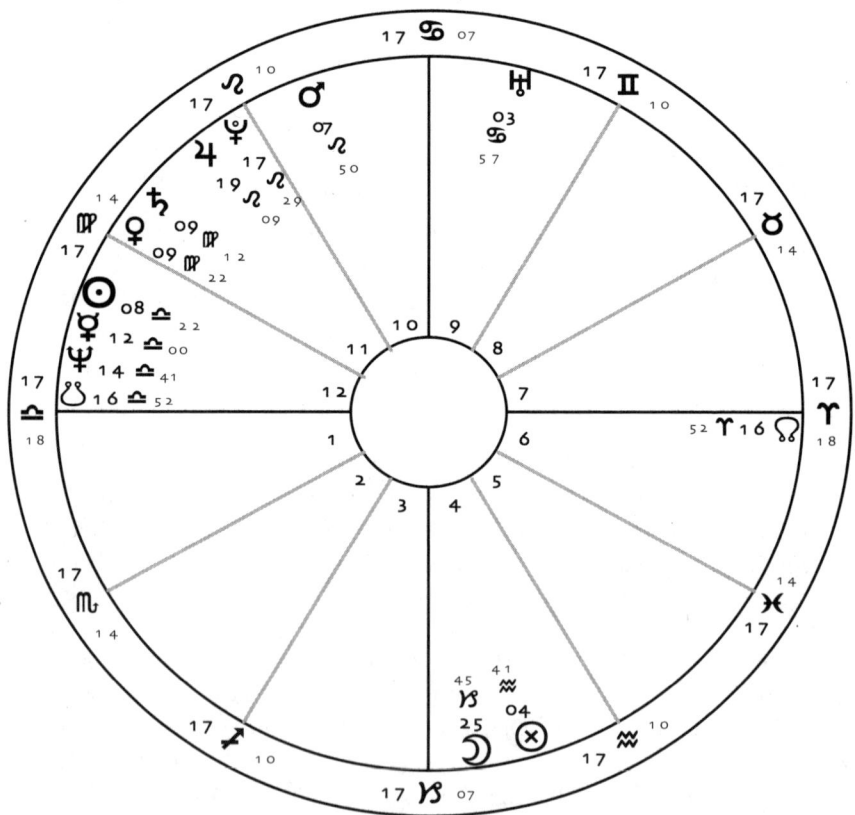

This couple has had a long-term stormy relationship with numerous break-ups, as can be seen in the square from Sun to Uranus. In synastry, each Venus is conjunct the other's Saturn, which also produces the conjunction of these two planets in the composite chart. Conjunctions with Saturn, whether in synastry or in composites, make it nearly impossible for a couple to ever really break up. The two truly love one another, even though they are not ideally compatible. A 12th house Sun, along with Neptune on the South Node, shows a deeply karmic relationship. They have not lived together, maintaining separate residences, attributable to the unaspected Moon. Upon closer scrutiny, however, that Moon is found at the far midpoint of Uranus and Pluto, exact within 02' of arc. The central reason they remain with one another is their highly satisfying and liberating sexual relationship. This intimate bond between them can also be seen in the 8th ruler conjunct Saturn.

There are several psychological theories of dubious value floating around in the world of astrology regarding the meaning of unaspected planets. In practice, these hypotheses often do not stand up to closer scrutiny. A basis for classifying planets as unaspected, as mentioned earlier, is that no Ptolemaic aspects are found to other bodies. This logic, I presume, is based on the rule for which the Moon is judged to be void-of-course. Following this line of reason, Farrow's Sun is unaspected.

In her nativity shown on page 18, astrologers find the Sun at 20° Aquarius 39'. A novile to the Moon exists, with an orb of 01° 01'. An octile to Venus is seen, with an orb of 01° 42'. Trioctiles are found from the Sun to both Saturn and Neptune; an orb of 01° 17' for the former, and an orb of 00° 29' for the latter. As no conjunction, sextile, square, trine or opposition is found to her Sun, astrologers might classify it as being unaspected. However, when two of the same aspect, major or minor, are found to any planet from different bodies, such as the 135° sesquiquadrates from both Saturn and Neptune, this alerts astrologers to a possible midpoint structure.

I recommend considering both the near and the far midpoint when looking to see if a Luminary, or planet, is integrated into the rest of the horoscope via midpoints. For Farrow, the axis of 20° Leo-20° Aquarius would be relevant for her natal Sun. Scrutinizing her nativity, find her Saturn/Neptune midpoint to be 20° Leo 15', exactly on this solar axis. Saturn rules her Midheaven, and Neptune rules film stars, and she is an actress by profession. As C.E.O. Carter has written, *the closest aspect to the Sun often determines the vocation;* here we find a midpoint to an unaspected Sun's axis also working according to Carter's law.[34]

In summary, I recommend that before appraising a planet or Light in the composite or Davison charts to be unaspected, first check to see if that planet is either at the near or far midpoint of any other two planets. If it is, then consider this planet to have a relationship with the other two, as if it were aspected. This is how a seemingly unaspected planet is integrated into the rest of the chart. These techniques, used in natal astrology, can also be applied to the relationship charts.

Second or Third Marriages and the Derivative House System

Since the 1970s, when divorce rates began to skyrocket during the Uranus and Pluto transits through Libra, it has become more and more common for astrologers to work with clients who are in their second, third, or even fourth marriages. This cultural fact of life has required the astrologer to adjust his techniques regarding the planetary influences affecting marriage relationships. Whereas, before divorce became so prevalent, the seventh house was always relevant to questions about marriage, this is no longer the case.

There exists in astrology a derivative house system, about which I wrote on page 15. This technique, also called *secondary house influences*, shows the connection between any one house and the other eleven. As far as marriage and divorce are concerned, there are very specific houses that astrologers should look at when fielding questions regarding marriages. The derivative houses to which I refer involve all of the odd numbered houses: 1, 3, 5, 7, 9 and 11.[35]

As mentioned in Chapter One, first marriages fall under the domain of the 7th house. Divorcing, one must go to court, a 9th house matter. The 9th house from the 7th is the 3rd house. Now divorced and in this 3rd house, for an individual to marry for a second time, he must then find the 7th house from the 3rd, which is the 9th. If the client divorces for a second time, the 9th from the 9th is the 5th house; if he marries for the third time, the 7th from the 5th is the 11th.

1. First marriage = 7th house. First divorce = 3rd house.
2. Second marriage = 9th house. Second divorce = 5th house.
3. Third marriage = 11th house. Third divorce = 7th house.
4. Fourth marriage = 1st house. Fourth divorce = 9th house.
5. Fifth marriage = 3rd house. Fifth divorce = 11th house.

From the table, astrologers can discern why third divorces are usually calamitous, as they involve the 7th house of open enemies. The hardest on children is a second divorce, as it is ruled by the 5th house. A third wife or husband will often involve an old friend, as is shown by the ruling 11th house of these marriages.

I am asked rather frequently about out-of-court financial settlements in divorce proceedings, with the client inquiring about a best date to negotiate a deal with the soon-to-be ex-spouse. This may involve alimony, child support, or the division of property and assets. When preparing for this type of consultation, to which house ruler should the astrologer look when searching for favorable transits or progressions to substantiate timing guidance for clients?

Since financial settlements occur *prior to the divorce,* the derivative house formula that I use involves not the 2nd house from the divorcing house, but the 2nd house from the relevant marriage house. If a client is negotiating a financial settlement in a first divorce, then the 2nd from the 7th, or the 8th house ruler, is the key planet.

If a client is ending a second marriage (9th house), and is negotiating financially with a spouse, then the ruler of the 10th is relevant, as the 2nd from the 9th shows the financial outcome of a second marriage. After determining this ruler, I then find the dates when transit Venus, ruling negotiations, either sextiles or trines that ruling planet, and I present these dates to my client as when to have the lawyer schedule the out-of-court settlement meeting. If there is child custody being settled, I use the 5th from the relevant marriage house, e.g., children from a second marriage are ruled by the 1st house, as this is the 5th from the 9th. In all cases, I am using the traditional rulers: Mars for Scorpio, Jupiter for Pisces, and Saturn for Aquarius.

When using this system, the astrologer can honestly inform his client that on these dates, the financial settlement will be as good as it gets and he should advise the client not to be greedy and demand more money from the divorcing spouse. I have heard of several lost opportunities involving tens of thousands of dollars when a client ignored my counsel and did not agree to the terms under a favorable Venus transit. The spouse then told the lawyer to play hardball, and the client got far less.

Other uses of these derivative houses are for clients who are between marriages. For example, a client, twice divorced and who has dated but not married for many years, now has the secondary progressed Moon, or transit Saturn, about to ingress into their 11th house of third marriages. Upon seeing this, the astrologer can bring up for discussion the possibility for marriage to occur over the next two to three years. Within that house passage, if the progressed Moon or Saturn also conjoins, trines or sextiles the 11th house ruler, marriage is a high probability.

If the astrologer offers this type of analysis to his clients, he must have a command of the practical house meanings, and of how to find reliable progressions or transits to their rulers. I must say that the best resource for this work is *The Rulership Book* by Rex E. Bills.

The Problems with Computerized Relationship Analysis

It is no secret among professional astrologers that computerized relationship analysis is often times hardly worth the paper it is printed on. Most self-employed astrologers cannot survive financially from clientele income alone as it is erratic and unpredictable, so multiple revenue streams are needed to earn a living as an astrologer. Besides consultation fees, astrologers can earn extra income by selling these computerized reports, by selling astrology software, by lecturing and teaching, and through selling their books, class tapes, or other mail order items.

Looking at sales of these computerized astrology reports from a realistic point of view, astrologers will have certain clients who either cannot afford or do not want to pay the fee for personal or telephone relationship analysis consultation. In some cases, it is practical to offer these clients the lower cost option of a computerized report. However, it should be made very clear that this is not an equivalent substitute for a professional consultation.

Several astrology books on relationship analysis published since the 1970s were written with an additional purpose in mind: to create stock interpretations that were used as text files in computer programs that produce reports. This cookbook approach to writing, with its emphasis on including all the different permutations and combinations of house overlays, synastry aspects, composite house positions, and composite aspects, has unfortunately diminished this branch of astrology.

A computer generated relationship analysis is a sequential list of synastry aspects, house overlay positions, and composite chart factors, without any discrimination given to what aspects are more or less important, or how the house overlays are modified by these aspects. It is not uncommon to find in these computerized reports some absurd contradictions, such as one paragraph describing person A's Mercury sextile to person B's Venus as meaning that a couple will have harmonious communication; then, the very next paragraph delineates that same Mercury is also in opposition to person B's Mars, and states they will fight like cats and dogs. What is the report customer to think?

Computerized reports are also being sold by inexperienced students of astrology, who have not set the orbs of the aspects correctly, thus their report customer has a product that treats a synastry sextile with a six degree orb as being in the same league with a synastry conjunction which is exact to the degree. I suppose it is fair to say that the client is getting what they pay for, yet computer-generated reports also reflect poorly on the accuracy of professional astrological technique.

So, as is usually the case with technology, one problem is solved, while others are simultaneously created. What are astrologers to do with computer reports? Some authors of these software program text files have attempted to include only what they perceive as the most important synastry aspects. Yet these text files, in the striving to reduce the number of permutations necessary to generate the report, are written and programmed into the software application in ways confusing to a typical report customer who has no knowledge of astrology. How can someone who has never seen a synastry analysis before understand an astrology report containing both *challenging* and *easier* aspects with no context?

In my observation of professional astrology over the last 30 years, computers are relentlessly diminishing the student's ability to discern which astrological technique is of greater importance and which is of lesser significance. Perhaps a plethora of Uranus in Gemini software programmers have set into motion an era in professional astrology where the quantity of calculation choices are legion, yet the relative quality of these multitudes of computations remain indiscriminate.

As is the life mission of those of us born with Uranus in Cancer who follow our elder brethren of the Uranus in Gemini generation, I now offer a new technique to help the advanced student or professional astrologer weed out the abundance of computer calculated synastry aspects, with a hopeful result of determining which are the most significant. Somewhat like the guy at the end of the tickertape parade for Mr. Peabody and Sherman on the *Rocky and Bullwinkle* show, with his broom and trash can, I will try to sweep up the tickertape of one too many calculations.

Holographic Links from Synastry to Progressions or Transits

In Chapter Three, in the section on synastry aspects, there is a ranking system that lists in order of importance, the relative significance of the interchart aspects. Starting with the closest orb conjunctions or oppositions involving the Lights, and continuing through six additional categories of synastric aspects, the list helps astrologers to prioritize while preparing for a consultation.

Even with this ranking system, however, the astrologer will still find some 35 to 50 interchart aspects for any given couple. Of all of these synastry aspects, which are most relevant to what a couple is presently encountering in the marriage?

It is my experience that some synastry aspects remain dormant for periods of time, while other interchart aspects are active. How can astrologers know which is which? I offer you an original technique, called *Holographic Links from Synastry to Progressions or Transits*. This multi-dimensional approach to synastry allows the astrologer to connect the time factor to any relationship.

This technique is actually quite simple. It links any current progressed aspects or transit influences affecting either individual in a relationship with the synastry aspects between the two horoscopes. If, for example, the man's Saturn is conjunct the woman's Mars, the aspect is only activated when either of the two individuals has transit Saturn aspecting their natal Mars, or transit Mars aspecting natal Saturn, or if either has progressed Mars aspecting natal Saturn.

A seasoned astrologer will see that of these example variations, the Mars transit will last, within a one degree orb, for about four days, a Saturn transit will have about a 17-20 day influence, while a progressed Mars episode lasts three years.[36] This explains not only how synastric aspects get activated, but also for how long.

The theoretical and metaphysical underpinning of this technique is akin to a Sun-Moon phase angle return. Each month after birth, the Sun and Moon replicate the angular separation found in the nativity. The positions of the Luminaries at birth create a hologram in the heavens, and, on a repeating monthly basis throughout the life of any soul, return to this celestial relationship. This is why this technique is used in calculating conception charts for women trying to get pregnant, as the life force of the female required for ovulation and seeding is regenerated monthly.

In a similar fashion, each synastry aspect between any couple is a hologram, and when those same two planets form progressed or transit aspects to either of the nativities, this causes a holographic activation of that specific synastry aspect. Using this technique, astrologers can discern which of the 35-50 synastry aspects are presently activated and which are in a dormant state.

Hillary Clinton
Oct 26 1947   8:00 PM CST
Chicago   Illinois
41N40   87W39
Oct 27 1947   02:00:00 GMT
Tropical Porphyry   True Node

Second Chart   Natal Chart
Bill Clinton
Aug 19 1946   14:51:00 GMT
Third Chart   Natal Chart
Saturn Stationary Rx
Aug 15 1998   19:08:29 GMT

An example of this technique was seen in the marriage of former President Clinton and his wife, Hillary. One of the leading synastry aspects for them is a Sun-Saturn conjunction, with a 04° 40' orb. During the Monica Lewinsky scandal of 1998, the marriage was put to its severest test, a Saturnian experience in life. That summer, from June 30th to October 2nd, Saturn stationed at 03° Taurus 37', holding a one degree stationary opposition to Mrs. Clinton's natal Sun for over three months. It is fair to say that this was a most painful period in her life. There was the public humiliation of the lies and the subsequent admission of the affair by her husband. Yet, she stood by him.

This holographic link between their Sun-Saturn synastric conjunction and Saturn in transit opposition to her Sun, illustrates how that essential interchart aspect, necessary for holding a troubled marriage together, was activated by a transit-to-natal episode involving the same two planets. These holograms are the time factor.

Chapter Six
Analyzing Relationships Moving Through Time

In the preceding chapter, I outlined a technique for determining which synastry aspects are operative and which are dormant by linking them to progressions and transits. This approach to relationship analysis takes into consideration the time factor. Similar to how a motion picture differs from still photography, the ability to analyze relationship moving through time is essential for meeting the needs of clients who not only want a compatibility evaluation, but also want perspective about what is currently affecting them.

There are several different methods that I use to accomplish this. I have always calculated the current progressions and transits for both individuals. Many times couples come to me thinking that something is wrong with their marriage and that they are no longer compatible. Often it turns out that one party has progressed Venus squaring natal Uranus, or the transit of Uranus aspecting natal Venus and that party just needs more independence. After 11 months (transit), or 19 months (progression), things return to normal.[37]

Besides transits and progressions to each natal chart, there are other techniques to help couples understand what influences are acting upon them at any given time. In this chapter, I will describe how to use progressed composite or Davison charts, transits to composite or Davison charts, transits to progressed composite or Davison charts, and synastric progressions. The condition of a solar return Venus will also be discussed, as will the annual 360° progression of the solar return angles. Lastly, I will share some thoughts on the solar return Sun-Venus eight-year cycle and how it coincides with major karmic relationships.

To illustrate these techniques, I am using our case study couple, Mia Farrow and Woody Allen; in particular, 13 January 1992[38] when Farrow found nude pictures of her daughter, Soon-Yi, in Allen's apartment, an episode that set into motion an entire sequence of events. I will show each of the various charts—natal, transit, progressed, composite and Davison—and if the charts had predictable planetary influences in effect when this happened.

Transits and Progressions to the Natal Chart

During the years of my astrological practice, I have consulted with hundreds of couples for relationship analysis. Early on, it became clear that assessing compatibility dynamics was only half of the total consultation experience. During our sessions together, I would invariably speak with both parties regarding how they were feeling about their lives as individuals. This part of the consultation was often most productive as it framed relationship issues in the context of each person's spiritual journey.

At first, it startled me how differently each spouse described his or her experience of the marriage. During my preparation for the consultation, I diligently recapped all of the synastry aspects, the house overlay positions, and the composite and Davison chart factors. I would approach the appointment as if I were to be talking to a third entity—*the relationship itself*. However, the reality of each consultation was that both individuals were experiencing the relationship differently and the synastric squares or oppositions were only part of the conflict in their marriage.

The other half of the story was usually like this: the husband had a progressed Venus in trine to natal Saturn and he was feeling very secure and committed in the marriage. However, his wife might have progressed Venus in aspect to her natal Neptune and she was either feeling quite platonic at the time and not very sexual, or she appeared lost to him as she fantasized about how perfect love should be. In these situations, our discussion about conflict and how best to resolve it had as much to do with each progressed chart as it did with the synastry aspects.

While there are *objective* factors that can affect the marriage experience, such as synastry aspects between the two nativities, the astrologer must also calculate the progressions and transits for each individual to perceive any *subjective* dynamics at work. In my experience, these factors, rather than incompatibility alone, can produce conflict.

The tri-wheel chart on page 113 shows the nativity of Farrow in the innermost wheel; in the middle wheel are secondary progressions calculated diurnally for 13 January 1992, and in the outer wheel are her diurnal transits[39] of that day. The derived ephemeris date for her progressions is 28 March 1945 at 16:39:02 GMT.[40]

Find, among other things, the following relevant aspects:

1. Progressed Full Moon activates natal Venus-Neptune opposition.
2. Progressed Venus stationary retrograde in Chiron discovery degree.[41]
3. Progressed Moon in fated 7th harmonic triseptile with progressed Venus.
4. Progressed Mercury, ruler of 5th, applies to square with Mars.[42]
5. Transit Uranus conjunct progressed South Node (and their composite Sun).
6. Transit Saturn opposite progressed Pluto; 4th—10th house interception.
7. Progressed Jupiter (rules 8th) has perfected inconjunct with natal Sun.

Note that the degree symbol (Charubel) for her progressed Full Moon on 30 January 1992, Libra 8, is: *A figure resembling what is called 'the true lover's knot.'* It is also noteworthy that her progressed Saturn returned to a partile conjunction with her natal Saturn in 1993, during the ensuing court battle over child custody.

Farrow's progressed Saturn had stationed direct on 15 April 1969; it then took 24 years for *The Reaper* to return to partile (exact to degree and minute) conjunction with its natal position. It is revealing that at the direct station, she was involved with a married man, conductor Andre Previn, having children with him before he was divorced. In true Saturnian parlance, *what goes around comes around*.

Mia Farrow
Feb 9 1945   11:27 AM PWT
Santa Monica   California
33N50   118W29
Feb 9 1945   18:27:00 GMT
Tropical   Porphyry   True Node

Second Chart   Secondary Progression
Mia Farrow
Jan 13 1992   18:27:00 GMT
Third Chart
Transit Chart
Jan 13 1992   18:27:00 GMT

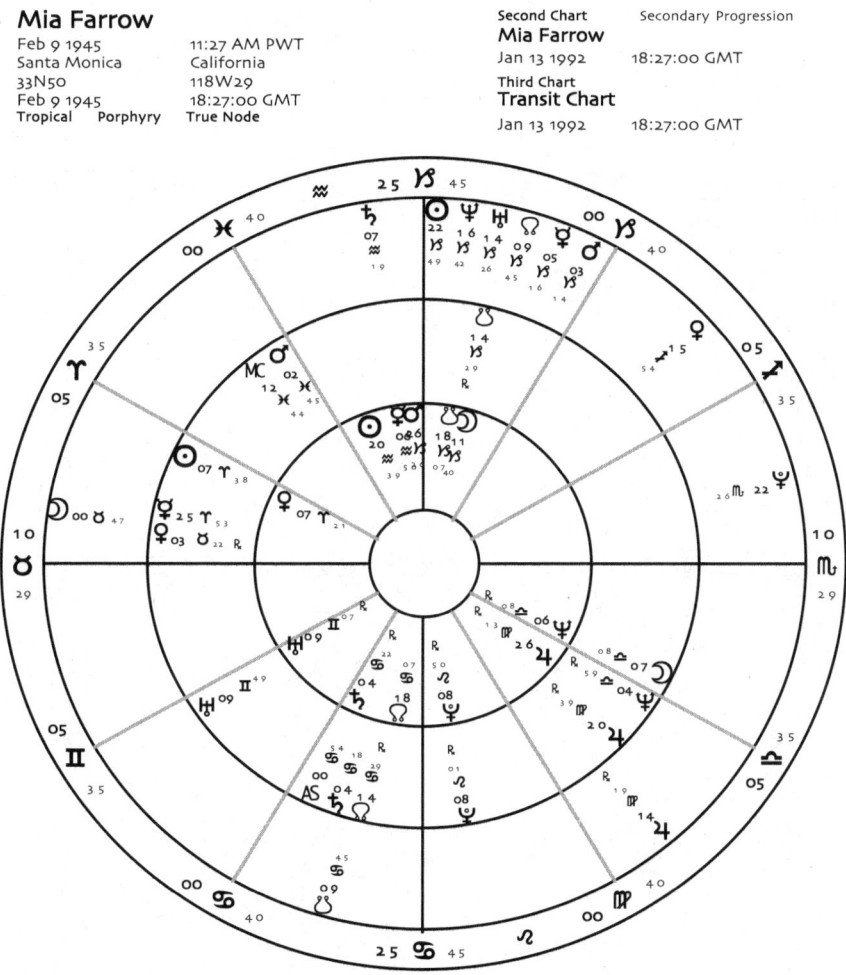

What the astrologer realizes by contemplating these various astrological factors is that none of this has anything to do with the synastry, composite or Davison charts. Often, when conflict arises in a relationship, it is due to one or both individuals having progressed chart activation, or transit influences to the natal or secondary progressed positions. While a solid relationship, built on the strength of synastric conjunctions and trines, can weather these passing storms, a weaker one may not.

This tri-wheel shows Allen's nativity in the innermost wheel, his secondary progressions calculated diurnally for 13 January 1992 in the middle wheel, and the transits for that day in the outermost wheel.[43]

Woody Allen
Dec 1 1935
Bronx
40N40
Dec 2 1935
Tropical Porphyry

10:55 PM EST
New York
73W54
03:55:00 GMT
True Node

Second Chart   Secondary Progression
Woody Allen
Jan 14 1992   03:55:00 GMT
Third Chart
Transit Chart
Jan 14 1992   03:55:00 GMT

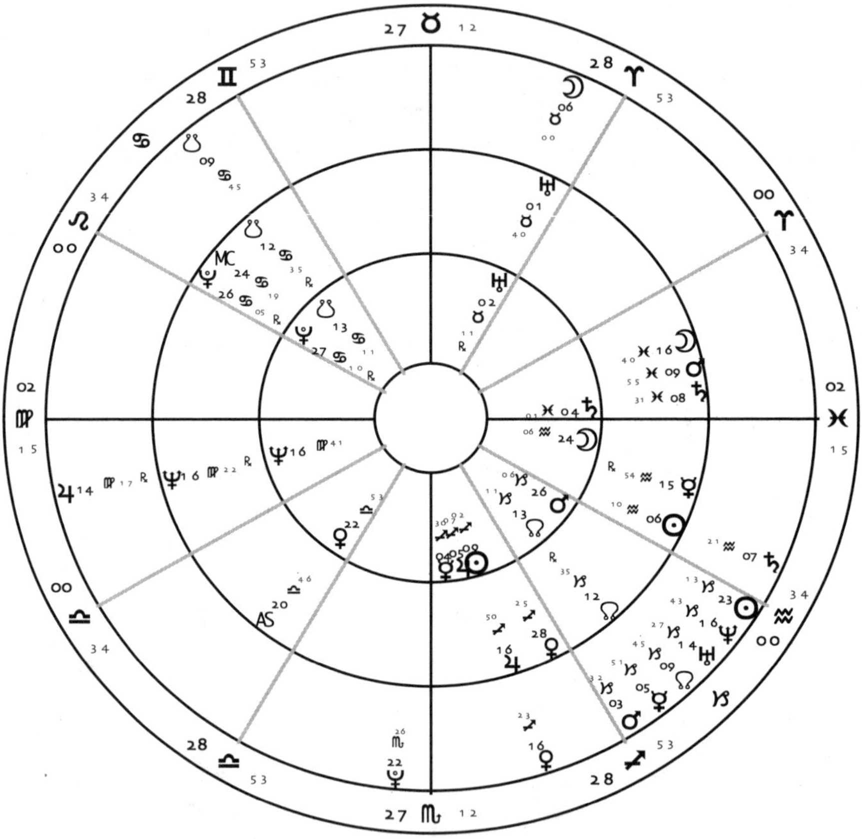

Find, among other things, the following pertinent aspects:

1. Progressed Moon perfecting an opposition to Neptune that very day.
2. Exact Mutable T-Cross forms to progressed Jupiter and transit Venus.
3. Both progressed malefics in < 1° orb square to natal Sun.
4. Natal Mars-Pluto opposition (01° 04' orb) has perfected by progression.
5. During 1993 child custody battle, progressed IC conjoins natal Mars.
6. Court verdict of 1994 damages reputation as progressed MC conjoins Pluto.
7. Progressed Ascendant conjoins Venus 1994; he's free to be with Soon-Yi.
8. Transit Mars, ruler of 8th, in fated 7th harmonic septile with natal Moon.

Woody Allen

Dec 1 1935　　10:55 PM EST
Bronx　　　　New York
40N40　　　　73W54
Dec 2 1935　　03:55:00 GMT
Tropical　Porphyry　True Node

Second Chart　　Minor Progression
Woody Allen
Jan 14 1992　　03:55:00 GMT

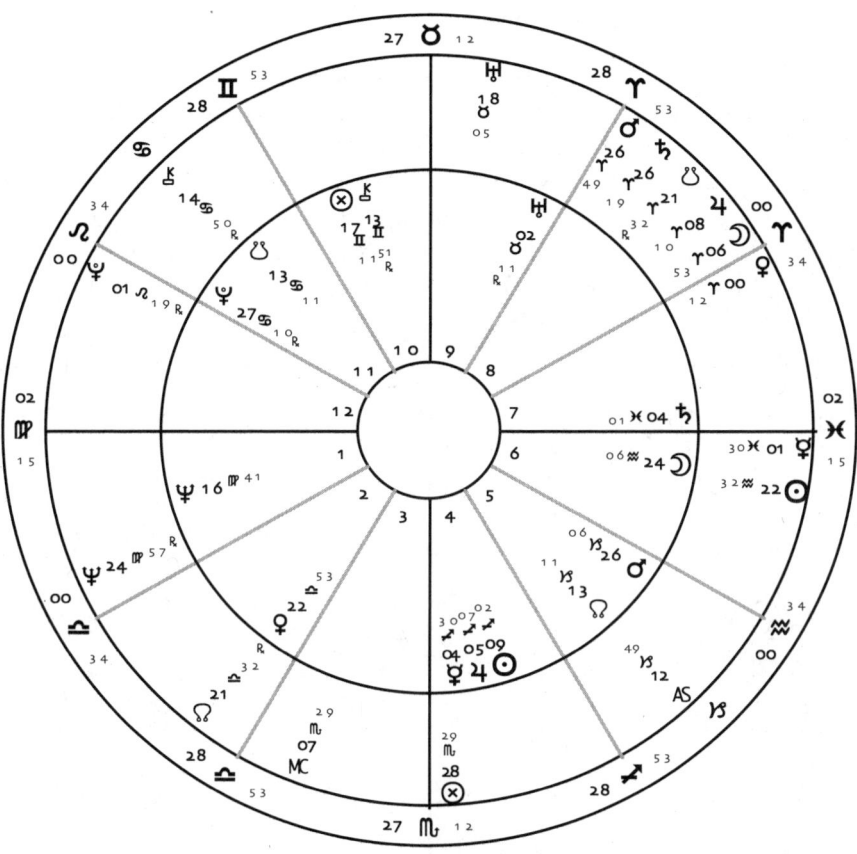

In this bi-wheel chart showing Allen's minor progressions for that day, there are both minor progressed malefics conjoined and filling in a Cardinal Grand Cross with his natal Venus-Mars-Pluto T-Square. It is also of note that C.E.O. Carter's problematic marriage degrees were occupied by both co-rulers of Allen's Descendant—Jupiter in 8° Aries, and Neptune in 25° Virgo.[44] The minor progressed derived ephemeris date is 12 February 1940, 09:50:55 GMT.

In summary, the astrologer should always calculate the progressions and transits for his clients when preparing for a relationship analysis consultation. It is never sufficient to try to assess compatibility dynamics from just the synastry aspects, house overlays, and composite or Davison charts, without also having taken into account the current progressions and transits for each individual in the marriage.

Progressed Composite Charts

Another way of fathoming relationship as it evolves over time is to consult the progressed composite chart. Many of my students have asked how this is possible to calculate as the composite chart does not exist in time or space, and thus its planetary positions cannot be found in an ephemeris.

To compute these charts, the astrologer must first progress each individual chart, and from these two progressed horoscopes, the composite chart. Just as in the progressed nativity for any individual, the rate of planetary motion for the Luminaries and planets remains the same, with a progressed composite Sun moving about one degree per year, and the progressed composite Moon moving about one degree per month. I often use this chart, calculated to the day of the first meeting, to help couples to understand the purpose of their relationship.

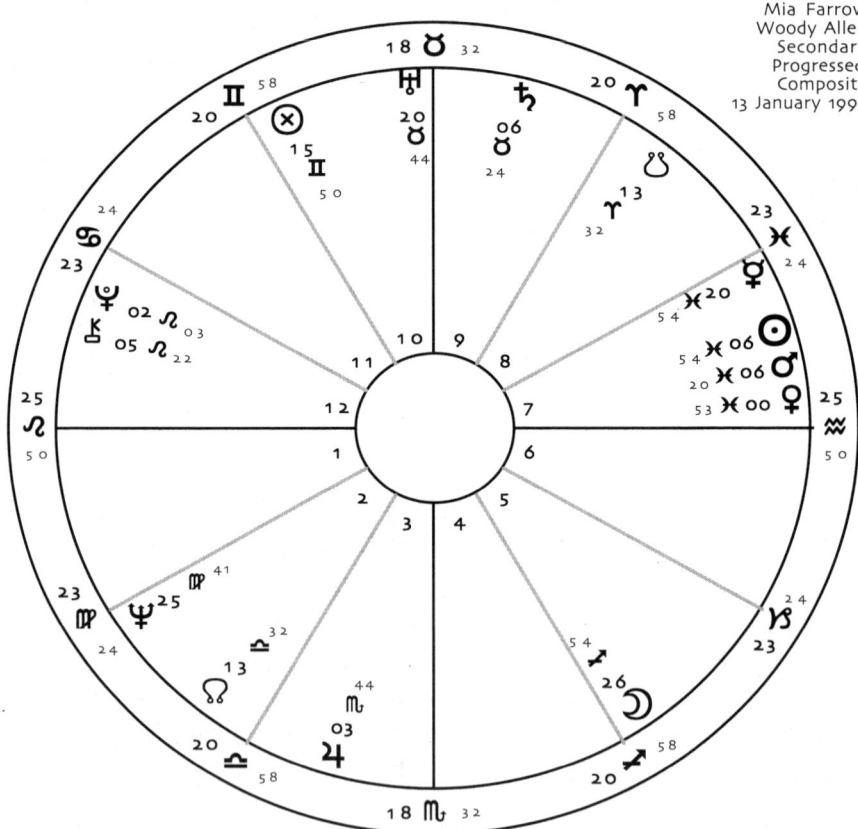

The secondary progressed composite chart for Farrow and Allen is shown here, calculated for 13 January 1992. The progressed composite Moon is just separating from a square with Neptune,[45] the planet associated with betrayal and deception. The Moon also opposes the Uranus/Pluto midpoint, these bodies occupying the

5th house of children, 10th house of public reputation, and 12th house of secret activities. It is of note that the Moon is in the degree of the Galactic Center, and Neptune is in one of C.E.O. Carter's marital problem degrees.

Readers familiar with *Volume I - Progressions* will recall that I first introduced my original metaphysical progression theory in that book. This theory correlated the secondary progressions with the physical body, the tertiary progressions with the astral body, and the minor progressions with the mental body. A *Mystic Time Ratio* of 1:13:27 was also elucidated, which corresponds with the relative rates of planetary movement in the three systems of progressions. These techniques can be applied to perceive relationship from the physical, astral or causal dimensions.

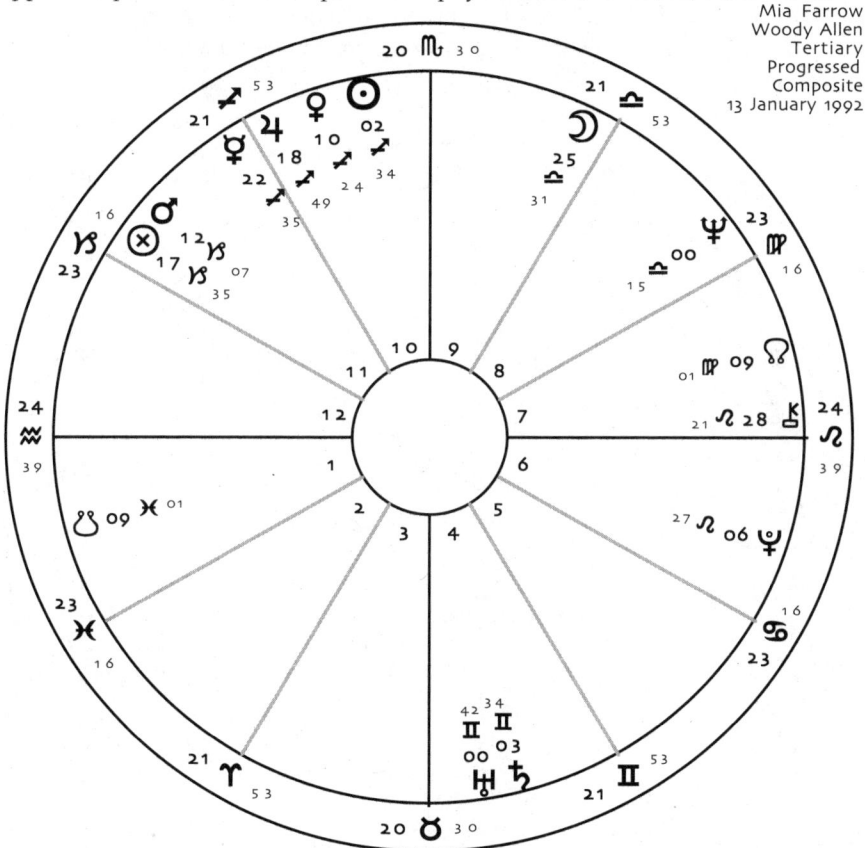

Mia Farrow
Woody Allen
Tertiary
Progressed
Composite
13 January 1992

This is the tertiary progressed composite chart for Farrow and Allen, calculated also for 13 January 1992. The plane of reality illustrated by these charts is of the astral, or the desire nature. The Sun exactly ingressed into a one degree applying orb with Saturn, a progressed-to-progressed aspect lasting for about two months.[46] This aspect is between the rulers of the horizon, with the quotidian Ascendant in the degree of Allen's Moon. As these angles progress quite rapidly, this is highly significant.[47]

The derived ephemeris date for Farrow's tertiary progressions, when calculated diurnally for 13 January 1992, is 30 October 1946 at 02:21:52 GMT. Her chart ruler, Venus, had stationed retrograde in her tertiary chart on 30 November 1991, just as the affair began between Allen and Soon-Yi. This tertiary Venus joined her secondary progressed retrograde Venus, which had stationed on 31 October 1988. I have repeatedly found that when the natal chart ruler becomes stationary in the tertiary or minor progressions, hidden internal forces then manifest externally.

The derived ephemeris date for Allen's tertiary progressions, calculated diurnally for 13 January 1992, is 21 December 1937 at 09:00:57 GMT. His chart ruler, Mercury, had stationed retrograde in his tertiary chart on 31 December 1991, the very month his affair began with Soon-Yi. Tertiary Neptune was also stationary when the tryst became unveiled, turning retrograde on 31 March 1992.

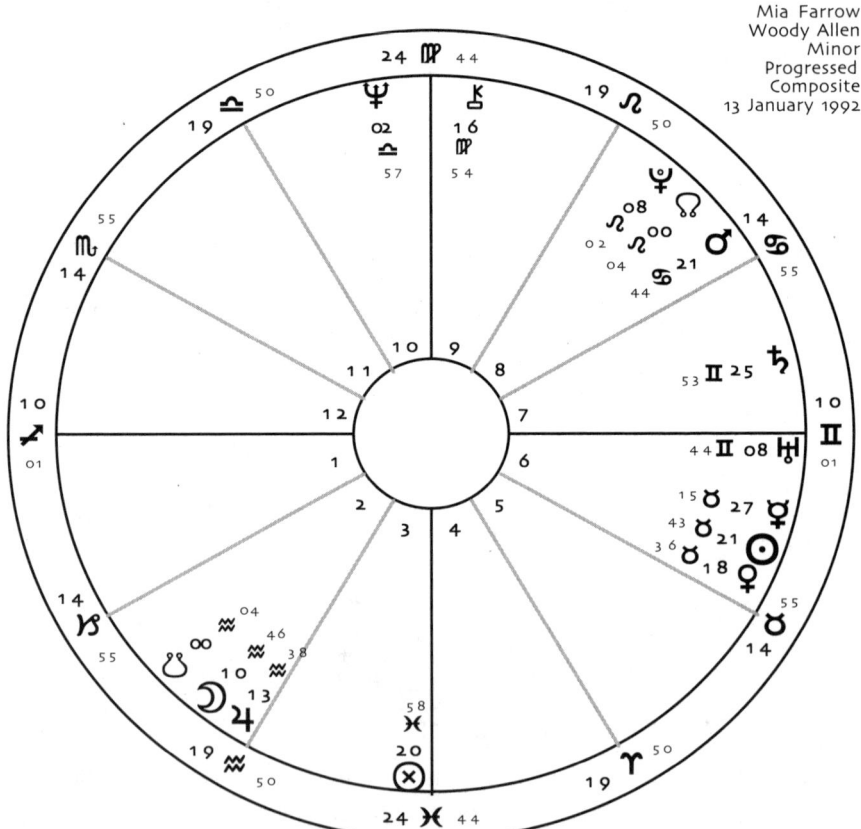

Mia Farrow
Woody Allen
Minor Progressed Composite
13 January 1992

This minor progressed composite chart for Farrow and Allen is again calculated for 13 January 1992. The causal plane is symbolized by the minor progressions, and this level of reality is where thought forms originate and how intention is set.

The Moon in this chart moves very rapidly, about a degree per day, and often is a trigger for relational upsets. The Moon had just opposed Pluto within the last 2-3 days, perhaps triggering suspicions that something was amiss. A nearly partile Sun-Mars sextile may have provided courage to confront a hunch. What I found most poignant in this progressed composite chart was the evidence of the painful wounds of a betrayal: minor progressed Chiron was in the degree of his natal Neptune, and minor progressed Neptune was in the degree of her Chiron.

Do the three different progressed composite charts symbolize events only, or do they reveal the inner life of a couple? I believe that tertiary and minor progressed composite charts show what a couple is experiencing on a private level. Desires, hopes, and fears can be seen in the tertiary composite, and changes of intention, which takes place at the causal level of consciousness, can be seen with the minor progressed composite chart, especially when the minor Luminaries change phases.

In summary, there are relevant planetary aspects in each of the progressed composite charts calculated for the date of a major relationship event. If my readers wish to pursue the more subtle dimensions of relationship analysis, I would recommend *Volume I*, wherein I describe secondary, tertiary and minor progressions in ample detail, and all from a metaphysical perspective.

Progressed Davison Time-Space Relationship Charts

Since the Davison chart exists in both time and space, the positions of the Lights and planets can be found in an ephemeris, just as if it were a nativity. This also means that the date and time midway between the two births, along with the median location, can be entered into your astrology software program just like natal chart data, calculated, saved, and progressed in any of the three ways. Our case study Davison chart (page 62) is calculated for 6 July 1940 at 23:10:59 GMT, and is located at 39N24 and 097W15.

This data can be entered like a natal chart and then secondary progressed to 13 January 1992 for the Davison-diurnal time of 23:10:59 GMT. Again, the difference between a time-space chart and a composite chart is: *a composite chart symbolizes the life force energy of a couple as if it were a third personality, a separate relationship entity; whereas the Davison chart, because it exists in both time and space, symbolizes forces working on a couple from outside of the relationship, be they from the family, children, financial pressures, or past life factors that are creating present karma.* It is also this author's belief that Davison charts show forces acting on relationship from the more recent past, such as heartaches, sexual betrayal, and other painful losses. The following is the secondary progressed Davison chart for Farrow and Allen, as of 13 January 1992.

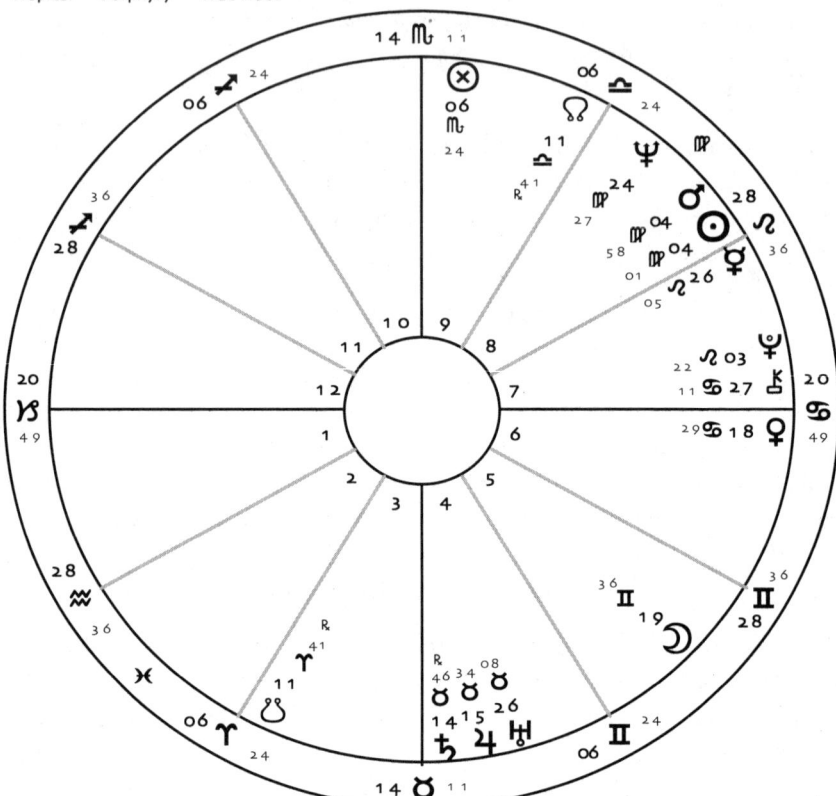

Farrow-Allen Davison Chart
Secondary Progression
Jan 13 1992   23:10:59 GMT
39N24   097W15
Derived Time
Aug 27 1940   11:42:37 GMT
Tropical Porphyry True Node

The chart ruler, Saturn, is both stationary retrograde and conjunct the progressed IC to the degree. Mercury, ruler of an intercepted Virgo in the 8th house of sex, is applying to a square with a stationary retrograde Uranus, exact within 03' of arc. This symbolizes a sudden, shocking revelation. Venus, the ruling planet of daughters, is in the exact degree of Farrow's North Node. Chiron is conjunct Allen's natal Pluto within one minute of arc, explicitly representing the sexual wounding that deeply pierced Farrow's heart. The nodal axis is also square to Farrow's Moon within one minute of arc, symbolizing the family disruption, and subsequent severing of the children's relationship with the father.

Also, every planet is in the Western hemisphere, indicating a situation where all matters are in the hands of others. In their case, it was the courts who decided the fates of the children; on the 9th cusp, ruling legal matters, is Libra 7, its Sabian Symbol: *An eccentric old witch is feeding her chickens, and seeking to allay their fear of a hawk whom she has just tamed.*[48]

This next chart is the tertiary progressed Davison chart for Farrow and Allen:

Farrow-Allen Davison Chart
Tertiary Progression
Jan 13 1992   23:10:59 GMT
39N24   097W15
Derived Time
May 26 1942   17:42:49 GMT
Tropical Porphyry True Node

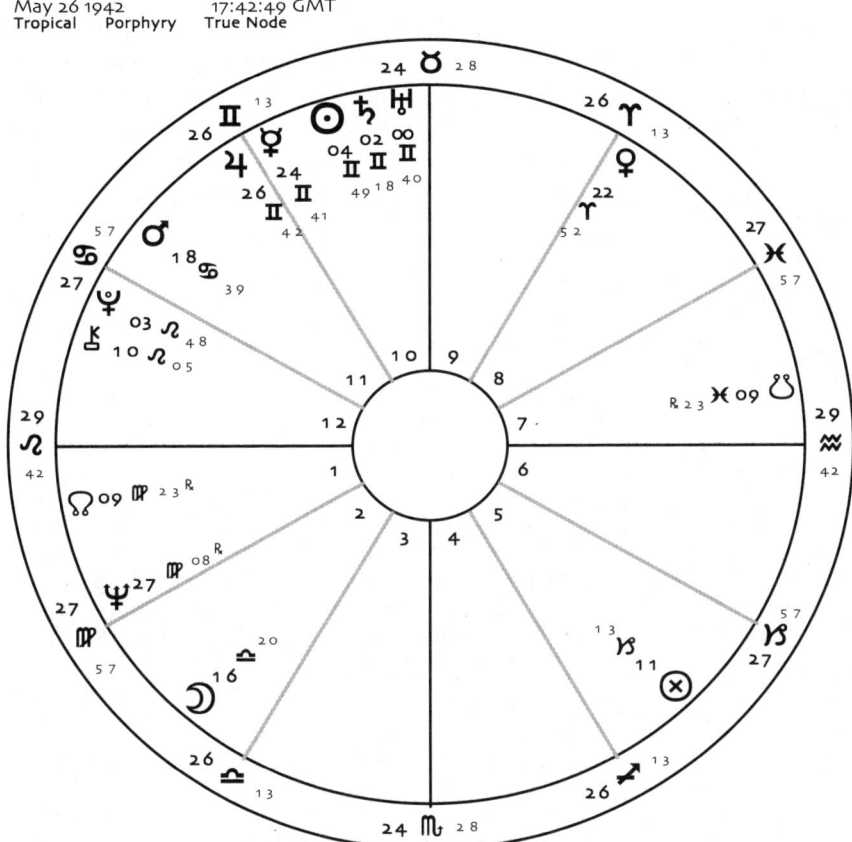

Here we find the Part of Fortune in the exact degree of Farrow's natal Moon. I would speculate that on an unexpressed inner level, her maternal instincts knew that Allen was not entirely safe for the children. Perhaps with a natal Mars-Pluto opposition, he was sexually molested as a little boy; this theory certainly explains his preoccupation as a film maker with sex and self-loathing. It is not uncommon for adults who were sexually mistreated as children to remember these traumas. Often this happens when their own children reach the same age that the adult was when he or she was molested.[49]

This point of view supports a protection theory for the tertiary progressed Part of Fortune being in conjunction with Farrow's Moon—that, on the astral plane, she knew he might not be safe around the younger children and an elder daughter was sacrificed for the greater good of the family. Just as in the secondary progressed Davison chart, where we saw Venus in the exact degree of Farrow's North Node, in the tertiary chart we find Mars at the apex of a T-Cross, also at Cancer 19. The Sabian Symbol for this degree: *A fragile miss, representative of proud old blood, is wed by a pompous priest to an eager youth of the new order.*

It is also worth noting that the tertiary progressed Davison Venus is opposite Allen's natal Venus, exact within one minute of arc. Venus is the ruling planet of daughters, and is also the ruler of this chart's Midheaven, attesting to the highly public scandal following the exposure of his lascivious infamy. The ruling planet of both the 5th house of children and the 8th house of sex, Jupiter, is in a close square with Neptune, the planet ruling betrayal and deception.⁵⁰

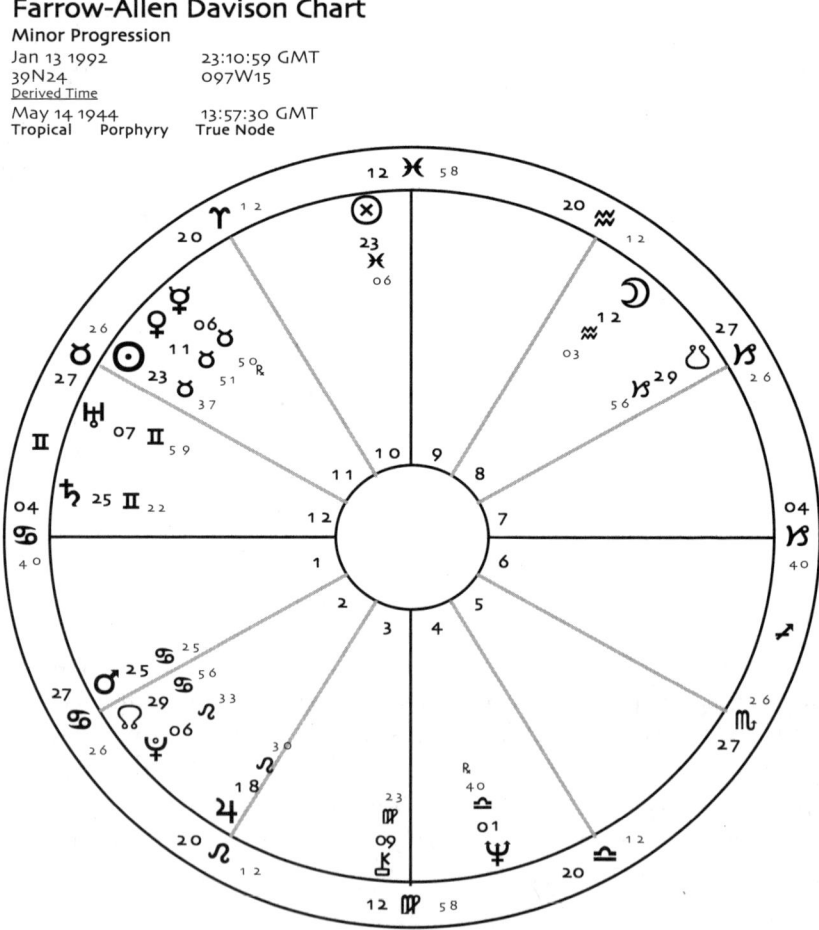

This minor progressed Davison chart has stationary direct Mercury ruling the IC, in a close square with Pluto, showing an externalization of a family secret. Mars is in the degree of Farrow's natal IC. Jupiter, ruling the custody battle in the courts that followed, is at the Neptune/ASC midpoint.[51] The rising degree, Cancer 5, is the most willful of the Zodiac, seen in its Sabian Symbol: *A man in an automobile, maddened by the lust for speed, races with a fast train and loses; he is killed.*

In summary, each of the three progressed Davison charts had relevant aspects and exact degree links with the individual nativities when calculated diurnally for the date when the clandestine affair between Soon-Yi and Allen became known to Farrow. The secondary progressed Davison chart corresponds with the physical dimension of relationship; the tertiary progressed with the astral, or emotional level; and the minor progressed with the causal, or mental level.

Transits to Composite or Davison Charts

In addition to using progressed composite or Davison charts to view relationships moving through time, I have also calculated transits to these two charts as well, to understand what the marriage was going through at the given time.

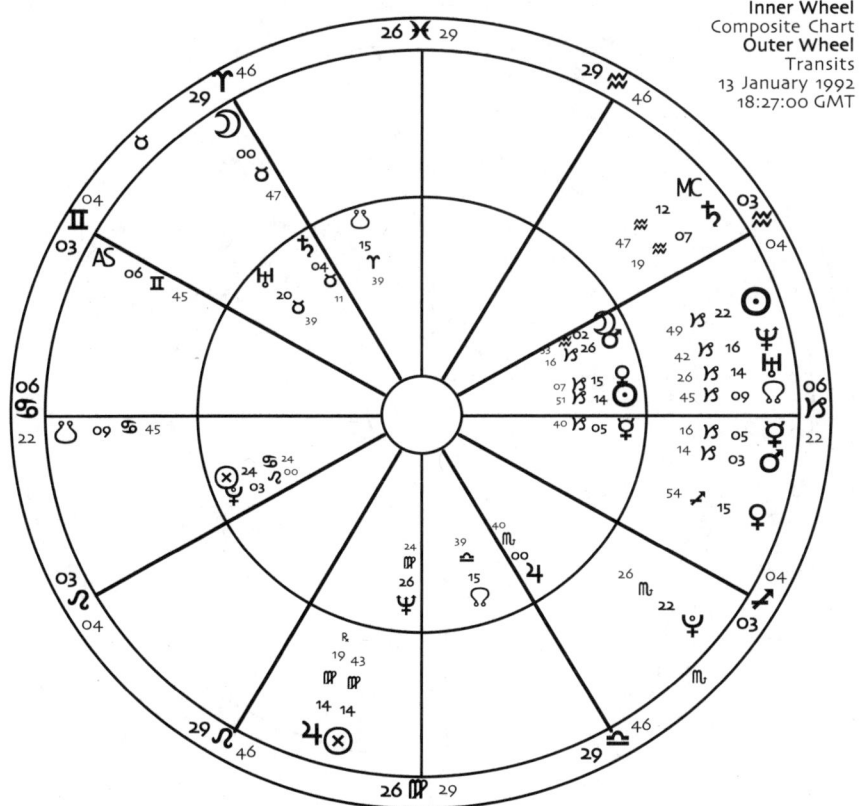

This bi-wheel chart shows the Farrow-Allen composite chart in the inner wheel, and in the outer wheel are the transits of 13 January 1992.[52] Immediately, the astrologer sees transit Uranus in exact conjunction with the composite Sun. There is also a Mercury return; Mercury rules the IC, symbol of the family, and the 12th house of secrets. The Moon (children) is opposite Jupiter, ruler of the courts.

Moreover, Jupiter is in exact trine to the composite Sun. Upon noticing this, astrologers may wonder if the hand of Divine Providence was also at work here. Just as in a death chart, when the soul leaves a body and Jupiter is found to be prominent in the progressions or transits, this union was perhaps brought to a merciful end by the discovery of the illicit sexual affair.

This bi-wheel shows the transits of 13 January 1992 acting on the Davison chart.

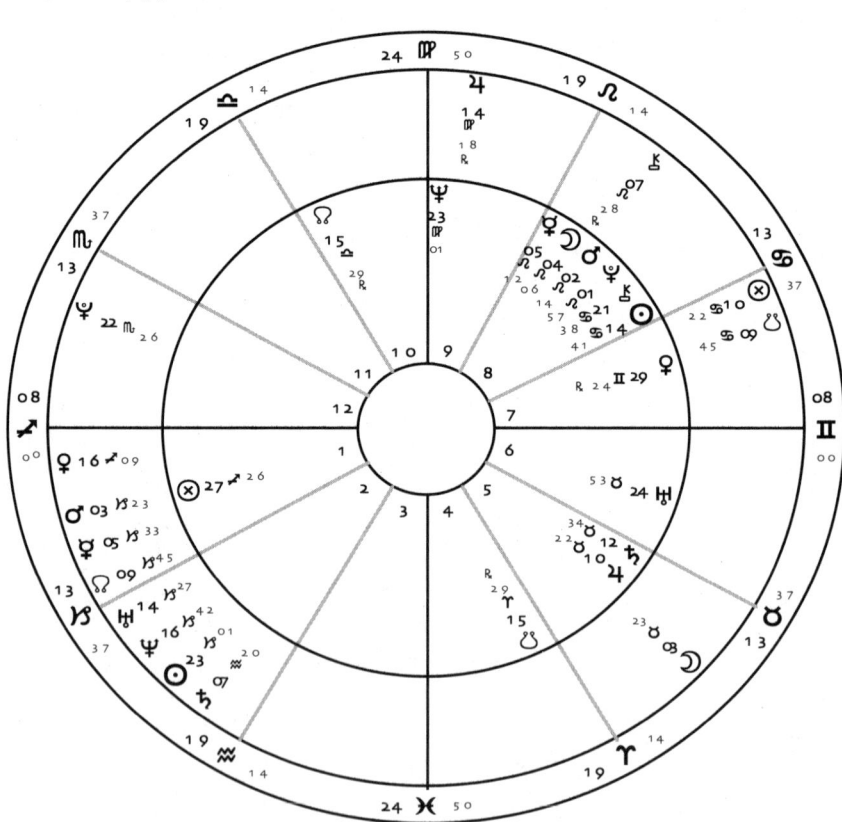

Uranus is now found to be in exact opposition to the Davison Sun, and, similar to the transits to the composite, the Uranus-Neptune conjunction closely squares the Lunar Nodes. Jupiter is again in aspect with the Sun, this time by sextile. It is also interesting how the transit Sun is in partile trine with the Davison Neptune, elevated as it is on the Midheaven, symbolizing the highly public sexual betrayal.

Transits to Progressed Composite or Davison Charts

Throughout my career as an astrologer, I have found transits to the progressed positions to be of equal, or greater merit than transits to natal planets. In particular, transits of the secondary progressed angles are remarkably precise. In relationship horoscopes, however, I have not found this technique to operate as accurately.

This is the bi-wheel chart showing transits of 13 January 1992 to the secondary progressed composite chart, calculated to that same date, for Farrow and Allen.

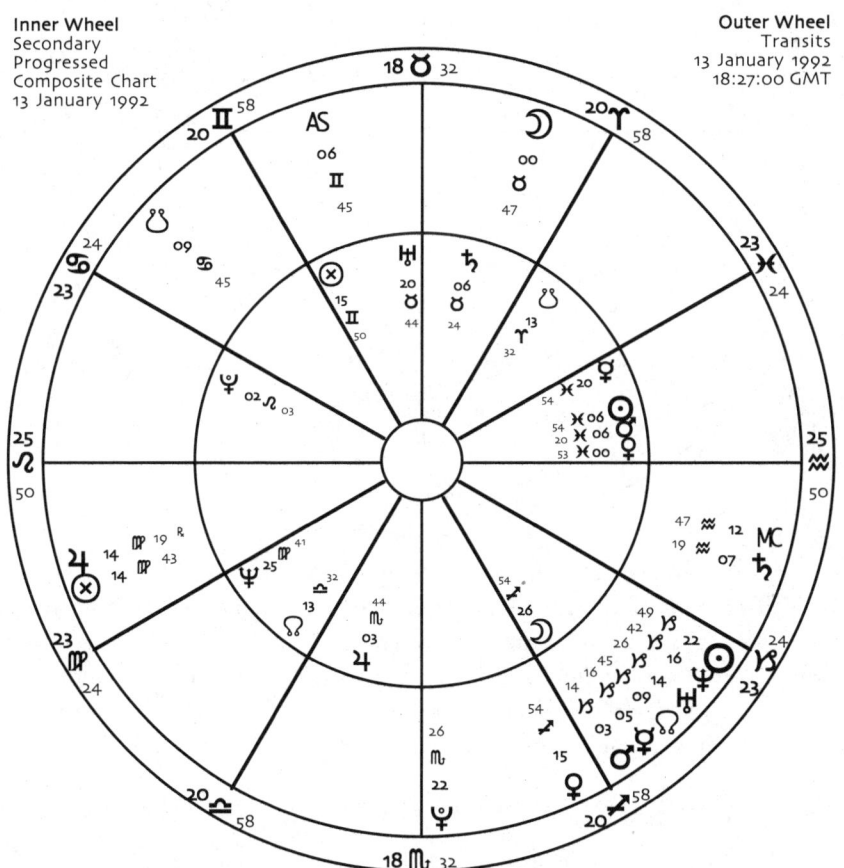

While astrologers could reasonably argue that an exposed secret love affair with a family member could be seen in a 5th house transit Stellium, and Pluto near the IC in the 4th, there are no exact-to-the-degree transit conjunctions or oppositions, other than Venus (daughters) opposing the progressed composite Part of Fortune.

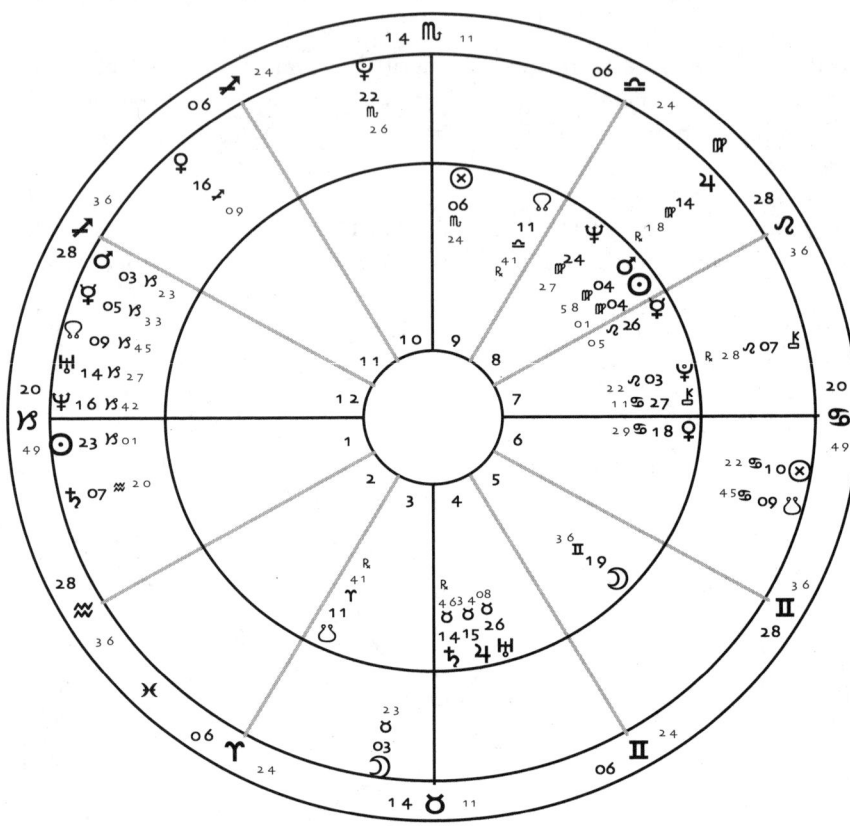

Looking at the transits of 13 January 1992 to the secondary progressed Davison chart,[53] the closest aspects are a transit quincunx from Mars to Pluto, exact within one minute of arc, and a square of the Moon to Pluto, also exact within one minute. Additionally, two very tight transit Grand Trines are forming, with Jupiter and Uranus trine to the progressed Davison Saturn/IC in the former, and a precise Moon-Mars trine in transit trine to the Sun and Mars in the latter.

C.E.O. Carter wrote rather unflatteringly of the Grand Trine configuration:

> Such a configuration was considered evil by medieval writers and unfortunately this view appears to be not without foundation. Often the fortunes seem to be greatly involved in those of others, both for good and evil, and the character may tend to weakness and lack of moral fibre. The element in which the Grand Trine falls may be too prominent in the temperament. - *The Principles of Astrology* (1925)

A relevant speculation regarding the effect of a transit Grand Trine to a Davison progressed chart, is that a relationship could be morally weakened and prone to infidelity under this influence, especially so if falling in the sensuous Earth signs. Allen's Mars-Pluto opposition, which had just perfected by progression, is arguably the one natal aspect that drove him into sexual compulsions. It is of interest to the psychological astrologer that these two planets formed a transit inconjunct when he was caught philandering.[54] One would also suspect that with a transit Moon in square to Pluto, Farrow's suspicions were heightened.

In researching transits to both the tertiary and minor progressed Davison charts, I did not find exact conjunctions or oppositions forming. As mentioned, I have found the transits to individual progressions to be extremely accurate, but less so the transits to progressions of a derived chart.

Synastric Progressions

Throughout this chapter we have looked at ways of analyzing relationship as it travels through time. So far, we've covered transits and progressions to the natal chart, progressed composite and Davison charts, transits to composite or Davison charts, and transits to the progressed relational charts. These techniques can be used to open windows of perception into either the current reality of individuals in a marriage, or into the structure of the relationship itself.

The astrologer who is consulted for a relationship analysis will naturally look at the synastry between the two nativities for information on how the individuals interact. Yet after entering into a relationship, both parties do not grow and evolve in the same way or at the same pace. If one's soul growth over time is seen in the progressed horoscope, then it is only logical that the original synastry must also be updated.

This can be accomplished by investigating the following three types of synastry:

1. Person A natal to person B progressed.
2. Person B natal to person A progressed.
3. Person A progressed to person B progressed.

Recalling my metaphysical progression theory—secondary progressed-to-natal synastry shows changes in physical aspects of relationship; tertiary progressed-to-natal synastry illustrates the developing astral, or feeling domains; and minor progressed-to-natal synastry corresponds with mutations on the mental level. For example, if person A's *secondary progressed* Venus comes to synastry conjunction with person B's natal Saturn, and person A has had some weight gain adversely affecting their appearance, person B might feel decreased physical attraction.

But if person A's *tertiary progressed* Venus arrives at a conjunction with person B's natal Saturn, person A would feel a deeper commitment to the partner and would also experience more security in the relationship. If person A has *minor progressed* Venus conjunct person B's Saturn, person B may have critical thoughts about some items of furniture recently purchased by person A. In addition to these three types of progressed synastry affecting different levels of reality—physical, astral or mental—the astrologer must remember that each system of progression moves Venus at various rates of speed. Secondary Venus holds a progressed conjunction for 19 months, tertiary Venus for 1 1/2 months, and minor Venus for just 3 weeks.[55]

Mia Farrow
Feb 9 1945   11:27 AM PWT
Santa Monica   California
33N50   118W29
Feb 9 1945   18:27:00 GMT
Tropical   Porphyry   True Node

Second Chart   Secondary Progression
Woody Allen
Jan 14 1992   03:55:00 GMT

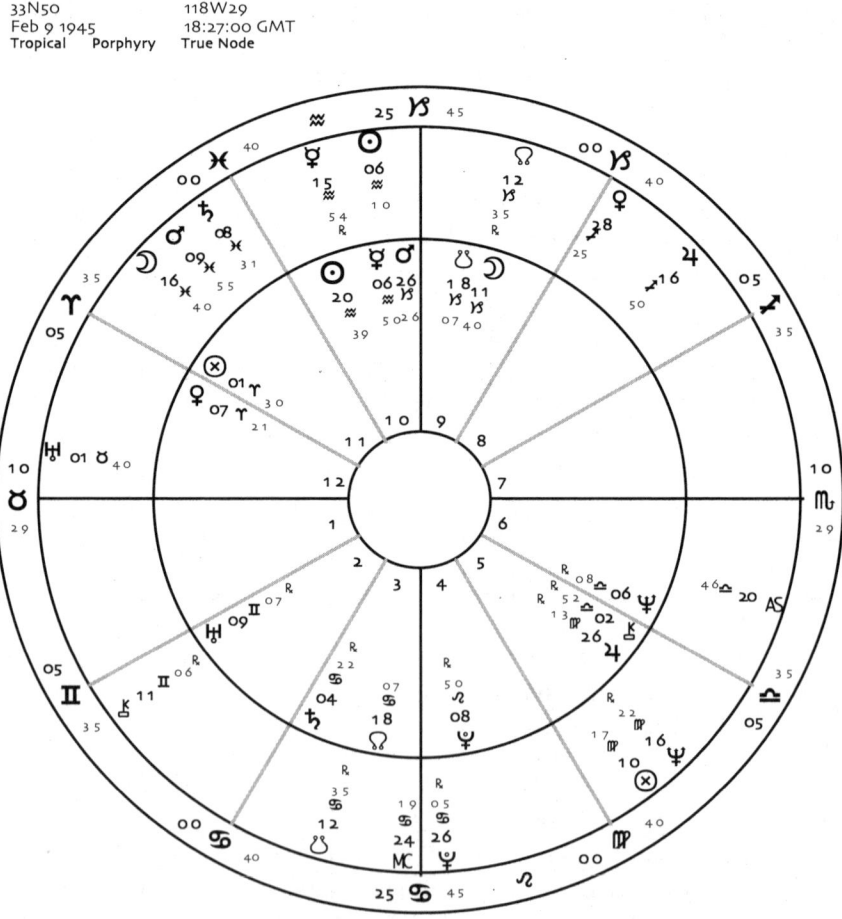

This bi-wheel shows Farrow's natal chart in the inner wheel, and Allen's secondary progressions, calculated for 13 January 1992, in the outer wheel. See how Allen's progressed Sun will move through an opposition with Farrow's natal Pluto over the next 2-3 years. The accusations of sexual molestation leveled against him were never substantiated in court, but the levels of bitterness and enmity between the two of them resulted in intense hatred. His progressed Sun was also conjoining her 5th house ruler (children), Mercury, at the time.

On page 114, when summarizing Allen's progressions, I noted the exact 16° Mutable T-Square forming between his secondary progressed Moon, Jupiter and Neptune. Seasoned astrologers may ponder if Farrow had any bodies at 16° of Gemini, thus filling in a progressed synastric Mutable Cross. I found no planets of hers in that degree, but her Arabic Part of Soul is 16° Gemini 47', and her Part of Ancestral Heritage is 16° Gemini 35'. One surmises some serious past karma here.[56]

Allen's progressed Mars was separating from a square to her natal Uranus at the time of the discovery of the affair, and one wonders if this aspect had strained the relationship during the previous 2-3 years with quarrels, bickering and the like. That progressed Mars had also just completed the separating 1° orb from a synastric quincunx to her natal Pluto, and was moving toward a synastric sextile with her natal Moon, thus forming a progressed synastric Yod. Since Farrow and Allen had natal Mars conjunct to the degree, his natal Mars-Pluto opposition also created a synastric opposition. For these two planets to again have linked by progressed synastry is similar to my hologram theory in the preceding chapter.

It is also of note that the most exact of the synastric progressions is his Sun trine to her natal Neptune, separating by only 02' of arc. This aspect had perfected just 12 days earlier, substantiating C.E.O. Carter's rule about *the two planets in aspect being more important that the specific aspect itself.* Neptune rules deceit and lies. His progressed Ascendant is also in close synastric trine with her Sun, not an aspect one would normally associate with what happened between them.

Also notice that Allen's progressed Midheaven is applying to a conjunction with Farrow's natal IC, and his natal retrograde Pluto, which is conjunct her IC with an orb of 01° 25', has now tightened to just 20' of arc by progressed synastry. The symbolism of Pluto overlaid into her 4th house is quite poignant considering what happened, akin to the fox guarding the henhouse. With past life connections associated with the IC, what unusual family karma these two had!

In the next bi-wheel chart (shown on the following page), we see Allen's natal chart in the inner wheel, and Farrow's secondary progressions, calculated to 13 January 1992, in the outer wheel. On page 112, I recapped her progressions and transits, pointing out a progressed Full Moon landing right on her Venus-Neptune natal opposition, a remarkable testimony to the unfailing accuracy of astrology.

Farrow's progressed Mars formed a synastric conjunction to Allen's Descendant, and ingressed into his 7th house of open enemies. Over the next two years as the custody battle and molestation charges played out in court, her progressed Mars arrived at a synastric conjunction with his natal Saturn.

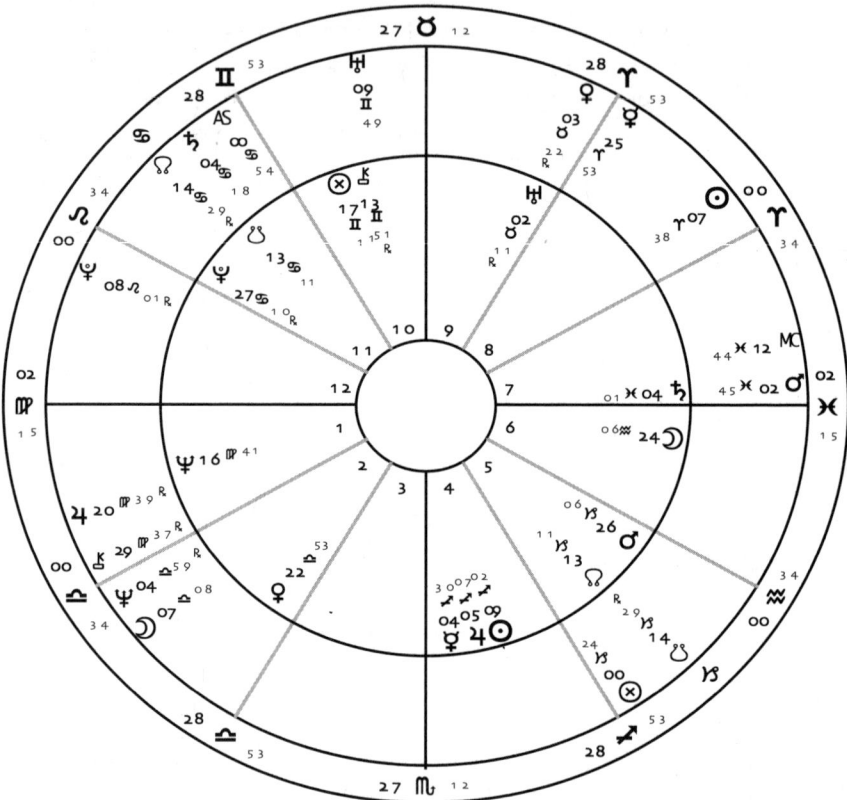

Also, her progressed Full Moon forms a quindecile axis with his natal Venus; the greater Luminary forms a 195° contraquindecile, and the lesser Light a 345° quindecile. In *Volume II*, I wrote about these aspects in Chapter Thirteen, using the Sabian Symbols for Aries 16, Virgo 16, Libra 16, and Pisces 16 to illustrate how the waxing and waning versions of these aspects function:

> Waxing and waning quindeciles (15° or 345°) are evidence of happy and secure childhood mystical experiences during play, solitude or contact with Nature that lead to pronounced inner peace or creative inspiration. The waxing and waning contraquindeciles (165° or 195°) are evidence of frightful agitation in the unconscious, such as borderline personality or post-traumatic stress disorders,

resulting from childhood physical, verbal and/or sexual abuse that may have somewhat crippled the functionality of the adult behaviors, yet also opened the consciousness to altered states of spiritually inspired genius or creative prowess.

One can only speculate that Allen was perhaps sexually molested as a child, and now having children of his own the same age as he was when this possible trauma occurred, he was unable to maintain his sexual balance and fell prey to predatory instincts that are associated with a natal Mars-Pluto opposition. The progressed synastric contraquindecile from her Sun to his Venus might have been the trigger.

Other noteworthy factors in the synastric progressions between his nativity and her secondaries are: 1) her stationary retrograde progressed Venus (in the Chiron discovery degree) conjunct his natal Uranus; 2) her progressed Mercury fills in a synastric Cardinal Grand Cross with his natal T-Square; and 3) during the next two years of the courtroom tragedy, her progressed MC squared his natal Chiron.

Mia Farrow
Secondary Progression
Jan 13 1992   18:27:00 GMT
33N50   118W29
<u>Derived Time</u>
Mar 28 1945   16:39:02 GMT
Tropical   Porphyry   True Node

Second Chart   Secondary Progression
Woody Allen
Jan 14 1992   03:55:00 GMT

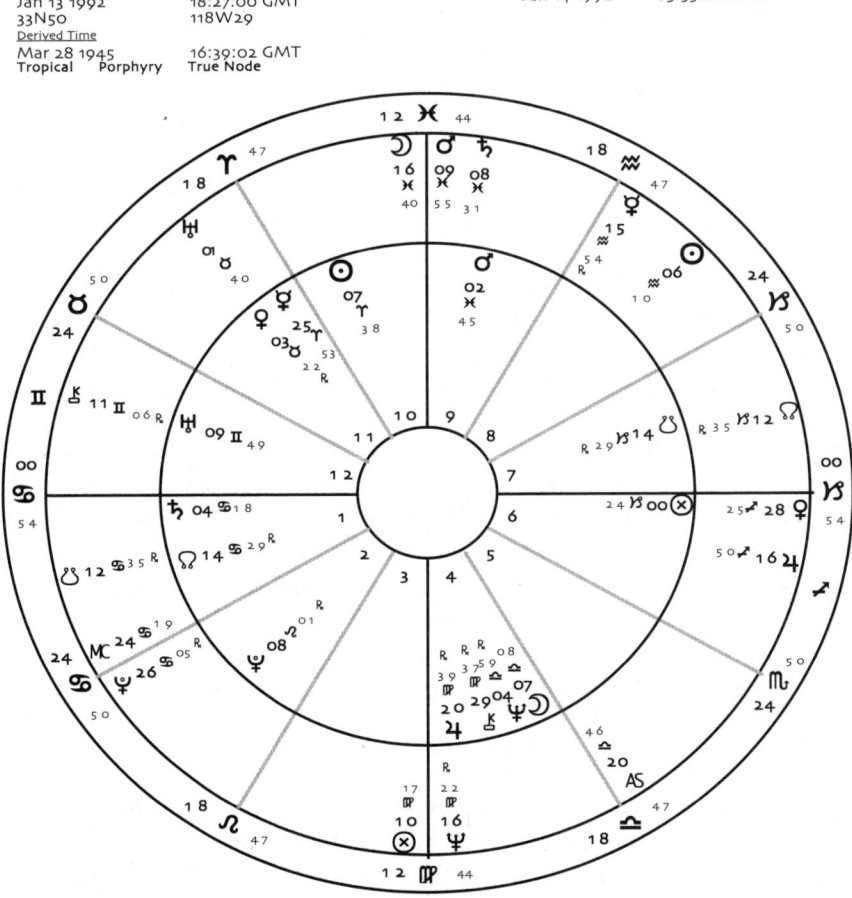

This third bi-wheel chart shows synastric progressions between each secondary chart, progressed diurnally to 13 January 1992. Farrow's progressed horizon was in the powerful cardinal ingress degrees of 00° Cancer-00° Capricorn, and as is the case with any progressed Full Moon, her Part of Fortune is conjunct the Descendant.[57]

Somewhat similar to the *Marriage Rule* (page 49), wherein rulers of the horizon must conjoin the Ascendant or Descendant in the other nativity, or each other, for marriage to occur, I have observed that when relationships end, the progressed horizon rulers may also be involved. During the two years of the bitter custody battle, Allen's progressed Venus, ruling planet of her Taurus Ascendant, became angular on Farrow's progressed Descendant.

Further testing this maxim about the progressed rulers of either horizon being angular, or the progressed horizon rulers being in aspect with each other during relational endings, one finds some of the more precise synastry upholding this law:

1. His SP Mercury, ruler of his natal ASC, trioctile her SP ASC; 00° 00' orb.
2. Her SP Saturn, ruler of her SP DSC, quintile his SP Neptune; 00° 04' orb.
3. His SP Jupiter, ruler of his natal DSC, quintile her SP Neptune; 00° 09' orb.
4. Her SP Mercury, ruler of his natal ASC, square his SP Pluto; 00° 12' orb.
5. His SP Saturn, ruler of her SP DSC, quincunx her SP Pluto; 00° 30' orb.
6. Her SP Pluto, co-ruler of her natal DSC, quintile his SP ASC; 00° 45' orb.
7. Her SP Moon, ruler of her SP ASC, quintile his SP Pluto; 00° 57' orb.

It is also of interest that a fated 7th harmonic aspect exists in their synastric progressions, with her secondary Sun in close septile to his secondary Mercury, his chart ruler, this aspect having an orb of 00° 18'. This family of aspects, which include biseptiles and triseptiles, are often seen in synastry between fated lovers.

In summary, astrologers can utilize progressed synastry to understand the changes that a relationship is currently going through. By comparing each natal chart to the other's progressed chart, or one progressed chart to another, the astrologer opens up a new world of insight beyond that found in the natal synastry. Some of the more powerful manifestations of this technique can also be seen at the beginning of a relationship, when two souls first meet. I have personally seen the progressed conjunction of a woman's Venus to her natal Sun, and with both in an exact conjunction with the author's natal Saturn, when the two of us first met.

The Condition of the Solar Return Venus

One other tool to reveal what is going on in an individual's relational life is the annual solar return Venus. I use two specialty horoscopes in my practice; a standard solar return that calculates the precise transit of the Sun over the natal

Sun, and a progressed solar return which calculates the exact passage of the transit Sun over the secondary Sun.

This means that any given client will have two *astrological birthdays* each year. The first one falls within a day or so of the actual birthday and is represented by the standard solar return chart; the second, called the *progressed birthday*, occurs as many days after the actual birthday as the person's age and is delineated with the progressed solar return chart. This second date advances one day each year.

For example, the tri-wheel chart shown on page 113 with secondary progressions for Farrow calculated to 13 January 1992 has a derived ephemeris date of 28 March 1945. This is 47 days after her birthday of February 9th. She turned 47 in 1992. One year later in 1993, the derived ephemeris date advances to March 29.

The transit of the Sun over this secondary progressed Sun has much relevance. In 1906, when Alan Leo first published *The Progressed Horoscope*, he spoke of these calculations as being quite significant. As I restated in *Volume I - Progressions*:

> Leo believed that increased importance should be attached to the transiting conjunctions that take place at the birthday, or progressed birthday, each year. In effect, any conjunction in the Solar Return chart to any natal planet is significant. Also of importance is any transit over a natal or progressed planet at the time of the year coinciding with the secondary progressed Sun. He felt that these transits would hold their influence over the next year.

What this means in practice is that if the astrologer finds a solar return planet or a progressed solar return planet in exact conjunction with the natal or secondary progressed Venus, then this influence will hold over the next year. Now, with the outer planets, this is a no-brainer, as the transits of Uranus, Neptune or Pluto will show up in solar return charts for several years running. But, what is less likely to be observed by the astrologer is, for example, a Mars position in either a solar return, or a progressed solar return, which is in the exact degree of either the natal Venus, or the progressed Venus. This conjunction's effects are felt for a full year.[58]

Astrologers must also apply some discernment when working with solar returns or progressed solar returns before making a judgment about a client's relationship experiences. I have rarely found influences in these solar revolution maps that could not also be seen in the client's current progressions or transits. In fact, as I write, I am under the rays of a current solar return Mutable T-Cross having as its apex planet a Venus-Pluto conjunction, with a Mars-Jupiter opposition. However, at the same time, I also have my progressed Venus in square with my natal Mars.

One thing that I have observed *which is unique* about these solar return charts is how they reveal exact degree synastry conjunctions to other soul's nativities with whom one comes into contact during the next year. I have repeatedly found that this *solar return synastry* shows up at the beginning of new relationships, and that the synastric conjunctions will usually involve the rulers of the horizon. This is even so for the author, as on his last birthday his solar return Mercury was in 4° Sagittarius; he met a girlfriend then who has Jupiter in that very same degree. Her progressed Mars, ruler of her 7th, had conjoined that Jupiter 10 days earlier.

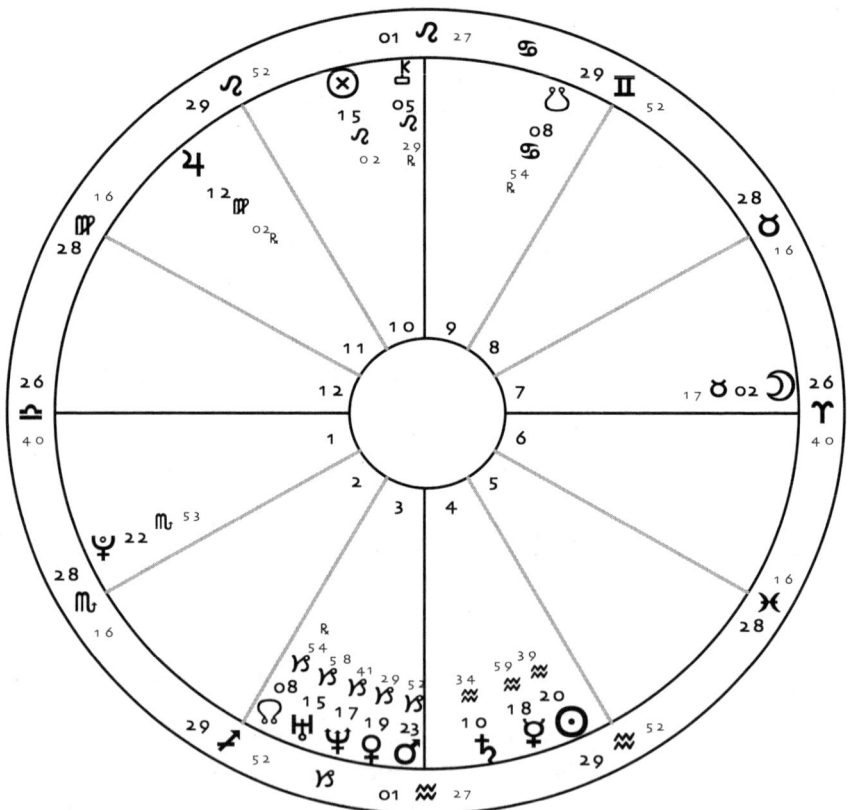

This is the solar return chart for Farrow, calculated on her 47th birthday in 1992. Her solar return Moon is in the exact degree of Allen's natal Uranus, attesting to the severe disruption that hit her family after the discovery of the sexual affair. The condition of solar return Venus tells the story rather well—the planet of relationship is intercepted in a 3rd house Stellium flanked by Uranus and Neptune on one side, and the malefic Mars on the other side. It would be pertinent here to state that the 3rd house is the 12th from the 4th (family life), and symbolizes any hidden conditions at home.

The astrologer also finds Saturn, ruler of the 5th house of children (with the anaretic 30th degree of Aquarius on its cusp) in exact square with Farrow's natal horizon. The solar return horizon is in exact square with her natal Mars. One cannot help but notice an elevated Chiron on the MC, showing the very public wounding that she endured during that year. The Sun, ruler of the solar return MC, is in a square to Pluto, and is found in the 4th house of private family matters.

Progressed Solar Return—Farrow

Mar 28 1992 1:37:23 AM EST
Manhattan New York
40N35 73W59
Mar 28 1992 06:37:23 GMT
Tropical Porphyry True Node

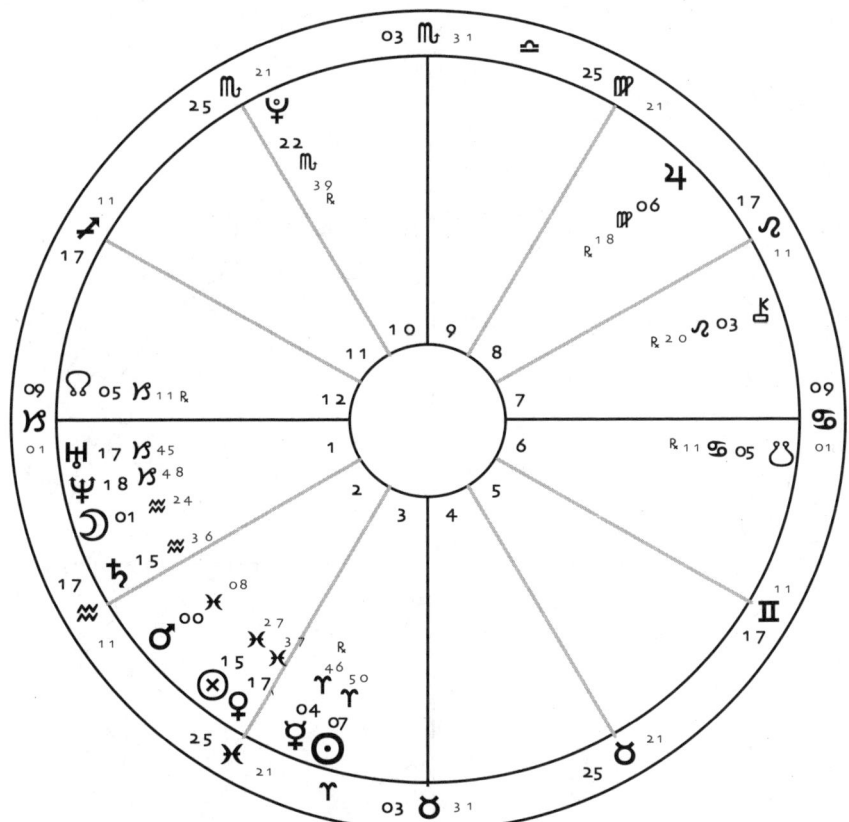

This is the progressed solar return for Farrow, calculated for the precise time that the transit Sun conjoined her secondary progressed Sun to the degree, minute and second of arc on 28 March 1992. Immediately, the astrologer sees that the IC is in exact conjunction with her progressed retrograde Venus, which had stationed in 1988 in the Chiron discovery degree, at 03° Taurus 35', 04' of arc from this IC. A scrutiny of the condition of progressed solar return Venus yields the fact that she is in the precise degree of the Mercury/Mars midpoint; Mercury ruling Virgo on the 9th (court cases), and Mars ruling Scorpio on the MC (for all the world to see).

The horizon is in the exact degrees of the Lunar Nodes on 13 January 1992, when she found the photographs. This can only occur for about 4 minutes on any given day. The astrologer will also notice that the progressed solar return Moon is also in the same degree as the standard solar return IC, exact within 03' of arc. Again, we find an interception in the 3rd house, the 12th from the 4th, this time the Sun. As Farrow was involved in a bitter legal struggle that year, the Sabian Symbol for Jupiter is: *The women's quarters of an Oriental palace are revealed; here are the bright and unafraid eyes of cloistered souls* (Virgo 7). I do not need to remind the reader that Soon-Yi is Korean.

Woody Allen
Solar Return
Dec 1 1991   18:07:17 GMT
Manhattan   New York
40N35   73W59
Tropical Porphyry True Node

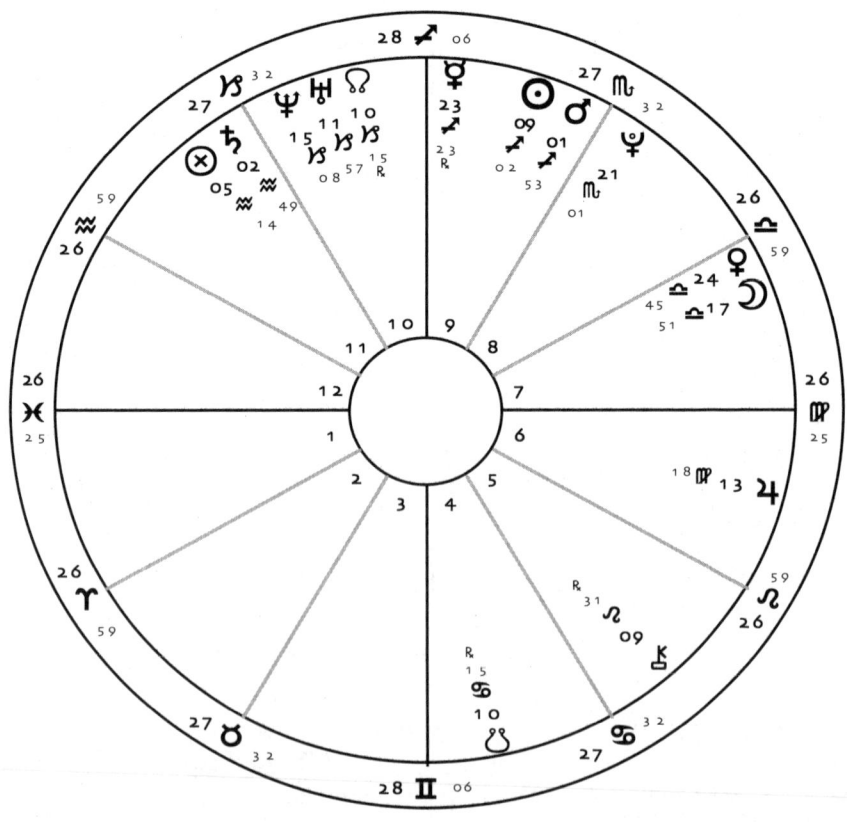

On page 136 is the solar return chart for Allen, calculated for his 56th birthday in December 1991, which had occurred about six weeks before the big eruption. On the 7th cusp, the house of open enemies and lawsuits, we find the exact degree of Farrow's natal Jupiter, ruler of the legal system. One also finds the Midheaven in the degree of his secondary progressed Venus in 1992.[59] Repeated conjunctions such as these are a powerful testimony to the efficacy of angularity in astrology.

With the painful betrayal that took place that year between Allen and Farrow, one would expect to find a Neptune connection in this solar return chart. The solar return Neptune/Ascendant midpoint is 20° Aquarius, her natal Sun. The Moon's closest aspect is a square to Neptune. The solar return Uranus is also found in the degree of her natal Moon, a transit for Farrow that coincided with sudden and dramatic upheaval in her family life.

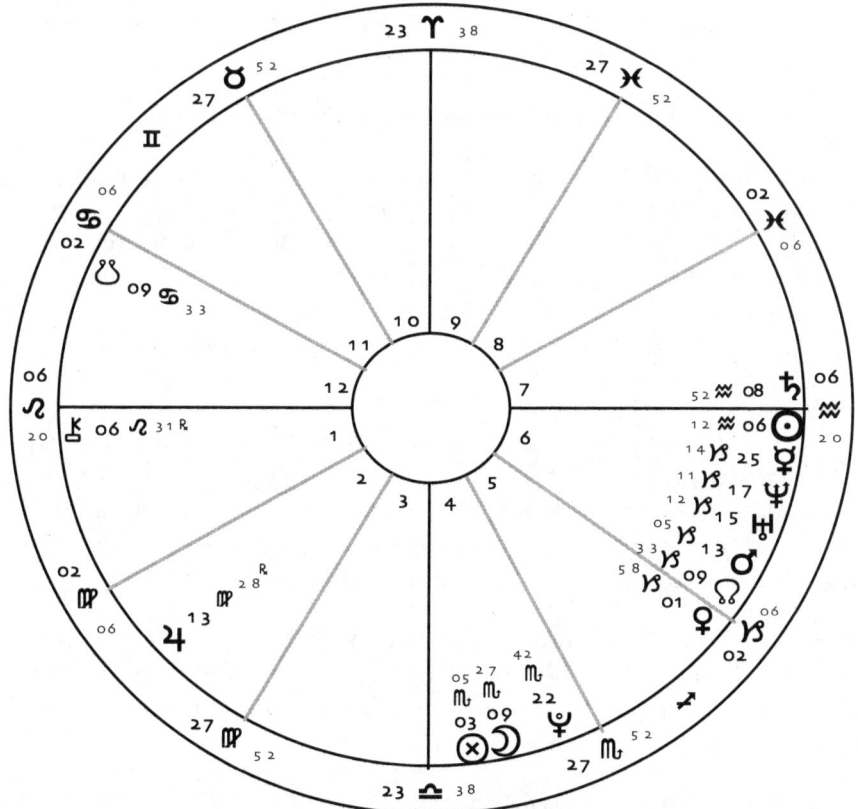

This is the 1992 progressed solar return for Woody Allen. Chiron is exactly rising and opposite the Sun, symbolizing the gaping wound that the illicit affair opened up. Saturn is angular in the 7th house of open enemies, and there is a Fixed T-Cross with an apex Moon, just a degree from Farrow's natal Descendant. The progressed solar return Venus/Neptune midpoint is in the degree of the North Node, again symbolizing the betrayal. Allen, having made his choice of the woman for his future—sure enough, the Moon/North Node midpoint is on his natal Sun.

Mercury is found in the degree of Farrow's natal Midheaven, representing the impossibility of keeping the whole affair hidden from the press. The court case did wind up costing Allen a lot of money, and it is of interest that a retrograde Jupiter in detriment is found in the progressed solar return 2nd house, with the cusp being 02° Virgo, the exact degree of Allen's natal Ascendant.

In summary, after examining these four solar return charts, the two standard, and the two progressed, astrologers find relevant aspects, angularity and midpoints in each of the horoscopes. As mentioned, any conjunction found between solar return charts and either a natal or secondary progressed chart, or synastry conjunctions to a partner's chart, will hold their influence over the entire year. The condition of Venus in either of the two solar return charts is important since it reveals the client's relationship karma for that year.

Annual Progression of the Solar Return Horizon

There is also another technique to calculate precisely when any planetary influence will act in the lives of clients. This method involves the solar return chart, and the progressing of its four angles a full 360° revolution during the birthday year. The angles are moved one degree per day and brought to each of the ten solar return planets. For our discussion of analyzing relationships as they move through time, I will concentrate now on just the solar return horizon.

I first used this technique after I read *The Solar Return Book of Prediction*, written by Raymond A. Merriman, in the late 1970s. For many years, I sent taped interpretations through the mail as birthday presents for the children of my clients. After making these calculations, I indicated which days of the year each of the four solar return angles would cross over the two Lights and the eight planets. These 40 dates were described as the most important during the next year.

Many times I received letters from the young adult writing me to say how bloody accurate the tape was, with events happening *to the exact day* of my predictions. To be perfectly honest, it was only by receiving this unsolicited feedback that I came to believe in this prediction method.

It was then only natural to isolate on one or two of the four angles progressing around a solar return chart, making its ten conjunctions to the Lights and planets.

When clients would inquire about prospects for a new relationship entering their lives during the next year, I would progress the solar return horizon to the dates it would conjoin the Luminaries, or the benefics, and inform the client of these days. I had several clients meet a new love when the progressing horizon was on Venus. I also had clients who separated from spouses with a progressed horizon on Mars.

This is the 1991 solar return chart for Mia Farrow, calculated on her birthday in the year just before her discovery of the affair between Allen and Soon-Yi. This chart was in the final month of its shelf life when she found the photographs on 13 January 1992. There is an exact square from the angular Sun on the Descendant to a 4th house Pluto, an ominous sign of what was to come, affecting her relationship, and from within her own family[60]. There is also a void-of-course Moon.

Mia Farrow
Solar Return

Feb 9 1991	22:14:58 GMT
Manhattan	New York
40N35	73W59
Tropical Porphyry	True Node

Applying this method of progressing her 1991 solar return angles a full revolution during the year between birthdays, let us now find the horizon progressed to 13

January 1992. Because there are 360° in a chart wheel, and 365 1/4 days in a calendar year, a conversion formula must be applied to the calculations. Astrologers will also have to refer to Tables of Houses, as this technique requires finding the specific degrees of the progressed Midheaven and its Ascendant.

For the conversion formula, calculate either 1.0142 days per degree (365.2422 ÷ 360), or 0.9856 degrees per day (360 ÷ 365.2422). From 9 February 1991 to 13 January 1992 is a total of 338 days. Converting this sum to degrees, we get 333.1328°. Converting the decimal to minutes of arc, we get 7.968' (60 x .1328). Rounding this figure, we now have 333° 08' of arc to add to the solar return MC of 11° Taurus 41'. Converting the original MC into a 360° value, it becomes 41° 41'. The sum is 374° 49'. Subtract 360° to give it a Zodiac value, and 14° Aries 49' is the progressed MC for that day.

Consulting a Tables of Houses, use the latitude of 40N35 for her residence in Manhattan, New York. Locating tables for the lower and higher Midheavens, find 14° Aries 07' for the former, and 15° Aries 12' for the latter. Rising degrees are given for either 40° or 41° north latitude, with the range from 29° Cancer 00' rising for the lower MC listing at 40° latitude, to 00° Leo 20' rising for the higher MC listing at 41° latitude. Through interpolation, the progressed horizon for 13 January 1992 is 00° 02' Leo-Aquarius. The progressed Descendant was exactly conjunct the solar return greater malefic, Saturn, on the day she found the pictures.

This example illustrates how this technique will produce 40 dates each year when each of the four solar return angles progress over the two Lights and eight planets. By applying the conversion formula, either converting days to degrees, or degrees to days, the astrologer can predict exactly to the day when progressed angularity will occur in the solar return chart. If the client inquires as to when there might be relational difficulties during the coming year, the astrologer can progress the solar return Descendant to the malefics, and advise his client to be careful on these days.

Some readers may be curious as to the progressed angles in Allen's 1991 solar return chart. The progressed Descendant conjoined his solar return Mars on that fateful day, 13 January 1992. Seasoned astrologers may value a reminder here about the difference in progressed motion between the meridian and the horizon. I recommend never *'guesstimating'* the progressing horizon, as it moves variably, as opposed to the progressing MC/IC axis, which moves about a degree per day. In the case of Allen's progressed solar return angles, the MC advanced from 28° Sagittarius to 09° Aquarius, some 41°, whereas the Ascendant advanced from 26° Pisces to 01° Gemini, a total of 65°. This is a 24° difference from the advanced MC.

I also realize that some readers may despair at the thought of having to use a Tables of Houses, and to have to interpolate the four different Ascendants to zero in on the precise degree and minutes of the horizon. I am pleased to inform you that, even though I still prefer the manual calculations, you can use the Solar Fire™ program to accomplish this. One need only calculate the solar return chart, then go to the 'Dynamic' menu and choose 'Animate Chart'. Click the blue arrows to advance the angles either by the day, or by the month, until they reach the degrees of the solar return Luminaries and planets. Ignore the changing degrees of the animated planets, however, as you are only looking for angularity with the original solar return Luminary and planetary degrees.

One last important detail about using this technique: the astrologer is faced with a choice of four latitudes and longitudes when calculating a solar return chart: 1) the place of birth; 2) the current location of residence; 3) the location at the birthday if away from home; or 4) the new location when a move occurs during the year between birthdays. In my experience with the progressed solar return angles, I have found that the current place of residence is more accurate than the birthplace. If a move occurs during the year, the location of residence at the last birthday is more accurate than the new location.[61]

The Solar Return Sun-Venus Eight Year Cycle

At the conclusion of this chapter, which has summarized various techniques for analyzing relationships moving through time, I want to share a final observation from my astrology practice with you. In the many consultations with clients during my career, I recognize that certain patterns repeat when it comes to karmic relationships. I research the progressed lunation cycle and Saturn transit cycle for a client as part of my standard preparation work prior to a consultation. I make notes of any key dates, such as when progressed New or Full Moons fall, or when transit Saturn forms conjunctions, squares or oppositions to the Luminaries.

I have heard many stories about relationships, which were karmic in nature, that appeared to follow an eight year pattern in the lives of clients. At first, I ascribed this to the Saturn transit cycle, which, because of its elliptical orbit, can produce differing lengths of time between conjunctions, first quarter squares, oppositions and last quarter squares. Some would occur six years apart, some eight, and so on.

However, upon closer scrutiny, I realized that every eight years the position of the planet Venus would replicate its natal position in the solar return chart, and that these were commonly birthdays that preceded a year of significant and dramatic relational change. This phenomenon is due to the synodic cycles of the Sun and Venus, which make inferior conjunctions when Venus is retrograde about every nineteen months. Five cycles are formed over an eight year period (see Chapter 11).

Therefore, every eight years the Sun and Venus return to very similar positions in the Zodiac relative to one's birth, and this pattern can be seen in the solar returns calculated for ages 8, 16, 24, 32, 40, 48, 56, 64, 72, 80, 88 and 96. These birthdays are often indicative of a coming year wherein major relationship changes occur, or new relationship enters into one's life. The condition of the solar return Venus in these charts is highly revealing regarding the upcoming eight year pattern for love.

In my own life, at the age of sixteen, I had a solar return chart that I would not wish on my worst enemy. Venus was back in the first decan of Scorpio, where she was at my birth, and part of a nasty cadent Fixed T-Cross involving an opposition to Saturn in Taurus, and a square to a Moon-Mars conjunction in Aquarius at the apex. I had met my first love the previous May, and she left me for another boy the month after my birthday. Devastated, I ran away from home and hitchhiked across country to Ohio, visiting her cousin, also a 1954 Gemini, born the day before her.[62]

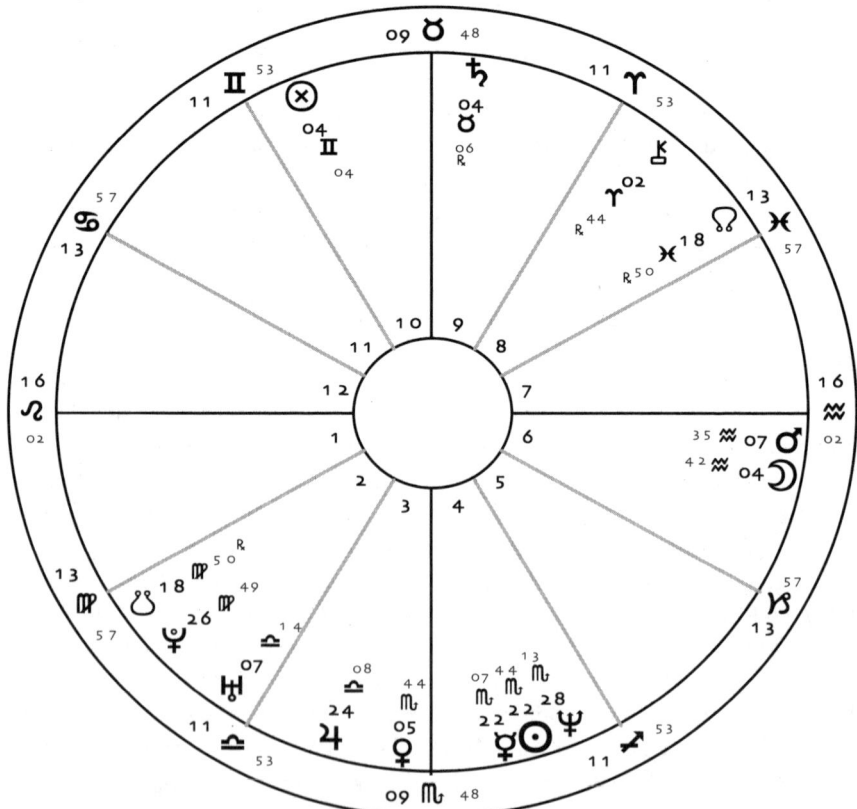

Beneath the surface reality of these stories from my youth is a recognition that this event established a pattern in relationship that lasted until my 24th birthday in

1977. My natal Venus-Saturn conjunction was under the transit opposition from Saturn during 1969, and whatever fears of rejection or feelings of unworthiness ingrained in my soul from past lives, were certainly reinforced by that adolescent experience. The good news was solar return Jupiter conjoined my natal Neptune, and trined my natal Jupiter, and I discovered a lifelong love of being on the road.

If the reader returns to the 1991 solar return for Woody Allen on page 136, one will see that this was the 56th birthday for him, a multiple of eight. Venus is found at 24° Libra 45', just two degrees from his natal Venus of 22° Libra 53'. Conjunct the Moon, and in a favorable sextile to Mercury, that Venus at age 56 was in good shape, attesting to the happiness which he shared with Soon-Yi until 1999.

The gist of this cycle is that there is important understanding to be gained about relationship by reviewing solar return charts from the client's last birthday that was a multiple of eight. For example, if your client is age 44, the solar return from the 40th birthday would show the karmic pattern of relationship between the ages of 40 to 48. A solar return for a birthday that is a multiple of eight, and which has favorable aspects to Venus, denotes a chapter of life with positive karma in love.

Conversely, a solar return for a multiple of eight birthday which has unfavorable aspects to Venus will denote an eight year chapter of life with challenging karma in love and relationships. The condition of Venus in each of the seven subsequent solar returns, lasting until the next birthday that is a multiple of eight, should be interpreted as a subplot within the context of a longer storyline. It is my belief that the solar return Venus, every eight years, holds key insights into patterns of love.

In the years immediately following these multiples of eight birthdays, at the ages of 1, 9, 17, 25, 33, 41, 49, 57, 65, 73, 81, 89 and 97, the astrologer will find Venus is sometimes retrograde in that year's solar return. My understanding of this pattern is that the soul may feel as if it has slipped backwards, and is revisiting relational karma that no longer produces spiritual growth. The urge to end relationship in the years with a solar return retrograde Venus is quite powerful, as the soul feels alienated from truth and seeks change to realign with its higher purpose. For long-married couples, the marriage will go through a year of intense soul searching during the years that either spouse has a retrograde solar return Venus.

In summary, this eight year cycle of Venus returning closely to her natal position can best be understood through an analysis of that year's solar return chart. After completing this chapter, it is hoped that my reader now has valuable techniques to use to help clients understand changing patterns in love and relationship.

Chapter Seven
Electing A Wedding Chart

Professional astrologers receive several requests each year from clients wishing to have a wedding date selected for them. Often this planning is done over a year in advance and the astrologer is contacted during the very beginning of the process. This electional work is highly personal and takes the astrologer into the inner circle of the families involved.

In the last fifteen years, I have developed a system for electing wedding charts. While there are books that teach election techniques in general (such as how to pick surgery dates or when to start a business), I will discuss wedding charts only. As a general rule, there are two approaches: 1) look for dates with signs and aspects that you want; or 2) eliminate days with the planetary dynamics that you don't want. As a Scorpio, I start with elimination.

For illustration, we will use a free calendar from *http://www.printfree.com*. You can either download an html file or print a calendar directly from the Web site.

Regarding fees for this work, the astrologer must be very careful here. Electional work usually takes longer than you think and if you quote a flat fee and wind up spending more hours than anticipated, it can turn out to be quite unprofitable. I recommend requiring a minimum retainer, with a stipulation for an additional fee should the project take longer than estimated. I have charged between $150 and $500 for wedding electionals; the higher fee was for clients who requested several dates to choose from, which is not uncommon.

Obtaining Date and Time Parameters From Your Clients

To elect a wedding chart, it is essential to ask some very basic questions about date and time parameters. Wedding ceremonies at the weekend are far and away the most popular. Some clients will even specify the exact weekend they want, having already booked a hall for the reception up to a year and a half in advance. These are the worst electional jobs, as sometimes these dates fall in retrograde personal planet periods. Yet, if the astrologer is brought on board early in the planning stages, he can attempt to persuade his clients to change the date to a more favorable weekend.

You will need to know what are acceptable times of day for the exchange of vows. The best wedding elections will have the Sun or Venus in the 7th house, and this occurs near sunset. However, some clients will insist on a morning or early afternoon ceremony and the astrologer has to remain flexible here. During your initial consultation, the critical thing to determine is *how flexible are your clients?* I recommend asking these questions:

1. If the ceremony is to be planned exclusively around the best astrological chart, are all days and all hours open for consideration? If not, only when?
2. Does the ceremony absolutely have to take place at the weekend?
3. Are Friday evening, and anytime Saturday or Sunday, acceptable options?
4. If not, which specific weekend day and time slot(s) will be acceptable?
5. What month(s) is the wedding planned this year, or next year?
6. Have reservations, deposits or bookings been made yet? Any penalty fees?
7. What is the approximate length of time from the start of the ceremony until the exchange of vows?

These are all obviously common sense questions but failing to ask them can cost you. The last thing you need is to have to redo wedding elections without compensation because of initial miscommunication with the client over date and time parameters.

I have included item (1) in the list of questions because I have literally elected wedding charts for the middle of the night when the planetary aspects were ideal. For these clients, getting married in the backyard at 3:15 AM was just fine, as long as I could guarantee an exalted Moon applying to a perfect trine with Venus.

Once these questions have been answered, your retainer paid, and any fees for extra work agreed to, you are ready to roll. Let's elect a wedding chart![63]

Elimination of Personal Planets in Fall or Detriment

As I have mentioned, I am from the school of astrological thought that believes that sign strength trumps aspect. As regards the election of a wedding chart, this means that before looking for desired aspects, eliminate Mercury, Venus and Mars from being in the signs of their detriment or fall. The following list summarizes these unwanted signs:

1. Mercury in Sagittarius or Pisces (both in detriment; Mercury has no fall).
2. Venus in Aries (detriment), Virgo (fall), or Scorpio (detriment).
3. Mars in Taurus (detriment), Cancer (fall), or Libra (detriment).

The most efficient way to organize electional work is to use a yearly calendar and an ephemeris.[64] To begin with, determine the dates that the personal planets are in the signs of their detriment or fall. Using calendar year 2005 for our wedding election, I have lined out the unwanted days.

Mercury is in Pisces from February 16th until March 4th; and in Sagittarius from October 30th until November 26th, and from December 12th until the end of the year. Venus is in Aries from March 22nd until April 15th; in Virgo from July 22nd until August 16th; and in Scorpio from September 11th until October 7th. Mars is in Taurus from July 27th until the end of the year. These dates are all lined out.

2005																				
January								February								March					
S	M	T	W	T	F	S	S	M	T	W	T	F	S	S	M	T	W	T	F	S
						1			1	2	3	4	5			~~1~~	~~2~~	~~3~~	~~4~~	5
2	3	4	5	6	7	8	6	7	8	9	10	11	12	6	7	8	9	10	11	12
9	10	11	12	13	14	15	13	14	15	~~16~~	~~17~~	~~18~~	~~19~~	13	14	15	16	17	18	~~19~~
16	17	18	19	20	21	22	~~20~~	~~21~~	~~22~~	~~23~~	~~24~~	~~25~~	~~26~~	~~20~~	~~21~~	~~22~~	~~23~~	~~24~~	~~25~~	~~26~~
23	24	25	26	27	28	29	~~27~~	~~28~~						~~27~~	~~28~~	~~29~~	~~30~~	~~31~~		
30	31																			
April								May								June					
S	M	T	W	T	F	S	S	M	T	W	T	F	S	S	M	T	W	T	F	S
					~~1~~	~~2~~	1	2	3	4	5	6	7				1	2	3	4
~~3~~	~~4~~	~~5~~	~~6~~	~~7~~	~~8~~	~~9~~	8	9	10	11	12	13	14	5	6	7	8	9	10	11
~~10~~	~~11~~	~~12~~	~~13~~	~~14~~	~~15~~	16	15	16	17	18	19	20	21	12	13	14	15	16	17	18
17	18	19	20	21	22	23	22	23	24	25	26	27	28	19	20	21	22	23	24	25
24	25	26	27	28	29	30	29	30	31					26	27	28	29	30		
July								August								September					
S	M	T	W	T	F	S	S	M	T	W	T	F	S	S	M	T	W	T	F	S
					1	2	~~1~~	~~2~~	~~3~~	~~4~~	~~5~~	~~6~~						~~1~~	~~2~~	~~3~~
3	4	5	6	7	8	9	~~7~~	~~8~~	~~9~~	~~10~~	~~11~~	~~12~~	~~13~~	~~4~~	~~5~~	~~6~~	~~7~~	~~8~~	~~9~~	~~10~~
10	11	12	13	14	15	16	~~14~~	~~15~~	~~16~~	~~17~~	~~18~~	~~19~~	~~20~~	~~11~~	~~12~~	~~13~~	~~14~~	~~15~~	~~16~~	~~17~~
17	18	19	20	21	~~22~~	~~23~~	~~21~~	~~22~~	~~23~~	~~24~~	~~25~~	~~26~~	~~27~~	~~18~~	~~19~~	~~20~~	~~21~~	~~22~~	~~23~~	~~24~~
~~24~~	~~25~~	~~26~~	~~27~~	~~28~~	~~29~~	~~30~~	~~28~~	~~29~~	~~30~~	~~31~~				~~25~~	~~26~~	~~27~~	~~28~~	~~29~~	~~30~~	
~~31~~																				
October								November								December					
S	M	T	W	T	F	S	S	M	T	W	T	F	S	S	M	T	W	T	F	S
						~~1~~			~~1~~	~~2~~	~~3~~	~~4~~	~~5~~					~~1~~	~~2~~	~~3~~
~~2~~	~~3~~	~~4~~	~~5~~	~~6~~	~~7~~	~~8~~	~~6~~	~~7~~	~~8~~	~~9~~	~~10~~	~~11~~	~~12~~	~~4~~	~~5~~	~~6~~	~~7~~	~~8~~	~~9~~	~~10~~
~~9~~	~~10~~	~~11~~	~~12~~	~~13~~	~~14~~	~~15~~	~~13~~	~~14~~	~~15~~	~~16~~	~~17~~	~~18~~	~~19~~	~~11~~	~~12~~	~~13~~	~~14~~	~~15~~	~~16~~	~~17~~
~~16~~	~~17~~	~~18~~	~~19~~	~~20~~	~~21~~	~~22~~	~~20~~	~~21~~	~~22~~	~~23~~	~~24~~	~~25~~	~~26~~	~~18~~	~~19~~	~~20~~	~~21~~	~~22~~	~~23~~	~~24~~
~~23~~	~~24~~	~~25~~	~~26~~	~~27~~	~~28~~	~~29~~	~~27~~	~~28~~	~~29~~	~~30~~				~~25~~	~~26~~	~~27~~	~~28~~	~~29~~	~~30~~	~~31~~
~~30~~	~~31~~																			

Elimination of Retrograde Personal Planets

The next process of elimination involves getting rid of the days on which Mercury, Venus or Mars are retrograde. Debilitated planets are those that are retrograde, in detriment or fall, or in bad aspect to a malefic. By eliminating sign weakness, we strengthen the wedding chart; by removing retrograde personal planets, the chart is made even stronger. The following dates will be removed from consideration:

1. Mercury retrograde from March 19th until April 12th; from July 22nd until August 15th; and from November 13th until December 3rd.
2. Venus retrograde from December 24th until the end of the year.
3. Mars retrograde from October 1st until December 9th.

As you can see, some of these unwanted dates will overlap each other. In the case of Mars in detriment in Taurus, it wipes out most of the second half of the year from consideration. What's left?

Finding Sign-Strength for the Moon and Venus

After eliminating all of the days when the personal planets are in detriment, fall, or retrograde, we turn our attention to the two heavenly bodies that symbolize domestic life and harmonious, loving companionship: the Moon and Venus. From the remaining days in 2005, we will search for the dates when the Moon is either dignified in Cancer, or exalted in Taurus, and for the dates when Venus is dignified in either Taurus or Libra, or exalted in Pisces. For the Moon, we note any of these dates falling at the weekend. We will also consider Mutual Reception of Venus in Cancer to Moon in Taurus.[65]

1. Moon in Taurus: January 17-19; February 13-15 (W); March 12-15 (W); May 6-9 (W); June 2-5 (W); June 30-July 2 (W).
2. Moon in Cancer: January 22-24 (W); March 17-18 (W); April 15-16 (W); May 11-13 (W); June 7-10; July 5-7.
3. Venus in Taurus: April 15-May 9.
4. Venus in Pisces: March 4-19.
5. Venus in Cancer in Mutual Reception with Moon in Taurus: June 3-5.

Next, from this list of dates showing when the Moon or Venus have sign strength, or are in Mutual Reception, we look for simultaneousness of dignity or exaltation.

1. March 12-15 (W) (Moon in Taurus and Venus in Pisces).
2. March 17-18 (W) (Moon in Cancer and Venus in Pisces).
3. April 15-16 (W) (Moon in Cancer and Venus in Taurus).
4. May 6-9 (W) (Moon in Taurus and Venus in Taurus).
5. June 3-5 (W) (Moon in Taurus and Venus in Cancer—Mutual Reception).

Some years, like wine, are better than others for electing wedding charts. Here we are fortunate, as all five windows of time contain at least one weekend day. From these five contending blocks of time, we continue, examining planetary aspects and the Sun-Moon phase to zero in on the very best day for a wedding chart.

Planetary Aspects and the Luminaries' Relationship

After eliminating any days when personal planets are in detriment, fall, or retrograde, we've found the dates during 2005 when the Moon and Venus are both strong by sign. Next, we will scrutinize these five windows of time to assess whether the Moon is waxing or waning and what aspects are in the sky.

Window of Time	Lunar Phase	Planetary Aspects
1. March 12-15	New to Crescent	Sun square Pluto
2. March 17-18	1st Quarter	Venus square Pluto
3. April 15-16	Crescent to 1st Quarter	Mars conjunct Neptune
4. May 6-9	Balsamic to New	Sun square Neptune
5. June 3-5	Balsamic	Sun square Uranus

It is preferable to have the Moon waxing in light for a wedding chart, placing her between the New Moon and the Full Moon. Because electional astrology is not an exact science, you will rarely ever find both sign strength for the feminine bodies, and no unfavorable planetary aspects in the heavens. To a certain extent, the bad aspects can be muted by choosing an Ascendant not ruled by one of the planets in square or opposition. However, no couple deserves an applying Sun-Pluto square!

Taking the dates which contain a waxing Moon, we will look for a conjunction, sextile or trine between the Luminaries. The Sun symbolizes a husband, the Moon a wife, and placing the Lights in good aspect is highly desirable. The 5th or 10th harmonic aspects between the Luminaries are also considered favorable. These include the 36° decile, 72° quintile, 108° tridecile, and 144° biquintile. Narrowing our dates:

1. March 14 (Monday): Sun in Pisces sextile Moon in Taurus.
2. May 8 (Sunday): Sun conjunct Moon in Taurus.

After only five steps into this process, we are down to just two days out of an entire year. And, only one of these days is at the weekend.

Using Decanates and Dwadashâmshas in Electional Work

Each sign of the Zodiac is broken down into three subsections of 10 degrees each, known as decanates, or decans. The first third of any sign, from 00° to 10°, is ruled by that sign itself. The middle third, from 10° to 20°, is ruled by the succeeding sign of that element. The final third of a sign, from 20° to 30°, is ruled by the last sign of that same element. Within the decanates, there is also a further partitioning of any sign into dwadashâmshas, or dwads. These are 2.5° divisions of a sign, and there are four dwads in each decanate, one of each element, and twelve dwads in a sign. Therefore, akin to fractal theory, each sign contains the entire Zodiac within it.

Table of Decanates and Dwadashâmshas

Sign	♈	♉	♊	♋	♌	♍	♎	♏	♐	♑	♒	♓
0° to 10°	♈	♉	♊	♋	♌	♍	♎	♏	♐	♑	♒	♓
0° to 2.5°	♈	♉	♊	♋	♌	♍	♎	♏	♐	♑	♒	♓
2.5° to 5°	♉	♊	♋	♌	♍	♎	♏	♐	♑	♒	♓	♈
5° to 7.5°	♊	♋	♌	♍	♎	♏	♐	♑	♒	♓	♈	♉
7.5° to 10°	♋	♌	♍	♎	♏	♐	♑	♒	♓	♈	♉	♊
10° to 20°	♌	♍	♎	♏	♐	♑	♒	♓	♈	♉	♊	♋
10° to 12.5°	♌	♍	♎	♏	♐	♑	♒	♓	♈	♉	♊	♋
12.5° to 15°	♍	♎	♏	♐	♑	♒	♓	♈	♉	♊	♋	♌
15° to 17.5°	♎	♏	♐	♑	♒	♓	♈	♉	♊	♋	♌	♍
17.5° to 20°	♏	♐	♑	♒	♓	♈	♉	♊	♋	♌	♍	♎
20° to 30°	♐	♑	♒	♓	♈	♉	♊	♋	♌	♍	♎	♏
20° to 22.5°	♐	♑	♒	♓	♈	♉	♊	♋	♌	♍	♎	♏
22.5° to 25°	♑	♒	♓	♈	♉	♊	♋	♌	♍	♎	♏	♐
25° to 27.5°	♒	♓	♈	♉	♊	♋	♌	♍	♎	♏	♐	♑
27.5° to 30°	♓	♈	♉	♊	♋	♌	♍	♎	♏	♐	♑	♒

Decanates and dwads can be used in electional astrology to further strengthen a planet or Luminary, by placing it within a specific degree range of any given sign. A Moon exalted in Taurus, between 05° 01' and 07° 30', is thus furthered fortified by being within the Cancer dwadashâmsha, the sign of her dignity. Conversely, an exalted Moon in Taurus from 20° 01' and 22° 30' is in the Capricorn dwad, and in the subsection of her detriment, and therefore this Moon would be made weaker.

Many times, the astrologer has to choose between two or three electional charts. If one chart has Mars in Virgo, for example, from 10° and 20°, this is the Capricorn decanate, and exalts Mars by decan. Elect the chart when that Mars is between 17° 31' and 20° 00', the Aries dwad, and Mars is even stronger.

On the two dates to which we have narrowed our 2005 wedding chart search, let us examine the decanates and dwads of the Moon as she nears her aspect with the Sun on both days. On March 14th, the exact sextile between the Luminaries occurs at 7:32:17 PM Pacific Time, or 03:32:17 GMT on the 15th, in 24° Taurus 39'. This is the Capricorn decanate of Taurus, and, as such, the astrologer would not want the Moon between 20° 01' and 22° 30', as this would also be the Capricorn dwad. Therefore, we have about two degrees before the perfecting sextile that are safe.

Sun Sextile Waxing Moon

Mar 14 2005 7:32:17 PM PST
San Francisco California
37N35 122W25
Mar 15 2005 03:32:17 GMT
Tropical Porphyry True Node

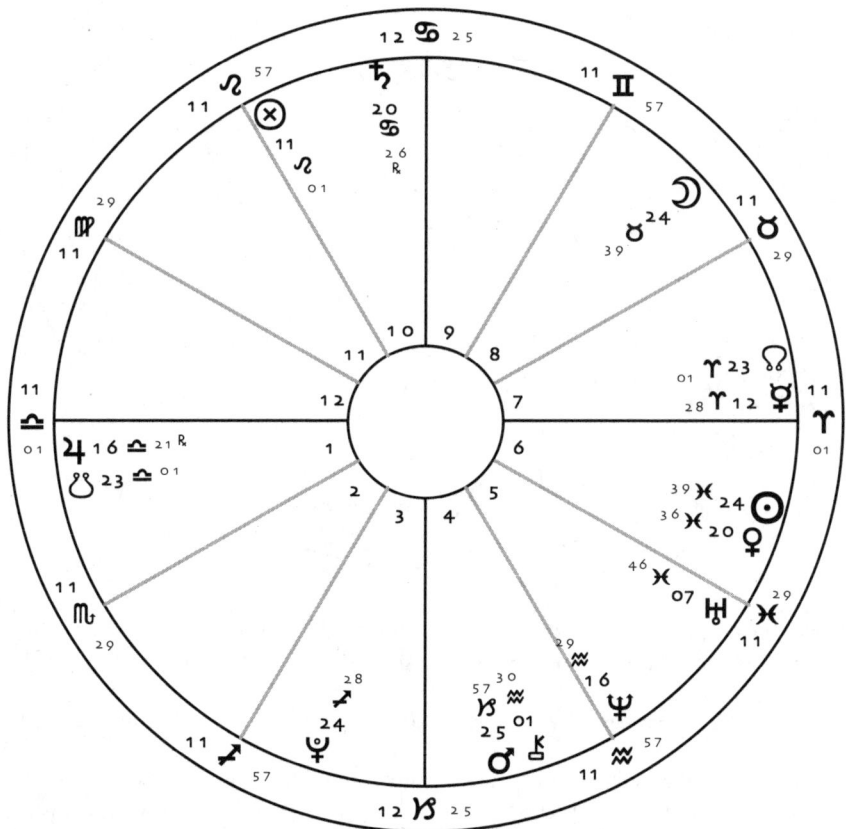

On May 8th, the New Moon in Taurus occurs at 01:45:21 AM Pacific Daylight Time, or 08:45:21 GMT, in 17° Taurus 51'. This is the Virgo decanate of Taurus, and the Sagittarius dwadashâmsha. To place the New Moon in the waxing phase, we need a separating conjunction; but to avoid the Capricorn dwad of Taurus, we would limit our orb to the first 2°, or wait until the Moon separates by over 5°.

New Moon in Taurus

May 8 2005   1:45:21 AM PDT
San Francisco   California
37N35   122W25
May 8 2005   08:45:21 GMT
Tropical   Porphyry   True Node

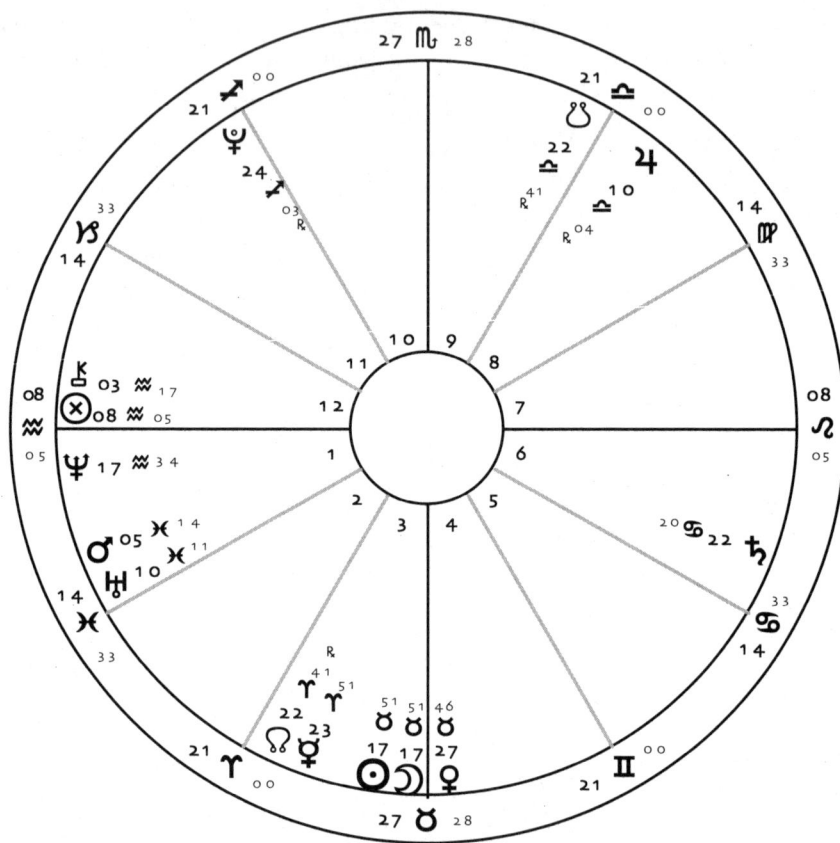

These charts are only the raw electional horoscopes for our two selected days. We will now proceed to choose the time of day, and the exact degrees of the angles.

The Lunar Degree and Her Applying Aspect to a Benefic

Now that we have narrowed our wedding chart search down to these two days, our next step is determine the lunar degree, and attempt to have the Moon apply to Venus or Jupiter by good aspect. In the March 14th chart, the Taurus Moon has a sextile relationship by sign with Venus in Pisces. But, if we go earlier into that day to get the Moon around 19°, just before the Capricorn dwad, but still applying to Venus by sextile, we solve one problem, but create another. We now have the Sun applying to a square with Pluto. Not good for marriage. The Sun perfects the square to Pluto at 03:12:50 PM Pacific Time, with the Moon at 22° Taurus 21'.

By 3:30 PM, the Moon has gotten to 22° Taurus 31', and left the Capricorn dwad. We do not have the opportunity for her to apply to a benefic, as Jupiter in Libra is in a quincunx relationship by sign with the Moon. However, the dispositor of the Moon, Venus in Pisces, is in Mutual Reception with Jupiter in Libra, and this will strengthen the Moon. Our Taurus Moon nows applies to the sextile with the Sun. At this stage, we work with the March 14th chart for any time after 03:30 PM.[66]

In the May 8th chart, the New Moon has already separated from the square with Neptune, and now applies to a sextile with Saturn in Cancer. This is an unwanted applying aspect, as Saturn is in detriment in Cancer. The Moon next applies to a conjunction with a dignified Venus. The sextile to Saturn perfects at 10:09:31 AM Pacific Daylight Time, and the conjunction with Venus occurs at 10:15:08 PM, so we now have a full twelve hours to work with on May 8th. Our dignified Venus is the sole dispositor for the entire chart, which is very good for marriage.[67]

Selecting an Ascendant and Fortifying the Ruler on an Angle

So now the astrologer is sitting with two charts to fine tune. This will involve the search for the right rising sign and degree, and if possible, to fortify the chart ruler on an angle. For our March 14th chart, we are looking at times after 03:30 PM; for our May 8th chart, we begin our search for the rising sign after 10:10 AM.

On March 14th, by the time Libra is rising in San Francisco, the Sun and Venus have already set, and are in the undesired 6th house. It is much more preferable to have the Sun or Venus in the 7th house for a wedding chart, so for this day, Virgo rising it will be. The ruler, Mercury, becomes angular in the 7th house at around 5:17 PM, and the Sun sets at 6:12 PM, so we have it narrowed down to 55 minutes.

On May 8th, the Sun enters the Porphyry 7th house in San Francisco at 5:29 PM, and Libra is rising, an ideal Ascendant for a marriage chart. Venus enters the 7th house at 6:16 PM with the 28th degree of Libra rising; the Ascendant moves into Scorpio at 6:29 PM, so we have this chart narrowed down now to 13 minutes.

At this point, the electional astrologer comes up for air amidst all of the detail, and looks to see if any planet is near a house cusp in which it would have accidental dignity. If, for example, Saturn is straddling the MC on the cadent 9th house side, a few minutes difference in time puts Saturn into the 10th, with accidental dignity. If Jupiter is on the 11th house side of the 12th cusp, a slightly earlier time fixes this.

Fine-Tuning the Ascendant Using Sabian Symbols

The electional astrologer is now honing in on the exact degree of the rising sign, and he smells blood like a shark, his finished chart nearly done. In the March 14th chart, we begin our search at 5:17 PM, with the 14th degree of Virgo rising, and at

6:12 PM we have the 25th degree of Virgo rising. This range of eleven degrees span the Aquarius, Pisces, Aries, Taurus and Gemini dwads of Virgo rising. With the benefics in Mutual Reception, we choose from either the Jupiter-ruled Pisces dwad or the Venus-ruled Taurus dwad. This selection further narrows down the rising degrees from 15° 01' to 17°30' of Virgo rising, or from 20° 01' to 22° 30' of Virgo.

I recommend using the Sabian Symbols at this stage of the fine tuning process. We pick a rising degree based on the positivity of its degree symbol. Our choices are:[68]

> Virgo 16: *The delighted children are crowded about a cage in the zoo; an orangoutang is sitting in a spot of afternoon sun.*
>
> Virgo 17: *A vast display of cosmic force is seen in the eruption of a volcano; dust clouds, flowing lava, earth rumblings.*
>
> Virgo 18: *Two giggling young girls are sitting facing each other, knees tightly touching, working an ouija board on their laps.*
>
> Virgo 21: *A large cheerful but bare room holds two teams of fresh young girls engaged in a laughing contest of basketball.*
>
> Virgo 22: *Upon rich velvet in a case, at an exhibition, is an exquisitely wrought miniature; a jewel-set royal coat-of arms.*
>
> Virgo 23: *A man, clad in gay colors of the circus, rushes into the barred arena, where unwilling animals await his bidding.*

The quasi-exact science of electional astrology ends here. Even a highly technical astrologer has an intuitional faculty, and in the selection of the rising degree, this part of the consciousness is used. Reading through these six symbols, one gets a feel for each rising degree. However, I must offer a disclaimer, as I have the 22nd degree of Virgo rising, and I must say that I choose either that degree, or Virgo 18.

Erecting our March 14th wedding chart with the 18th degree of Virgo rising gives us a time of 5:36 PM in San Francisco. Jupiter is exactly on the Porphyry 2nd cusp, and in exact trine to Neptune on the 6th cusp. If either spouse is involved in the music world for a living, or perhaps is a photographer, this aspect would be ideal. Their perfect trine involves the rulers of the IC and Descendant: home and partner.

The Sun-Venus conjunction is setting in the 7th house, which is what we wanted, and the 9th house Moon, symbolizing mutual spiritual understanding, applies to a sextile with the Sun. The exalted Moon at 23° Taurus 37' is safely in the Aquarius dwad. The Sun separates from the square to Pluto, and this aspect would actually favor a second marriage, where the couple is rebuilding their new lives together. A renovation project on an older home would be favored with that 4th house Pluto.

Saturn is accidently dignified in the 11th house, conferring lasting friends on the marriage. The ruler, Mercury, is angular in the 7th, and exalted Venus is in a close trine with Saturn, good for longevity, exact within 04' of arc. The Part of Fortune is exactly conjunct the 3rd cusp, helping the brothers and sisters-in-law to be a joyful part of the extended family circle. An exalted Mars, sextile the Sun, is in the 5th house of physical lovemaking (Scorpio dwad), which is great for their sex life.

March 14 Wedding Chart

Mar 14 2005　　　5:36:00 PM PST
San Francisco　　California
37N35　　　　　　122W25
Mar 15 2005　　　01:36:00 GMT
Tropical　Porphyry　True Node

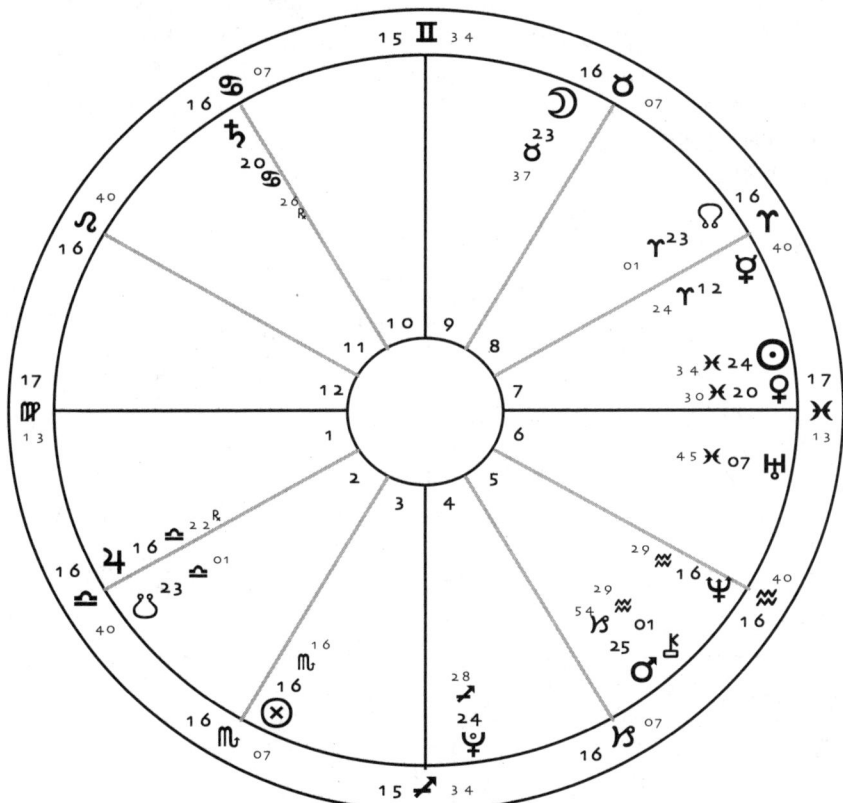

Erecting this wedding chart with the 22nd degree of Virgo rising gives us a time of 5:56 PM in San Francisco. Venus has set, is in the 6th house, and is no longer accidentally dignified in the 7th. For this reason alone, I choose the 5:36 PM chart.

Now we turn our attention to fine tuning the Ascendant for the May 8th wedding chart. We begin our work at 6:16 PM, with the 28th degree of Libra rising, and we also consider the final two degrees of a Libra Ascendant. However, Scorpio rising is not acceptable, as the ruler, Mars, applies to a conjunction with Uranus, ruling self-centeredness, separation and disruption. The rising sign changes at 6:29 PM.

Libra 28: *A man stands alone in surrounding gloom; were his eyes open to spirit things he would see helping angels arriving.*

Libra 29: *It is a seer's dream: vast masses of humanity push forward in frantic effort to cross the black chasm to knowledge.*

Libra 30: *The phrenologist is reading "bumps" for his clients; he explains three mounds of knowledge on a philosopher's head.*

The Virgo dwad of Libra rising is preferred for this chart as its ruler, Mercury, is conjunct the North Node, symbolizing the couple's future together. That eliminates the first 30' of the 28th degree of Libra rising, which is still in the Leo dwad. The Sabian Symbol for that degree is also quite depressing, even with angels arriving. Of the two remaining rising degrees, I choose Libra 29 for its evolutionary theme.

May 8 Wedding Chart

May 8 2005	6:21:00 PM PDT
San Francisco	California
37N35	122W25
May 9 2005	01:21:00 GMT
Tropical Porphyry	True Node

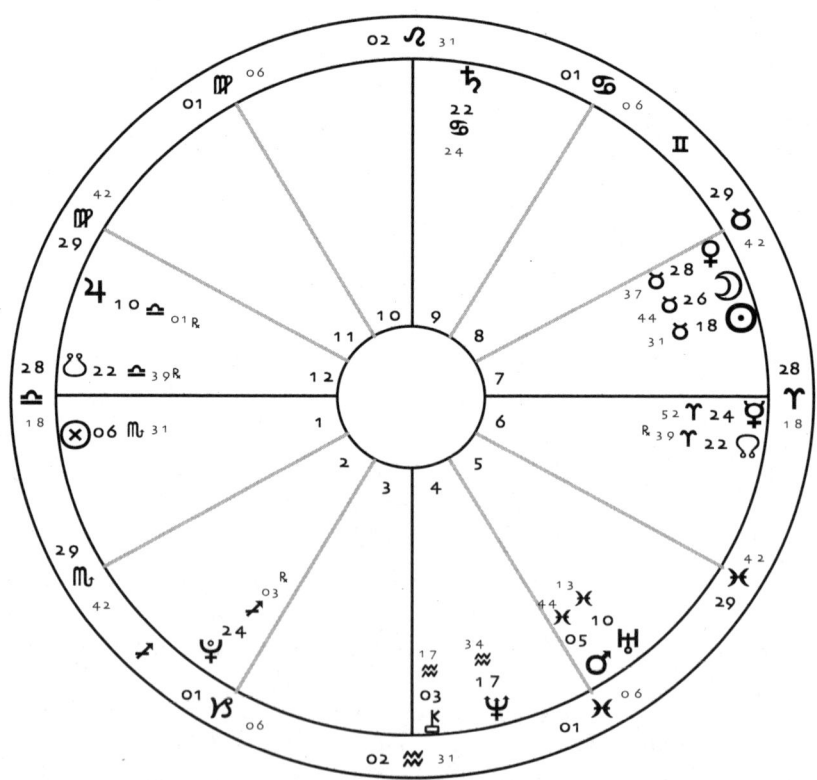

As the Ascendant changes one degree approximately every four minutes, to get our preferred Sabian Symbol we have the time range of 6:20 PM to 6:24 PM for getting this degree to rise in San Francisco. However, at 6:22:20 PM, Taurus intercepts in the 7th house, which would hide the Lights and Venus within its cloaking effects. For this reason, I use 6:21 PM, giving Libra 29 rising, before the 1-7 interceptions.

The separating and waxing New Moon is in the 7th, which is what we want, and our dignified Venus, ruler of the wedding chart, is also angular in the 7th, and is a sole and final dispositor for the entire horoscope, quite powerful for marriage. A 1st house Part of Fortune trines Mars, ruler of the Descendant. Accidental dignity is found with Jupiter in the 12th house. The astrologer also finds a Yod forming to an intercepted Pluto in the 2nd house, with the Moon and Saturn at its base. This aspect configuration would need to be explained to a couple as a transformational influence, with the marriage drawing out hidden, deeper values which both share.

Linking the Wedding Part of Fortune with the Nativities

Frequently, when electing wedding charts for clients, I have been faced with the choice of two or three rising degrees during the final steps of this whole process. I have also had the situation arise where each of the contending Sabian Symbols is of a positive nature, with no clear favorite. In these cases, I then turn to the Part of Fortune as the final arbiter in the choosing of the exact Ascendant for the election.

The Part of Fortune moves a degree about every three to five minutes, and it can be used to determine both the rising degree, and exact minutes of arc within the degree on the wedding chart Ascendant. With the nativities of the bride and groom in front of me, side by side with my wedding electional, I look to see if the Part of Fortune in either nativity is near a conjunction or trine with the wedding chart Ascendant or if the Part of Fortune in the wedding chart is close to conjunction or trine with the Ascendant in either nativity. I have been surprised how often this happens.

One metaphysical explanation for this is that the astrologer, when working on a wedding election, is entering into the hopes and dreams of his clients for a happy and prosperous marriage. If an astrologer has his heart open when doing the work he is transported into the astral plane, and sees connections in the charts which he would not ordinarily perceive. I believe, and I realize that this will sound rather bizarre to my readers, that if this Part of Fortune link is discovered at the very end of all of the detailed efforts to erect the right chart, it is a confirmation from above.

The Diurnal Moon and Her Connection to the Nativities

At the conclusion of this chapter, I would like to share one final technique I have used to choose between competing dates for wedding elections. I have often found that the transit diurnal Moon, when calculated for the date of a life event, is precisely conjunct one of the angles in the nativity. When rectifying a horoscope for a client who has a suspect time of birth, on the dates given to me for major life events, I always calculate the progressions and transits diurnally, using the presumed, rectified time for these event dates. Once I believe that I have precise angles, I use the diurnal Moon for the dates of these life events to test these angles.

In a similar way, if the astrologer has two or three wedding electionals to give to his clients as marriage date options, they will often ask him which is his favorite. What I do then is take the two or three different wedding dates, and on these days I calculate diurnal charts for the bride and groom, using their time of birth on each of the wedding date charts. I have frequently found that the Moon in one of these diurnal wedding charts is in the exact degree of their Ascendants or Descendants. I then choose the elected chart which has a linked diurnal Moon as the one to use.

The last step in this entire process is to present the elected wedding chart to your clients. If just the rising degree is critical, the astrologer explains that the minister has a 3-4 minute margin of error for timing the sequence of the wedding ceremony so as to get the exchange of vows at the elected time. If the critical time range is less that four minutes, such as when an interception occurs only two minutes into the rising degree, or when the Part of Fortune changes degrees, then astrologers should advise the clients to ask the minister to be very precise with the timing of the vows.

In summary, the astrologer has now proceeded through a very detailed process of elimination of any unwanted days during a given year, with careful choices of dates then made from the remaining days that year. The electional astrologer will come to realize that there are no perfect wedding charts, and that we do the very best we can within the date and time parameters given to us by our clients. After getting the Moon and Venus in dignity or exaltation at the weekend, one usually finds a planetary aspect in the heavens that he wishes wasn't there. Astrologers can mitigate bad aspects by choosing angles that are not ruled by either planet.

If any reader should choose to get married on either March 14th or May 8th of 2005, the first full year after this book's publication, the author will be delighted to hear of your wedding, and wishes you much happiness in your life together. If the wedding is to take place in a different time zone, make sure to find a good rising degree for that location, and adjust your local time to obtain these angles.

Chapter Eight
Partners Who Activate Our Shadow

> The *shadow* is a moral problem that challenges the whole ego-personality, for no one can become conscious of the *shadow* without considerable moral effort. To become conscious of it involves recognizing the dark aspects of the personality as present and real. This act is the essential condition for any kind of self-knowledge.
> *Aion;* Collected Works of Carl Gustav Jung; Volume 9; Part ii; 1951

In 1994, I developed a new lecture for the Vision '94 conference in San Diego entitled *Partners Who Activate Our Shadow*. The lecture synopsis was:

> *Why do we attract relationship into our lives with individuals whose planets form stressful synastry aspects to the most psychologically sensitive points in our birth chart? Can these relationships be seen as agents of transformation in bringing our woundedness into the light? Or do they only perpetuate a cycle of non-growth by triggering shadow content over and over again? We will examine the attraction-friction dynamic found in synastric squares and oppositions, as well as the difficult reality of living with a partner whose planets synastrically activate our T-squares, Yods, 12th house, midpoints of squares, unaspected planets, or produce a challenging composite chart.*

The lecture was very well received. Several in the audience responded to the question about the value of personal relationships that seem to trigger *shadow* content over and over again. The gist of my talk was to evaluate when it would be appropriate to exit such relationships, or when to remain and continue to do the personal growth work necessitated by this *shadow* activation.

The tape of the lecture became quite popular and I subsequently expanded the talk into a full-day workshop. I have taught this material to local astrology groups around the country and have lectured on it at conferences in the USA and abroad. Many times over the last ten years I have been asked if I had written more about these concepts.

As in all areas of specialization in the healing arts, there is often personal history involved in the subject matter. This is certainly the case for the author, as material in the *Partners* lecture and workshop is derived from my own relational history. I often feel that with a Moon in Pisces and a Venus-Saturn conjunction in Scorpio, I have had the karma in this lifetime to experience relationships that require the development of compassion and an understanding of trauma.

The women I have been involved with could easily fill a manual of astrological indicators of childhood wounding. Many times in my life I have felt like God was sending me all of the stray cats and broken souls; my initial feelings being, *somebody has to love them.* I have known women with retrograde Venus or Mars, Venus or Mars in the 12th house, Venus or Mars in hard aspects to Saturn or Pluto, Venus or Mars at the apex of a T-Cross or Yod, and with Venus or Mars in detriment or fall, or unaspected. Several of these souls had been sexually abused as children, raped during adolescence, or subjected to domestic violence.

If one attracts a relationship with another soul who is wounded or traumatized by past pain and suffering, it can be presumed that an emotional resonance exists between the two souls, with each reflecting the *shadow* side of the other. The old adage *"it takes one to know one"* certainly applies here, and it is a testimony to the power of love how two broken and hurt souls can help each other heal by giving of their love. However, the road to a healed heart is a long one.

During my three Saturn returns in 1982-83, it dawned on me that I was just as broken as the women I had known and loved. I married in 1983 and shortly thereafter, Pluto began the transit over my natal Saturn and Venus. During the five Pluto conjunctions to Venus in 1985-86, I was escorted by Spirit into the underworld to face my damaged self and to begin to heal. My wife at the time had Scorpio rising with the ruler, Mars, conjunct Saturn in Scorpio in the 12th house. She was working on her master's degree in psychology, and I was her number one guinea pig. Pluto was, of course, in Scorpio then, and psychotherapy was in vogue.

Over the years I have worked with many clients who had issues similar to mine. I observed several astrological correspondences that helped me see the connections between one's family of origin experiences and one's adult relationships. In this chapter, I will define the *shadow* in astrological terms, provide some examples of how one's *shadow* can be perceived in the natal chart, and how the *shadow* can be triggered in synastry and composite charts. I will discuss Saturn transits to the secondary progressed Moon and how the astrology of anger and transformational relationships is understood. I will conclude with a technique using the midpoint vector of natal or synastric squares.

The Shadow Defined in Astrological Terms

The Sun in astrology symbolizes the Light and Love of God, our Almighty Father. The planets are all held in their orbits by the gravitational pull of the Sun, and they receive their light and warmth from this central star of our solar system. The Earth and its Moon are held in a joint orbit around the Sun by a combined center of gravity located some one thousand miles beneath the surface of the Earth.

In other words, the Moon does not orbit the Earth *but rather shares a center of gravity with the Earth*, with which it makes a joint orbital path around the Sun. The following diagrams illustrate these solar system dynamics.

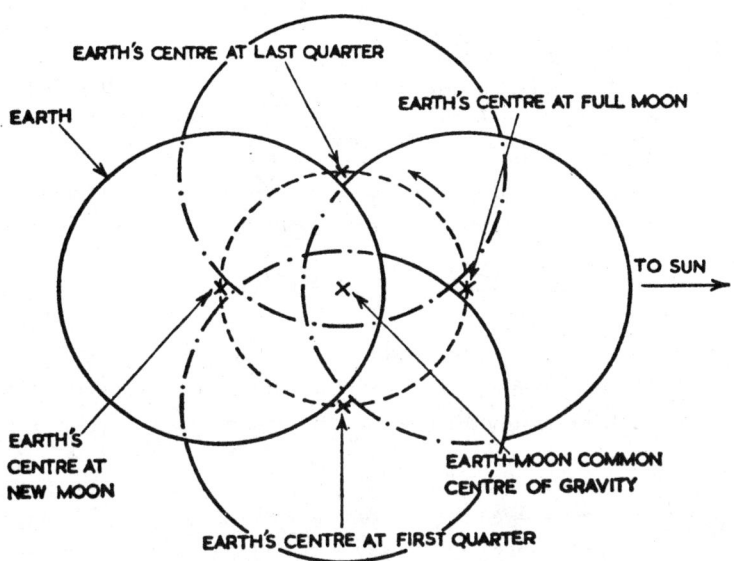

Fig. 8. Earth–Moon Common Centre of Gravity

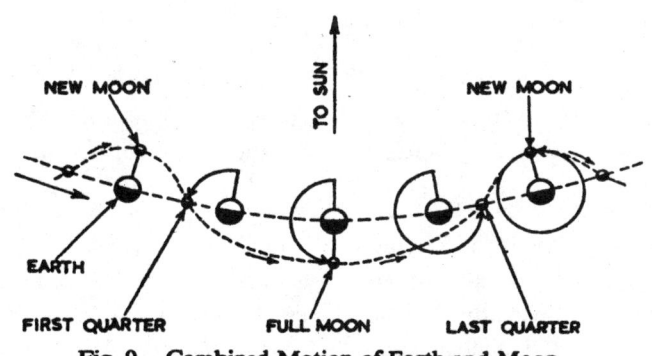

Fig. 9. Combined Motion of Earth and Moon

The Astrologer's Astronomical Handbook by Jeff Mayo (L.N. Fowler & Co., Ltd.; London; 1965)

These illustrations from Jeff Mayo show how the center of the Earth is pulled in four different directions each month and that a Cross is formed by these changes in position of the Earth's center at each of the Lunar Quarters. Therefore, while still held firmly in its orbit by the Sun, Earth is slightly oscillated by the mass of the Moon, which is tugging at its central core.

For astrological symbolism this is quite profound, as it defines three dimensions of Self and their interrelationship. Incarnating, the soul enters a body (Earth), and begins to revolve again and again around the Light and Love of God (Sun), yet the residual effect of the soul's past (Moon) causes it to waver and vacillate. True to form, our past travels with us, just as the Moon orbits along with the Earth, until the soul (Moon) aligns itself with the personality (Earth) through the heart (Sun).

The *shadow* as defined by Carl Jung, is the same concept, only secularized, as *Evil* is to all of the world religions. Jung's moral advice to confront the *shadow* while on the road to self-knowledge is identical to a priest admonishing his parishioner to resist evil and do good. What role does human relationship play in all of this? Is the power of the Sun, which holds Earth and Moon together in their orbits, the force of Good in our Solar System? Is *shadow* only the separation from this Light?

The childhood experiences produce memory, which is stored in the subconscious, a lunar domain within astrology. The spirit of a child, his happiness and creativity, comes from the love and praise bestowed by both parents, a solar domain in astrology. If traumatic memory during childhood outweighs love and praise, the result is an unbalanced individual whose lunar instincts can overpower the solar nature through fear and hurt.

In astrology we refer to a weak central core as a solar deficiency. When one either cannot reveal his own inner Light due to a wounded core, or one chooses not to because of a distorted spiritual philosophy which dictates self-abnegation, the result is the same—one perceives himself as if in darkness, and through projection feels to be in the *shadow* of other people's Light.

Now operating from within this *shadow*, the individual may reject all that is good and loving coming toward him and subconsciously choose relationships that reflect a low self-esteem, fears of rejection, and underlying sense of unworthiness.

The *shadow*, which can be defined in relationship analysis as *an aversion to love* is quite similar to evil, which in religious thinking is seen as *rejection of goodness*. Looking at human partnership from this point of view, the great tragedy in life is a heart that remains closed due to fear. The great triumph in love is to open one's heart, thus receiving all of the goodness which is being given.

When working with clients who have partners who activate their *shadows*, the astrologer must first assess the client's nativity to understand the childhood origin and any past life indications of the internal discord. Only then can one begin to analyze the stressful synastry aspects that trigger the *shadow*.

We will now examine examples of natal *shadow* content and how astrologers are able to identify these forces that operate deep within the unconscious mind.

Some Examples of Natal Shadow Content

Certain horoscopic factors are referred to when seeking to understand a client's unconscious mind:

   1. Planets in the 4th, 8th or 12th houses that are in square or opposition.[69]

2. Square, quincunx or opposition aspects from the Luminaries to Pluto.
3. Retrograde personal planets in square, quincunx or opposition.
4. T-Squares, Yods or Grand Crosses with interceptions in the watery houses.
5. Unaspected Luminaries or personal planets (Ptolemaic: 0°-60°-90°-120°-180°).
6. Predominance of bodies in water signs (especially if deficiency in fire or earth).
7. South Node conjunctions to the outer planets within 5° orb.
8. Progressed lunations falling in the *shadow* degrees of the Zodiac.[70]

When preparing for a relationship analysis, and while examining the individual nativities, you find one or more of these eight categories in either horoscope, it is likely that *shadow* activation by a partner will be an issue. Let us review the eight different classifications that pertain to the unconscious.

The 4th, 8th and 12th houses are of the water element, and planets within them render any soul extremely impressionable to outside vibrational forces. I have often referred to these houses as causing *psychic absorption.* This is certainly true when planets in these watery houses are squared or opposed by other bodies, especially the Lights. These hard aspects cause invasive, rather than invited, entry of other's emotional and psychic energies into the soul.

Therefore, *shadow* content associated with stressed planets in watery houses is of *feelings which are not one's own, but mistakenly thought to have personal origins.* Healing this condition requires enacting virtues of the opposite houses. Thus, planets in the 4th receiving squares or oppositions (which usually produce torment in the family during childhood, and which can leave the individual emotionally unhinged at the slightest stimuli) require souls to concentrate on achievement and accomplishment (10th house polarity). This helps individuals to overcome blaming others for disrupting and upsetting one's emotional composure.

Stressfully aspected planets in the 8th house, especially the Lights, often result in childhood sexual confusion or trauma, due to either actual physical molestation, or inappropriate sexual thoughts coming at the child from a parent, sibling or relative. On a subconscious level, these are frighteningly invasive to the child. The *shadow* associated with the 8th house is the individual who seeks to attract sexual attention through provocative dress or manner in an unconscious response to this kind of attention received during childhood. Healing of the *shadow* involves a gradual development of physical comfort and trust with a monogamous, reliable and faithful sexual partner (2nd house polarity).

Planets in the 12th house that are squared or opposed by other bodies, especially the Luminaries (usually in the cadent 3rd, 6th or 9th houses), affect the mental development of the child. Often there is family history of mental illness, depression, or suicidal tendencies within the ancestral bloodlines. The childhood trauma associated with stressful aspects to the 12th house is one of intense fear of losing control and plunging into personal emotional chaos. The *shadow* is thus one of a projection of weakness onto people around him, with an individual viewing others as disorganized, sloppy, slovenly or confused. Healing the *shadow* requires that these souls work to develop a compassionate understanding of other's fears and a desire to be of helpful service to those who struggle (6th house polarity).

In our second category of horoscopic factors producing turmoil in the unconscious mind, we have the Sun or Moon in a square, quincunx or opposition aspect with Pluto. These aspects often cause a childhood trauma which is of the severest kind, such as repeated beatings, ritualistic abuse involving evil and perverted religious ceremonies, or sexual molestation containing domination and submission themes.

These souls can reach adulthood with surprising behavioral functionality, having had to develop survival instincts from a very young age. Yet, a deep scarring can often be found with these aspects, such as post traumatic stress disorder (PTSD) or borderline personality disorder. With the solar aspects, it is as if the ego structure has been demolished during childhood and must regenerate itself in adulthood. With lunar aspects to Pluto, I have observed that it is often the entire family system that is violent, rather than violence being perpetrated on just one child.

The *shadow* inherent in the bad aspects from Pluto to the Lights is self-destruction. Deep in the unconscious mind, having been grooved through repeated abuse, is a belief system of personal shame and worthlessness. As if in a trance, the souls with these aspects somehow sabotage everything that is good and true for them, apparently feeling undeserving of love, kindness and human consideration.

I do not fully understand this urge to destroy, even after having had to heal from it myself. I believe that it is most certainly due to past life factors in which the owner of these dreadful natal aspects in this lifetime must have caused the brutalization of others in a previous incarnation. I also feel psychotherapy is somewhat unable to treat these aspects, with rather spiritual surrender, or a conversion experience necessary for the horoscope to transform and now operate from a different level. This point of view was first elucidated by C.E.O. Carter over 75 years ago:

> When we view the question in this light, we see why it is often very hard to decide what is incorrectly called "the age of the soul." It is a question, not of age, but of self-realisation; and this may come at any moment and alter the entire tenor of the horoscope, throwing the operation of an aspect or of several aspects from one plane to another. I do not say for one moment that a change of this nature, called in some circles conversion, will occur without directional influences of an appropriate nature, but it would be a matter of considerable delicacy of judgment to foretell when this would happen, or even that an event of that kind would happen at all. - The Zodiac and the Soul; 1928.

Healing of the *shadow* involving the squares, quincunxes or oppositions from the Luminaries to Pluto is to be found in the forgiving of one's parents, or of the one who victimized the soul during childhood. There is no other way.

Here is my story. In 1996, in a chapel at a Catholic retreat center called *The Grotto* in Portland, Oregon, I was kneeling in a pew with a woman with whom I would have a child the following year. The chapel was called *Our Lady of the Sorrowful Mother*, and it had a huge mural above the altar depicting Jesus, dead (having just been taken down from the cross). He was in the arms of his mother, Mary.

I heard Mary say to me, *"You must forgive your mother."* I started to weep and felt a surge of energy radiate up my spine. Until that very moment, I had been unable to reach that place in my heart despite years of therapy and the fervent desire to let go of the lingering hatred for having been repeatedly slapped in the face as a young child. I had no conscious memory of this at that time.

In an instant, the Divine Power of Mary changed me. A month later, I traveled to my parent's home for a visit which had already been planned. I felt much lighter, but I did not understand why. My mother asked me to go on a long walk by the sea with her, and on this walk she told me what had happened to me as a young child.

This was the first time I was able to connect the dots between my history of rage and anger and what was actually at its source. Seven years earlier, while in a 12-Step recovery group, I had demanded to know about the years in my childhood of which I had no memories, but nothing was disclosed to me then. It was only after I found forgiveness for my Mom that she was free to tell me. At the time of this religious experience, my progressed Sun was precisely conjunct my natal Part of Spirit, which is in 05° Capricorn 24'.[71]

A third category of chart factors that can produce turbulent *shadow* content in the unconscious mind are retrograde personal planets, either in the nativity, or in a progressed horoscope, and which are also in square, quincunx or opposition aspect. With Mercury, Venus or Mars retrograde, the planetary consciousness is turned inward, with a vibrational frequency quite different than direct motion bodies. From *Volume I - Progressions:*

> *In my experience, retrograde planets produce alienation, introspection, delay, indirectness, repetition and time-disorientation. The effect natally is to turn a planetary process subconsciously inward, delaying its outward manifestation and making it more powerful from a self-conscious standpoint, but rendering it less effective, at least early in life, for worldly interaction and accomplishment.*

Souls with three or more retrograde planets, especially when Mercury, Venus or Mars are among them, can feel especially alienated. They often have inner lives that are more real to them than their outer involvements. External behaviors are performed with a robotic detachment, so as to protect the vulnerable interior self. It is common to find individuals with an active *shadow* to have stressful aspects to these retrograde bodies, with deep levels of frustration over being misunderstood.

The astrologer will consistently hear stories from female clients with a retrograde Mars in stressful aspect about relationships with men who have been very aggressive toward them, sometimes even physically violent. Conversely, astrologers will also hear stories from men with a natal retrograde Venus in hard aspect by square, quincunx or opposition who are mistreated by women, either in the work place or at home in their personal lives. I have also heard many times of women, when having the secondary progressed station of Mars, being raped or battered in their marriages. What is at the root of this pain?

It is my understanding that retrograde personal planets create *shadow* content in the unconscious mind through a relentless repetition syndrome. The person who possesses these retrograde bodies can be found to endlessly repeat to themselves a mantra of circular thought, the nature of which is an expectation of failure or loss. I feel that this pattern is highly karmic, where a soul *has experienced* this sorrow in past lives and now must overcome fear and transform these echoes and beliefs. This is especially the case when retrograde Mercury, Venus or Mars is in square, quincunx or opposition aspect with *another retrograde planet*.

Healing the *shadow* and getting free from circular loops requires years of contemplative prayer or concentrated meditation, or dedicated efforts to focus on the now. I have also observed that women with a retrograde natal Mars will love men with Aries or Scorpio planets, as a sort of synastric dispositorship in lieu of retrograde Mars dispositing its own nativity. Retrograde Venus for a man often puts him in relationship with a Taurus or Libra Sun woman, or with one of those signs rising.

There is another observation I would like to share with you regarding retrograde personal planets in bad aspect. Both of the women with whom I have had a child possessed a natal retrograde Mars in the 7th house opposite Jupiter on the Ascendant. One has Cancer rising and retrograde Mars in Capricorn, the other has Virgo rising and retrograde Mars in Pisces. Still another woman, an ex-wife, also has retrograde Mars in Pisces opposite Jupiter in Virgo. Why did I attract a pattern of women such as this? The dispositors of my Sun in Scorpio and Moon in Pisces are Mars and Jupiter. Perhaps the split-off *shadow* in me was being reflected by the opposition of those two planets in the nativities of these women.

So far, we have analyzed three of the eight categories of horoscopic factors that can produce *shadow* activation in the unconscious mind. Recalling our case study of Mia Farrow and Woody Allen, here is her chart again.

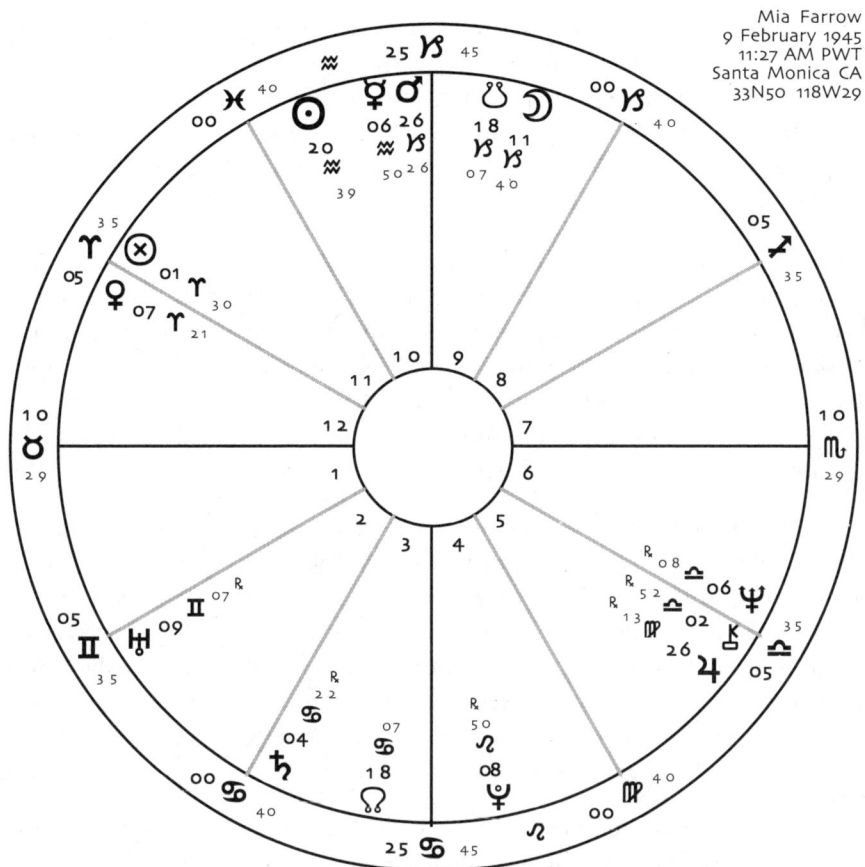

From category 1, we find a 4th house Pluto in an opposition with Mercury, and a 12th house Venus in an opposition with Neptune. From category 2, the Moon is in a quincunx with Pluto. From category 3, recall that Farrow had a progressed stationary retrograde Venus at 3° Taurus during her relationship with Allen. In category 4, she has a 4th house interception involving a Yod planet. Category 5 is seen in an unaspected Sun with no conjunction, sextile, square, trine or opposition aspect to it. These are what I add up and term *The Shadow Count.* If a person has three or more of the eight categories, there is a very active *shadow*.

A fourth category of horoscopic factors that activate a *shadow* are stressful aspect configurations such as T-Squares, Yods and Grand Crosses containing planets in the watery 4th, 8th or 12th houses. This is especially so when interceptions exist.

When working with clients who are in relationships that trigger their *shadows*, it is more effective to first assess the nativity rather than the synastry, to determine what is activated in a relationship. This approach emphasizes the client taking responsibility for him or herself.

Helping clients to know their *shadow* begins with identifying components in the unconscious mind that are unstable, causing imbalance. This is often like peeling an onion. Once clients are familiar with the basic structure of their nativity, most are sincere about their healing journey and want to know more of what lies deeper. Here, astrologers have unprecedented advantage over a psychotherapist in that there is a map of the soul.

The water element 4th, 8th and 12th houses are the doors to the unconscious mind. Within these chambers lie both the source of childhood, or past life, trauma and its cure. Multiple planetary configurations such as a T-Square, Yod or Grand Cross, with planets in watery houses, are likely to be at the root of psychic disturbances that plague the client. When these planets are intercepted in the water houses, they are even tougher to bring to the surface. It is my belief that a timing factor is necessary in the effort toward self-knowledge.

Natal aspect configurations with intercepted planets in watery houses are subject to periodic activation by the secondary progressed Moon. It is at this time that the astrologer is most likely to have success in helping a client to integrate more of the *shadow* into the conscious Self. During the progressed Moon's 27-year cycle, she will activate a T-Square four times, yet the most potent of these is when the fourth leg of the Cross is filled in. I have repeatedly found that when clients are genuinely sincere about healing some part of their *shadow,* they seek out an astrologer very close in time to when progressed Moon aspects occur.

I have often viewed this phenomenon as the *self-guidance system of the client.* Any soul with an open heart and in touch with intuition, hears inner promptings when the time is right to further integrate spiritually. It is the job of the astrologer to perceive which part of the nativity is ripe for deeper self-understanding and to articulate these dynamics to the client. In similar fashion, Yods and Grand Crosses with planets intercepted in the watery houses are also activated four times during the progressed Moon cycle and can be transmuted during these periods.

The fifth category of chart factors contributing to *shadow* content are planets that are Ptolemaically unaspected. This means that there is no conjunction, sextile, trine, square or opposition to this planet in a nativity, and that it functions somewhat out of the loop as regards the gestalt of the rest of the chart. Unaspected Luminaries, Venus or Mars appear to have the greatest affect on relationship, as is also the case when the chart ruler or the 7th house ruler is unaspected.

In *Volume II*, I introduced a radical new technique for aspect interpretation using the Sabian Symbols. In this model, all planets are seen as being in aspect with all other planets as the angular separation between any two bodies is measured, and this arc then corresponds with a particular degree symbol. All 360° of the Zodiac are assigned an aspect, with each aspect's separating orb touching the next one's applying orb. However, it must be said that, despite the many valuable insights the Sabian Aspect Orb method has evinced for its users, when it comes to the *shadow*, and its integration into the higher Self, only planets without major aspects count.

What often happens in relationship is that unaspected Luminaries or planets will attract synastry aspects to them, as was seen where Farrow had an unaspected natal Sun which synastrically conjoined Allen's Moon. It is quite possible that a *Law of Compensation* is somehow at work here, because if a planet or Light has no major aspect relationships with the other bodies in its own nativity, it is logical that it will seek out aspect connection with other horoscopes.

Experienced astrologers may naturally wonder if 45° octiles, 135° trioctiles, 150° quincunxes, or 30° semisextiles qualify as aspects to a so-called unaspected body. I think not, and perhaps it is similar to the formula for the void-of-course Moon, where only the five Ptolemaic aspects are considered. Several astrologers, notably Robert Hand, have written of geometric rationales substantiating this position.[72]

Other astrologers may argue that a so-called unaspected planet or Luminary that is at the midpoint of two or more other bodies is thus integrated into the nativity. I would only support this reasoning up to a certain point, because I have heard stories from too many clients with unaspected planets who described lives where the part of human experience symbolized by that planet was disconnected from the rest of their existence. It is commonly held that these planets either overfunction or underfunction. This is precisely why unaspected planets can trigger the *shadow*.[73]

In my own life, I have an unaspected Mars in detriment in Libra, yet accidentally dignified in the 1st house. While having no Ptolemaic aspect within allowable orb, this Mars does form a quincunx to my Moon in Pisces, and is octiled by both Pluto and the Sun. Moreover, that Mars is in the exact midpoint degree of a Sun-Pluto square. In relationship, this Mars has received some dreadful synastry aspects.

In my longest lasting marriage, my wife had a Stellium in Capricorn involving the Sun, Moon, Mercury and Venus between 4° and 13°, and all square to my Mars. In two other marriages, both wives had natal Suns in 9° or 10° Libra, in synastric conjunction with that Mars. The mother of my first daughter has a Cancer Stellium with Moon, Mercury, Venus, Jupiter and the Ascendant all between 2° and 14°, in synastric square with my Mars. It gets worse. She has retrograde Mars in the 7th in 7° Capricorn, conveniently forming a synastry T-Square with my Mars. It is no coincidence that we seek to understand partners who activate our shadows.

For me, that Mars has been both the blessing and the curse of my life. When I was a younger man, I could not control the anger which I attributed to its position at the Sun/Pluto midpoint, doing a lot of damage in relationships with my volcanic eruptions. But conversely, I never would have lasted as a self-employed astrologer and author on a full-time basis without the drive and determination of that Mars.

The *shadow* I have had to integrate has been the life lesson of transmuting intense passion into personal creativity and accomplishment. Simultaneously, I've had to learn how to neutralize anger through forgiveness, compassion and tenderness. I have failed miserably many times in my attempts to do this, but I am still trying and I will never quit. I only became aware of the depth of my *shadow* through the stressful synastry to my unaspected Mars that I encountered in relationships. As Jung has written, *"There is no coming to consciousness without pain."*

Our sixth category of horoscopic factors that can produce an active *shadow* is a predominance of planets in the water signs, and especially so when there is also a deficiency in earth and fire. The water-air combinations, like myself, are identified by psychological astrologers as the most sensitive; and yes, as the most neurotic. A lack of feeling grounded in life, combined with hypersensitivity to outside stimuli, is the lot of those of us with much water but no earth. With many planets in water and no fire, memories from the past can interfere with hope for the future.

In his 1975 book, *Astrology, Psychology & the Four Elements,* Stephen Arroyo wrote very precisely about the different combinations of elements in natal charts. His description of a predominance of planets in water signs should be read carefully by astrologers working with these sensitive souls who struggle with their *shadows*. Overwhelming fear is very real to them and is a paralyzing factor until they develop a deep faith and trust in Divine Guidance.

Watery souls measure reality through their feelings. They will often sacrifice personal comforts for a spiritual vision, or for love and human connectedness. The *shadow* in the unconscious mind is more likely to be one of despair and fatalism when idealistic adventures fail to build a lasting and concrete security. The projection of the *shadow* therefore is aimed toward those who appear happy and content, and there is self-pity at its root.

Those souls with a predominance of planets in water signs have especially active imaginations and the line dividing fantasy and reality is often very difficult to discern. Memories of significant life events are regularly occluded by sentiment, and painful losses can be altered in the subconscious mind to fit a self-image of one who has given and sacrificed for the higher good. The *shadow* in all of these inner machinations can be one where complete truth and honesty do not prevail, because to sustain the inner self-image of goodness, injurious deeds are minimized.

Of the four elements in astrology, water most closely resembles the functioning of the *shadow*. In a religious sense, the unconscious mind is where *evil lurks in the shadows,* and it can only be made pure by its absorption into the Light of the Holy Spirit. Watery souls often feel that they are being absorbed into the vibrations of others, or, on a transpersonal level, into forces beyond control. If this absorption is into the Light and Love of Christ Consciousness, it is blissful; but absorption into the Darkness of the *shadow* can feel like a scary descent into hell.

The seventh category of chart factors contributing to *shadow* content are the conjunctions to the South Node from the outer planets, Uranus, Neptune or Pluto. At death, the soul vacates the body accompanied by its astral and causal minds. Almost all of the memory of physical experience from previous lives is erased upon reincarnation, with only slight traces of residual feeling and thought being carried into the next birth. This residue of memory is symbolized by the South Node, and this is the most sensitive degree in the nativity regarding previous incarnations.

If a soul incarnates with Uranus, Neptune or Pluto conjunct the South Node, past life events over which the individual had absolutely no control dominate the soul memory and are firmly lodged in the innermost astral and causal mind. Retrograde outer planets conjunct the South Node symbolize a repeating pattern spread over multiple incarnations, whereas direct outer planet conjunctions represent the most immediate past life only. The nature of the past life events permeates the thinking.

Uranus conjunct the South Node occurs in the horoscopes of waves of souls who incarnate about every fifteen years. Conjunctions during the 20th century were:

1. 26 January 1908   14° Capricorn 08'
2. 26 May 1923   17° Pisces 14'
3. 24 January 1939   13° Taurus 50'
4. 12 April 1954   19° Cancer 07'
5. 3 January 1969   04° Libra 00'
6. 12 February 1984   13° Sagittarius 03'
7. 16 May 1999   16° Aquarius 47'

These conjunctions hold a 5° orb for about four to seven months. However, this 5° orb is not equidistant on either side of the exact conjunction, as was the case when I was born. Uranus and the South Node entered the 5° applying orb on 28 October 1953; the conjunction perfected on 12 April 1954; and the separating 5° orb lasted until 25 May 1954. Conjunctions occur about every 55° to 75° apart in the Zodiac.

One presumes that these waves of souls are reincarnating after previous lives that contained much disruption, sudden shock, and abrupt separation from those whom they loved. If the astrologer researches the past just prior to a Uranus-South Node conjunction, he find events in world history that caused large scale disruption.

In the years before Hitler invaded Poland in September 1939 at the onset of WWII, for example, many Jews in Europe emigrated to the United States, fleeing their homes and leaving everything behind. It is likely that many in the wave of souls who were born at the Uranus-South Node conjunction of 1939 may have died in their immediate previous life during the chaotic upheaval of the late 1930s.

The *shadow* inherent in Uranus conjunct the South Node is one of perpetuating the pattern of disruption carried over from the previous life. Sudden separation and shock during a past life created a groove in the innermost mind. The residual effect remains mostly unconscious, operating through the *shadow* in a self-sabotaging way. Being born myself at one of these conjunctions, and having moved over 55 times between the ages of 18 and 50, it is as if I do not expect any home to abide.

Neptune conjunct the South Node occurs in the horoscopes of souls who incarnate every sixteen to seventeen years. Conjunctions during the 20th century were:

1. 31 August 1899   26° Gemini 47'
2. 27 May 1916   00° Leo 28'
3. 25 December 1932   10° Virgo 08'
4. 13 November 1949   16° Libra 11'
5. 27 August 1966   19° Scorpio 36'
6. 25 March 1983   29° Sagittarius 13'
7. 15 January 2000   03° Aquarius 42'

These conjunctions also hold a 5° orb for between four and seven months. It is of interest how they occur like bookends at the beginning and end of each century. If one does the math, one can see that six 16 2/3 year cycles equal one hundred years. The souls who incarnate with the South Node conjunctions to Neptune have had a past life wherein they were financially swindled or embezzled, and a *shadow* that contains deep issues around financial mistrust. This past life event may also have been exacerbated by the resulting despair from the thievery leading to alcoholism.

The essential *shadow* content within the Neptune conjunction to the South Node is one of broken dreams. Projection takes the form of seeing others as having given up in life, and no longer having any fighting spirit left inside to carry on. Depression and morbidity have to be overcome through sheer willpower for the soul to believe in all of life's possibilities again. Making financial donations to charity can help heal the lingering feelings of having lost money in a previous incarnation. Displaying innocence, naiveté and guilelessness will also help to heal the *shadow*.

Pluto conjunct the South Node occurs in the horoscopes of groups of souls who incarnate every seventeen years. Conjunctions during the 20th century were:

1. 14 March 1900   14° Gemini 44'
2. 3 October 1917   05° Cancer 32'
3. 12 May 1935   24° Cancer 06'
4. 24 August 1952   21° Leo 31'

5. 15 July 1969	22° Virgo 53'
6. 31 December 1985	06° Scorpio 55'
7. 22 August 2002	14° Sagittarius 54'

Similar to Neptune, these conjunctions remain within 5° orb for about six months. The souls who are born with Pluto conjunct the South Node have deep scars in the unconscious mind from either having been involved in a criminal underworld, and responsible for crimes of violence against others, or from having been victimized themselves by organized crime, or by multiple robberies while living in dangerous neighborhoods. The *shadow* in this life revolves around issues of protection from law enforcement, and fears of a breakdown in overall public safety on the streets.

The essential *shadow* content with Pluto conjunct the South Node is one of intense fear of personal violence. Projection occurs through an unconscious expectation of violent retaliation from others, with strangers in public places appearing to look menacing, threatening and frightening. Healing of the *shadow* lies in a willingness to socially engage, without fear, with strangers in public environments. Extending warmth and trust toward others through relaxed facial expressions is key. Doing volunteer work in a religious ministry serving prisoners would also be healing.

The eighth and final classification of horoscopic factors which pertain to *shadow* activation are progressed lunations occurring in certain degrees of the Zodiac whose Sabian Symbols contain references to "shadow". These are the 10th degree of Virgo, the 15th degree of Sagittarius, and the 28th degree of Pisces. I refer also to tertiary or minor progressed lunations, in addition to secondary progressed.[74]

The astrologer who works with the Sabian Symbols will often find that there is a literal manifestation of the wording contained within a particular degree symbol. I have observed through the years that several of my clients, after having a lunar phase ingress in the progressed chart in one of these three degrees, experienced an activation of *shadow* material arising from within their unconscious mind. In some cases, this *shadow* triggering took the form of bad dreams and nightmares; in other instances it was similar to an inner struggle with mental illness symptoms such as chronic depression, severe self-doubt, or irrational feelings of hatred or jealousy.

From *Lecture~Lessons* (1931) by Marc Edmund Jones, the three Sabian Symbols are:

> Virgo 10: *As if in a moment of vision a man is seen possessed of two heads; both of these look out and beyond the shadows.*
> Sagittarius 15: *The time is at hand to determine whether winter shall end; the groundhog comes forth looking for its shadow.*
> Pisces 28: *Night has seemed light as day, and in the odd shadows of diffused whiteness the fertile fields appear quite alive.*

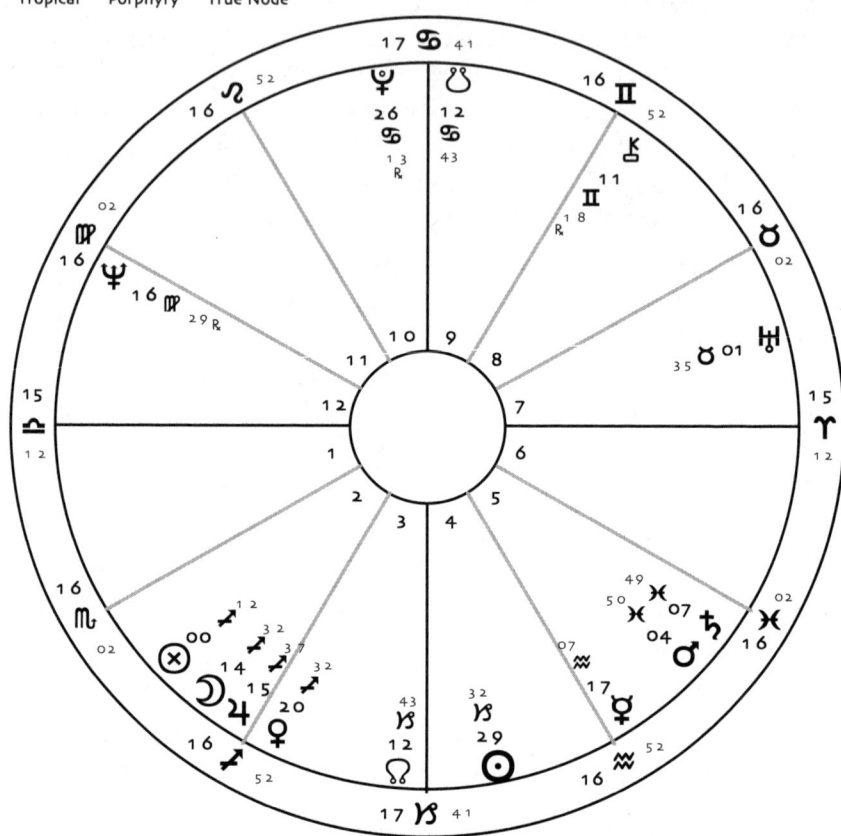

During the bitter litigation and child custody battle between our case study couple in August 1992, it was alleged that between the years of 1985 and 1988, Allen had sexually molested his adopted daughter, Dylan (now called Eliza). The charges were never proven, but he was barred from spending any more time with the child.

The above chart shows the ingress of Allen's secondary progressed lunation cycle into the balsamic phase, in which it remained for three and one half years until his progressed New Moon in January 1989. His progressed Moon has perfected a waning octile (315° semisquare) with his progressed Sun, and the Moon is in Sagittarius 15 at this balsamic phase ingress, one of the *shadow degrees*.

In summary, the past eight examples of potential *shadow* triggers provide specific horoscopic factors indicating what lies within the unconscious mind of clients. All can produce psychic turmoil, and before astrologers begin comparing charts for a relationship analysis, both of the individual nativities should be scrutinized to see if these *shadow* factors exist.

The Shadow in Synastry and Composite Charts

The very nature of the unconscious mind is that it is concealed. A mystic will seek to penetrate the veils through constant and arduous meditation practice, whilst the lover, through his feelings for the beloved, will arrive there in his heart. In this sense, *human relationship is spiritual practice,* with benefits of equal value.

However, just as a beautiful pearl can be found within the rather ugly oyster, and that one must dive to the bottom of the sea to find one of these mollusks, so, too, is it necessary to plumb the depths of one's emotional core to find true love. Astrologers will often find that the most unstable relationships produce the finest experience of exquisite and soulful intimacy, yet at times tearing the heart asunder.

These relationships are the ones that have synastry or composite chart dynamics that not only can activate the *shadow* of both participants, but which can also take each soul into parts of themselves previously unknown and uncharted. When the astrologer finds synastric or composite T-Squares, Yods or Grand Crosses, he knows that the energy generated by the couple can take them into hidden depths.

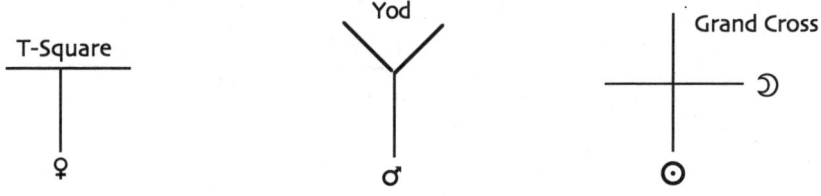

These three aspect configurations, when found synastrically or in the composite chart, and if comprised of the Luminaries, Venus or Mars, will have a significant impact on the souls of both individuals in the relationship. Their effect is to render a partnership unstable, while simultaneously opening up doors to consciousness. The rhetorical question posed in my *Partners Who Activate Our Shadow* lecture was whether to remain in a relationship such as this, reaping benefits of higher awareness, or to exit because of repeated *shadow* activation.

After ten years of teaching and lecturing about this material, not to mention having personal experience with this dimension of love, I am now convinced that there is no one, easy answer. The capacity of a given soul to withstand and endure stress, while also growing spiritually, will vary by the inner strength, life experience, desire, and willingness to seek self-knowledge of the person involved. The natal condition of Venus, along with the 7th house ruler, inform astrologers about an individual's capacity to perceive relationship as a vehicle for spiritual growth.

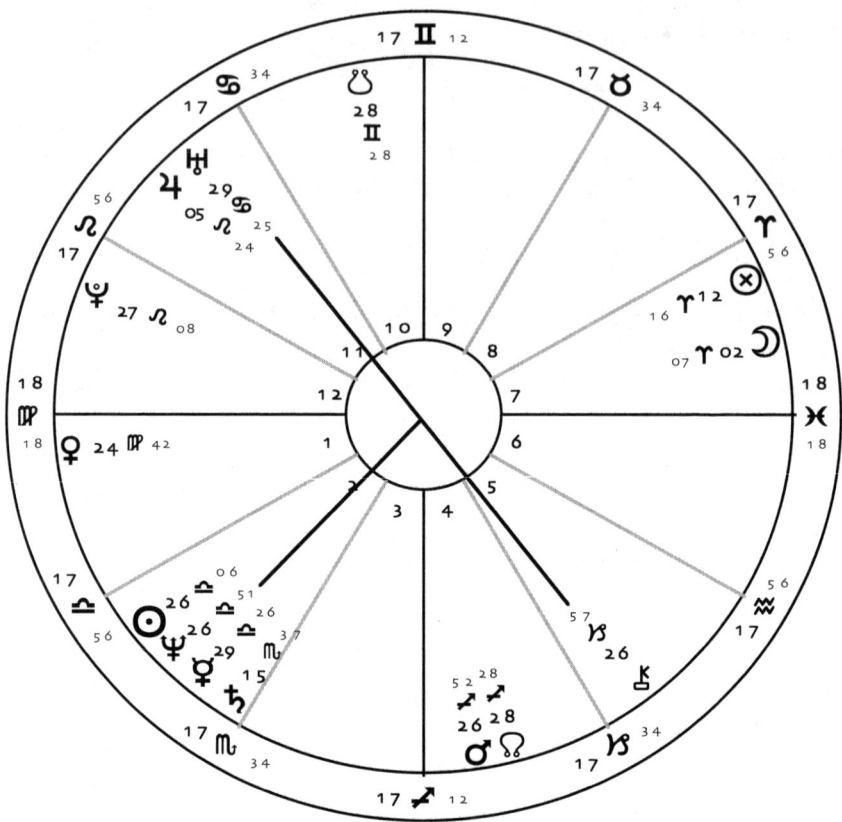

This is the composite chart of the author and the mother of his younger daughter, with whom he had a two-year relationship during 1996-98. The partnership was completely unstable, but was also filled with a deep love. A beautiful child came to this earth through them, yet in the end, a tragic and painful parting occurred.

The astrologer finds a succedent T-Cross with a Sun-Neptune conjunction at its apex. Chiron in the 5th house of children, and Uranus, in exact square to the ruler, are in opposition, and square to the Sun, Mercury and Neptune. While, at first, the love seemed perfect, with Neptune joined to the Sun, during the time that they were together, many chaotic separations occurred, indicated by the Uranus squares.[75]

Both the love shared and the birth of a daughter can be seen with Venus rising and with the Moon in a fertile trine with the benefic, Jupiter. A planet conjunct the North Node usually defines the purpose of any relationship; with Mars conjoined the Dragon's Head, an ultimate separation it was to be. Just as our eight categories of horoscopic factors defined activation of the *shadow* in the natal chart, these methods can also be used to analyze composite charts. Pluto in the 12th house, along with Mars in the 4th forming a square with Venus, activated much *shadow* material for both parties, and in the end it was more than could be handled. Saturn is the planet necessary for stability and longevity, and here we find it unaspected.

Woody Allen
Dec 1 1935 10:55 PM EST
Bronx New York
40N40 73W54
Dec 2 1935 03:55:00 GMT
Tropical Porphyry True Node

Second Chart Natal Chart
Mia Farrow
Feb 9 1945 18:27:00 GMT

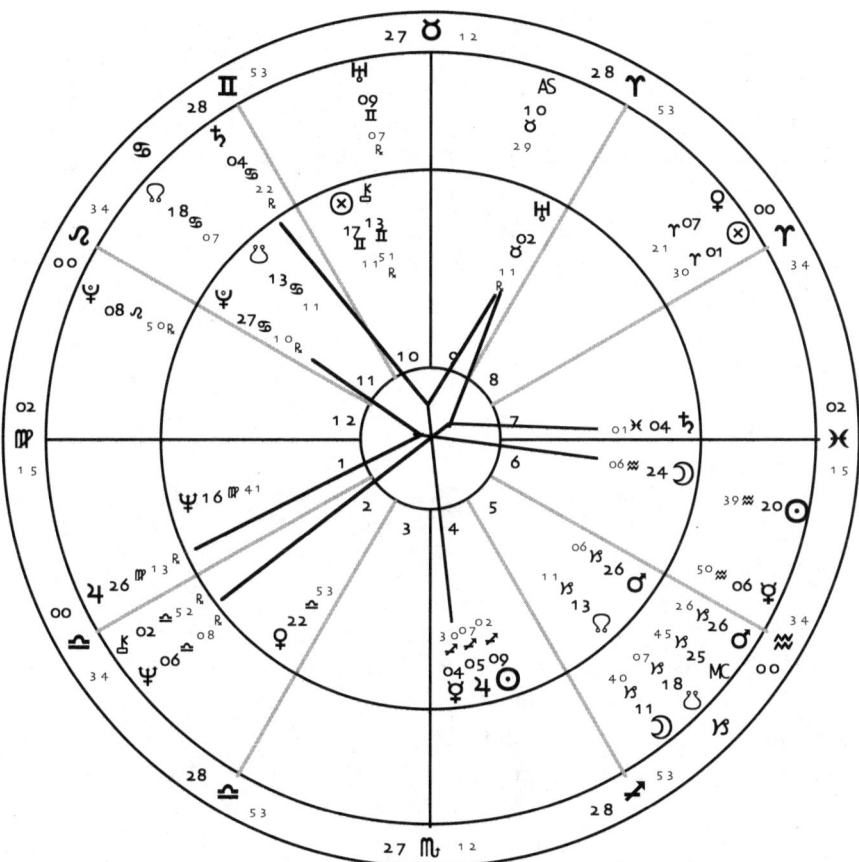

Referring once again to our case study couple, this bi-wheel chart has Allen's natal chart in the inner wheel, and Farrow's planets in the outer wheel. There are three synastric Yods forming between their two sets of Luminaries and planets, with one of the Yod's having Allen's Moon as the apex planet. A second Yod has Farrow's Chiron-Neptune conjunction in Libra at its apex, a poignant symbol for the wound from a deceptive relationship betrayal. A third Yod has as its apex the rulers of Allen's horizon, Mercury and Jupiter.

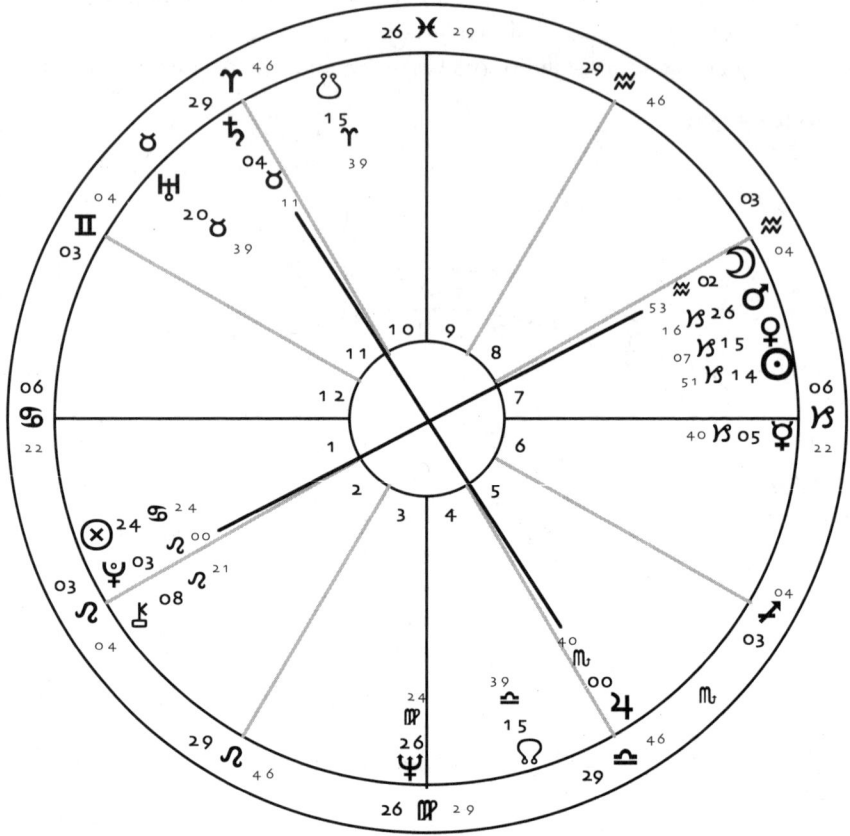

This is the composite chart for Farrow and Allen, originally shown on page 56. A Fixed Grand Cross is found, with the Moon-Pluto opposition forming a transverse arm and a Jupiter-Saturn opposition making up the vertical axis. Considering the court battle and litigation over child custody and molestation allegations (Jupiter) which led to reputational damage to Allen (Saturn), and the hidden sexual liaison within the family (Moon-Pluto), each planet in the Cross is tragically represented.

If the astrologer is working with clients whose *shadows* are activated in their relationships and he finds there are indeed synastric or composite T-Squares, Yods, or a Grand Cross, he must assess the planets involved in these stressful aspect configurations to understand the particulars of the *shadow* trigger.

The Lights, Venus and Mars, when in these dreadful aspect configurations, are the primary bodies that will feel the effect of the *shadow* at the deepest levels. Other planets in the configuration will give an astrologer insight into what the trigger is. Saturn, Chiron, Uranus, Neptune or Pluto have a different triggering mechanism.

1. Saturn = intimacy fears, armoring, inhibition or repression issues.
2. Chiron = shame, humiliation, sexual trauma or forgiveness issues.
3. Uranus = commitment fears, narcissism or emotional disconnection issues.
4. Neptune = disillusionment, fantasy, addiction or romantic perfection issues.
5. Pluto = power, control, anger, manipulation or broken trust issues.

After identifying which planets, and therefore which issues are the triggering mechanism, cross-check these individual aspects that make up the stressful synastric or composite configuration against the natal aspects in each person's horoscope. A link suggests the trigger to the *shadow* material. For example, both Allen and Farrow had the natal Moon in quincunx to Pluto;[76] in the composite chart, the Moon opposed Pluto. This will immediately alert the astrologer that broken trust issues from childhood are likely, but have not yet been confronted openly (150° quincunx). With the composite opposition between Moon and Pluto, the issue is brought out into the open.

In summary, the eight classifications of horoscopic factors producing *shadow* material within individuals, when also found in synastry or in composite charts, will trigger psychic turmoil buried in the unconscious mind. Therefore, astrologers finding either an overlay Pluto in the 4th house, a synastric Moon in square or opposition to a partner's Pluto, or a composite square or opposition between the Moon and Pluto, will have specific clues as to the nature of the relational *shadow*.

Transit Saturn Aspecting the Secondary Progressed Moon

Many clients have asked me over the years if there is a timing factor involved in the activation and subsequent coming to awareness of one's *shadow*. Astrologers know that Saturn is the planet that rules time and space, the former through his domain over the earth sign, Capricorn, and the latter through his sovereignty over the air sign, Aquarius. The unconscious mind is governed by the Moon, including childhood memories, as well as past life experiences affecting the present incarnation. At some point in every soul's life, the transit of Saturn will lock into a repeating aspect pattern with the progressed Moon. This will last for years.

The Saturn transit cycle is 29.5 years while the progressed Moon cycle is 27.3 years. Due to fluctuating motion of the Moon and the elliptical nature of Saturn's orbit, the two lock into sequences of repeated aspects at different times in every life. When this occurs, the contents contained in the unconscious mind are capable of becoming crystallized, brought into perceptible form, and worked with in a healing manner. If this repeated aspect sequence between transit Saturn and the progressed Moon is a sextile or a trine, the integration of the *shadow* can be accomplished much like voluntary therapy. However, if the repeating aspect from Saturn to the progressed Moon is a conjunction, square or opposition, integrating the *shadow* may have to be achieved much like court ordered therapy—painfully.

I have ongoing personal experience with this phenomenon, as transit Saturn forms forty-three oppositions to my progressed Moon from August of 1989 to February of 2011, ultimately lasting for over 21 years. Saturn and the Moon rule my North and South Node, respectively, and any soul who has either of these two bodies ruling an angle or a nodal axis sign or house, or as the dispositor of a Luminary, will be affected by this transit-to-progressed scenario. Jung's dictum that a moral effort is required to confront one's shadow along the road to self-knowledge is an echo of this astrological symbolism: Saturn rules effort, the Moon rules the soul.

DYNAMIC REPORT

Dynamic Chart (2):
Mia Farrow – Female Chart
Feb 9 1945, 11:27 am, PWT +7:00
Los Angeles California, 34°N03'08", 118°W14'34"
Geocentric Tropical Zodiac
Porphyry Houses, True Node

Selection: Transit Saturn Tracking Progressed Moon

♄ (3)	☍	☽ (9)	(X)	Tr-Sp	Aug 7 1945	18°♋21' D	18°♑21' D
♄ (3)	☍	☽ (9)	(X)	Tr-Sp	Dec 17 1945	23°♋24' ℞	23°♑24' D
♄ (4)	☍	☽ (10)	(X)	Tr-Sp	Aug 27 1946	03°♌09' D	03°♒09' D
♄ (4)	☍	☽ (10)	(X)	Tr-Sp	Dec 25 1946	07°♌48' ℞	07°♒48' D
♄ (4)	☍	☽ (10)	(X)	Tr-Sp	Sep 26 1947	18°♌44' D	18°♒44' D
♄ (4)	☍	☽ (10)	(X)	Tr-Sp	Dec 24 1947	22°♌17' ℞	22°♒17' D
♄ (8)	△	☽ (4)	(X)	Tr-Sp	Aug 12 1988	26°♐11' ℞	26°♌11' D
♄ (8)	△	☽ (4)	(X)	Tr-Sp	Oct 29 1988	28°♐46' D	28°♌46' D
♄ (9)	△	☽ (5)	(X)	Tr-Sp	Aug 9 1989	08°♑08' ℞	08°♍08' D
♄ (9)	△	☽ (5)	(X)	Tr-Sp	Nov 27 1989	11°♑45' D	11°♍45' D
♄ (9)	△	☽ (5)	(X)	Tr-Sp	Aug 10 1990	20°♑09' ℞	20°♍09' D
♄ (9)	△	☽ (5)	(X)	Tr-Sp	Dec 21 1990	24°♑29' D	24°♍29' D
♄ (10)	△	☽ (5)	(X)	Tr-Sp	Aug 14 1991	02°♒11' ℞	02°♎11' D
♄ (10)	△	☽ (6)	(X)	Tr-Sp	Jan 11 1992	07°♒04' D	07°♎04' D
♄ (10)	△	☽ (6)	(X)	Tr-Sp	Aug 19 1992	14°♒15' ℞	14°♎15' D
♄ (10)	△	☽ (6)	(X)	Tr-Sp	Jan 28 1993	19°♒33' D	19°♎33' D
♄ (10)	△	☽ (6)	(X)	Tr-Sp	Aug 27 1993	26°♒23' ℞	26°♎23' D
♄ (11)	△	☽ (6)	(X)	Tr-Sp	Feb 14 1994	01°♓57' D	01°♏57' D
♄ (11)	△	☽ (6)	(X)	Tr-Sp	Sep 6 1994	08°♓37' ℞	08°♏37' D
♄ (11)	△	☽ (7)	(X)	Tr-Sp	Feb 28 1995	14°♓17' D	14°♏17' D
♄ (11)	△	☽ (7)	(X)	Tr-Sp	Sep 19 1995	20°♓57' ℞	20°♏57' D
♄ (11)	△	☽ (7)	(X)	Tr-Sp	Mar 10 1996	26°♓38' D	26°♏38' D
♄ (11)	△	☽ (7)	(X)	Tr-Sp	Oct 3 1996	03°♈27' ℞	03°♐27' D
♄ (12)	△	☽ (8)	(X)	Tr-Sp	Mar 21 1997	09°♈03' D	09°♐03' D
♄ (12)	△	☽ (8)	(X)	Tr-Sp	Oct 19 1997	16°♈09' ℞	16°♐09' D
♄ (12)	△	☽ (8)	(X)	Tr-Sp	Mar 30 1998	21°♈36' D	21°♐36' D
♄ (12)	△	☽ (8)	(X)	Tr-Sp	Nov 5 1998	29°♈07' ℞	29°♐07' D
♄ (12)	△	☽ (9)	(X)	Tr-Sp	Apr 8 1999	04°♉25' D	04°♑25' D
♄ (1)	△	☽ (9)	(X)	Tr-Sp	Nov 23 1999	12°♉23' ℞	12°♑23' D
♄ (1)	△	☽ (9)	(X)	Tr-Sp	Apr 18 2000	17°♉36' D	17°♑36' D
♄ (1)	△	☽ (10)	(X)	Tr-Sp	Dec 8 2000	26°♉01' ℞	26°♑01' D
♄ (1)	△	☽ (10)	(X)	Tr-Sp	May 1 2001	01°♊18' D	01°♒18' D
♄ (2)	△	☽ (10)	(X)	Tr-Sp	Dec 21 2001	10°♊02' ℞	10°♒02' D
♄ (2)	△	☽ (10)	(X)	Tr-Sp	May 18 2002	15°♊38' D	15°♒38' D
♄ (2)	△	☽ (10)	(X)	Tr-Sp	Jan 1 2003	24°♊26' ℞	24°♒26' D
♄ (2)	△	☽ (10)	(X)	Tr-Sp	Jun 9 2003	00°♋41' D	00°♓41' D
♄ (3)	△	☽ (11)	(X)	Tr-Sp	Jan 7 2004	09°♋11' ℞	09°♓11' D
♄ (3)	△	☽ (11)	(X)	Tr-Sp	Jul 5 2004	16°♋29' D	16°♓29' D
♄ (3)	△	☽ (11)	(X)	Tr-Sp	Jan 9 2005	24°♋13' ℞	24°♓13' D
♄ (4)	△	☽ (11)	(X)	Tr-Sp	Aug 8 2005	02°♌57' D	02°♈57' D
♄ (4)	△	☽ (12)	(X)	Tr-Sp	Jan 8 2006	09°♌22' ℞	09°♈22' D
♄ (4)	△	☽ (12)	(X)	Tr-Sp	Sep 17 2006	19°♌57' D	19°♈57' D
♄ (4)	△	☽ (12)	(X)	Tr-Sp	Jan 1 2007	24°♌25' ℞	24°♈25' D

This Dynamic Report was calculated using Solar Fire™ for Windows, and shows two periods in the life of Mia Farrow when she has transit Saturn forming repeated Ptolemaic aspects to her secondary progressed Moon. Because she was born with a natal Moon separating from an opposition to Saturn, and the Moon and Saturn in Mutual Reception, this transit-to-progressed pattern is critically important to understand her childhood.[77]

Saturn stationed direct on 5 March 1945 in 03° Cancer 49', less than a month after she was born. Saturn then moved through the Zodiac all the way to 24° Cancer 54' before stationing retrograde on 6 November 1945. The Dynamic Report shows that Saturn caught up to Farrow's progressed Moon on 7 August 1945, forming an exact opposition with it. A little over a month after Saturn turned retrograde, another opposition formed to her progressed Moon on 17 December 1945. This pattern repeated during her childhood in 1946 and 1947, as Farrow received four more oppositions of Saturn to her progressed Moon.

The astrologer then sees that there were no more aspects formed until 1988, when Farrow was now in her early 40s, and Saturn started to form repeating trines with her progressed Moon. A total of 37 trines will form over 18.5 years. A break in the pattern occurred from 1947 until 1988 because the progressed Moon began moving faster than Saturn. Many years passed until the trine aspect formed.

It took almost 41 years for these two bodies to again align by Ptolemaic aspect. It would be perfectly legitimate for astrologers to question whether there was possible sexual molestation during the first three years of Farrow's life, while the six Saturn oppositions to her progressed Moon were taking place. It is also logical to speculate that, during her relationship with Woody Allen, which was in effect in 1988 when Saturn began to again aspect her progressed Moon, she experienced crystallizing of the *shadow*, and started having subconscious fears of sexual molestation between Allen and their adopted daughter, Dylan.

Also in the Dynamic Report, on 11 January 1992, Saturn is perfecting its 8th trine to her progressed Moon, and *two days later* is when she discovered the pictures. I obviously cannot judge whether actual incest was taking place with Dylan, or if Farrow was reliving her own memories of having been a victim of incest and projecting that *shadow* content onto Allen. In either case, surmise that the contents of her unconscious mind (progressed Moon) are being crystallized into perceptible form (Saturn) for facilitating healing and integration.

Astrologers will encounter clients who are having *shadow* content triggered in a relationship, such as a fear of sexual molestation between a child and a spouse. It is essential for the astrologer to then calculate a lifetime report of any Saturn transits to the client's secondary progressed Moon before he can judge if a *shadow* activation may be occurring or if actual molestation may be taking place.

This is a very delicate subject to discuss with a client, as often there is no memory of their own incest experience. But, if the astrologer sees that there was indeed a pattern of Saturn aspecting the progressed Moon during childhood, then a gap of time with no aspects being formed, and now the client has aspects forming anew, it is reasonable to presume that Saturn is crystallizing contents in the unconscious. In no case should astrologers doubt a client's suspicions, but if a pattern between Saturn and the progressed Moon exists, it indicates likely unconscious projection.

To calculate a lifetime Dynamic Report of Saturn aspects to the progressed Moon, follow these easy steps in your Solar Fire™ for Windows program:

1. Select chart in the 'Calculated Charts' window.
2. Open 'Dynamic' menu and click 'Transits & Progressions'.
3. In 'Saved Selections' pop-up window, choose 'Transits'.
4. Change 'Start Date' to birthday of client.
5. Change 'Period' to 85 years.
6. In 'Event Selection', click off the 'x' in 'Transits to Radix'.
7. Click on 'Transits to Progs', with no other boxes selected.
8. In 'Point Selection', click 'Transits' field.
9. Click 'Create', and name file 'SATURNONLY', click OK.
10. Remove all planets in 'Selected Points', leaving Saturn only.
11. Click 'Save', then click 'Select'.
12. In 'Point Selection', click 'Progs' field.
13. Click 'Create', and name file 'MOONONLY', click OK.
14. Remove all planets in 'Selected Points', leaving Moon only.
15. Click 'Save', then click 'Select'.
16. In 'Aspect Selection', click 'Transits' field.
17. Choose 'MEDIEV.ASP', and click 'Select'.
18. Click 'Save Selection'; type 'Transit Saturn Aspecting Progressed Moon'.
19. New calculation routine name shows in 'Saved Selections', click 'View'.
20. 'Dynamic Events Report' displays on screen, sorting aspects by decades.

The Astrology of Anger and Transformational Relationships

Perhaps the most unpleasant part of the *shadow* to deal with is anger. Anger is a secondary emotion, with primary states of hurt or fear preceding it. Children are often told sternly not to display anger. Even worse, children are frequently spanked or slapped when showing anger, which further confuses them. Upon becoming an adult and entering into a personal relationship, one's emotions and attachments are triggered at a level comparable to childhood and anger surfaces. Is astrology useful for identifying and explaining the different dimensions of anger?

Yes, and the four main patterns of anger can be defined by the stressful aspects to Mars, Saturn, Uranus or Pluto in the nativity. Some souls express anger through impatience and aggressiveness, while others attempt to repress anger until it can no longer be held within and it boils over. Still others show anger by being rebellious and willfully going to extremes, and some struggling souls occasionally blow up into a ferocious rage, completely out of control as if possessed by demons.

As an astrologer with four planets in Scorpio, you can be sure that I have known many clients with anger issues. I have Mars at the midpoint of Sun and Pluto, so I have always been interested in how individuals sometimes just lose their cookies and blow up, going absolutely out of control. These struggling souls need a safe place to talk about the demons within, without being shamed or judged. My own personal experience with anger has given me a deeper understanding of its nature.

I have carefully listened to my clients during consultation as they discuss their feelings of anger. I tried to hear exactly what was making them angry, and its origins. In Oriental Medicine, each organ of the body is correlated with a specific emotion, and in turn that organ corresponds with a ruling planet. Thus we have grief stored in the lungs and ruled by Mercury. Fear is contained in the kidneys and is ruled by Venus. Anger is held in the liver, which is ruled by Jupiter.

As in alchemy, wherein the poison contains the cure, Jupiterian forgiveness is the only antidote to anger. I have taught Astrology and Anger workshops since 1997 to help individuals understand the origins of their anger, and to learn more about a spouse's anger patterns. I recommend virtues opposite from the planetary vices.

I have a handout from my workshop that includes interpretive material found in the books of C.E.O. Carter and Stephen Arroyo, and also from my experience with clients. These definitions of anger are included for you here. Let us review the four patterns of anger found in natal charts, and how astrologers can offer clients alternate means of self-expression in order to transform darkness into Light. The stressful natal aspects referred to include 0° conjunctions, 45° octiles, 90° squares, 135° trioctiles, 150° quincunxes, and 180° oppositions. It must also be stated that even the sextiles and trines will produce these behaviors, albeit to a lesser degree.

Mars' stressful aspects: [Virtues = courage; conviction; purpose; determination]
    a) impatience   d) threats, aggressiveness
    b) willfullness   e) egocentric and subjective
    c) improper use of force   f) anger as release of emotion

☉ ♂ Aggressiveness, ego gratification, arrogance, strong desires
☽ ♂ Strong emotional reactions, restlessness, takes everything personally
☿ ♂ Disputatious, argumentative, challenging, accusatory
♀ ♂ Impatience, irritability, abrupt and forceful, demanding

Anger pattern: Ego centered reactions, use of power or aggressiveness to protect self.

Individuals with Mars in hard aspect to personal planets face a lifelong test to transform impatience, aggression, and threatening behaviors toward others into personal courage, purposeful living, healthy determination and moral conviction.

The anger pattern associated with Mars is predominantly an ego-based reaction, and much of the aggressive behavior has an underlying fear. I have observed a pattern in clients with stressful aspects to Mars who have brothers who picked on them mercilessly as children. The anger in childhood was necessary for self-protection. But, in adult relationship, it is no longer needed, nor appropriate.

Healing of the *shadow* associated with Mars is most difficult for souls who have the Sun in opposition or quincunx to a retrograde Mars. An admission to oneself of underlying hurt or fear underpinning the anger is a first step. Fairness and reliability need to be inculcated into the personality, as these are virtues of the polarities (Libra and Taurus) of the Mars-ruled signs, Aries and Scorpio. Great depth, a good intellect, and a passion for hard work are found with these aspects.

It is usually not until the client's Sun (who has a natal opposition or quincunx to retrograde Mars) secondary progresses to the trine with Mars that he or she finally gets a handle on the anger. Those with a natal waning quincunx between the Sun and retrograde Mars are the most fortunate, because by age 10 Mars stations direct, and by age 33 the progressed Sun forms a trine with Mars.[78]

However, those born with the waxing quincunx between retrograde Mars and the Sun have the most difficult karmic task laid out for them. Their natal Sun will have to first progress through the opposition with Mars at age 22, then a waning quincunx at age 45. At age 63 progressed Mars stations direct. It is not until age 74 that this soul would finally reach the progressed trine with Mars. This is why some individuals may karmically struggle with anger for most of their lives. In the case of a natal Sun-Mars opposition, the progressed trine comes at age 52.

The Moon in hard aspect with Mars produces an active *shadow*, and a difficult struggle with anger. Stressful lunar aspects to Mars are notorious for producing a person who takes everything personally and is defensive. I had an ex-wife with the natal opposition and one wrong word and a conversation went immediately down the toilet. These poor souls usually had a lot of aggression directed at them in the family system, and, as a result, have very strong emotional reactions. I have the quincunx between Moon and Mars, and I get an upset stomach at the slightest hint of stress. Suppertime arguments were quite frequent as I was growing up.

Mercury in hard aspect with Mars produces a disputative person who will take exception with anything that you say. Here, the anger in the *shadow* is verbal and while these souls are extremely glib and mentally quick, they can drive others to madness with a headstrong and contrary demeanor. I have observed clients with these aspects usually coming from family systems with many siblings, and where the individual had to verbally spar with the brothers and sisters to be accepted.

Venus in hard aspect to Mars produces a sad condition wherein the individual directs anger at those closest to him or her. While these souls would never think of yelling at a waitress or at a gas station attendant, they have no problem unloading on their spouse, children, or closest friends. There is often an irritable nature, social impatience, and a surprising forcefulness with friends and family.

To transform darkness into Light when one struggles with *shadow* issues related to Mars' specific pattern of anger, one must turn the poison on oneself. With the same combative aggressiveness often directed at others, these souls must perform surgery on themselves, relentlessly attacking their inner demons until subdued.

In relationships where synastry or composite chart squares or oppositions with Mars exist, couples need to make friends with anger, developing a sense of humor about it. It is usually for the best if these couples take a southern Mediterranean approach: yell at each other periodically, then passionately kiss and make up. A transformational relationship means just that—one is forever changed by loving another soul. Blockages in the *shadow* can run so deep that it takes the power of anger and passion to penetrate the veils, reaching the truth at the core of the soul.

Saturn's stressful aspects: [Virtues = patience; responsibility; character; prudence]
   a) fearfully inhibited   d) rigidity, control
   b) overly self-reliant   e) suppression, repression
   c) overly self-disciplined   f) anger turned inward = depression

☉ ♄ Self-esteem, perfectionism, self-criticism, low self-confidence

☽ ♄ Defensiveness, fear of criticism, lonely childhood, depression

☿ ♄ Rigid opinions, inferiority complexes, intellectual self-doubt

♀ ♄ Fear of closeness or vulnerability, difficulty expressing affection, armored

♂ ♄ Fear of self-assertion, sexual inhibitions, repressed anger *(stuffs it)*

Anger pattern: *Slow boil, holds it in until unbearable, then explodes with pent-up rage.*

Those born with the personal planets in hard aspect with Saturn face a journey of transformation on which they must convert rigid repression and fearful inhibition into patience, personal responsibility, maturity of character, and prudent actions. The anger pattern associated with Saturn is one that is like a slow boil, where the person holds anger simmering inside, then explodes with pent-up rage. I must say that these aspects are the hardest on human health, as anger turned inward causes not only mental depression, but also physical ailments such as arthritis, gallstones and spleen disease, all of which are Saturn-ruled. Releasing resentments is the key.

Healing of the *shadow* associated with Saturn requires a soul to overcome a lonely childhood devoid of affection and carefree playfulness. These individuals need to accept the fact that they have a melancholic temperament, and that there is nothing wrong with this. Taking time out when with family members, going off to be alone for awhile, and learning to appreciate that lonely, soulful place inside is essential.

I have observed that even the sextiles and trines to Saturn produce these feelings.

Usually on the receiving end of much criticism, especially from parents or teachers, these souls have to go inside of the *shadow* and make peace with their natural gift of discernment and critical thinking. Self-doubt is nearly always present, and low self-esteem and a lack of confidence plague these poor souls well into midlife. The author has a Venus-Saturn conjunction, and knows this psychic territory well. I have only felt good about myself since becoming an author, as accomplishments are ruled by Saturn and represent the transformation of this darkness into the Light.

As with Mars, those born with the Sun in quincunx or opposition with retrograde Saturn will struggle the most with these karmic patterns contained in the *shadow*. Past life factors exert a strong hold over the soul. Psychotherapy is not always effective in healing the personal armoring, fears of criticism, and perfectionism. I have observed that the antidote to this *shadow* is found through Saturn's rulership of the positive sign, Aquarius. When these souls involve themselves in groups and volunteer work in the community, they are the happiest and become transformed. A natural inclination for viewing reality as a hierarchy favors church involvement.

In relationships where synastry or composite chart conjunctions, oppositions or squares with Saturn exist, couples sometimes need to express affection formally, such as giving a greeting card that says *"I love you."* The healing of the *shadow* can occur in these relationships when appropriate boundaries are strictly maintained. Each individual, feeling safe within formal dimensions of love after a childhood with severe criticism, can then slowly emerge and regenerate their spontaneity.

Uranus' stressful aspects: [Virtues = innovation; originality; romanticism; intelligence]
    a) restless impatience   d) extremism
    b) willfulness   e) self-centeredness
    c) rebelliousness   f) anger toward any restrictions

☉ ♅ Excitable, unpredictable, self-centered, dislikes routine, erratic
☽ ♅ Inflexibility, difficulty adjusting to change, restlessness, nervous irritation
☿ ♅ Conversational impatience, high strung, nervous, eccentric *"know it alls"*
♀ ♅ Insensitivity, coldness, self-centeredness, fear of commitment
♂ ♅ Excitability, impatience, extremism, willfulness, wants own way

Anger pattern: Impatient irritation, self-centered annoyance, unpredictable reactions.

Individuals with Uranus in hard aspect to the personal planets face the challenge of transforming feelings of alienation, self-centeredness, rebellious willfulness, and perverted extremism into constructive innovation, original thinking, romantic risk-taking, and using their God-given intelligence for the awakening of others. Anger patterns associated with Uranus are an impatient irritation, a self-centered annoyance with all restrictions or limits, and unpredictable violent reactions if others try to control or confine the person in any way. I have observed that these individuals[79] experience life as if everyone else around them is functioning in slow motion, moving at a pace agonizingly beneath their high strung mental bandwidth.

Healing of the *shadow* associated with Uranus requires these souls to commit their lives to intellectual work, such as writing, lecturing or teaching, that reaches into the minds of others and awakens them to higher truths. This will take some effort as these souls are often content existing in their mental world of extreme ideas, looking at society as being full of sedated sheep who cannot think for themselves.

There is a coldness toward others that is found in these individuals who have the hard aspects from the personal planets to Uranus. I have observed that these souls have past life memories of having lived during times of advanced consciousness on Earth, such as during the Atlantis era, and are literally appalled at the low levels of human spiritual development predominant in society during this current epoch. It appears that the karma in this lifetime is to heal the Uranus *shadow* through an eradication of attitudinal cynicism, replacing that with creativity and originality.

As with Mars or Saturn, those born with the Sun in quincunx or opposition with retrograde Uranus will struggle the most with the karmic patterns contained in the *shadow*. A softening of the soul ideally takes place gradually over the lifetime. At secondary progressed sextiles or trines from the Sun to Uranus is usually when a soul who was born with the natal hard aspects is able to transform these energies. My mother, who was born with a Virgo Sun opposite Uranus retrograde in Pisces reached her progressed trine in 1977 at the age of 55. She became a grandmother in 1978 for the first time when my nephew was born, and softened considerably then.

In relationships with synastry or composite conjunctions, oppositions or squares to Uranus there are often many separations and abrupt endings. I have personally experienced the composite Sun-Uranus square in at least three major relationships and I must say that, realistically, these unions show the karma of each individual being changed by the relationship, but not destined to remain together over time. A freeing of the soul takes place, but this usually comes amidst stressful instability.

Pluto's stressful aspects: [Virtues = depth; passion; analytical skills; insight]

   a) compulsively controlling   d) abuse of power
   b) willfulness   e) volcanic eruptions
   c) ruthlessness   f) immediate escalation to rage

   ☉ ♇ Secretive, willful, intense, ruthless, demanding, controlling

   ☽ ♇ Compulsive reactions, fear of loss, hypersensitivity, intense emotions

   ☿ ♇ Compulsive talking, opinionated, forceful expression, fearful suspicions

   ♀ ♇ Judgmental, jealous, possessive, impersonal, attraction-repulsion

   ♂ ♇ Cruelty, abuse of power, compulsive willfulness, sexual domination

Anger pattern: Explosions of rage, intense emotional upheavals, violent intimidation.

The souls born with personal planets in hard aspect with Pluto inherit lifetimes of transformation wherein compulsive and destructive urges must transmute into the passionate pursuit of meaningful work, and the development of insight and depth. The anger pattern associated with Pluto is one where there are explosions of rage, intense emotional upheavals, and the use of violent intimidation to regain control. These aspects produce behaviors that are not only shocking to those who love the individuals who have them, but also to the individuals themselves as it may feel as if one is possessed by demons when erupting into intense fits of rage and anger.

Healing of the *shadow* associated with Pluto demands that the soul achieve self-mastery in this lifetime, learning how to harness intense forces within that are on the edge of spinning out of control. This perhaps is the most difficult anger pattern to overcome, as it is usually accompanied by severe childhood trauma and abuse. I believe that spiritual surrender, rather than psychotherapy, is needed for healing the Plutonian *shadow*. This may take the form of a conversion experience, or of a psychic meltdown (like a nervous breakdown) in order to truly redeem the soul.

With both my Sun and chart ruler, Mercury, in square with Pluto, I have wrestled with these demons all of my life. It is as if there is this incredible power buried in the core of the soul, but it is somehow contaminated, and needs a purification to be fully used with others in the most beneficial and effective way. Certainly, *peeling the onion* is an apt metaphor for those of us who possess these natal aspects.

The natures of those with stressful aspects to Pluto are secretive, intense, ruthless, demanding and controlling. Often referred to as ticking time bombs with legs, souls with these aspects are usually prodded and goaded by other children when they are young, as if the other kids sense the magnetism and power within and want to feel it come exploding out. Mothers and fathers of children who have these aspects need special parenting skills—firm discipline while not crushing the willful spirit.

As with the other planets, those born with the Sun in quincunx or opposition with a retrograde Pluto have very hard work cut out for themselves in this lifetime. The waxing square from Pluto to the Sun occurs about ten days before the retrograde station, while the waning square from Pluto to the Sun comes about ten days after the direct station of Pluto. When any of these aspects are found in the natal chart, the astrologer knows that deep personal loss has been written into the life script. This loss is part of the healing of the Plutonian *shadow,* as it appears that only pain can penetrate the ruthlessness and willfulness of souls with these aspects.

In relationships with synastry or composite conjunctions, oppositions or squares to Pluto a pronounced intensity is found with the couple. If this energy can be put into creativity, a business, self-employment goals, or otherwise channeled into constructive pursuits, it can hold a couple together for years unless control issues sink the relationship. In the case of Farrow and Allen's composite opposition of the Moon to Pluto, astrologers can see how these energies can also manifest with sexual improprieties, hateful cruelty, suspicion, broken trust, and bitter endings. I would say that Pluto pushes couples to the edge to either transform or break up.

In summary, the emotion of anger is part and parcel of any relationship. Astrology can define four distinct patterns of anger through the stressful aspects with Mars, Saturn, Uranus or Pluto. It is important to know that anger is a secondary emotion with primary states of hurt or fear preceding it. Working with clients with anger issues, astrologers can be of helpful service by describing the specific aspects that underpin their anger, and by recommending positive virtues as an antidote.

The Midpoint Vector of Natal or Composite Squares

Of all the aspects, the 90° square is responsible for the build-up of internal tension and stress. Unlike the 180° opposition, defined by C.E.O. Carter as a *passive force*, squares are highly motivational, dynamic and driven. However, as with all active forces, an outlet for energy release is required, or a rupture of its container occurs. The square aspect is akin to a tea kettle, where boiling water needs to release its steam or blow up the canister. Can astrologers specify the dynamics of squares?

Yes, and it is accomplished by investigating the midpoint vector of any square. For each of these aspects, a line can be drawn from the degree of the near midpoint to the degree of the far midpoint. This vector slices the square right through its heart and informs the astrologer, through the two degree symbols, of its peculiar nature. The near midpoint, I have observed, is the release point of tension generated by the square. The far midpoint is where the soul learns self-control and emotional poise.

An aspect configuration called a Minor T-Square is an ideal illustration of these midpoints. In this three planet pattern, two are in square and a third planet occupies the near midpoint of the other two planets.

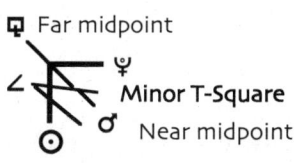

The aspect configuration shown is the author's natal Sun-Pluto square with Mars at its near midpoint. Mars thus forms 45° octile aspects with the Sun and Pluto. In my case, Mars occupies the exact degree of the midpoint, but this is not always so. In some nativities with Minor T-Squares, astrologers will find that the third planet does not exactly occupy the near midpoint degree. In these cases, the exact degree of the near midpoint must be calculated separately. The astrologer also sees that a far midpoint degree exists that is 135° away from each planet in square. It is rare to find a planet in this degree, but it does occasionally occur. Most rare of all is a nativity with a pair of planets in opposition that exactly occupy the midpoint of two different planets in square. I have only seen this a few times in my career.

Regardless of whether or not a planet(s) occupies the near or far midpoint of any square, the important calculation required for this technique is the pair of polar opposite degrees that occupy the exact midpoint vector of any square.

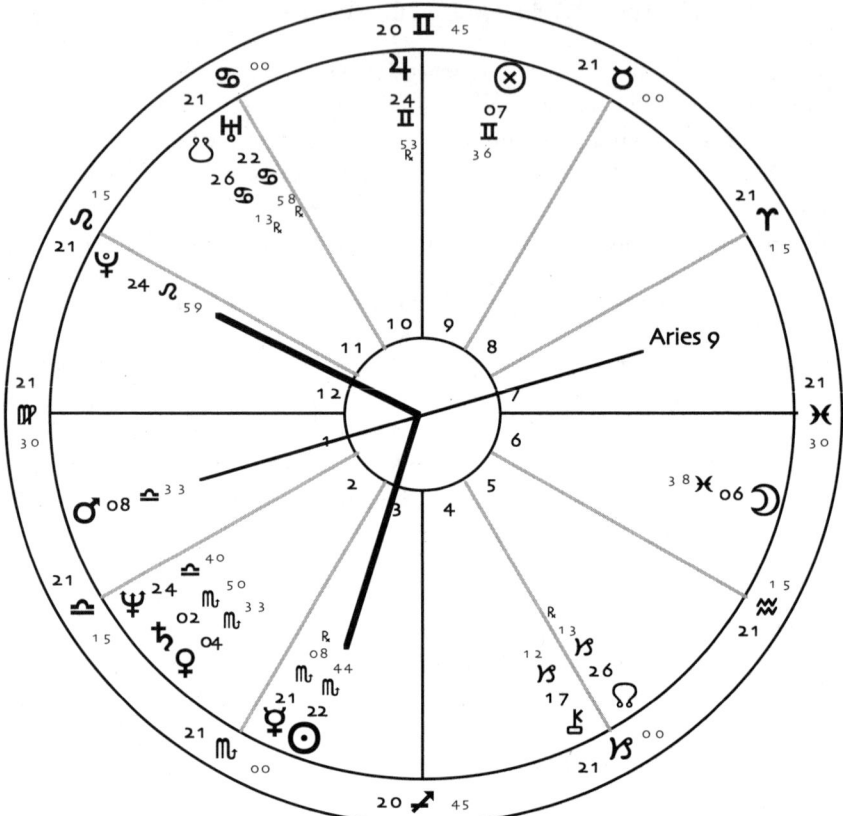

This is the nativity of the author, showing his Sun-Pluto square with Mars at its exact near midpoint, Libra 9. Directly opposite is an unoccupied degree, Aries 9. This far midpoint degree holds the key to development of self-control and poise, whereas the near midpoint degree is the release point of tension generated by the square. When I was a younger man, you can imagine how my tea kettle boiled over.

From Charubel, Aries 9:

> *A straight road, going in a direct line up to a point from which lead a number of branch roads, parting in four different directions. There is a finger-post which points but one way—the primal way, the direct one, alluded to.*

> *This denotes one who will miss his way in life, but who will eventually recover, and will become a teacher of others, or may prove a reformer, either as a public speaker or writer.*

The degree symbol for the far midpoint of any square holds the key to its control and ultimate success. The symbol for the near midpoint of any square illustrates how a soul will have to release stress and tension from these dynamic aspects. If a third planet occupies this degree, such as in my case, it will play a leading role in this process. For me, the independence (Mars) of self-employment has been crucial. I must say that the symbolism for Aries 9 certainly tells the story of my life. It may also interest the reader to examine the degree symbol from Charubel for Libra 9:

> *A man standing on the top of a high mountain; on the one side a perpendicular rock; he is standing near this precipice with a red flag in his hand, which he is waving by way of signalling a promiscuous crowd, who appear to be rushing on horseback at a gallop towards this rock.*
>
> *Denotes one who will be endowed with great powers of discernment, much forethought. One able to detect a fault where another would see nothing wrong. An excellent critic, and may become a proficient analyst.*

This midpoint vector technique can also be employed to assess composite chart squares. This is the composite for the USA and President George W. Bush:

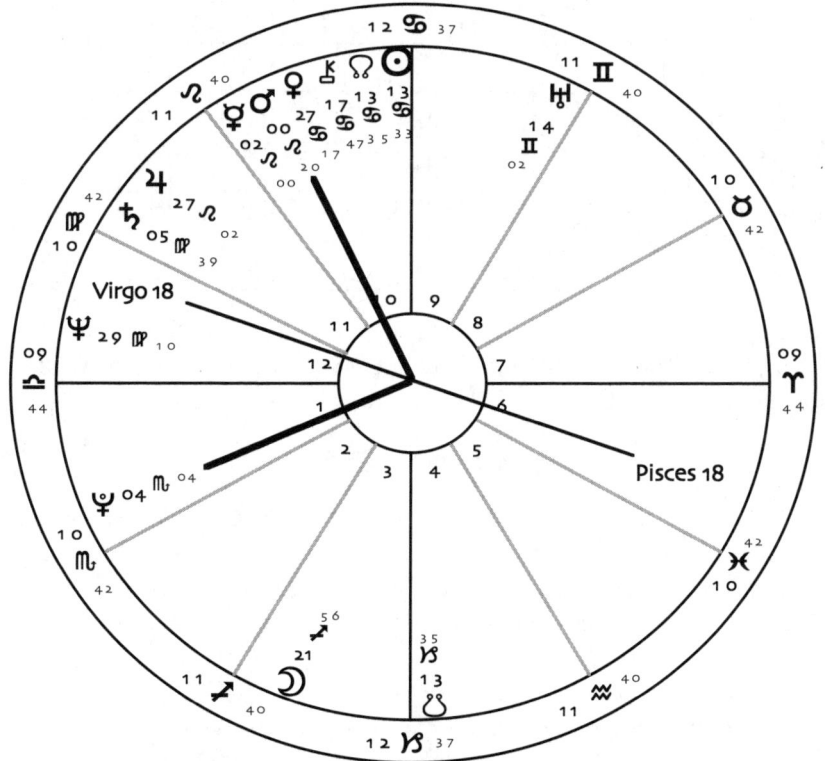

A key aspect is the violent Mars-Pluto square with an orb of 03° 44'. Mars rules the 7th house of open enemies, symbolizing the War on Terrorism declared by this president after the 9/11 attacks. Mars also rules the 2nd house of the nation's economy and this president presided over the largest budget deficit in U.S. history.

Midpoint & Arc Table

	☉	☽	☿	♀	♂	♃	♄	♅	♆	♇	MC	AS	IC	DS	☊
☉		02 ♎ 44	22 ♋ 46	20 ♋ 25	21 ♋ 56	05 ♌ 17	09 ♌ 36	28 ♊ 47	21 ♌ 21	08 ♍ 48	13 ♋ 05	26 ♌ 38	13 ♎ 05	26 ♉ 38	13 ♋ 34
☽	158 23		11 ♎ 58	09 ♎ 37	11 ♎ 08	24 ♎ 29	28 ♎ 47	17 ♓ 59	10 ♏ 33	28 ♏ 00	02 ♎ 17	15 ♏ 50	02 ♑ 17	15 ♒ 50	02 ♎ 46
☿	018 27	139 55		29 ♋ 39	01 ♌ 10	14 ♌ 31	18 ♌ 50	08 ♋ 01	00 ♍ 35	18 ♍ 02	22 ♋ 19	05 ♍ 52	22 ♎ 19	05 ♊ 52	22 ♋ 48
♀	013 44	144 38	004 ☌ 42		28 ♋ 49	12 ♌ 10	16 ♌ 28	05 ♋ 40	28 ♌ 14	15 ♍ 41	19 ♋ 57	03 ♍ 31	19 ♎ 57	03 ♊ 31	20 ♋ 26
♂	016 47	141 35	001 ☌ 40	003 ☌ 02		13 ♌ 41	17 ♌ 59	07 ♋ 11	29 ♌ 45	17 ♍ 12	21 ♋ 29	05 ♍ 02	21 ♎ 29	05 ♊ 02	21 ♋ 58
♃	043 ∠ 29	114 △ 54	025 01	029 ⚺ 44	026 41		01 ♍ 20	20 ♋ 32	13 ♍ 06	00 ♎ 33	04 ♌ 50	18 ♍ 23	04 ♏ 50	18 ♊ 23	05 ♌ 18
♄	052 06	106 17	033 38	038 21	035 18	008 36		24 ♋ 50	17 ♍ 24	04 ♎ 51	09 ♌ 08	22 ♍ 41	09 ♏ 08	22 ♊ 41	09 ♌ 37
♅	029 ⚺ 30	172 ☍ 05	047 58	043 ∠ 15	046 ∠ 18	073 00	081 37		06 ♌ 36	24 ♌ 03	28 ♊ 20	11 ♌ 53	28 ♓ 20	11 ♉ 53	28 ♊ 48
♆	075 37	082 □ 45	057 ⚹ 09	061 ⚹ 52	058 ⚹ 50	032 08	023 31	105 08		16 ♎ 37	20 ♌ 54	04 ♎ 27	20 ♏ 54	04 ♋ 27	21 ♌ 23
♇	110 31	047 ∠ 52	092 □ 03	096 46	093 □ 43	067 01	058 ⚹ 24	140 01	034 53		08 ♍ 21	21 ♎ 54	08 ♐ 21	21 ♑ 54	08 ♍ 49
MC	000 ☌ 55	159 18	019 22	014 40	017 42	044 ∠ 24	053 01	028 ⚺ 35	076 32	111 26		26 ♌ 11	12 ♎ 37	26 ♉ 11	13 ♋ 06
AS	086 □ 11	072 Q 11	067 43	072 Q 26	069 24	042 42	034 05	115 △ 42	010 34	024 19	087 □ 06		26 ♏ 11	09 ♋ 44	26 ♌ 40
IC	179 ☍ 04	020 41	160 37	165 19	162 17	135 ⚼ 35	126 58	151 ⚻ 24	103 27	068 33	180 ☍ 00	092 □ 53		26 ♒ 11	13 ♎ 06
DS	093 □ 48	107 48	112 16	107 33	110 35	137 17	145 54	064 17	169 25	155 40	092 □ 53	180 ☍ 00	087 □ 06		26 ♉ 40
☊	000 ☌ 02	158 20	018 25	013 42	016 44	043 ∠ 26	052 03	029 ⚺ 33	075 34	110 28	000 ☌ 57	086 □ 09	179 ☍ 02	093 □ 50	

The Midpoint & Arc Table shows that Mars-Pluto square and its near midpoint of 17° Virgo 12'.[80] The crucial far midpoint of this square is Pisces 18, the key for its ultimate success or failure. Sepharial's translation of *La Volasfera* for Pisces 18:

A horse and its rider falling at a fence.

This symbol denotes one whose career will be broken either in some foreign land or in the pursuit of an enterprise that is strange and foreign to his nature and capacity. He will be adventuresome and headstrong, and will pursue his course regardless of consequences. His taste for outdoor sports will be prominent and will lead him into dangers, especially if he should follow equestrian pleasures. To some who are born under this degree calamity will accrue from transgression of the law. Let all such keep their passions in subjection by the power of the will and bridle their desires. It is a degree of CATASTROPHE.

Chapter Nine

Mirror Degree Synastry

As the Sun appears to travel through the 360 degrees of the Zodiac, it reaches four crucial points in its annual journey. The Solstices and Equinoxes that occur at the Cardinal Ingress degrees of 0° Capricorn—0° Cancer and 0° Aries—0° Libra are not just the beginning of each of the four seasons, but also key turning points in the Sun's declination. The measurement of the Sun's distance above or below the celestial equator reaches its maximum at the Solstices, and at the Equinoxes the ecliptic, or the apparent path of the Sun, intersects the equator.

This astronomical phenomenon creates pairs of degrees in the Zodiac that are equidistant from the Solstices and Equinoxes, and reflect the two days of the year when the Sun is in identical declination. A week before the Summer Solstice,[81] for example, the Sun is in the 24th degree of Gemini and at 23° N 16' declination. A week after the Summer Solstice, the Sun is in the 7th degree of Cancer, and is again at 23° N 16' declination, after having peaked at 23° 27' of maximum declination.[82]

One way to visualize this is to calculate a nativity using Natural Houses.

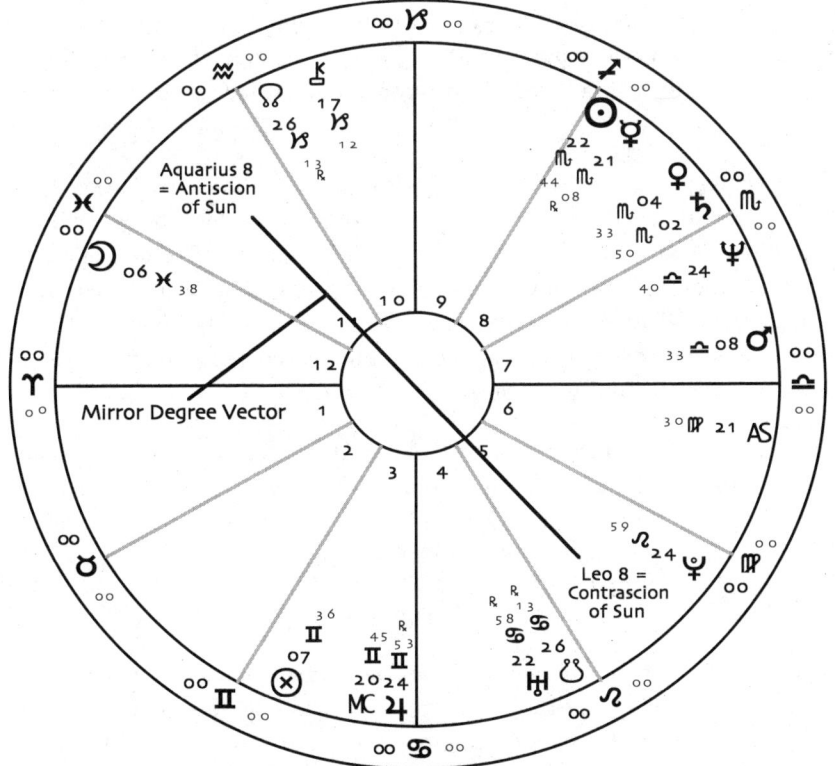

The chart on the previous page is the nativity of the author erected with Natural Houses. This places 0° Aries on the Ascendant, 0° Cancer on the IC, 0° Libra on the Descendant, and 0° Capricorn on the MC. If the reader can visualize folding this chartwheel in half with the vertical meridian as the seam (creating what I call the *taco shell Zodiac*), one can picture the 180 degrees along the circumference of the left hemisphere of the wheel perfectly overlaying onto the degrees along the right side. Each of these pairs of degrees are the antiscion (plural = antiscia), or Solstice Point of the other. The pairs of degrees are thus either equidistant from 0° Cancer, or from 0° Capricorn. I refer to these Zodiac pairs as *Mirror Degrees*.

Similarly, if one visualizes folding the chartwheel in half with the horizontal axis as the seam, the 180 degrees along the circumference of the upper half of the wheel will perfectly overlay onto the degrees around the bottom half. Each of these pairs of degrees are the contrascion (plural = contrascia), or Equinox Point, of the other. These pairs of degrees are thus either equidistant from 0° Aries, or from 0° Libra.

Each degree of the Zodiac therefore is linked to two other sensitive degrees, its antiscion and contrascion. These two degrees are always the exact opposite of the other, and produce what I call a *Mirror Degree Vector*. In the author's nativity on the preceding page this vector is shown. The author's Sun is in the 23rd degree of Scorpio—its antiscion is the 8th degree of Aquarius (equidistant to 0° Capricorn), and its contrascion is the opposing 8th degree of Leo (equidistant from 0° Libra). I have observed that progressed conjunctions to the Mirror Degrees of the natal Luminaries are very powerful, as well as outer planet transits over these degrees.

In this chapter, I will discuss how these Mirror Degrees can be used in synastry to identify spiritual connections in relationship that are hidden from view if using conventional synastry technique alone. It is quite common to find the natal Lights, planets or angles in one nativity having exact-to-the-degree conjunctions to a partner's mirror degrees. If a synastry conjunction is found from Person A's natal Moon to the mirror degree of Person B's Neptune, a conjunction also exists from Person B's natal Neptune to the mirror degree of Person A's natal Moon.[83]

I will introduce DNA theory, showing Mirror Degrees as an astrological Double Helix. I believe that genetic characteristics are transferred from parents to their children through mirror degree synastry conjunctions between the spouses. I will also include statistics from my research into Solstice and Equinox Point synastry.

Solstice Points (Antiscia)

When working with mirror degrees, astrologers must familiarize themselves with the six pairs of Zodiac signs comprising the antiscion degrees, or Solstice Points. One must also get in the habit of equating the degrees of one sign in ascending order with the degrees of its mirror sign in descending order, e.g., 1 = 30, 2 = 29, 3 =

28, etc. As in working with the Sabian Symbols, always round up to the next higher degree. A planet at 22° Scorpio 44' is thus in the 23rd degree of Scorpio.[84]

Solstice Points

Capricorn	Sagittarius
Aquarius	Scorpio
Pisces	Libra
Aries	Virgo
Taurus	Leo
Gemini	Cancer

The astrologer may also visualize a chartwheel with natural houses to perceive the symmetrical pairs of signs. Houses 9 and 10 make a pair of solstice point signs, as do houses 8—11; 7—12; 1—6; 2—5; and 3—4. Each of these pairs of houses are equidistant from the horoscopic vertical axis. The following table shows the Solstice Point degrees of the Zodiac (Antiscion).

♑	♐	♒	♏	♓	♎	♈	♍	♉	♌	♊	♋
1	30	1	30	1	30	1	30	1	30	1	30
2	29	2	29	2	29	2	29	2	29	2	29
3	28	3	28	3	28	3	28	3	28	3	28
4	27	4	27	4	27	4	27	4	27	4	27
5	26	5	26	5	26	5	26	5	26	5	26
6	25	6	25	6	25	6	25	6	25	6	25
7	24	7	24	7	24	7	24	7	24	7	24
8	23	8	23	8	23	8	23	8	23	8	23
9	22	9	22	9	22	9	22	9	22	9	22
10	21	10	21	10	21	10	21	10	21	10	21
11	20	11	20	11	20	11	20	11	20	11	20
12	19	12	19	12	19	12	19	12	19	12	19
13	18	13	18	13	18	13	18	13	18	13	18
14	17	14	17	14	17	14	17	14	17	14	17
15	16	15	16	15	16	15	16	15	16	15	16
16	15	16	15	16	15	16	15	16	15	16	15
17	14	17	14	17	14	17	14	17	14	17	14
18	13	18	13	18	13	18	13	18	13	18	13
19	12	19	12	19	12	19	12	19	12	19	12
20	11	20	11	20	11	20	11	20	11	20	11
21	10	21	10	21	10	21	10	21	10	21	10
22	9	22	9	22	9	22	9	22	9	22	9
23	8	23	8	23	8	23	8	23	8	23	8
24	7	24	7	24	7	24	7	24	7	24	7
25	6	25	6	25	6	25	6	25	6	25	6
26	5	26	5	26	5	26	5	26	5	26	5
27	4	27	4	27	4	27	4	27	4	27	4
28	3	28	3	28	3	28	3	28	3	28	3
29	2	29	2	29	2	29	2	29	2	29	2
30	1	30	1	30	1	30	1	30	1	30	1

Equinox Points (Contrascia)

A second arrangement of the Zodiac into symmetrical halves also exists. Here, the degrees that are equidistant from 0° Aries and 0° Libra are paired into Equinox Points, or Contrascion degrees. To visualize these signs through the natural house chartwheel, remember houses 1—12; 2—11; 3—10; 4—9; 5—8; and 6—7. The signs that comprise the Equinox Points are:

Equinox Points

Aries	Pisces
Taurus	Aquarius
Gemini	Capricorn
Cancer	Sagittarius
Leo	Scorpio
Virgo	Libra

The following table shows the Equinox Point degrees of the Zodiac (Contrascion).

♈	♓	♉	♒	♊	♑	♋	♐	♌	♏	♍	♎
1	30	1	30	1	30	1	30	1	30	1	30
2	29	2	29	2	29	2	29	2	29	2	29
3	28	3	28	3	28	3	28	3	28	3	28
4	27	4	27	4	27	4	27	4	27	4	27
5	26	5	26	5	26	5	26	5	26	5	26
6	25	6	25	6	25	6	25	6	25	6	25
7	24	7	24	7	24	7	24	7	24	7	24
8	23	8	23	8	23	8	23	8	23	8	23
9	22	9	22	9	22	9	22	9	22	9	22
10	21	10	21	10	21	10	21	10	21	10	21
11	20	11	20	11	20	11	20	11	20	11	20
12	19	12	19	12	19	12	19	12	19	12	19
13	18	13	18	13	18	13	18	13	18	13	18
14	17	14	17	14	17	14	17	14	17	14	17
15	16	15	16	15	16	15	16	15	16	15	16
16	15	16	15	16	15	16	15	16	15	16	15
17	14	17	14	17	14	17	14	17	14	17	14
18	13	18	13	18	13	18	13	18	13	18	13
19	12	19	12	19	12	19	12	19	12	19	12
20	11	20	11	20	11	20	11	20	11	20	11
21	10	21	10	21	10	21	10	21	10	21	10
22	9	22	9	22	9	22	9	22	9	22	9
23	8	23	8	23	8	23	8	23	8	23	8
24	7	24	7	24	7	24	7	24	7	24	7
25	6	25	6	25	6	25	6	25	6	25	6
26	5	26	5	26	5	26	5	26	5	26	5
27	4	27	4	27	4	27	4	27	4	27	4
28	3	28	3	28	3	28	3	28	3	28	3
29	2	29	2	29	2	29	2	29	2	29	2
30	1	30	1	30	1	30	1	30	1	30	1

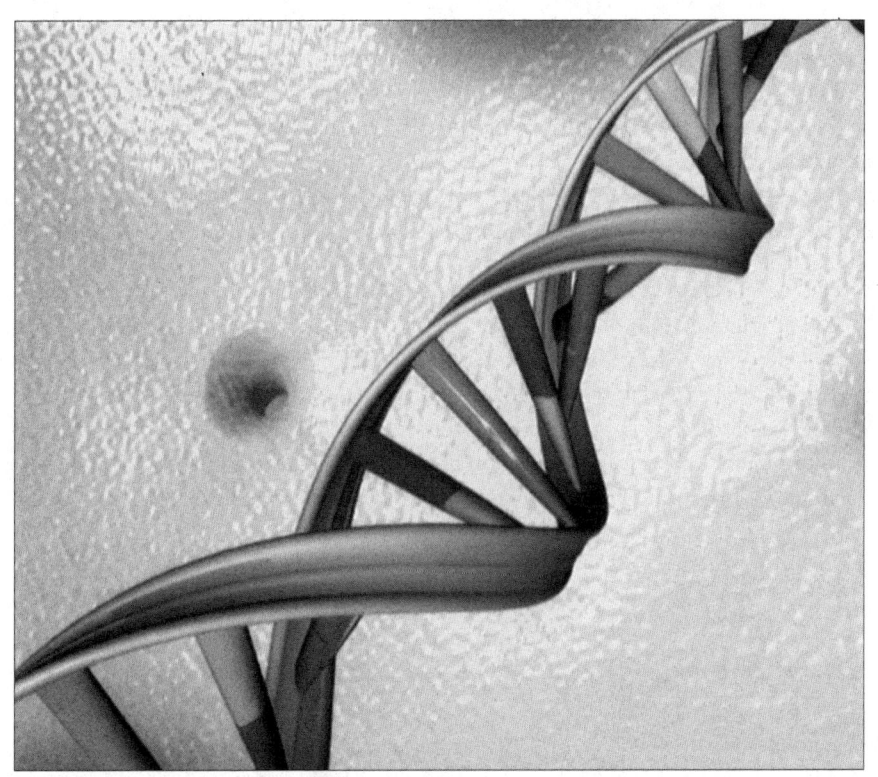

The Astrological Double Helix and DNA Theory [85]

On 2 April 1953, with Mercury stationary direct in Pisces at the finger of a Yod, and a Saturn-Neptune conjunction in Libra sextile to Pluto in Leo as its base, two scientists, James Watson & Francis Crick, working at Cambridge University in the UK, published a paper, "Molecular Structure of Nucleic Acids." They proposed a radical structure for Deoxyribose Nucleic Acid (DNA), which consisted of two helical chains, each coiled round the same axis. Perpendicular to this central axis, in Watson and Crick's theoretical model, were strands of nitrogenous bases. Two of the chemical bases, Adenine and Thymine, only bonded with one another; two others, Guanine and Cytosine, similarly bonded exclusively with each other.

Also that year, Uranus and Neptune approached the 270° waning square of their 172-year cycle. This radical breakthrough in understanding of the human chemical architecture was brought into visible form by the Saturn-Neptune conjunction, and the ability of Watson and Crick to think outside the box was a gift of Uranus. By the Uranus-Neptune conjunction in February 1993, a Human Genome project was underway to map a complete set of human chromosomes, comprised of about 30,000 genes made up of three billion chemical nucleotides labeled C, G, A or T. Is there also an astrological equivalent to this chemical design of a human being?

Yes, and it is my belief that an astrological counterpart to DNA can be found in Antiscia and Contrascia degrees. Genetic characteristics transmitted from parents to their children may possibly be traced to the synastry conjunctions between one parent's natal planet, and a planet in its Antiscion in the second parent's nativity. Can astrology illustrate the metaphysical underpinnings of this conceptual model for the Double Helix? Is this model limited to genetics, or can karma be seen, too?

I have contemplated the theoretical underpinnings of an astrological equivalent to the Double Helix. A hologram exactly replicating the atomic structure of DNA should therefore exist on the macrocosmic level. I believe that this pattern can be perceived in a figure-eight curve forming around the central axis of an Analemma, which is a plotting of the Sun's position in the sky at regular daily intervals. This geometric figure produces an equation of time, as well as tracking the annual solar declination from Winter Solstice to Summer Solstice, and then back again.[86]

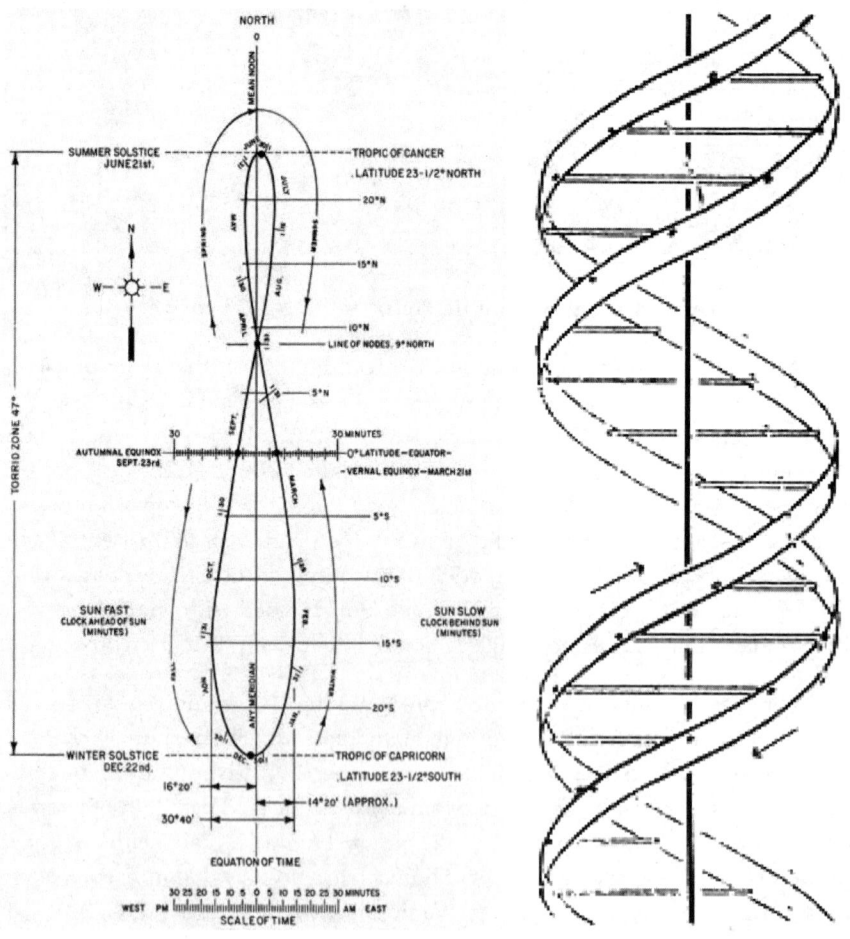

Watson and Crick's 1953 theory about DNA structure expounds that each helical chain ran in opposite directions. For astrologers, it is a simple perceptual leap to visualize how the annual journey of the Sun traces a pattern identical to the structure of DNA. A link between macrocosm and microcosm is found in ascending and descending declination of the Sun. Each degree of the Zodiac from Winter Solstice to Summer Solstice represents the helical chain in its ascending journey, while each degree from Summer to Winter Solstice is the helical chain in its descending journey. Solstice Points, or Antiscia, are identical to the perpendicular strands of nitrogenous bases bonding in exclusive pairs. It is my belief that this solar declinational model is the macrocosm to DNA's Double Helix microcosm.[87]

This image shows an Analemma as displayed on a *Cram's Imperial World Globe*. Earth's equator is seen to intersect the figure-eight curve at the Equinoxes, and the top reach of the figure-eight depicts the Summer Solstice at the Tropic of Cancer, while its lowest point is the Winter Solstice at the Tropic of Capricorn (23° S 27'). The ecliptic, or the apparent path of the Sun, is seen to intersect the equator at the International Date Line in the Pacific Ocean; this being the Autumnal Equinox.[88]

I have not yet formulated a permanent working theory of how the Antiscia degrees differ from the Contrascia degrees. Just as the Double Helix has four nitrogenous bases bonding in two exclusive pairs, C—G and A—T, it would be only logical if the mirrored pairs of Equinox Point degrees comprised one exclusive bonding, while the mirrored Solstice Point degrees made up the second set of bonded pairs.

This theoretical model for astrology opens a vast window for research into what I call *Genetic Synastry*. I invite the astrological community to go forward with this research. The technique I recommend consists of exact conjunctions from the natal planet of one parent to a planet in the second parent's nativity occupying the former's antiscion or contrascion degree. *The gist is that planetary connections in synastry from one Zodiac degree to its antiscion or contrascion degree show the genetic framework between the mother and father being transferred to their child.*[89]

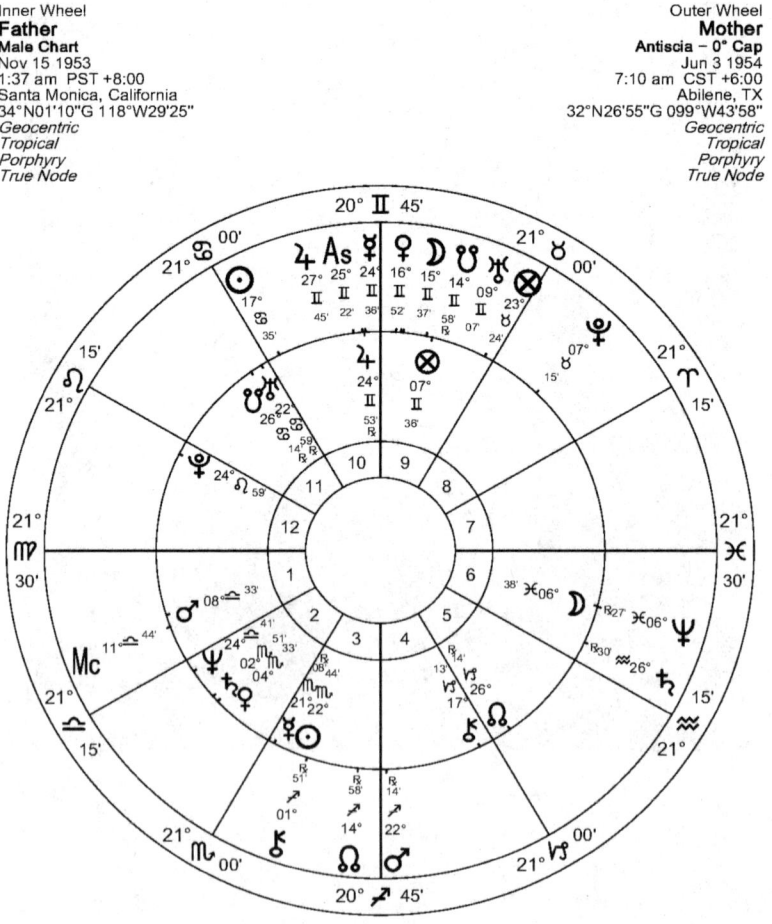

This bi-wheel chart shows the author's nativity in the inner wheel. In the outer wheel are Antiscion degrees of the mother of his older daughter. His natal Moon is in the 7th degree of Pisces, which is the Antiscion of the 24th degree of Libra. His daughter's mother has her natal Neptune at 23° Libra 32' Rx. In a second Mirror Degree synastry conjunction, the author's Jupiter in the 25th degree of Gemini is conjoined with the Antiscion of Mercury in the chart of the daughter's mother. Her natal Mercury at 05° Cancer 24' has its Solstice Point in the 25th degree of Gemini.

Their daughter is a musician who released two CDs by the age of 23, symbolized by an exact Antiscion conjunction to Neptune. She has a melancholic temperament, and is prone to depression, also a Neptunian proclivity. Her Mercury-Jupiter genetic link received from the father and mother is illustrated by the involvement both parents had with an Eastern spiritual path, which resulted in the child being raised as a vegetarian since birth. As a singer-songwriter, her mind has received both the spiritual imprint of the father, and the verbal skills of the mother.

Whether Mirror Degree synastry conjunctions between parents represent genetic links only, or if they additionally symbolize karmic manifestations, is a question unanswered in my mind. Much more research into this Antiscion and Contrascion synastry is required before astrology can definitively state the scope of relevance for this technique. The specific differences between Solstice Point and Equinox Point synastry will require additional research to clarify. To calculate a Mirror Degree bi-wheel chart with your Solar Fire™ program, follow these easy steps:

1. Open both parent's nativities in the "Calculated Charts" opening screen.
2. Click on the mother's natal chart and go to the "Chart" menu.
3. Open menu and select "Harmonic".
4. Under "Chart Type to Generate", select "Antiscia - 0° Cap" and click OK.
5. After being returned to the opening screen, go to the "View" menu.
6. Open menu and select "BiWheel".
7. In "Selected Charts" you will find "Inner Wheel" highlighted.
8. Click the Natal chart of the father; it will become the "Inner Wheel".
9. Click the Antiscia chart for the mother; it will become the "Outer Wheel".
10. Click "View".
11. Scrutinize bi-wheel chart for any exact-to-the-degree conjunctions.
12. These are the *Mirror Degree* conjunctions between the parents.

Existing Theory and Applications of Antiscia and Contrascia

A minority of astrologers are already using Solstice Points and Equinox Points as an interpretive technique. Chief among these practitioners are Horary astrologers. If a malefic, for example, is opposing the degree of a significator's Antiscion in a Horary chart, it is considered improvident to advise the client to act on his or her query at that time. In my experience, this branch of astrology appears to have the largest percentage of practitioners who are familiar with these *Mirror Degrees*.

I have found that planets or angles secondary progressing to the Mirror Degrees of the Luminaries are quite powerful. This includes both the Antiscion degree and the Contrascion degree. For this reason, I advise my readers to become familiar with the *Mirror Degree Vectors* for their natal Sun and Moon. These four degrees will be extremely sensitive to progressed conjunctions. In your author's case, his progressed MC arrived at a conjunction with his natal Sun's Contrascion, Leo 8, when his first book on Progressions began to receive its positive reviews in 1999.

I have also observed that the outer planets, Jupiter through Pluto, transiting over the Antiscion or Contrascion degree of the natal Luminaries will produce major life events, or significant internal shifts in consciousness. When Uranus conjoined the author's Antiscion of his Sun in March 1997, he left an Eastern spiritual path he had been a disciple on since 1978, and returned to his mystical Catholic roots.

I have seen Solar Return planets in Antiscion or Contrascion degrees of the natal Lights or Ascendant result in years with major life changes when no other leading progressions or transits were indicated. While I lectured on the topic in Australia in 2003, a professional astrologer in the audience, unsure of her husband's time of birth, and thus his exact rising degree, found that the Antiscion of her Sun was a degree away from her rectified Ascendant for him. She adjusted the time to create an exact conjunction. These *Mirror Degrees* can thus be used for rectification.

In the United States, there is a group of astrologers in Michigan who have been using Antiscia and Contrascia for many years. Richard J. Smoot, Cynthia Cornell, and Bette Denlinger are some of my Michigan colleagues who have corresponded with me about using this technique. Mr. Smoot, in particular, has his own theory of how Antiscia and Contrascia technique works for his clients.

In response to a research request for data that I sent out on the Internet in August 2002, in which I proposed a *Twin Soul* theory as a basis for how *Mirror Degree* synastry joins two souls in love, Smoot wrote a highly articulate response:

> I've been using Antiscia and Contrascia for many years with amazing results. I've felt it has been "my little secret" for a long time. Even my students and peers think I'm wasting my time. Not so, says I. I've also used "Antiscia Synastry" or "Contrascia Synastry" and it works great. I have a bit of a different result (and theory) about them, which I would love to discuss with you.
>
> Briefly, these points and charts seem to connect us with our inner self, and for lack of a better term, our unconscious self. They represent our motives and intentions and seem to foretell (via transits and progressions to the Antiscia chart) trends and cycles in our life prior to the actual natal chart

events (transits and progressions). It is almost as if a different entity "lives" within us, although more accurately it seems that the collective is at work and is helping us integrate itself with our individual self.

I've found them amazingly accurate in foretelling "premonitions" and "feelings" we get when we "sense" something is about to happen. These charts tell you what those events are. I have one case study (a former boss of mine) where he felt "the need" to get life insurance for himself. He was very impatient, saying he wanted to "protect" his wife, although he was very young, healthy and never sick in his life. He went to the hospital with "indigestion" that lasted 2 days and died there 3 days later with leukemia. He apparently had the cancer only 2 months and did not know it. His wife (of one year) received $250,000. Sad story.

My own research uses them for synastry and supports the natal couples' charts if they are a match in terms of motive and intention to marry, and "inner connections." The Antiscia charts describe the subconscious as another person, and a mate and their Antiscia chart also needs to match. They match in different ways than do natal charts, however, they need to match. Those that don't have the connection appear to be in the relationship for reasons other than personal and, in my view, selfish in motive. The other person may be taken advantage of, or have other motives.

In some respects, I've come to a thought that these charts and the actions within us that they promote are our "guiding lights" and they watch out for us in life. I feel we need to pay attention to them as they know what is in store for us and can help us quell our over-extended egos. I feel that the Antiscia chart can tell us how to shape our ego for integration with the collective unconscious and not be renegades acting out on our own (out of control egotist).

These are some of my brief thoughts and I suspect there are many other ways these charts can be viewed and used. I'm intrigued with your approach and it makes a lot of sense.

One can visualize *Mirror Degrees* as a pattern of elegant symmetry through which the life force energy of the Sun is transmitted to the Zodiac during its annual journey. On its way into human consciousness, solar energy creates pairs of dichotomies. Each possible reality in life, represented by a Zodiac degree, has a *mirrored counterpart.* Astral imprints exist in Antiscia and Contrascia degrees that are symbolic of choices made prior to impending physical manifestation. When *Mirror Degrees* are triggered by synastry, electrical impulses (forewarning) are sent by the soul into the personality. This is perhaps how the "premonitions", to which Smoot refers, get activated on an inner level in unhealthy relationships.

What Smoot has observed in his experience with Antiscia and Contrascia charts appears to parallel my DNA theory. These charts may symbolize the *pre-cognitive wiring* of an individual. There is a metaphysical premise that Spirit manifests into Matter (Sun + Uranus interpenetrating Saturn) in a manner similar to a lightning strike. The spiritual energy flowing into earthly manifestation passes from one electrical polarity to the other (+/- zigzag), imitating the Double Helix of DNA.[90]

Revealing Invisible Synastry from Behind the Veil

This overlay chart has the nativity of Prince Charles in the inner wheel; planets of the late Princess Diana are in the outer wheel.[91] Perhaps the most astrologically analyzed couple of recent times, their synastry has been used often in case studies. One finds the marriage rule referred to on page 50 perfectly illustrated. Diana had Sagittarius rising; her ruler, Jupiter, is conjunct Charles' Descendant to the degree.

Prince Charles
Nov 14 1948 9:14 PM GMT
Buckingham Pal. England
51N19 00W08
Nov 14 1948 21:14:00 GMT
Tropical Porphyry True Node

Second Chart Natal Chart
Princess Diana
Jul 1 1961 18:45:00 GMT

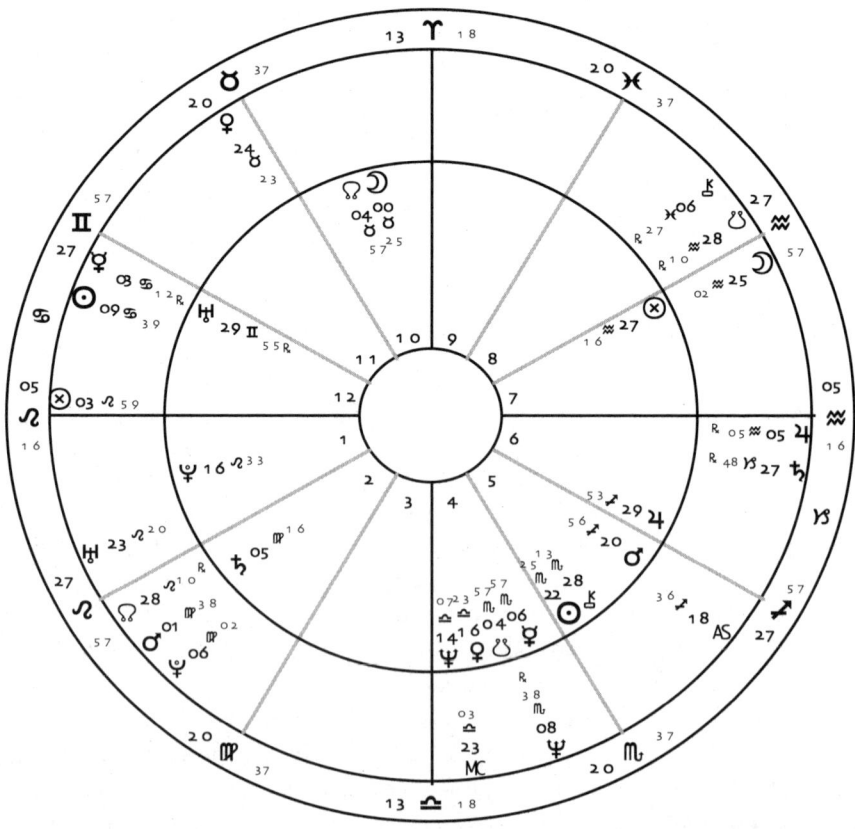

Using conventional synastry technique with a maximum orb of 5°, astrologers find the following key synastric conjunctions:

1. Diana's Moon conjunct Charles' Part of Fortune.
2. Diana's Mercury conjunct Charles' Uranus.
3. Charles' Mercury conjunct Diana's Neptune.
4. Diana's Mars conjunct Charles' Saturn.
5. Charles' Mars conjunct Diana's Ascendant.
6. Diana's Jupiter conjunct Charles' Descendant.
7. Charles' Saturn conjunct Diana's Pluto.
8. Diana's Neptune conjunct Charles' South Node.
9. Diana's Part of Fortune conjunct Charles' Ascendant.

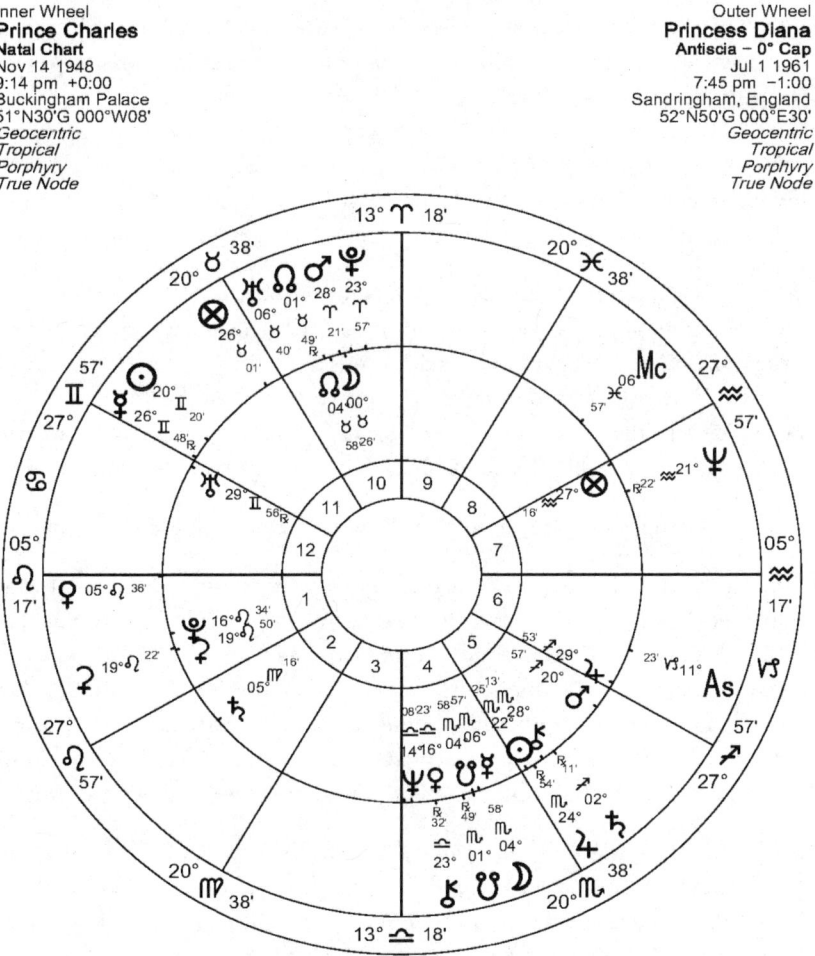

Inner Wheel
Prince Charles
Natal Chart
Nov 14 1948
9:14 pm +0:00
Buckingham Palace
51°N30'G 000°W08'
Geocentric
Tropical
Porphyry
True Node

Outer Wheel
Princess Diana
Antiscia – 0° Cap
Jul 1 1961
7:45 pm −1:00
Sandringham, England
52°N50'G 000°E30'
Geocentric
Tropical
Porphyry
True Node

Every couple has *invisible synastry*—conjunctions forming between natal planets in one nativity and Antiscion or Contrascion degrees of planets in the other chart. This overlay chart again has the nativity of Prince Charles in the inner wheel, but

205

this time the Antiscia chart for Princess Diana is shown in the outer wheel. A planet's Antiscion opposing a spouse's natal planet is the same as the Contrascion degree of that planet being conjunct the spouse's natal planet.

Revealed are the *invisible Mirror Degree synastry conjunctions and oppositions:*

1. Charles' Mars opposite the Antiscion of Diana's Sun.[92]
2. Charles' South Node conjunct the Antiscion of Diana's Moon.[93]
3. Charles' Mercury opposite the Antiscion of Diana's Uranus.[94]
4. Charles' Ascendant conjunct the Antiscion of Diana's Venus.
5. Charles' Ceres conjunct the Antiscion of Diana's Ceres.

Readers may speculate, as I do, about the differences between a standard synastry conjunction and Mirror Degree connections. Charles and Diana's most remarkable Antiscia synastry is the exact-to-the-minute-of-arc conjunction of his natal South Node with the Antiscion of her Moon. The South Node symbolizes what exits our life, in addition to being a powerful degree of past-life connection. The Moon rules the wife, mother, family and children in a man's horoscope. One can only ponder if a soul contract was in place between these two prior to incarnation. The fact that she bore him two sons can be genetically seen in Mars conjunct Sun's Contrascion.

This Moon-South Node conjunction appears to substantiate Smoot's theory about motives and intentions being seen in Antiscia synastry. Diana was accepted by the Royal Family as a wife (Moon) for Charles in order to produce male heirs for the throne. With Charles already emotionally attached to another woman, he and Diana were perhaps not in love, nor completely committed to making the marriage work. Less than honorable intentions thus led to painful losses (South Node).[95]

Using Sabian Symbols with Mirror Degree Synastry

Continuously since the 1890s, astrologers have investigated various sets of degree symbols for the Zodiac. The publication of Alan Leo's Astrological Manual No. 8 in 1898 was the first in recent times. Entitled *The Degrees of the Zodiac Symbolised* by Charubel, this little book also contained a translation by Sepharial of the *La Volasfera* degree symbols, originally divined by Antonio Borelli. In 1925, the great American astrologer, Marc Jones, in collaboration with a gifted clairvoyant, Elsie Wheeler, produced the 360 Sabian Symbols. These are now the most widely used.

Concurrently, first Marc Edmund Jones and later, Dane Rudhyar in the 1930s, began to search for an underlying mathematical structure of the Zodiac. As I wrote in *Volume II - Sabian Aspect Orbs,* each found a repeating sequence of five degree symbols replicating 72 times throughout the Zodiac. Are there other patterns of degrees to be found underpinning the Zodiac? Yes, the Antiscion and Contrascion pairs of degrees also reveal hidden connections through their respective symbols.

When working with the degree symbols for Antiscion or Contrascion, which are relevant? Because Mirror Degrees form vectors from opposing pairs of degrees, I recommend looking at all four. In the previously cited example for Charles and Diana, the relevant natal degrees are Taurus—Scorpio 5 (Charles' Nodal Axis) and Leo—Aquarius 26 (Diana's Moon axis). These two pairs of degrees are the Solstice and Equinox Points, or Antiscion and Contrascion, of one another.

From *Lecture~Lessons* (1931), the Sabian Symbol for Taurus 5:

> *A youthful widow, fresh and soul-cleansed from grief, kneels at a grave to receive the secret of eternal life.*

For Scorpio 5:

> *A massive rocky shore presents its unchanging face of the centuries to the furies and coaxing calms of the sea.*[96]

For Leo 26:

> *A perfect rainbow forms slowly in the summer rain as the sun begins to break through the rather thin cloudbanks.*

For Aquarius 26:

> *The battery man at the automobile service station has his hydrometer in hand, about to inspect a customer's car.*

In these four degree symbols we see both the beauty of Diana (Leo 26), a reference to her death (Taurus 5), possible mechanical problems with the car she was being driven in at the time of her death in Paris (Aquarius 26), and the probable marital demeanor of Charles coping with an emotional and volatile wife (Scorpio 5).

I wrote in *Volume II*, when introducing a radical method for aspect interpretation using Sabian Symbols for distance arcs separating planets, that a marriage of technique and symbolism occurs when using this approach to delineation. I advise astrologers who wish to contemplate the meaning of Mirror Degree synastry connections to meditate on the four Sabian Symbols involved in the conjunction.

It is quite clear to me that each degree of the Zodiac possesses a relationship with the other 359. The pairs of degrees that are each other's Antiscion or Contrascion have a combined symbolic message that is only understood when placed in context of the individual relationship being analyzed. Many of my students and clients have asked me about differences between the Sabian Symbols, Charubel's degree symbols, and Sepharial's translation of *La Volasfera*. My understanding is that all three have relevance. The older sets of symbols, e.g., Charubel and Sepharial, were the essence of the soul during prior lifetimes, especially the Lights and Ascendant.

Research Statistics

In August 2002, when I began the research for this book, I sent out a request on the Internet for volunteers to provide data of themselves, spouses, parents, children, siblings, friends, enemies, employers, or employees. I wanted to research Mirror Degree synastry conjunctions between individuals in all human relationships. I wish to thank the many hundreds who replied with birth data, and who completed a questionnaire containing a list of the Antiscia or Contrascia synastry, and their relevant Sabian Symbols. Many wrote very poignant stories about loved ones.[97]

As was the case with the research project that I undertook for *Volume II*, I had no idea of what to expect. I wound up calculating over 700 individual nativities (plus their Antiscia and Contrascia counterparts), and I analyzed approximately 360 relationships of all possible types. I was looking for the following factors:

1. What percentage of relationships had exact Mirror Degree conjunctions?
2. What percentage of relationships had no Mirror Degree conjunctions?
3. Did conjunctions occur more in spousal or parent-child relationships?
4. Were these conjunctions occurring between the same bodies in each chart?
5. Were these conjunctions occurring between different bodies in each chart?
6. If occurring between the same bodies, which were the most prevalent?
7. What is the ratio of Antiscion to Contrascion conjunctions occurring?
8. Did particular types of relationship have either Antiscion or Contrascion?
9. No orb was allowed. Either a body was in the exact Mirror Degree, or not.

My findings, from 359 total relationships analyzed, were:

1. 314 relationships had exact mirror degree conjunctions (87.5%).
2. 45 relationships were without exact mirror degree conjunctions (12.5%).
3. An even distribution was seen in spousal vs. parent-child synastry.
4. 23% of relationships had same-planet Mirror Degree conjunctions.
5. 77% of relationships had different-planet Mirror Degree conjunctions.
6. Most common same-planet: ASC; Vertex; Juno; Sun; North Node; Chiron.
7. A roughly even distribution was seen between Antiscion and Contrascion.
8. Insufficient data to form conclusion about this.
9. Some research respondents preferred to use an orb of 2° for conjunctions. This would alter the results, as only exact conjunctions were used.

In conclusion, I wish to encourage others in the astrological community to pursue this research into Antiscia and Contrascia synastry. I discussed with Richard Smoot the possibility of a research article for the ISAR *International Astrologer* if more data can be collected, calculated and analyzed. It is hoped that readers will add this technique to their astrological repertoire, as I believe it holds much value.

Chapter Ten
Social, Cultural and Historical Perspectives

The Transits of Uranus, Neptune and Pluto Through Libra

Over the last 60 years, all three outer planets have had a transit through Libra, the sign of marriage. Uranus, Neptune and Pluto, with orbits of 84, 165 and 248 years, respectively, correspond with evolutionary societal and cultural changes affecting entire generations. What has been the effect of these transits on human relationship?

Neptune was in Libra from 1942 until 1957 and involved an idealization of marriage. During the opening decanate of this transit (0°-10°), which occurred between 1942 and 1947, the first wave of the baby boom was birthed, as hundreds of thousands of returning soldiers got married, finished college on the GI Bill, bought homes with government loan guarantees, and started families.

Within the Aquarian decanate (10°-20°), between 1946-7 and 1951-2, many of these post-war couples, my parents included, moved westward within the USA to seek better communities in which to raise their families. There was migration to California and other western states, as job opportunities there were plentiful.

During the Gemini decanate (20°-30°), from 1951-2 until 1956-7, many of the wives from these post-war marriages began to teach pre-school, kindergarten or grammar school, as the sheer numbers of babies being born created a huge demand for teachers in the marketplace. This development thus led to a gradual eroding of the stay-at-home wife which had marked the early post-war marriages.

As with all things Neptunian, beside the ideal lay an undermining disillusionment. This dimension was perhaps most clearly seen in the rapid post-war development of suburban housing tracts, which were relatively few until the mid to late 1940s. Husbands began commuting to jobs in the downtown areas of cities, thus isolating many wives and mothers in their homes, away from the emotional support circles of the extended family system. Alcoholism and drug dependency became common.

Before the post-war migration from farms into urban areas, and from the eastern U.S. to western states, families shared homes with grandparents and other close relatives or lived closer to them. A breakdown in this social structure ran parallel to the growing idealization of marriage and a nuclear family as the preferred social unit. This began to occur as Neptune squared the natal Pluto in Cancer of this generation.

Astrologers can analyze periods of history in two ways: *a) what occurred during an outer planet's transit through a sign;* and *b) what were the accomplishments or failings of the souls born during that period, seen most clearly at their first or second Saturn returns?* As the first wave of the Neptune in Libra generation turned 29 in 1971-2, the divorce rate began to increase, and continued during that generation's maturation period, with the youngest members reaching Saturn returns in 1986.

Older members of the Neptune in Libra generation are now reaching their second Saturn return at age 59. With a history of dissolved relationships for many in this age group, they have been learning to derive emotional needs outside of marital or committed relationships. Despite satisfying spiritual relationships with other souls on the mystical path, it is clear that there can be no substitute for intimate love and companionship. A fear of facing old age alone without a partner is a real concern, and a second Saturn return has transformed attitudes about commitment.

While Uranus passed through Libra between 1968 and 1975 conjoining the natal Neptunes of this generation, the institution of marriage began to be ridiculed as unnecessary by these young cultural revolutionaries. Born with Uranus in Gemini trine to their Neptunes in Libra, one of their heroines, Joni Mitchell (born Roberta Anderson; 7 November 1943), a musician from that time, could be heard singing *'My Old Man'* from her 1971 *'Blue'* album, with the lyrics *"we don't need no piece of paper from the city hall keeping us tied and true . . . "*

The souls born during the Uranus in Libra period are now between the ages of 29 and 36, and in that critical life passage between the first Saturn return and the subsequent waxing square of the second Saturn cycle. (My hope for them is that they weather marital difficulties, stay together as husband and wife, and lead a societal reawakening about the value of marriage). Many of these individuals have sad memories from childhood of mothers and fathers breaking up.

Other evidence of this generation and their unusual views on marriage is reflected in the openness that they feel toward same-sex unions. Almost unheard of until recent times when homosexuals began coming out of the closet more and more after the Uranus-Neptune conjunction in 1993, legitimizing gay unions became an aspiration during the years of Chiron's transit through Libra between 1995 and 1997. Note that the final egress of Chiron out of Libra on 2 September 1997 occurred with Venus dignified in Libra opposing a retrograde and fallen Saturn.

As if the traditional institution of marriage was not already being challenged enough by the rebellious youth during the late 1960s and early 1970s, Pluto also joined Uranus in the sign of Libra in 1971, remaining there until 1983-84. Intense power struggles between husbands and wives marked this era as rapid societal change now demanded a complete restructuring of spousal roles and expectations. Many marriages did not hold up under the demanding transformational dynamics of that time period and ended in bitter divorces.

By the time of the Saturn-Pluto conjunction in Libra in November 1982, marriage was an exhausted tradition battered by divorce, cynically derided by many, and devolved into a theatre of the absurd with cold and calculating pre-nuptial agreements that betrayed an absolute lack of romantic hopefulness. It is no small coincidence that the three recent Saturn-Pluto oppositions that were occurring as the devastating terrorist attack on the USA took place in September 2001 have produced a secondary effect. Both men and women now place more value on lasting personal relationships and the family unit.

What has been the cumulative outcome of the transits of the three outer planets in Libra? Has the institution of marriage been forever changed? Or has it only gone through an aberration brought on by a self-centered and rebellious generation? It is too early to tell, but there are other astrological indicators that can shed more light on these questions. An examination of the progressed USA horoscope is next.

Progressed Venus and Mars in the USA Sibly Chart

Clues to comprehending change in the social institutions of marriage and family can be found in the progressed national horoscope for a country. America came into existence with its Declaration of Independence on 4 July 1776 at 5:10 PM in Philadelphia, Pennsylvania. The first horoscope for the United States was published in 1787 by the British Freemason and physician, Dr. Ebenezer Sibly (who was acquainted with our Founding Fathers) in his four-volume *New and Complete Illustration of the Occult Sciences*. Although his horoscope used mundane techniques of the day such as the prior cardinal ingress angles for London with planetary positions for July 4th, the local Philadelphia time of 5:10 PM was clear.

The foundation of American democracy is freedom and the United States has been the spiritual Light of the world. The U.S. has a sacred destiny as outlined in the Constitution and Bill of Rights and has been looked up to and emulated by all nations. Jupiter and Saturn, which serve as cultural anchors and core values for any civilization, are exalted in signs of family (Jupiter in Cancer) and marriage (Saturn in Libra) in the USA Sibly chart.

The radical cultural changes that American men and women have gone through over the last 40 years can be understood through an investigation of the USA chart and any sign ingress, aspect or retrogradation involving progressed Venus and Mars. The following bi-wheel chart shows the Sibly horoscope in the inner wheel, and secondary progressions calculated diurnally for 1 November 2004 in the outer wheel (derived ephemeris date for the progressions is 18 February 1777 at 06:02:54 GMT). On this day the USA progressed Sun ingressed into Pisces.

In 1968, as transit Uranus entered Libra, progressed Venus ingressed into her exaltation in Pisces, remaining there for 25 years until the entry into her detriment in Aries in March 1993. During that 25-year era, many countercultural American women of the Pluto in Leo generation sought universal love by living in spiritual ashrams and through spiritual initiation by powerful father-figure gurus of the various religious cults.

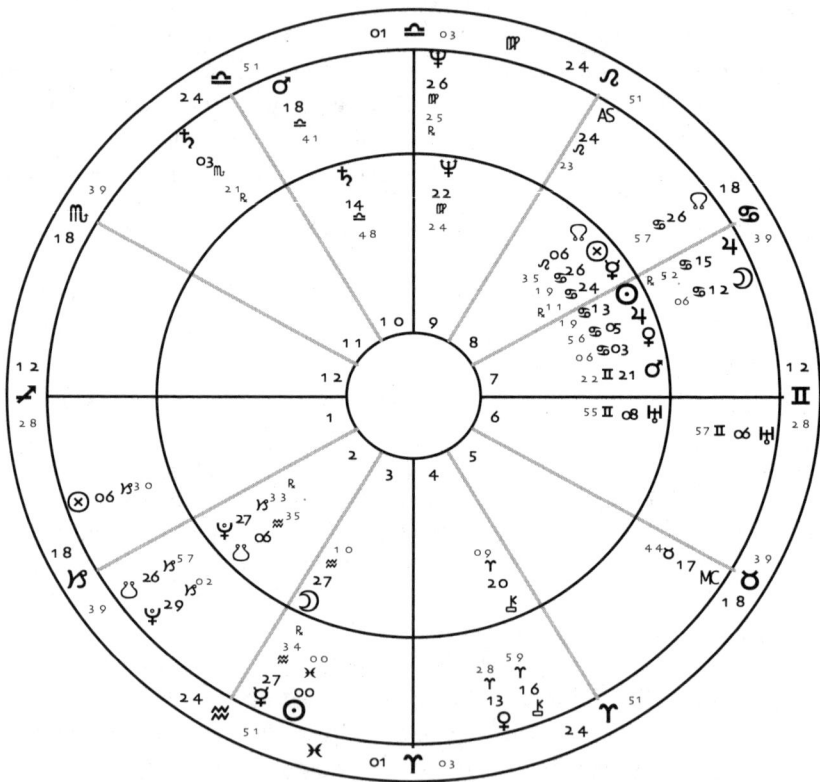

More traditional women seemed to long for perfection through "having it all" in their roles as wives, mothers and career women. Men, too, were influenced by this dream of the ultimate feminine. Whenever there is idealization of a person, place, or institution, there is also the inevitable letdown when the object of the illusion is revealed as it truly is.

During these 25 years of American social change, the progressed Mars was in its detriment, and, more importantly, slowing towards a retrograde station in July of 2006 in the 19th degree of Libra (for the first time in American history). This progressed Mars will remain retrograde for eighty years until its direct station precisely on the powerful cardinal point (00° Libra 01') in March 2086, which is, fascinatingly, also the same year that progressed Venus stations retrograde for the first time in U.S. history.

What has happened to the American male psyche during the last 40 years? Even though progressed Mars ingressed into detriment in Libra in September of 1940, right as the country was about to enter World War II, in recent years, as it has slowed while nearing its progressed station, many American men have been doing some deep soul-searching about their radically changed roles in this society.

It appears as if a regression of the masculine archetype has slowly taken place. Since progressed Mars entered the Aquarius decanate of Libra (10°-20°) in July of 1964, and in which it shall remain until December of 2044 when it opposes the U.S. progressed Sun, a sort of *techno-effeminacy* has besieged middle class American males. Unlike their ancestors in the 19th and early 20th centuries who physically toiled on farms or in factories, U.S. males have since become enslaved by electronics and technology in their work, both Aquarian manifestations.

Additionally, in the following year, on 1 April 1965, the USA experienced a progressed Solar Eclipse at 19° Capricorn 51', which opposed progressed Jupiter. Many of the young American men of the Uranus in Gemini generation over the next several years, dreading their injury or death in combat in Vietnam, broke the law (solar eclipse opposite Jupiter) by dodging the draft, and missed a traditional male initiation into adult masculinity by facing death in war and overcoming fear. Interestingly, this progressed eclipse degree would later be triggered by the Uranus-Neptune conjunction of 2 February 1993 at 19° Capricorn 34', right as the poster boy of draft dodging, William Jefferson Clinton, took office as president.[98]

With the U.S. progressed Venus in her detriment in the masculine sign of Aries since 1993 and approaching an opposition with the progressed Mars in detriment in Libra in May 2009, American culture is now experiencing an unusual gender role-reversal. With competitive and highly educated women working in corporate careers, delaying marriage or choosing not to have children altogether, or while some of their husbands stay home with the babies, how different society has become in the last forty years! Will these trends continue indefinitely?

The degree of progressed Mars' station (18° Libra 42' on 20 July 2006) falls in the Taurus dwadashâmsha of the Aquarius decan of Libra, arguably the weakest sector of the Zodiac for Mars. What will be the upcoming changes to the American male archetype with a national retrograde Mars? Can these be seen beforehand?

A likely scenario is that minority American males (symbolized by retrograde Mars) will continue to assume greater roles in societal, cultural and spiritual leadership. The huge population growth of Latinos in many areas of the USA, along with their admirable manual work ethic, could prove pivotal in shaping national masculine role models during the century ahead of us.

Black men, too, so prominent in sports and entertainment fields in U.S. culture, should also play an increasingly important leadership role in American society. Homosexual men, another symbol of a retrograde Mars in Libra, can be counted on to be a big part of an artistic and cultural renaissance in this country, with a national progressed Sun is in Pisces for 30 years between 2004 and 2034.

It is this author's belief that the cultural conflict between men and women today is drawing nearer to a crucial point in the not-too-distant future when the progressed Venus-Mars opposition takes place on 30 May 2009. Gender-based polarities, which have been escalating over the last few decades, should peak at this time leading to a broader societal awareness for limits on any further role changes for men and women. Hopefully, combative relations between the sexes will improve soon afterwards.

Before reaching that progressed opposition with the stationary Mars, Venus is creating a Cardinal T-Cross in the USA horoscope squaring the Sun and opposing the USA Saturn. This configuration remains in effect until November 2006. As this book goes to press, the USA progressed Moon is about to trigger this T-Cross.

One manifestation of this upcoming progressed Venus-Saturn opposition could regard the health of American children (since Venus rules the Sibly 6th house, and a 4th-10th house opposition highlights families versus careers). The country has a growing epidemic of children with attention deficit disorder (ADD). These children exhibit abnormally aggressive social behavior during the pre-school years. Treatment involves Ritalin or other medications to help calm them down. Therapists are now determining that these children suffer from a condition known as *attachment disorder*, which results from a lack of bonding with the mother since, from infancy, these children grew up in day care centers.

By having to compete with other toddlers for the attention of their caregivers, many of whom do not remain in these low paying jobs for any sustained length of time, these children became behaviorally disturbed simply because they needed their mothers with them, not away at the office while an employed nanny looked after them. As this connection between absent mothers and hyperactive kids is brought to a wider awareness in society during the progressed Venus-Saturn opposition of 2005-06, American mothers who work outside the home will have to reconsider their choices, values and priorities.

If astrologers take into consideration the length of the U.S. progressed stationary Uranus, which turned direct in June 1999 after having been retrograde since 1849, a clearer picture emerges regarding social change in America at the present time. In February 1777, Uranus was in the same degree and minute of its direct station, 06°

Gemini 57', from the 7th of that month until the 19th, a total of twelve days. In secondary progressions, wherein days equal years, this is a total of 12 years (which began with the first term of President Clinton in 1993). In 2005, just after the U.S. progressed Sun ingress into Pisces, the long progressed station of Uranus finishes, and the recent cultural radicalism will surely subside.

As the USA progressed Venus remains in Aries until August 2019, one appreciates how many fearless women have become police chiefs in major U.S. cities, who have served in combat in the Iraq War, or who have been elected to political office in Congress and as governors of different states. When the USA Venus progresses into her dignity in Taurus in 2019, it would be expected that American women will return to more traditional feminine roles and behaviors. With the progressed USA Mars in Libra for 230 years until 2170, American men will continue to evolve into even more polite, charming, literate and artistic souls.

There has been much cultural change over the past 40 years. Flexible life philosophy is required during this era of rapid transformation and one must look above and beyond gender considerations to appreciate the societal mutations from a humanistic perspective. Souls who are alive on the planet now are participating in an evolution toward an Aquarian Age where a true brotherhood of man will come to be, and all will be seen as equal brothers and sisters in the Family of God.

Chiron and Homosexuality

During the 1970's, as Uranus and then Pluto transited through the sign of Libra, it became quite clear to astrologers that the traditional institution of marriage was undergoing a fundamental transformation. Male and female roles were questioned, and society saw the frequency of divorce rising at an alarming rate. Right as Pluto was conjunct the North Node in 15° Libra, the exact middle of the sign of marriage, Chiron was discovered by the astronomer, Charles Kowal, on 1 November 1977.

Retrograde when first detected, at 03° Taurus 08', the heavenly body went through two identity reversals before it became clear exactly what kind of moving object it was. First thought to be a planet, then an asteroid, finally astronomers determined that it was a comet. With a highly elliptical orbit of 50.7 years, when closest to the Sun, Chiron is within the orbit of Saturn. When furthest from the Sun, Chiron can actually be beyond the orbit of Uranus. As such, this comet connects the seen and the unseen solar system. Chiron returns to the birth position between age 49 to 51.

On 10 February 2005, the progressed Moon in the discovery chart of Chiron will conclude its first cycle, and return to a conjunction with the discovery date Moon. This will open new windows for the understanding of Chiron and how it can be interpreted in individual nativities and in relationship analysis.

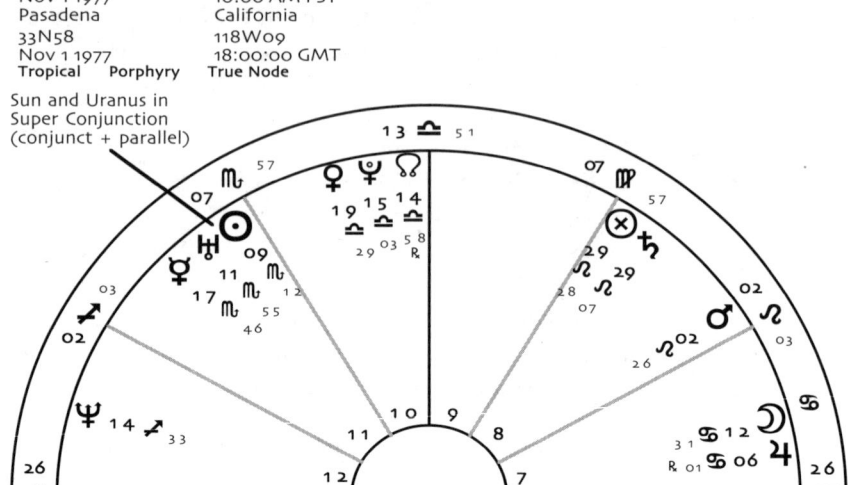

Contemplating the discovery chart for Chiron, first notice that all planets are above the horizon save Chiron, as if he was a lonely and alienated creature from the Underworld. The Galactic Center degree rises, and the Venus-Pluto-North Node conjunction in the marriage sign of Libra is elevated on the Midheaven. The Sun, conjunct the Awakener, is in Mutual Reception with Mars. The Moon and Venus are both in dignity, with Jupiter in exaltation. A direct reference to the Tantric sexual energy of the Kundalini is detected in the IC degree.

What I have found most significant about this chart is that both the Sun/Moon midpoint and the Venus/Mars midpoint are in the exact same degree, Virgo 11. This unusual phenomenon implies that powerful integrative forces designed to align the masculine and feminine principles of humanity, were released at the time of Chiron's discovery. How can astrologers understand this societal evolution?

It has become entirely clear that there have been changing relationship paradigms since 1977—not just in relationships between men and women, but also a rapid increase in visible homosexual relationships. A review of the degree symbols for Virgo 11 will be instructive for understanding this. From the Sabian Symbols in *Lecture~Lessons* by Marc Edmund Jones:

> *A beautiful boy is revealed; he is 'all boy' in every way, but in him lives too the idealization of a wise mother.*

From *The Degrees of the Zodiac Symbolised* by Charubel, Virgo 11:

> *A pyramid of red, very conspicuously situated on a large open plane.*

This denotes one of a strong character; much strength of will, great energy; he seldom fails to accomplish what be takes in hand to do. Strong animal passions; and these, unless well regulated, may occasion some trouble. This person will "never say die".

From Sepharial's translation of *La Volasfera*, Virgo 11:

> *A man's hand, with the index finger pointing upward as if in command.*

It denotes a nature of the most high utility. A flexible nature, capable of fulfilling many and various positions in life; generous, kind disposition; a high order of intelligence; always seeking after the uses of things; ingenious, inventive; one who will succeed in life, and will have many tributes to his intelligence and usefulness. It is a degree of UTILITY.

For any midpoint vector to be fully understood, the astrologer must also meditate on the degree symbols for its far midpoint, which is the opposing degree, Pisces 11:

> *A group of serious-eyed, earnest-faced men are seeking illumination; they are conducted into a massive sanctuary.* (Lecture~Lessons; Marc Jones; 1931)

> *The ascendant enveloped in gloom and blackness.*

This is the degree of death. I think few live, or come to maturity who have this ascendant. If they do, their life will be a misery so far as this world is concerned. I advise such to devote their energies to the spiritual side of their nature. Here they may find comfort, even when walking through the way where the shades of death abound. (Charubel; 1898)

> *A wild horse leaping a barrier.* (Sepharial's translation of *La Volasfera*)

This denotes a man of considerable freedom and energy of nature, one who will be restless under restraint, free and open in expression of his thoughts and feelings and very emphatic in his dealings with others. He will show aspiration and may incline to forensic study. His nature will be adventurous and his actions will be characterized by a supreme contempt for danger and peril. If he should incline to law, literature or ecclesiastical work, be will have distinction. It is a degree of LIBERTY.

In addition to intuitively absorbing the six preceding degree symbols, astrologers may also draw nearer to the essence of Chiron by contemplating three symbols for its discovery degree, Taurus 4. From the Sabian Symbols, Charubel and Sepharial:

> The rainbow's pot of gold is revealed in the midst
> of a shower of sparkling and flashing colors.

> A ram standing alone, looking towards a flock of sheep in the distance.

Denotes one in whom the male principle predominates *excessively*, the female being nearly nil, sympathies towards the opposite sex wanting. If a man he rarely ever marries. If a woman, she ought not to marry.

> A burning brand beneath the paw of a lion, whose rage is against it.

It denotes a person in whose life much sedition will prevail, whose affairs will be marred by his own violence, and whose house will be dismembered through strife, in whom wrath will effect great evils, and whose force will be turned against himself. It is a degree of DISINTEGRATION.

Recalling the Sun and Mars in Mutual Reception in the Chiron discovery chart, I ask the reader to consider their Sabian Aspect Orb from my *Volume II*. Angular separation between Mars and the Sun is 096° 46', which equates to the 7th degree of Cancer. The Sabian Symbol from *Lecture~Lessons* for Cancer 7 is:

> In a fairy glade, in a quiet circle of moonlight,
> two of the little people are executing a fanciful dance.

After pondering these degree symbols and thinking deeply about their relevance, in the courts of celestial reasoning a case may be argued for Chiron as governing homosexuals and the healing dimensions of love between man and woman. Allow me to state the points for this case, disingenuous as it may at first appear.

Point One: By 1977, the institution of marriage was becoming severely challenged, with women in society rising up against domestic violence, an imposition of power and control by husbands, and a financial inequality that made women dependent on men, so that leaving a bad marriage was sure to result in a life of near poverty. By the time that Pluto reached the middle of Libra, this socioeconomic system was crumbling, and a cultural rebalancing of male and female roles was sorely needed.

Enter Chiron. It was sighted on a day and hour when both pairs of masculine and feminine bodies, the Sun and Moon, Mars and Venus, shared the same midpoint. The purpose of Chiron entering public consciousness thus was to bring back the balance between men and women in society. But how would this come about?

Point Two: In the discovery chart, both feminine bodies are in dignity, the Moon in Cancer, and Venus in Libra. These dignities symbolize the goodness of femininity: strong families and marriages. The Sun and Mars, representing men, are in Mutual Reception, and the Sun is conjunct the Awakener, Uranus. Men needed to awaken to a higher plane of masculinity, to ultimately become better at being husbands and fathers. With Mutual Reception between the two masculine bodies, they would need to learn some of this refinement from each other. With the Sun conjunct unorthodox Uranus, straight men would need to learn from gay men.

By 1977, many men in the West had become disciples on various Eastern spiritual paths, the author included. This is seen in the far midpoint of Pisces 11: *A group of serious-eyed, earnest-faced men are seeking illumination; they are conducted into a massive sanctuary.* Through meditation and yoga, Western men learned spiritual practices from the East to raise their consciousness to universal levels. In their attempt to become more spiritually enlightened, men inched closer to the ideal of the Chiron discovery Sun/Moon midpoint, Virgo 11: *A beautiful boy is revealed; he is 'all boy' in every way, but in him lives too the idealization of a wise mother.* In other words, what I call a *Buff Buddha*, a "real" man, yet also gentle and spiritual.

Point Three: Eastern spiritual practice did not remove violence against women by men. In Fairfield, Iowa, for example, home of Maharishi International University since 1974 (now called Maharishi University of Management) where a large number of the town's men practiced TM, there was a higher percentage of domestic violence there than in just about every other city in America.[99] How could this be? Why didn't meditation practice bring out the gentleness and kindness in Fairfield's men?

To understand, we turn to the symbols for Taurus 4, the degree in which Chiron was discovered. *The rainbow's pot of gold is revealed in the midst of a shower of sparkling and flashing colors.* In this symbolism, we can see men who had already turned to drugs in the 1960s, especially LSD and other psychedelics, to expand their consciousness and to rise above societal expectations of masculinity placed on them, such as serving in combat in the Vietnam War, or entering a career to provide security for families. Many men in the 1970s rejected these male ideals.

A burning brand beneath the paw of a lion, whose rage is against it. In the symbol for Taurus 4 from *La Volasfera*, we see an angry animal (the masculine archetype) rage against the stereotype put on him by society for having lived up to cultural norms—the Vietnam Veterans who returned home only to be called criminals and butchers. Branded as bad men for having served in the military, they were shamed by feminist women if they didn't turn away from traditional masculine behaviors.

A ram standing alone, looking towards a flock of sheep in the distance. As Charubel has written, *"Denotes one in whom the male principle predominates excessively, the female being nearly nil, sympathies towards the opposite sex wanting. If a man he rarely ever marries. If a woman, she ought not to marry."* This symbol for Taurus 4, the discovery degree of Chiron, shows how some men and women turned away from one another and entered into same sex relationships, having become less able to relate to each other. In each of the three symbols for Chiron's discovery degree, we can understand the cultural dynamics in place in the late 1970s.

Point Four: In mythology, Chiron was the Immortal Wise King of the Centaurs and was wounded with a poisoned arrow by Hercules. In the symbol for Pisces 11, the far midpoint of the Sun/Moon, we have *A wild horse leaping a barrier.* This refers to the Centaur, half horse and half human, who wished to jump over a barrier and be free—in the 1970s gay men wished to escape from the societal stigma placed on them and explore their animal sexual energy without cultural fences or restraints.

But in mythology, Prometheus had already released the fire from the Underworld. He was a Titan who stole fire from Olympus and gave it to humankind, for which Zeus chained him to a rock and sent an eagle to eat his liver, which grew back daily. Chiron, moved by his intense pain, gave up immortality to relieve the shame, suffering and humiliation of Prometheus. It is my belief that gay men who died from the AIDS epidemic that spread like wildfire shortly after the discovery of Chiron, were the souls who gave their lives to appease the wrath of Zeus which was directed at the men who evaded the draft to avoid death or injury in Vietnam. This resulted in the only war the United States has ever lost, and shamed America.

The far midpoint of the Sun and Moon, representing husband and wife in Chiron's discovery chart, is Pisces 11. Charubel's symbol is: *The ascendant enveloped in gloom and blackness.* He writes, *"This is the degree of death. I think few live, or come to maturity who have this ascendant. If they do, their life will be a misery so far as this world is concerned. I advise such to devote their energies to the spiritual side of their nature. Here they may find comfort, even when walking through the way where the shades of death abound."* It is my belief that this symbolizes the homosexual men who died of AIDS at such a young age, and who stood as surrogates for straight men who had incurred the wrath of Zeus by refusing to serve in the military.

The development of "the spiritual side of their nature" by gay men was the love and compassion they showed to one another while so many were dying. Grief and bereavement counselors served the community and many others tended to the terminally ill in their last days. These kindred souls showed how men could be compassionate in the face of misery and suffering, and they are to be commended.¹⁰⁰

Point Five: In the discovery chart for Chiron, the 14th degree of Aries is found on the IC, the very root, or base of the horoscope. The Sabian Symbol for this degree: *A serpent is circling a man and woman who are very engrossed in each other*. This is a direct reference to Kundalini, the Tantric sexual energy which lies coiled like a serpent at the base of the human spinal column. If awakened, it travels upward, illuminating each chakra until it reaches the third eye, and at that point a soul achieves inner enlightenment. If a disciple is not properly trained and a premature activation of the Kundalini occurs, one can experience insanity or commit suicide.

A degree symbol for Virgo 11, midpoint of the Luminaries, and of Venus and Mars, in the Chiron discovery chart is: *A man's hand, with the index finger pointing upward as if in command*. An Eastern spiritual guru will usually be seen making this gesture, as if he were pointing to God above to make his case. Many men who became disciples of the Eastern gurus of the various cults in the 1970s abdicated their male authority, and then struggled with resentment because of emasculation. This often took the form of domestic violence, or passive-aggressive behaviors.

At the time of Chiron's discovery, therefore, with the Kundalini degree on the IC, intense sexual energy was released into the society and culture. Much of this was due to a once-in-84-year passage of Uranus through Scorpio from 1974 until 1981, which resulted in vast numbers of souls awakening to their sexual selves. It is no coincidence that the Sun is conjunct Uranus in Scorpio at Chiron's discovery.

This release of sexual energy into society is illustrated by the third degree symbol for Virgo 11, from Charubel: *A pyramid of red, very conspicuously situated on a large open plane*. Red is a color of sexual passion, and since 1977 western society has been inundated with open sexuality. This has taken the form of homosexuals asserting themselves more openly in society, after having been in the closet for so many years, and is seen in the graphic sexuality in the media and on the Internet.¹⁰¹

Chiron, therefore, is a symbol for homosexuality, a subculture of men and women whose primary identity is not race, religion or gender, but sexual orientation. This has made many in society very uncomfortable, especially if their own sexuality is repressed. The point is that society at large has, through the influence of gays and lesbians, now brought sexual considerations front and center in social discourse.

Point Six: Why has a Chironic sexual revolution happened? What is its purpose? Chiron orbits between Saturn and Uranus, symbolizing conventional society and non-traditional culture; the relationship between heterosexuals and homosexuals. What can we straight men learn from gay men? How can homosexual women teach heterosexual women? It is the author's belief that damaged relationships between women and men are somehow being healed by gays and lesbians in society. If that which we see around us is created by God, and since 1977 we have seen a visible increase in homosexuality in society, it must therefore be for a spiritual purpose.

The Sabian Symbol for Cancer 7, which symbolizes the angular separation from Mars to the Sun in the Chiron discovery chart, is: *In a fairy glade, in a quiet circle of moonlight, two of the little people are executing a fanciful dance.* This symbol is one of magic and innocent wonder. Fairies and nature spirits can only be seen by children or adults who have open hearts and open minds. The mystical entities of the plant kingdom are made of astral stuff, with only a Light body, and a refined consciousness is required to perceive them. Perhaps the ultimate impact of gay men on heterosexual men is to help them open to the sacred feminine within. It may also be that Lesbians are helping straight women to learn masculine self-assertion.

Chiron is therefore as much about the healing dimensions of love as it is about the sexual revolution that has occurred since its discovery in 1977. With every step toward the Light, humanity must shed the old ways and this brings suffering. On 11 August 1999, there was a Grand Cross Solar Eclipse for the first time since the 14th century. At that time (during the decade of the 1340s) the Black Death swept across Europe, killing one third of its population. Twenty-five million people died in the five years between 1347 and 1352. Now, at the dawn of the 21st century we have a modern Bubonic Plague sweeping across the planet: HIV-AIDS.[102]

The celestial attorney now rests his case for Chiron as the ruler of homosexuality, and for Chiron representing the healing dimensions of love. In practical synastry and composite chart work, however, in what way can astrologers view Chiron? From mythology, we have learned that Chiron took on the shame, humiliation and suffering of Prometheus. From this point of view, in composite charts the house position of Chiron identifies where both parties share a common painful injury. A man and woman, for example, with a 5th house composite Chiron will come together with a shared wound around children. She may never have had a child, yet always wanted one, whereas the man may have had a child that he couldn't be with because of a terminated relationship with the mother. These two souls, then, have an ability to compassionately understand each other's "hole in the soul."

In the house overlays, the Chiron person can help heal the house person's shame, suffering or humiliation. If person A has Chiron in person B's 4th house, for example, person B may have lived alone for a long time, yet had fervently wished for a domestic companion to share life with. Person A, by having Chiron in person B's 4th house, can bring healing simply by living with person B. When conducting a synastry and composite chart consultation, the important spiritual lesson about Chiron that astrologers should discuss is that one must voluntarily and without complaint, step into the suffering of their partner.

The close synastric aspects between Chiron in one nativity and the Luminaries in the second horoscope illustrate which parent had the injurious effect and how a partner can help to heal the memories of that difficult childhood relationship. For example, it is common to see a woman's Chiron in hard aspect with her husband's Sun when she had an especially challenging relationship with her father. In some way, her husband possesses both a similar vibrational pattern as her father, and also patience and love to help her rise above instinctual reactions to male energy which remind her of her father. As in alchemy, the poison likely contains the cure.

Chapter Eleven
Epilogue

While I was writing this book, my mother passed away from a malignant brain tumor. She was just three days shy of her 82nd birthday when she died, and I was with her at her last breath. As a result of her death, I have moved home to care for my father. The emotional and spiritual impact of this loss is still sinking in. It has given me opportunity to contemplate my first, and most important earthly relationship. As she was dying, I thanked her for bringing me into this world.[103]

In this closing chapter, I will discuss how the spiritual purpose of relationship can be understood through the Sun-Venus synodic cycle. I will also share thoughts about soul groups and the astrology of families. Friendship, becoming widowed or divorced, and preparing one's heart for love will also be appraised.

The Sun-Venus Synodic Cycle

When another heavenly body conjoins the Sun, it begins what astrologers call a *synodic cycle*. This cycle lasts until their next conjunction. These cycles are to be distinguished from a *sidereal cycle*, wherein a planet's orbit is measured from 0° Aries to 0° Aries. Each month we see this phenomenon with the New Moon, as the two Luminaries align in the Zodiac. In other planet cycles, orbital lengths are:[104]

Planet	Distance from Sun	Sidereal Period	Synodic Period
Mercury	36 million miles	87.97 days	115.88 days
Venus	67.2 million miles	224.7 days	583.9 days
Earth	92.9 million miles	365.26 days	n/a
Mars	141.5 million miles	687 days	779.9 days
Jupiter	483.3 million miles	11.86 years	399 days
Saturn	886.1 million miles	29.46 years	378 days
Uranus	1,783 million miles	84.02 years	370 days
Neptune	2,797 million miles	164.79 years	367.4 days
Pluto	3,670 million miles	248.4 years	366.7 days

Through the years I have observed that the impact of a personal planet's synodic cycle conjunction to the nativity of a client can be quite far-reaching. For example, if the exact degree of a Sun-Mars conjunction is precisely conjunct a client's Light or Ascendant, I have noticed that these individuals will uniformly have a difficult two-year period, even with no corresponding progressed or transit aspects which would suggest such challenges. One would expect a transit conjunction of Mars to only be felt for a few days. In these cases, however, where the synodic cycle degree is exactly conjunct the chart, its effect will last for the full two years of that cycle.

Similarly, when the degree of a Sun-Mercury or Sun-Venus inferior conjunction falls exactly conjunct the Luminaries or Ascendant in a client's chart, this transit conjunction will have effect for the entire 116-day period in the case of Mercury, or for an entire 19-month cycle in the case of Venus.[105] In *Appendix I*, you will find a table of the Sun-Venus inferior and superior conjunctions from 1900 to 2020.

If the astrologer closely examines the retrograde inferior conjunctions of Venus to the Sun, he will find that Venus cycles form an eight-year pattern. Five complete synodic cycles of Venus, each lasting 584 days, equal almost exactly eight years. Plotting these five conjunctions of retrograde Venus with the Sun onto a Zodiac wheel, one finds a five-pointed star, or pentagram, forming in the heavens. Degrees of the five conjunctions are not always within orb of quintile or biquintile aspect.

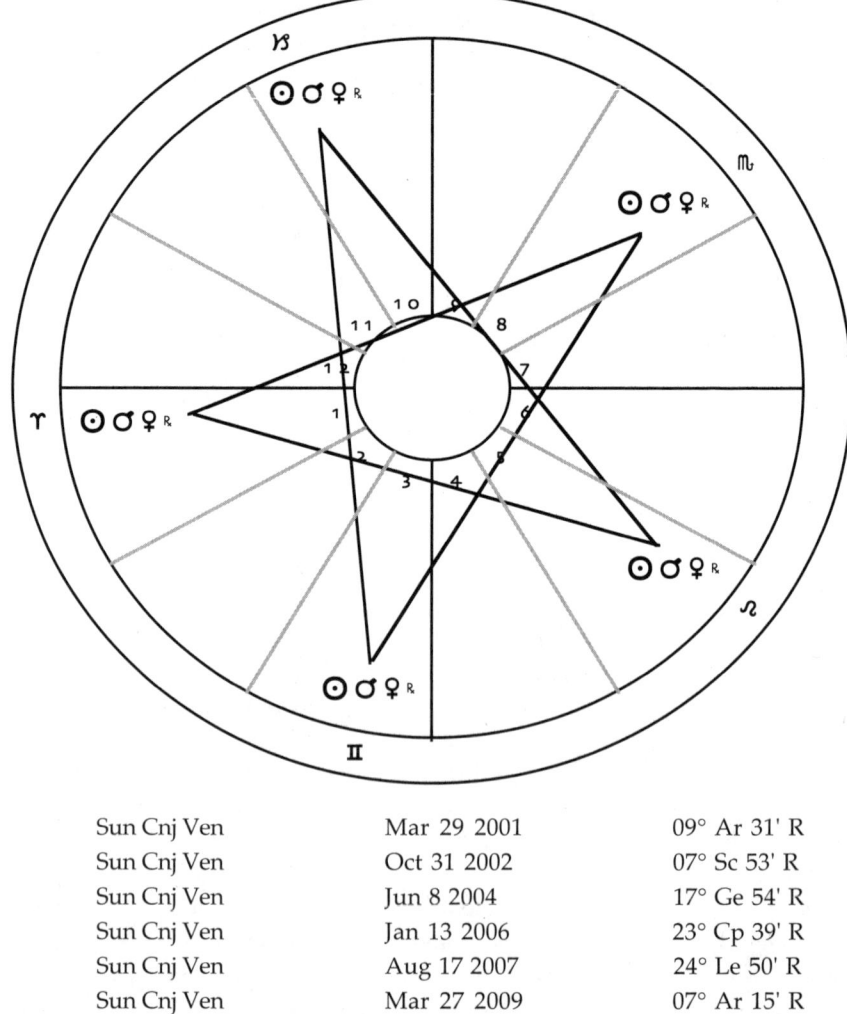

Sun Cnj Ven	Mar 29 2001	09° Ar 31' R
Sun Cnj Ven	Oct 31 2002	07° Sc 53' R
Sun Cnj Ven	Jun 8 2004	17° Ge 54' R
Sun Cnj Ven	Jan 13 2006	23° Cp 39' R
Sun Cnj Ven	Aug 17 2007	24° Le 50' R
Sun Cnj Ven	Mar 27 2009	07° Ar 15' R

The above chartwheel and table of Sun-Venus inferior conjunctions of this decade illustrate how this five-pointed star is inscribed in the heavens during the eight-year Sun-Venus cycle. Astrologers can see how the sixth conjunction in 2009 falls within two degrees of its cycle-opening counterpart of 2001, and that the dates of the two inferior conjunctions are within two days of an exact eight-year cycle.[106]

This is the most important synodic cycle regarding relationships. It is similar to how prenatal solar eclipses shed light on the karma of an individual, especially so when synastry conjunctions to that eclipse degree result in karmic relationships of the most painful, yet life-changing category. The degree of one's prenatal synodic cycle conjunction of retrograde Venus to the Sun is also very sensitive to synastric conjunctions or oppositions with the nativities of important souls in one's life.

For example, in *Appendix I* the reader finds that the degree of the author's prenatal Sun-Venus synodic cycle conjunction is 23° Aries 07', occurring on April 13th of 1953, some seven months prior to his birth. The mother of his elder daughter has natal Neptune in 23° Libra, exactly opposite this degree. This prenatal degree is also the Contrascion, or Equinox Point, of the author's natal Moon.

When the superior conjunction of direct motion Venus with the Sun precedes the birth, the soul is establishing new karmic contacts in personal relationship during the lifetime. If the inferior conjunction of retrograde Venus to the Sun is before the birth, one is completing karma in relationship with souls from past lifetimes. If the secondary progressed Sun-Venus synodic cycle changes from inferior to superior, or superior to inferior during the life, a new era of relational karma will occur.[107]

If the transit Sun-Venus inferior conjunction degree is exactly conjunct one's natal Luminary, planet, angle or nodal axis, the result is a key relationship entering the life. For example, the author had the inferior conjunction of Venus and the Sun of June 1980 fall exactly on his Jupiter in 24° Gemini. His elder daughter was born just four months later on 19 October 1980. She is a most beloved child, every bit a manifestation of the greater benefic, Jupiter, that any father could ever hope for.[108]

The Sun-Venus inferior conjunction that occurred before the birth of the author's younger daughter in September 1997 was in 20° Gemini 03' on 10 June 1996. This is the exact degree of the author's natal Midheaven. An ill-fated relationship with the child's mother was very hard on his career, resulting in an inability to work for two months in 1997 because of a broken heart. The entire length of that Sun-Venus synodic cycle, from June 1996 to January 1998, was the precise bookends in time for the destabilizing of his career due to the relationship. It is of interest that the degree of the new Sun-Venus inferior conjunction of 16 January 1998 was 26° Capricorn 07', conjunct his North Node within 06' of arc.

Astrologers will also find instances where the superior conjunction of Venus and the Sun (where Venus is in direct motion) forms an exact conjunction to the client's chart. This conjunction occurs about halfway through the 19-month synodic cycle, and can result in actions taken to break free from a karmic relationship which no longer is a vehicle for positive growth. The author had this occur in January 1994 when the Sun-Venus superior conjunction fell exactly on his natal North Node in 26° Capricorn. His second marriage to the same wife ended that very month.

Astrologers can help clients, and themselves, to understand the spiritual purpose of their relationships by studying the degree symbols for the Sun-Venus cycle that precedes the birth. If the birth takes place after the superior conjunction but before the inferior conjunction, this lifetime is about establishing new relationships with souls to whom fresh attachment is forming. These relationships have qualities of innocence, lightness and discovery. A sense of foreboding with other souls is rare.

If the birth takes place after the inferior conjunction but before the next superior conjunction, this lifetime is about completing relational karma with souls to whom there has been deep attachment for lifetimes. Upon first meeting the other soul, the individual feels a sense of familiarity immediately followed by an inner knowing that there is karmic work to be done here. A sense of dread, hand-in-hand with feelings of security, can be felt after being in the relationship for only a short time.

I recommend reflecting on the degree symbols for the Sun-Venus conjunctions just prior to birth since key insights into the spiritual purpose of relationships may be divined from them. These are the Sabian Symbols, Charubel, and Sepharial's translation of *La Volasfera*. To illustrate this technique, we turn to our case study to investigate the degree symbolism of their prenatal Sun-Venus conjunctions.[109]

1. Mia Farrow born 9 February 1945.
2. Immediate prenatal Sun-Venus conjunction = Superior (Cancer 6).
3. Prenatal Sun-Venus synodic cycle inferior conjunction degree = Virgo 13.
4. Sabian Symbol for Cancer 6: *It is in the flush of spring, and innumerable wild or game birds are seen feathering their nests.*
5. Sabian Symbol for Virgo 13: *A statesman stands before the mob; his "strong hand" can be seen in a transforming of hysteria into new enthusiasm.*
6. Cancer 6 from Charubel: *A large tract of land mapped out and enclosed with posts and rails, intended for a farm and homestead in the near future.*
7. Virgo 13 from Charubel: *A naked infant, exposed, sleeping alone in an open and dreary place. Around and above that helpless form are beasts and birds of prey. But, by some strange power, unseen, this embodied picture of innocence is protected.*
8. Cancer 6 from *La Volasfera*: *A woman clothed in gaudy apparel, plays with some jewels in her lap.*
9. Virgo 13 from *La Volasfera*: *A broad tract of open fields under the moon's rays; a river winds its way through them.*

Farrow's life now revolves around her thirteen remaining children, some of whom are physically handicapped. Virgo 13 from Charubel is especially poignant, as it reveals the spiritual purpose of her relationships with her children—she is the mother angel of protection for these poor abandoned souls whom she adopted. The strong emphasis on home and family life with her many children is clearly seen in the Sabian Symbol for Cancer 6 and its *feathered nest* symbolism. Her home life on a farm in rural Connecticut is found in Cancer 6 from Charubel, and in Virgo 13 from *La Volasfera*. She has said that her children have given her a "meaningful life."

Mia Farrow
Feb 9 1945   11:27 AM PWT
Santa Monica California
33N50   118W29
Feb 9 1945   18:27:00 GMT
Tropical   Porphyry   True Node

Second Chart   Secondary Progression
Mia Farrow
Nov 4 2004   18:27:00 GMT

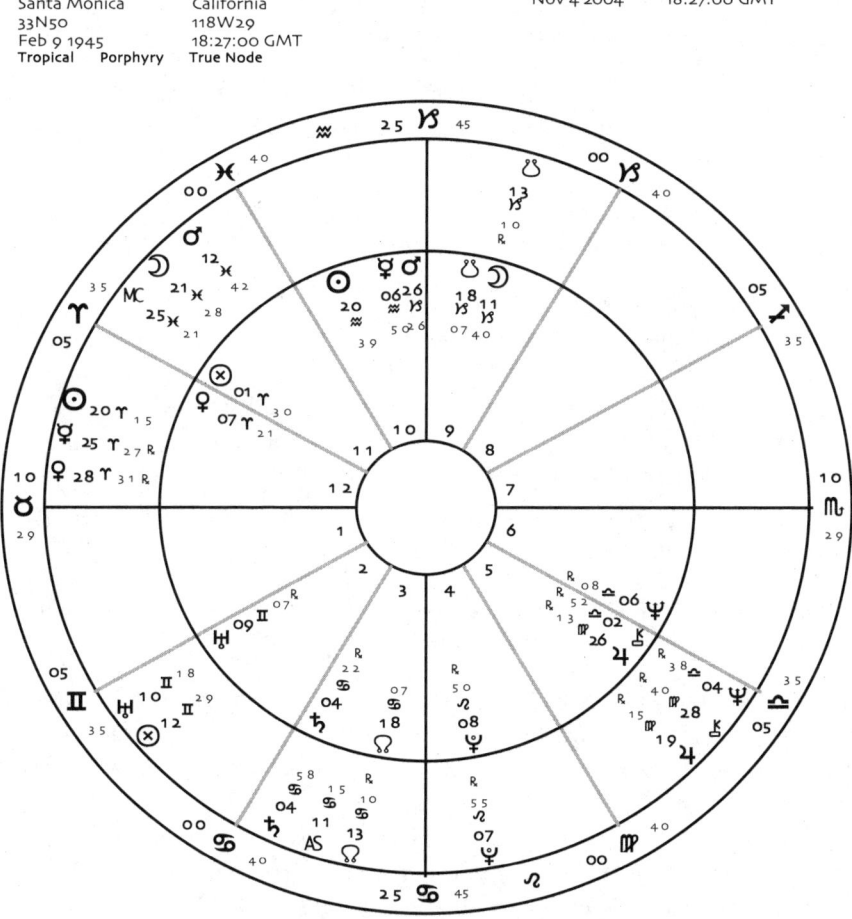

This bi-wheel chart has the nativity of Farrow in the inner wheel, and secondary progressions for the publication date of this book are in the outer wheel. One sees that her progressed retrograde Venus has passed through its heliacal setting and has disappeared into the rays of the Sun, no longer visible as the Evening Star. She will have an inferior conjunction of progressed retrograde Venus to progressed

Sun on 14 January 2010 in the 26th degree of Aries, just before her 65th birthday.

If astrologers see that clients have an upcoming progressed Sun-Venus synodic cycle change, it is quite informative to discuss with them the degree symbol for their arriving inferior or superior conjunction. It can provide a beacon of hope in some cases, when the symbol is of a positive nature; and if the client has had many heartaches in the past, it can regenerate the belief for them to find love again. In the case of Farrow, this astrologer expects more accomplishments and honors for her, as the degree symbols for Aries 26 will attest (Sabian, Charubel, *La Volasfera*):

> *A man is seen, burning to incandescent heat with the wealth of that which he has to give.*

> *The person born with this degree ascending will make a discovery; a new idea will dawn on the world through his agency.*

> *A kingly person, presenting a sceptre to one kneeling.*

Investigating the degree symbolism of Allen's prenatal Sun-Venus conjunction:

1. Woody Allen born 1 December 1935.
2. Prenatal Sun-Venus synodic cycle inferior conjunction degree = Virgo 15.
3. Sabian Symbol for Virgo 15: *A handkerchief, of the finest linen and oldest lace, lies folded near milady's mirror, by a bottle of rare perfume.*
4. Virgo 15 from Charubel: *A man standing, resting lightly on the end of his bow, with his quiver full of arrows on his back.*[110]
5. Virgo 15 from *La Volasfera*: *A beautiful woman nesting two doves upon her breast, one in each hand.*

Sepharial's interpretation of Virgo 15 addresses the caliber of women Allen has known and loved in his life (Louise Lasser, Diane Keaton, Farrow and Soon-Yi):

> *It indicates a person of the most tender and humane instincts, imbued with gentleness, love and devotion; capable of service in the meanest capacity, providing it to be an office of usefulness to others. The native will be remarkable for his womanly tenderness and gentleness. His life will be successful, but on account of his timidity, he will be in danger of being pushed into the background at critical junctures, and will thus lose credit where it will often be due to him. It is a degree of DEVOTION.*

Astute astrologers will have noticed that the age difference of Allen and Farrow is nine years and two months. Each was born after an inferior conjunction of the Sun and retrograde Venus in the middle decan of Virgo. The two conjunctions are the opening and closing arms of the five-pointed pentagram forming in the heavens between their two births. Studying the pattern of an eight-year Sun-Venus synodic cycle, one finds that superior conjunctions occurring four years (half way) into these cycles are also located in the exact area of the Zodiac (e.g., 12° Virgo 24' in September 1939). I have observed that couples who have the prenatal Sun-Venus conjunctions falling in the identical Zodiac area have highly karmic relationships.

Soul Groups and the Astrology of Families

Many clients and students have asked me if astrology can identify other souls as being part of one's "spiritual tribe" or "soul group." Some of these individuals had read the channeled teachings of Saint Germain. Others had read treatises by Alice Bailey and different leading Theosophists regarding the division of Creation into *Soul Groups,* each of which consists of 144,000 *Monads*. References were made to *Oversouls* that have domain over 1/12 of each *Soul Group*. As I researched some of these writings, I found many astrological and Biblical parallels; especially the prominence of the number 12, the key to the division of the Zodiac.

After my lengthy and abstract metaphysical discussions with clients and students about these matters, in practical terms, what they really wanted to know about was one other person whom they loved dearly. Somehow, to them, it was a comfort if an astrologer could point out a powerful synastry connection between the two charts which indicated past life connections belonging to the same "soul group."

For these requests, I research two things: a) synastric conjunctions to the natal IC; and b) synastric conjunctions to the progressed IC at the time of the first meeting. It is my belief that this birthchart angle not only symbolizes the ancestral lineage of an individual soul, with its family bloodlines or racial heritage, but also that the IC is the point of connection to other souls who are part of our "spiritual tribe."

I have observed, when analyzing birthcharts of several members of a family, that not all individuals have synastry contacts to the IC of the other family members. I have found that this is the metaphysical underpinning of why a person feels closer and more connected to certain family members than to others. This is especially so in large families with five or more children. Some are more bonded to the mother, while other children are closer to the father, or a sibling. It does not appear to follow the pattern of birth order, which is a theory put forward by psychologists.

My understanding of this phenomenon is that, esoterically, a soul enters the body at incarnation through the IC. This degree is the most sensitive in the horoscope to a soul contact from past lives that involves others from one's ancestral lineage. As I wrote in Chapter Four, the IC, South Node and Vertex are the most consequential degrees in the nativity for assessing past life connections. Of these three, the IC is the single most important for determining "soul history." Just as it is quite common to find exact conjunctions between the Draconic Zodiac planets of family members with the Tropical charts of their parents or siblings, it is equally common to find exact synastry conjunctions to the IC of the family member we love the deepest.[111]

Many clients have reported to me about non-family members that they felt closer to than any of the souls in their biological family. In these cases, I would invariably find a synastric conjunction to the IC. I also observed that the degree of the IC in one nativity was often exactly conjunct the 12th house cusp in the second chart. In my mind, this is a powerful past life connection between two souls.[112]

In practice, the astrologer will regularly get asked to analyze relationships with family members. This often poses an ethical dilemma, because the client cannot get permission from the other family member to use their birth data in the consultation. What does the astrologer do in these cases? My recommendation is to go back to the chart of the individual client, and by using house rulerships, the astrologer can appraise relations with any of the client's specific relatives by using the nativity.

For the benefit of professional astrologers and advanced students, I have compiled a summary of these family member—house rulership correspondences. As a rule of thumb, the natal houses which contain the malefics, Mars and Saturn, will point to the family members with whom one has the most challenging relationships. The houses containing the benefics, Venus and Jupiter, will signify the relations that one has the happiest and most affectionate relationships with. Rulers of these houses that are in bad aspect with malefics will also show vexed relationships.[113]

Parents & Grandparents
a) Mother/mother-in-law/stepmother of a man = 4th house
b) Mother/mother-in-law/stepmother of a woman = 10th house
c) Father/father-in-law/stepfather of a man = 10th house
d) Father/father-in-law/stepfather of a woman = 4th house
e) Grandmother of a man/grandfather of a woman = 1st house
f) Grandmother of a woman/grandfather of a man = 7th house

Children & Grandchildren
a) First child = 5th house
b) Second child = 7th house
c) Third child = 9th house
d) Fourth child = 11th house
e) Fifth child = 1st house
f) Sixth child = 3rd house
g) Stepchildren = 11th house
h) Adopted/foster child = 5th house
i) Grandchildren = 9th house
j) Great grandchildren = 1st house
k) Grandchildren through stepchildren = 3rd house

Siblings
a) Brother or sister (including half-brother or sister), first = 3rd house
b) Brother or sister (including half-brother or sister), second = 5th house
c) Brother or sister (including half-brother or sister), third = 7th house
d) Brother or sister (including half-brother or sister), fourth = 9th house

e) Brother or sister (including half-brother or sister), fifth = 11th house
f) Brother or sister (including half-brother or sister), sixth = 1st house
g) Brothers or sisters-in-law = 9th house
h) Stepbrothers or stepsisters from stepmother of a man = 8th house
i) Stepbrothers or stepsisters from stepmother of a woman = 2nd house
j) Stepbrothers or stepsisters from stepfather of a man = 2nd house
k) Stepbrothers or stepsisters from stepfather of a woman = 8th house

Relatives

a) Aunts and uncles from the mother's side of a man = 6th house
b) Aunts and uncles from the mother's side of a woman = 12th house
c) Aunts and uncles from the father's side of a man = 12th house
d) Aunts and uncles from the father's side of a woman = 6th house
e) Cousins from the mother's side of a man = 10th house
f) Cousins from the mother's side of a woman = 4th house
g) Cousins from the father's side of a man = 4th house
h) Cousins from the father's side of a woman = 10th house

In some of these house rulerships, the astrologer finds that the Derivative House System has been employed. For example, the 9th house rules one's sister-in-law because it is the 7th (spouse) from the 3rd (brother). Remember to count houses beginning with the house in question to arrive at the relevant derived house. One practical value of using family member house rulerships is that an astrologer can inform the client, by researching what houses the malefics are presently transiting, of which relations are most likely to be problematic and require careful handling.

Friendship

In Chapter One, I wrote about a tripartite concept of love from the Greeks. *Philos* is the form of brotherly or sisterly love that I associated with the sign of Aquarius and the 11th house. When placing a Fixed Cross into the succedent houses, *Philos*, or non-sexual love, is found opposite of *Eros* (sexual love) in the 5th house. In the synastry of friendship, it is very common to find the Luminary of one individual in the 11th house of the other. Dear friends usually also have synastric conjunctions to the Ascendant from the Sun, Venus, or the chart ruler. Synastry trines to Jupiter are prevalent, especially when two friends enjoy traveling extensively together.

While astrologers are consulted in the vast majority of cases about family and intimate relationships, occasionally a client will request a consultation for a relationship analysis with a friend. In my practice, this has usually been when the two were considering going into business together and wanted an assessment of compatibility issues regarding delegation of responsibilities, and communication.

In these synastry analyses, I recommend bringing in Jupiter and Saturn to a greater degree than one would normally pay attention to in personal synastry. Saturn, as the natural ruler of the 11th house, is often overlooked by astrologers as a major component in friendship analysis and as a consideration in business partnership. I have repeatedly found that lasting friendships, such as an old high school buddy who remains a lifelong friend, will have synastric trines to and from Saturn.[114] It is also ideal for business partners to have synastric sextiles or trines to Saturn.

Jupiter, on the other hand, is a primary influence supporting growth. If synastric conjunctions, sextiles or trines to Jupiter exist between friends, a relationship will continue to grow and remain meaningful for many years. I have observed that the transits of Jupiter or Saturn through the natal 11th house, along with the secondary progressed Moon entering the 11th house, are the most crucial times in a person's life for assessing existing friendships. I have repeatedly found that friendships are terminated when Jupiter or Saturn transits the 11th house, if that friend can no longer grow along with the individual having the transit.

When analyzing charts of friends who consider going into business together, I am often asked who should handle the finances or the advertising, and who should manage the office or employees. With these questions, I revert back to the nativities of the two individuals. Natal 3rd house planets are necessary for managing marketing and advertising, while natal 6th house planets are ideal for supervising employees. The one with a benefic in the natal 2nd house gets the recommendation to manage the company finances, and the friend with any 10th house planets gets my suggestion to be the public face of the business. In all cases, I point out synastry squares or oppositions involving Neptune or Pluto, as the former wreaks havoc on communication and understanding, while the latter activates control issues.

The composite chart of friends also provides insight into the primary focus of the relationship. If a 5th house Sun is found, the friendship revolves around children and their activities. If the composite Sun is in the 9th house, the friendship centers around the discussion of politics, or the sharing of spiritual growth experiences. A 1st house Sun between friends in found when outdoor activities are the norm.

When analyzing relationship between friends, astrologers employ the identical techniques, such as synastry, house overlays and the composite chart, that they use when assessing a personal relationship. The only real differences are looking at relational dynamics from a non-sexual perspective, with increased importance given to the synastry aspects involving Jupiter and Saturn.

Widowhood, Divorce and Being Single

It is as if two parallel universes exist side by side in this wonderful Creation in which we live. Never in my life have I experienced this awareness so profoundly as when I transitioned from being in relationship to being alone again. By divorce, or by a relationship with a girlfriend ending, I was catapulted from one sphere of reality into another. A grocery store aisle once walked down hand-in-hand with a lover now felt like a deserted street in the middle of the night, devoid of all life and meaning. Such is the power of the mental and emotional universes within us—they are every bit as real as the physical creation that we inhabit.

In my practice, I have consulted with many clients whose primary concern was if a relationship looked likely for them in the near future. Always wanting to provide hope for my single clients, during my preparation for the consultation, I would search for the "good news" progressions or transits. Seeing a progressed Venus arriving at a conjunction with the natal Sun, or having the client's progressed Ascendant arrive at a trine with the natal Venus, always filled my heart with happiness as I could report hopeful news about love to them.

But as many times as I found hope in the progressions and transits, I also found the dismal aspects, such as a progressed Venus opposing natal Saturn for 19 months, or the arrival of transit Neptune forming five squares to the client's natal Venus. I, as any astrologer must, have to deliver both the good news and the bad. How can astrologers speak truth to their clients, while also providing hope and meaning?

First, it is important to develop a life philosophy wherein there is no shame about life's losses. When the transit South Node conjoins a malefic, it is almost universal for individuals to experience loss. When a progressed Moon ingresses into the 8th house, client's will invariably have painful losses of one sort or another. Divorce is almost as common as marriage in modern Western society, and spouses will one day have to die and leave behind a bereaved widow or widower. This is life.[115]

My role as an astrological counselor is to accurately and objectively communicate to clients the meaning of any current planetary influences under which they labor. Simultaneously, I endeavor to be sympathetic toward any pain or loss that they have recently experienced, and to be joyful for them when happiness blesses their lives. I have observed that transits through the 1st house will usually require the client to become more self-reliant, regardless if in relationship or not. Similarly, a transit of Jupiter or Saturn, or the progressed Moon through the 7th house, will be a chapter of life for the client to learn how to share and appreciate partnership.

When my mother died while I was writing this book, my father lost his wife of 58 years. I have moved home to help care for him, and to try to relieve the suffering of his widowhood during the remaining years of his life. In choosing to do this, as his son, I had to accept the ending of a relationship that I was in. Life will bring us these types of decisions about relationship; sometimes we can have it both ways, other times we must choose between one priority and another. When I made this choice, transit Saturn was about to station on my natal South Node in Cancer. It is simply the right thing for a son to do.

As I wrote in Chapter Five, clients who are widowed, divorced or single will ask quite often about relationship or marriage prospects. In the case of single clients who have not yet married, a transit of the 7th house significator over the Arabic Part of Marriage is about as good as it gets for a prediction of marriage, and most certainly so when backed up by a favorable progressed aspect to Venus or the 7th house ruler. For divorced or widowed clients inquiring about marriage prospects, I recommend using the Derivative House System, wherein the 9th house rules a second marriage, and the 11th house a third marriage (see page 104). A progressed Moon ingress into these houses, combined with a sextile or trine to its ruler from that Moon, is as good as it gets for a prediction of a second or third marriage.

Preparing One's Heart for Love

As I arrive at the conclusion of this book, it is my hope that the techniques written about will be useful to my fellow astrologers in their work with individuals and couples. For the students of astrology who have read this volume, it is my wish for you to begin a professional practice with confidence and conviction. Astrology is unequaled in its ability to analyze relationships, and it was my intention to write a book that detailed most of the existing methods for comparing nativities, and for understanding the derived composite and Davison charts.

Whether a soul is blessed with a loving and faithful partner, or one is enduring the burden of an unhappy marriage for the sake of the children, or if one is single and wishing to know love again, there is one common denominator that unites us all—we can work to further prepare our hearts to be vessels for greater and deeper love. Love is everywhere in this Creation, literally all around us. It can be seen in the tired eyes of an elderly woman who strains to lift her groceries from the shopping cart to the checkout stand, but when a helping hand is offered a light comes into her eyes that reveals the timelessness of the soul. One never knows if one is the only loving human contact that another soul may receive during the course of a day, so in those moments of interaction with another human being, the choice to love is always before us. God bless you, my friend.

Appendix I

These tables were calculated using Solar Fire for Windows, v.5
© 1994-2001 Esoteric Technologies Pty. Ltd.

Sun-Venus Inferior (R) and Superior (D) Conjunctions 1900 to 2020

Sun Cnj Ven	Jul 8 1900	15° Cn 48' R
Sun Cnj Ven	Apr 30 1901	10° Ta 00' D
Sun Cnj Ven	Feb 14 1902	25° Aq 22' R
Sun Cnj Ven	Nov 28 1902	05° Sg 57' D
Sun Cnj Ven	Sep 17 1903	23° Vi 47' R
Sun Cnj Ven	Jul 8 1904	15° Cn 42' D
Sun Cnj Ven	Apr 27 1905	06° Ta 27' R
Sun Cnj Ven	Feb 14 1906	24° Aq 48' D
Sun Cnj Ven	Nov 29 1906	07° Sg 07' R
Sun Cnj Ven	Sep 14 1907	21° Vi 04' D
Sun Cnj Ven	Jul 5 1908	13° Cn 38' R
Sun Cnj Ven	Apr 28 1909	07° Ta 47' D
Sun Cnj Ven	Feb 12 1910	22° Aq 57' R
Sun Cnj Ven	Nov 26 1910	03° Sg 27' D
Sun Cnj Ven	Sep 15 1911	21° Vi 31' R
Sun Cnj Ven	Jul 5 1912	13° Cn 38' D
Sun Cnj Ven	Apr 24 1913	04° Ta 15' R
Sun Cnj Ven	Feb 11 1914	22° Aq 18' D
Sun Cnj Ven	Nov 27 1914	04° Sg 40' R
Sun Cnj Ven	Sep 12 1915	18° Vi 54' D
Sun Cnj Ven	Jul 3 1916	11° Cn 30' R
Sun Cnj Ven	Apr 26 1917	05° Ta 34' D
Sun Cnj Ven	Feb 9 1918	20° Aq 32' R
Sun Cnj Ven	Nov 23 1918	00° Sg 57' D
Sun Cnj Ven	Sep 12 1919	19° Vi 17' R
Sun Cnj Ven	Jul 3 1920	11° Cn 34' D
Sun Cnj Ven	Apr 22 1921	02° Ta 01' R
Sun Cnj Ven	Feb 8 1922	19° Aq 46' D
Sun Cnj Ven	Nov 24 1922	02° Sg 11' R
Sun Cnj Ven	Sep 10 1923	16° Vi 42' D
Sun Cnj Ven	Jul 1 1924	09° Cn 22' R
Sun Cnj Ven	Apr 23 1925	03° Ta 20' D
Sun Cnj Ven	Feb 7 1926	18° Aq 06' R

Sun Cnj Ven	Nov 21 1926	28° Sc 27' D
Sun Cnj Ven	Sep 10 1927	17° Vi 00' R
Sun Cnj Ven	Jul 1 1928	09° Cn 31' D
Sun Cnj Ven	Apr 20 1929	29° Ar 48' R
Sun Cnj Ven	Feb 6 1930	17° Aq 13' D
Sun Cnj Ven	Nov 22 1930	29° Sc 43' R
Sun Cnj Ven	Sep 7 1931	14° Vi 33' D
Sun Cnj Ven	Jun 28 1932	07° Cn 13' R
Sun Cnj Ven	Apr 21 1933	01° Ta 05' D
Sun Cnj Ven	Feb 4 1934	15° Aq 42' R
Sun Cnj Ven	Nov 18 1934	25° Sc 59' D
Sun Cnj Ven	Sep 8 1935	14° Vi 46' R
Sun Cnj Ven	Jun 29 1936	07° Cn 27' D
Sun Cnj Ven	Apr 17 1937	27° Ar 35' R
Sun Cnj Ven	Feb 3 1938	14° Aq 41' D
Sun Cnj Ven	Nov 19 1938	27° Sc 16' R
Sun Cnj Ven	Sep 5 1939	12° Vi 24' D
Sun Cnj Ven	Jun 26 1940	05° Cn 04' R
Sun Cnj Ven	Apr 18 1941	28° Ar 51' D
Sun Cnj Ven	Feb 2 1942	13° Aq 16' R
Sun Cnj Ven	Nov 16 1942	23° Sc 31' D
Sun Cnj Ven	Sep 5 1943	12° Vi 33' R
Sun Cnj Ven	Jun 26 1944	05° Cn 22' D
Sun Cnj Ven	Apr 15 1945	25° Ar 20' R
Sun Cnj Ven	Feb 1 1946	12° Aq 08' D
Sun Cnj Ven	Nov 17 1946	24° Sc 50' R
Sun Cnj Ven	Sep 3 1947	10° Vi 14' D
Sun Cnj Ven	Jun 24 1948	02° Cn 55' R
Sun Cnj Ven	Apr 16 1949	26° Ar 36' D
Sun Cnj Ven	Jan 30 1950	10° Aq 51' R
Sun Cnj Ven	Nov 13 1950	21° Sc 03' D
Sun Cnj Ven	Sep 3 1951	10° Vi 19' R
Sun Cnj Ven	Jun 24 1952	03° Cn 18' D
Sun Cnj Ven	Apr 13 1953	23° Ar 07' R
Sun Cnj Ven	Jan 29 1954	09° Aq 34' D
Sun Cnj Ven	Nov 14 1954	22° Sc 24' R
Sun Cnj Ven	Sep 1 1955	08° Vi 07' D
Sun Cnj Ven	Jun 21 1956	00° Cn 47' R
Sun Cnj Ven	Apr 14 1957	24° Ar 20' D

Sun Cnj Ven	Jan 28 1958	08° Aq 25' R
Sun Cnj Ven	Nov 11 1958	18° Sc 37' D
Sun Cnj Ven	Aug 31 1959	08° Vi 05' R
Sun Cnj Ven	Jun 22 1960	01° Cn 13' D
Sun Cnj Ven	Apr 10 1961	20° Ar 53' R
Sun Cnj Ven	Jan 27 1962	07° Aq 00' D
Sun Cnj Ven	Nov 12 1962	19° Sc 58' R
Sun Cnj Ven	Aug 29 1963	05° Vi 59' D
Sun Cnj Ven	Jun 19 1964	28° Ge 37' R
Sun Cnj Ven	Apr 11 1965	22° Ar 03' D
Sun Cnj Ven	Jan 26 1966	05° Aq 57' R
Sun Cnj Ven	Nov 8 1966	16° Sc 10' D
Sun Cnj Ven	Aug 29 1967	05° Vi 52' R
Sun Cnj Ven	Jun 20 1968	29° Ge 08' D
Sun Cnj Ven	Apr 8 1969	18° Ar 37' R
Sun Cnj Ven	Jan 24 1970	04° Aq 27' D
Sun Cnj Ven	Nov 10 1970	17° Sc 34' R
Sun Cnj Ven	Aug 27 1971	03° Vi 51' D
Sun Cnj Ven	Jun 17 1972	26° Ge 29' R
Sun Cnj Ven	Apr 9 1973	19° Ar 47' D
Sun Cnj Ven	Jan 23 1974	03° Aq 30' R
Sun Cnj Ven	Nov 6 1974	13° Sc 45' D
Sun Cnj Ven	Aug 27 1975	03° Vi 39' R
Sun Cnj Ven	Jun 17 1976	27° Ge 04' D
Sun Cnj Ven	Apr 5 1977	16° Ar 21' R
Sun Cnj Ven	Jan 21 1978	01° Aq 52' D
Sun Cnj Ven	Nov 7 1978	15° Sc 08' R
Sun Cnj Ven	Aug 25 1979	01° Vi 44' D
Sun Cnj Ven	Jun 14 1980	24° Ge 20' R
Sun Cnj Ven	Apr 7 1981	17° Ar 28' D
Sun Cnj Ven	Jan 21 1982	01° Aq 03' R
Sun Cnj Ven	Nov 3 1982	11° Sc 20' D
Sun Cnj Ven	Aug 24 1983	01° Vi 25' R
Sun Cnj Ven	Jun 15 1984	24° Ge 58' D
Sun Cnj Ven	Apr 3 1985	14° Ar 06' R
Sun Cnj Ven	Jan 19 1986	29° Cp 18' D
Sun Cnj Ven	Nov 5 1986	12° Sc 43' R
Sun Cnj Ven	Aug 22 1987	29° Le 37' D
Sun Cnj Ven	Jun 12 1988	22° Ge 12' R

Sun Cnj Ven	Apr 4 1989	15° Ar 09' D
Sun Cnj Ven	Jan 18 1990	28° Cp 35' R
Sun (Cnj Ven	Nov 1 1990	08° Sc 57' D
Sun Cnj Ven	Aug 22 1991	29° Le 14' R
Sun Cnj Ven	Jun 13 1992	22° Ge 53' D
Sun Cnj Ven	Apr 1 1993	11° Ar 49' R
Sun Cnj Ven	Jan 16 1994	26° Cp 44' D
Sun Cnj Ven	Nov 2 1994	10° Sc 18' R
Sun Cnj Ven	Aug 20 1995	27° Le 29' D
Sun Cnj Ven	Jun 10 1996	20° Ge 03' R
Sun Cnj Ven	Apr 2 1997	12° Ar 51' D
Sun Cnj Ven	Jan 16 1998	26° Cp 07' R
Sun Cnj Ven	Oct 29 1998	06° Sc 33' D
Sun Cnj Ven	Aug 20 1999	27° Le 01' R
Sun Cnj Ven	Jun 11 2000	20° Ge 48' D
Sun Cnj Ven	Mar 29 2001	09° Ar 31' R
Sun Cnj Ven	Jan 14 2002	24° Cp 07' D
Sun Cnj Ven	Oct 31 2002	07° Sc 53' R
Sun Cnj Ven	Aug 18 2003	25° Le 23' D
Sun Cnj Ven	Jun 8 2004	17° Ge 54' R
Sun Cnj Ven	Mar 30 2005	10° Ar 31' D
Sun Cnj Ven	Jan 13 2006	23° Cp 39' R
Sun Cnj Ven	Oct 27 2006	04° Sc 11' D
Sun Cnj Ven	Aug 17 2007	24° Le 50' R
Sun Cnj Ven	Jun 8 2008	18° Ge 43' D
Sun Cnj Ven	Mar 27 2009	07° Ar 15' R
Sun Cnj Ven	Jan 11 2010	21° Cp 32' D
Sun Cnj Ven	Oct 28 2010	05° Sc 30' R
Sun Cnj Ven	Aug 16 2011	23° Le 18' D
Sun Cnj Ven	Jun 5 2012	15° Ge 45' R
Sun Cnj Ven	Mar 28 2013	08° Ar 10' D
Sun Cnj Ven	Jan 11 2014	21° Cp 11' R
Sun Cnj Ven	Oct 24 2014	01° Sc 49' D
Sun Cnj Ven	Aug 15 2015	22° Le 38' R
Sun Cnj Ven	Jun 6 2016	16° Ge 36' D
Sun Cnj Ven	Mar 25 2017	04° Ar 56' R
Sun Cnj Ven	Jan 8 2018	18° Cp 58' D
Sun Cnj Ven	Oct 26 2018	03° Sc 06' R
Sun Cnj Ven	Aug 13 2019	21° Le 12' D

Appendix II
Lecture, Class & Workshop Tapes by the Author

UAC 2002 Conference Orlando "**Introduction to Progression Theory**" Lecture $9.95

UAC 2002 Conference Orlando "**Pragmatic Guidance for the Self-Employed Astrologer**" Lecture $9.95

South Florida Astrological Association 2002 "**The Spiritual Dimension of the Ascendant**" Lecture $9.95

ISAR 2000 "**Progression Theory & Transit Triggers**" Lecture $9.95

ISAR 2000 "**Secondary, Tertiary & Minor Progressed Client Counseling**" Lecture $9.95

Astrological Conference of Western Canada 1997 "**The Ascendant**" Lecture $9.95

Astrological Conference of Western Canada 1996 "**Secondary Progressions**" Lecture $9.95

UAC '95 Conference Monterey "**Multiple Levels of the Outer Planets**" Lecture $9.95

Vision '94 Conference San Diego "**Solar System Model of Planetary Consciousness**" Lecture $9.95

Vision '94 Conference San Diego "**Partners Who Activate Our Shadow**" Lecture $9.95

South Florida Astrological Association 2002 "**Mundane Astrology**" Workshop (3 tapes) $16.95
Cardinal ingress charts; Jupiter-Saturn conjunctions; geodetic methods; eclipses; Saros cycles, 9/11

South Florida Astrological Association 2002 "**The Astrology of Relationship**" Workshop (3 tapes) $16.95
How to prepare for a relationship analysis consultation (synastry & composite); case history

Astrological Association of St. Petersburg 2002 "**Multi-Dim. of Progressions**" Workshop (3 tapes) $16.95
Secondary, Tertiary & Minor inter-relationship with natal & transits; lunations; retrogradation; stations

Ast Research Guild of Orlando 2001 "**Partners Who Activate Our Shadow**" Workshop (3 tapes) $16.95
Karmic relationship theory; relationship as transformation; Chiron and healing dimensions of love

Earthwalk School of Astrology 1999 "**Esoteric Astrology**" Workshop (2 tapes) $16.95
Spiritual meanings of the different levels of planetary intelligence revealed to us through their glyphs

Earthwalk School of Astrology 1999 "**Sabian Aspect Orbs**" Workshop (2 tapes) $16.95
Sabian Symbols define angular separation between planets; waxing, waning, applying and separating

Earthwalk School of Astrology 1999 "**Sabian Symbols**" Workshop (2 tapes) $16.95
Origin and history; significant natal degrees; meaningful current progressed degrees

Earthwalk School of Astrology 1999 "**Medical Astrology**" Workshop (2 tapes) $16.95
Constitutional analysis; body-mind connection; planetary weakness; Yods; hard natal aspects

Earthwalk School of Astrology 1998 "**Neptune in Aquarius (1998-2012)**" Workshop (2 tapes) $16.95
Previous Neptune in Aquarius periods (1506-1520, 1670-1684, 1834-1848); plus generational effect

Earthwalk School of Astrology 1998 "**The Ascendant**" Workshop (2 tapes) $16.95
12 versions of each rising sign; chart ruler; prog. ascendant; transits to the ascendant; Sabian symbols

Earthwalk School of Astrology 1998 "**Karmic Astrology**" Workshop (2 tapes) $16.95
Nodes; retrograde planets; twelfth house; interceptions; eclipses; ascendant; the Moon; Saturn; Pluto

Earthwalk School of Astrology 1998 "**Jupiter & Saturn**" Workshop (2 tapes) $16.95
Realms of social and spiritual involvement; by sign, house, aspect, house rulership, transit and prog.

Earthwalk School of Astrology 1998 "**Transforming Loss to Gain**" Workshop (2 tapes) $16.95
Pluto; Scorpio; 8th house; loss, death and renewal in life; emotionally ravaged soul coming back to life

Earthwalk School of Astrology 1998 "**The Lunar Nodes**" Workshop (2 tapes) $16.95
Patterns from past lives; soul purpose; transiting nodes; nodes in synastry and composite charts

Earthwalk School of Astrology 1998 "**Electional Astrology**" Workshop (2 tapes) $16.95
Techniques for picking a wedding date; scheduling medical surgery; starting a business & more

Astrological Conference of Western Canada 1997 "**Astrology & Anger**" Workshop (2 tapes) $16.95
Examines the four patterns of anger as defined by the stressful aspects to Mars, Saturn, Uranus & Pluto

Astrology: A Language of Life • **Complete Set of Eight Two-Hour Beginning Class Tapes $89.95**
Week 1: Elements, Modes & Zodiac Signs • Week 2: Planets • Week 3: Houses • Week 4: Aspects I
Week 5: Aspects II • Week 6: Patterns & Configurations • Week 7: Chart Synthesis • Week 8: Examples

Chart Interpretation Handbook **by Stephen Arroyo** • **Beginning Class Textbook $12.95**

<u>*see next page for ordering instructions*</u>

Intermediate Astrology Class • **Complete Set of Eight Two-Hour Class Tapes $109.95**
Week 1: Retrogrades • Week 2: Transits • Week 3: Progressions • Week 4: Lunar Nodes & Life Purpose
Week 5: Relationship Analysis Techniques • Week 6: Aspects & 360° Cycle Analysis
Week 7: Solar Returns • Week 8: House Rulerships, Interceptions & Dispositors

Class Tapes Include Handouts, Reading Assignments, Written Essays & Recommended Book List

To Order by Mail or Phone:

Add $1.00 postage per lecture; $2.00 per workshop; or $7.50 per class up to maximum $10 postage
Earthwalk School of Astrology PO Box 3435 Santa Monica CA 90408 USA 1.800.778.8490
ewastro@earthlink.net • MasterCard/VISA accepted • e-mail for a postage quotation abroad
California residents please add 8.25% sales tax

Appendix III
Astrology Software Programs

For Windows

Solar Fire 5: The Complete Professional Calculation Program	call for current price
ACS PC Atlas: American & International	call for current price
Order Solar Fire 5 & PC Atlas together—1/2 off of Atlas price	call for current price
Solar Maps: Relocation Interpretations; Eclipse Paths	call for current price
JigSaw 2: Rectification; Research; Family Patterns	call for current price
Kepler 7.0: The Complete Professional Calculation Program	call for current price
Kepler Report Options: Dozens of Report Writers in Many Languages	call for current price

For Macintosh

Io Edition: The Complete Professional Calculation Program	call for current price
Star*Sprite: Time Machine; Research; Event Searching	call for current price
Io Detective: Search Chart Files For Like Criteria (signs, houses, aspects)	call for current price
Io Atlas: American & International Atlas For Macintosh	call for current price
Io Series Interpreters: Io Horoscope Io Forecast	
Io Relationship Io Child	call for current price
Specially Priced Packages: Multiple Programs @ Substantial Savings	call for current price

To Order Programs or Request Catalogues:
call or write
Earthwalk School of Astrology
PO Box 3435
Santa Monica CA 90408 USA
1.800.778.8490
ewastro@earthlink.net

MasterCard/VISA accepted

Appendix IV
Computer Chart Services

Natal Chart + Data Page
Yearly Progressed Hit List
Monthly Transit Search (Sun thru Mars)
90° or 360° Midpoint Sort
Natal/Transit Bi-Wheel
Lunar Return (Standard or Precessed)
Synastry Table (Interchart Aspects)
Composite Chart

Yearly Transit Search (Mars thru Pluto)
Progressed Chart
6-Month Graphic Ephemeris
Natal/Progressed/Transit Tri-Wheel
Solar Return (Standard or Precessed)
End of Life Chart
Davison Time-Space Relationship Chart
Lifetime Secondary Lunations

1 or 2 charts ordered - $5.00 ea. • 3 or more charts ordered - $4.00 ea. + $1.00 postage/order

Lifetime Tertiary Lunations Lifetime Minor Lunations

$10.00 ea. + $1.00 postage

Complete Natal Chart Sabian Aspect Orb Summary
(Includes every angular separation between all planets along with the corresponding Sabian Symbols)

$25.00 + $1.00 postage

Specify Options

House Division System: Placidus   Koch   Equal   Porphyry   Campanus   Natural
Planets/Chiron/Asteroids: Planets Only   Planets & Chiron   Planets, Asteroids & Chiron
Aspect Lines: Ptolemaic Only (Conjunction, Sextile, Square, Trine, Opposition)
Add Quincunxes; Add Semi-Squares; Add Sesquiquadrates; No Aspect Lines (Hub Chart)
Chartwheel Style: American (houses equally sized)   European (houses shown in actual size)
Lunar Nodes: True Node   Mean Node
Other Options: Add Part of Fortune   Add Node Aspects   Add ASC & MC Aspects

To Order Charts:
call or write
Earthwalk School of Astrology
PO Box 3435
Santa Monica CA 90408 USA
1.800.778.8490
ewastro@earthlink.net
MasterCard/VISA accepted

The Sacred Heart of Astrology Correspondence Course

A Two-Year Correspondence Course Designed to Transform
the Student into a Self-Employed Professional Astrologer

Taught by Robert P. Blaschke of Earthwalk School of Astrology

Internationally respected and trusted as a full-time
professional consulting, lecturing & teaching astrologer

Business Skills ~ Personal Support ~ Practical Guidance

As Uranus enters the sign of the Fishes: a Christ-centered approach to astrology.

You can study astrology forever, but an intention to love and serve clients
will transform your heart and make you into a professional astrologer.

Module I - Client Preparation
Lesson I-I: A Christ-centered approach to client work
Lesson I-II: Preparing for your natal consultation
Lesson I-III: Preparing for your progressed & transit consultation
Lesson I-IV: Preparing for your solar return consultation
Lesson I-V: Preparing for your relationship analysis consultation
Lesson I-VI: Preparing for your electional consultation

Module II - Advanced Technique
Lesson II-I: Retrograde planets, the Lunar Nodes & Karmic astrology
Lesson II-II: The Midheaven & Vocational astrology
Lesson II-III: Medical astrology
Lesson II-IV: Esoteric astrology & Sabian Aspect Orbs
Lesson II-V: Multi-Dimensional Progressions
Lesson II-VI: Chart Rectification

Module III - Astrological Self-Employment
Lesson III-I: Creating your multi-faceted astrology business plan
Lesson III-II: Establishing your professional practice
Lesson III-III: Handling income, expenses & taxes
Lesson III-IV: Marketing & advertising
Lesson III-V: Navigating the client relationship
Lesson III-VI: Overcoming occupational hazards & fostering personal growth

Module IV - Establishing Yourself as a Professional
Lesson IV-I: Teaching astrology & local public speaking
Lesson IV-II: Researching & writing astrological articles
Lesson IV-III: Writing your first book
Lesson IV-IV: Starting your publishing company
Lesson IV-V: Joining the lecture circuit & earning income on the road
Lesson IV-VI: Participating in local and national astrological organizations

Four six-month modules ~ Twenty-four lessons in all ~ One taped lesson a month
Self-paced ~ Subsequent lessons are sent only after completion of prior lesson

Tuition: $2,400+
MasterCard or VISA accepted
+10% discount for pre-payment in full.
Tuition payable in four $600 payments; one due at the start of each module.

www.earthwalkastrology.com

Appendix VI
Contacting the Author

To Write the Author

Correspondence may be sent to:

Earthwalk School of Astrology
PO Box 3435
Santa Monica CA 90408 USA

ewastro@earthlink.net

Author Availability for Lectures/Workshops

Mr. Blaschke is available to lecture and teach workshops on Relationship Analysis and many other astrological techniques and topics.

To request lecture/workshop synopses for your local astrological association, conference faculty or symposium, please write the publisher.

Author Availability for Telephone Consultation

Mr. Blaschke is available for personal consultation over the telephone. Relationship analysis appointments can be scheduled with the author. Call 1.800.778.8490 for appointment scheduling.

Bibliography

The Book of Instruction in the Elements of the Art of Astrology
Al-Biruni, (R. Ramsay Wright, translator) • Kessinger Publishing • 2004

Astrology, Psychology & The Four Elements • Stephen Arroyo • CRCS • 1975

Astrology, Karma & Transformation • Stephen Arroyo • CRCS • 1978

Relationships & Life Cycles • Stephen Arroyo • CRCS • 1979

The Rulership Book • Rex E. Bills • Macoy Publishing • 1971

Astrology: A Language of Life; Volume I - Progressions
Robert P. Blaschke • Earthwalk School of Astrology • 1998

Astrology: A Language of Life; Volume II - Sabian Aspect Orbs
Robert P. Blaschke • Earthwalk School of Astrology • 2000

An Encyclopædia of Psychological Astrology • Charles E.O. Carter • L.N. Fowler & Co. • 1924

The Principles of Astrology • Charles E.O. Carter • L.N. Fowler & Co. • 1925

The Zodiac and the Soul • Charles E.O. Carter • L.N. Fowler & Co. • 1928

The Astrological Aspects • Charles E.O. Carter • L.N. Fowler & Co. • 1930

Some Principles of Horoscopic Delineation • Charles E.O. Carter • L.N. Fowler & Co. • 1934

The Degrees of the Zodiac Symbolised • Charubel • L.N. Fowler & Co. • 1898

Synastry: Understanding Human Relations Through Astrology • Ronald Davison • ASI • 1977

Side Lights of Astrology • Thyrza Escobar • Golden Seal Research Headquarters • 1968

Skymates • Jodie & Steven Forrest • Seven Paws Press • 2002

Planets In Composite • Robert Hand • Whitford Press • 1975

Planets In Transit • Robert Hand • Whitford Press • 1976

Horoscope Symbols • Robert Hand • Schiffer Publishing • 1981

Lecture~Lessons • Marc Edmund Jones • Sabian Assembly • 1931

Aion (Collected Works of C.G. Jung Vol. 9; Part 2)
C. G. Jung • Princeton University Press • 1979

The Progressed Horoscope • Alan Leo • L.N. Fowler & Co. Ltd. • 1906

The Astrology of Self-Discovery • Tracy Marks • CRCS • 1985

The Art Of Chart Interpretation • Tracy Marks • CRCS • 1986

The Astrologer's Astronomical Handbook • Jeff Mayo • L.N. Fowler & Co. Ltd. • 1965

The Solar Return Book of Prediction • Raymond A. Merriman • Seek-It Publishing • 1977

Astrology, The Divine Science • Marcia Moore & Mark Douglas • Arcane • 1971

The Astrology of Personality • Dane Rudhyar • Lucis Press • 1936

An Astrological Mandala: The Cycle of Transformations and Its 360 Symbolic Phases
Dane Rudhyar • Random House • 1973

Cycles of Becoming • Alexander Ruperti • CRCS • 1978

The Astrology Of Human Relationships • Frances Sakoian • Harper & Row • 1976

How To Handle Your Human Relations • Lois Haines Sargent • AFA • 1958

Karmic Astrology, Volume I: The Moon's Nodes and Reincarnation
Martin Schulman • Samuel Weiser • 1975

Karmic Astrology, Volume II: Retrogrades & Reincarnation
Martin Schulman • Samuel Weiser • 1977

Karmic Relationships • Martin Schulman • Samuel Weiser • 1984

A New and Complete Illustration of the Occult Sciences • Ebenezer Sibly • London • 1787

Footnotes

[1] Ecclesiastes 12:6
[2] See author's nativity on page vi.
[3] If the final result of these calculations is a negative sum (less than zero), then one must add 360° to the sum of ASC + DSC; and from this subtract the number value of natal Venus.
[4] Geocentric latitude used for the Ascendant of his nativity.
[5] A full-size (8.5" x 11") version of this worksheet can be e-mailed to you as a PDF file. Go to my web site, *www.earthwalkastrology.com*, click the *info link* and send an e-mail request.
[6] From: http://wv.essortment.com/miafarrowbiogr_rxox.htm. Written by Kelly Wittmann; Copyright 2002 by PageWise, Inc.
[7] From: http://www.srfboy.com/james-lucas/html/celebrities/ab/allenw.shtml.
[8] It is taken for granted that signs of the same element are always compatible.
[9] The exception to this, of course, is a conjunction of two planets receiving the same synastry aspect from a third planet in the second chart.
[10] The septile glyph is ✱.
[11] Transit Uranus was conjunct the author's Sun in 1980!
[12] The Clintons also have a Sun-Saturn synastric square exact within 40' of arc.
[13] For this to occur in a composite, the natal aspects must both be either waxing or waning.
[14] In these calculations, the natal positions of both Farrow's and Allen's planets have been converted to 360° values, e.g. her Sun at 20° Aquarius 39' shown as 320° 39'. In the third column, degree values are the lower of the two arcs separating pairs of planets, e.g. the near midpoint, which is always less than 180°. This lesser arc is halved, and then added to, or subtracted from, one of the two natal positions to get the composite position.
[15] Io Relationship; © 2001 Time Cycles Research; Waterford CT.
[16] Bill Clinton 19 Aug 1946 8:51 AM Hope AR; Hillary 26 Oct 1947 8:00 PM Chicago IL.
[17] Paul Newman; 26 January 1925; 6:30 AM EST; Cleveland OH; AA.
Joanne Woodward; 27 February 1930; 4:00 AM; Thomasville GA; AA.
[18] Dr Alfred C. Blaschke; 20 January 1924; 7:32 PM; Bronx NY; B.
Clarine M. Blaschke; 10 September 1922; 3:30 PM; Cleveland OH; AA.
[19] See page 62.
[20] See page 64.
[21] Software programs such as Solar Maps™ for Windows, or Io Cartography™ for Apple, are available for calculating the angular positions of Lights and planets in other locations.
[22] Truly, blood is thicker than water. Perhaps husbands and wives come and go from life to life, whereas family members remain together for seven consecutive incarnations.
[23] See page 49 in Chapter Three.
[24] See page 96.
[25] This was also the discovery degree of Chiron in November 1977.
[26] MEJ = Sabian Symbols; Marc Edmund Jones; *Lecture~Lessons;* 1931.
[27] Even though Farrow has her natal Mars in the same degree as Allen, the minutes of arc are higher, thus, synastric angular separation is one degree greater than the natal.
[28] Or their derivatives, e.g., the 144° biquintile, 154 2/7° triseptile, 160° quadrinovile, etc.
[29] I do not use aspects with Chiron, nor with the angles, in these assessments.
[30] Either the near or far midpoint.
[31] The power of auto-suggestion, certainly an occupational hazard in this profession!
[32] Venus and Neptune have an angular separation of 276° 23', greater than a 6° orb which is customarily used for a planet-to-planet square.
[33] See page 62.
[34] It is also of note that a Grand Conjunction of Jupiter and Saturn at 25° Capricorn landed exactly on Farrow's Midheaven in February 1961. She got the role of Alison MacKenzie on *Peyton Place* shortly thereafter.
[35] In this system, one always begins the house counting from inside the house of relevance, and not from the adjacent house. Thus, the 8th house is the 2nd from the 7th, and so on.
[36] Except when a stationary transit occurs. Stationary Mars in aspect to a natal planet lasts about a month; while stationary Saturn can hold an aspect for up to three months. Rare, but occasionally seen, are progressed stationary Mars aspects, which last over 25 years.
[37] Transit Uranus, unless forming stationary aspects, forms three aspects over 11 months. Secondary progressed Venus, unless stationary, holds a 1° orb aspect for about 19 months.

38 Source: http://pathfinder.com/People/daily/97back/970113.html.
39 Diurnal transits are calculated for the birth GMT on the day of any life event.
40 This derived ephemeris date is 47 days after her birth and corresponds with age 47. It is important to always look at this date in the ephemeris to see if planets are stationary.
41 Farrow's secondary progressed retrograde station of Venus, her chart ruler, occurred on 24 October 1988 at 03° Taurus 35', during the time she was involved with Allen.
42 Farrow's progressed Mercury completed a synastric Cardinal Grand Cross with Allen.
43 For his diurnal calculations, 10:55 PM EST = 03:55 GMT the next day (14 January 1992). The derived ephemeris date for his progressions is 27 January 1936 at 06:46:15 GMT.
44 See page 48.
45 The affair between Allen and Soon-Yi is reputed to have begun in December 1991, just as the secondary progressed composite Moon was exactly square to Neptune.
46 A tertiary progressed composite Sun moves about 13 degrees a year, ± a degree a month.
47 A quotidian progression of the angles in tertiary calculations is commonly used; whereas in secondary progressions, I recommend progressing the MC by Solar Arc in longitude.
48 This is also the degree of Farrow's natal Neptune.
49 The Mars-Pluto opposition is frequently found in the nativities of sexual predators.
50 One often hears of men with Mars in Capricorn, as has Allen, as being *randy old goats*.
51 Interestingly, Jupiter is in the degree of the once-in-650-year solar eclipse with a Grand Cross, which then occurred seven years later in August 1999.
52 In my research, I could not find any news accounts of what time on January 13th the pictures were found; the transits are calculated diurnally for Farrow's time of birth.
53 Davison chart has also been secondary progressed to 13 January 1992 at 23:10:59 GMT.
54 The operation of the quincunx, I have observed, can be seen in individuals who can, as it were, "look around the bend." This aspect, skewed as it is 30° from an opposition, seems to give the ability to see that which is hidden, or obscured from view.
55 1° applying orb, perfection, 1° separating orb.
56 Part of Soul = IC + Moon - Sun. Part of Ancestral Heritage = ASC + Moon - 8th cusp.
57 When there is a progressed New Moon, the Part of Fortune is conjunct the Ascendant.
58 In a progressed solar return, the full year effect lasts until the next progressed birthday.
59 28° Sagittarius is also the cusp of Allen's natal 5th house of love affairs and children.
60 This square echoes the Pluto transit to her Sun which she was experiencing at the time.
61 The author's birthday in 2001 occurred while living in Ashland, Oregon. He subsequently moved to Safety Harbor, Florida, to get married in June 2002. Progression of the Ashland angles to the wedding day of 8 June 2002 advanced the ASC to 19° Scorpio, conjoining the solar return Moon exactly to the degree. The relocated Florida solar return did not.
62 The author hitched a 1700 mile ride from Barstow, California, to St. Louis, Missouri! It is also of note that the 6th (apex of T-Cross) is the 8th from the 11th (loss through a friend). The other boy who stole my girlfriend was a friend I had known since the age of four.
63 I have had a Merchant Services account for many years now and receive payment by MasterCard or VISA for electional work. If the work exceeds my retainer, I ask the client to authorize the additional charge to their credit card *before* I proceed any further.
64 Software programs such as Star*Sprite for the Macintosh, or Solar Spark™ for Windows, can move the planets through time, stopping on the day of the unwanted sign ingress.
65 Dates shown as (W) refer to a Friday, Saturday or Sunday.
66 In any wedding election, a void-of-course Moon is to be avoided (pun intended).
67 I use only the Lights and the five classical planets to determine dispositors.
68 Sabian Symbols are from *Lecture~Lessons* by Marc Edmund Jones; Sabian Assembly; 1931.
69 Often ruling planets of these watery houses, if squared or opposed, act in similar fashion.
70 Secondary, tertiary or minor progressed lunations falling in these *shadow* degrees:

Virgo 10: As if in a moment of vision a man is seen possessed of two heads; both of these look out and beyond the shadows.

Sagittarius 15: The time is at hand to determine whether winter shall end; the groundhog comes forth looking for its shadow.

Pisces 28: Night has seemed light as day, and in the odd shadows of diffused whiteness the fertile fields appear quite alive.

71 Part of Spirit = ASC + Moon - Sun for nocturnal charts (Sun in houses 1-6).
72 See *Horoscope Symbols* by Robert Hand.
73 Many of these clients had the unaspected planet at the midpoint of two others.

[74] Progressed lunation phase ingress occurring with the Moon in 09° 01' to 10° 00' Virgo; or in 14° 01' to 15° 00' Sagittarius; or in 27° 01' to 28° 00' Pisces. The author, while writing this Chapter, experienced a progressed New Moon Solar Eclipse, ending a lunation cycle that had begun in December 1974 with a New Moon in Sagittarius 15. From a relational point of view, it has felt like a thousand miles of bad road (six divorces in thirty years).

[75] It is of interest that the mother has her natal Moon in 27° Aries, filling in a Grand Cross.

[76] She has a separating waxing quincunx; he has an applying waning quincunx.

[77] See her natal chart on page 167.

[78] Ages shown in this, and the subsequent paragraph, are approximate; based on natal orbs.

[79] Especially so if there are no natal Lights or planets in earth.

[80] This vector is also the Saturn/Neptune and Moon/Uranus midpoint, ruling the IC/MC.

[81] In the Northern Hemisphere.

[82] This is also identical to the tilt of the Earth's polar axis.

[83] Composite chart planets at 0° Cardinal are created by synastry Antiscion or Contrascion.

[84] To quickly compute a Mirror Degree, subtract the degrees and minutes from 30° 00'.

[85] Image courtesy of National Human Genome Research Institute (www.genome.gov/11006909).

[86] Images courtesy of www.company7.com/geochron/principles.html and www.biocrs.biomed.brown.edu/Books/Chapters/Ch%208/DH-Paper.html.

[87] Globe image courtesy of www.analemma.com/Pages/Introduction/globe.html.

[88] Vernal Equinox occurs when the ecliptic intersects the equator at the Prime Meridian.

[89] No orb is allowed. The synastry conjunction must perfectly match the Mirror Degree.

[90] Perhaps the reader now feels as if he has been on Mr. Toad's Wild Metaphysical Ride. This sensation is to be expected when traveling to the theoretical dimensions of astrology. It is hoped that the reader finds some value in using these techniques.

[91] They had a legendary synastric Fixed Grand Cross of the Lights, Venus and Uranus.

[92] Conjunct the Contrascion of Diana's Sun.

[93] Exact to the minute of arc.

[94] Conjunct the Contrascion of Diana's Uranus.

[95] The author was married when he began the research for this book. His natal Venus is in the Contrascion of his former wife's Venus (Scorpio 5—Leo 26). The composite Venus is 0° Cardinal (Libra). His first theory was that Mirror Degrees reflected *Twin Souls*. During the marriage, it became clear that the Venus connection had more to do with motives and intentions, as per Mr. Smoot's theory. The author, having had a number of marital failures, married quickly in his last marriage, and did not do enough soul-searching over his motives and intentions for marrying. The desire to be a husband and homeowner was there, to be sure, but those needs or desires are no substitute for true love. It is unclear if the ex-wife had motives and intentions to benefit from the author's astrological stature.

[96] The beautiful cover art for this book (and degree of the author's natal Venus).

[97] Several individuals even wrote with birth data for their beloved pets! The author, with a Moon in Pisces in the 6th house of small pets should have seen this one coming!

[98] A case can be made for the conscientous objectors whose initiation into adult masculinity was to stand up for their beliefs, refusing to participate in a war that they opposed.

[99] Source: http://unstress4less.org/maharishi_effect-mdefect-fairfield.htm.

[100] This is identical to the male bonding experience from injury or death in military combat.

[101] The enormous proliferation of pornography on the Internet is directly attributable to the Uranus in Scorpio generation, born between 1974 and 1981. Called *techno-sluts* for their performance of graphic sexual acts in front of videocams in order to earn money, one is struck by the spiritual emptiness of this generation during their youth. However, as in all things Scorpionic, one must hit bottom before rising to the eagle's height. I predict that this generation, after their Saturn oppositions at age 45, will be a highly spiritual group of souls.

[102] The Grand Cross Solar Eclipse of the 14th century was in Cardinal signs (14 June 1341).

[103] The author had a progressed New Moon Solar Eclipse on 29 July 2004 and less than two weeks later his mother was diagnosed with brain cancer. From the MRI to the surgery to hospice care at home to her death was all less than a month. Uranus stationed on the author's Moon in 2004, and Pluto stationed on his IC as his mother passed away. His progressed chart ruler, Mercury, was square to Mars as he lost his mother. Saturn stationed on his South Node in Cancer as he moved home to care for his father.

[104] Astronomical facts from: *The Astrologer's Astronomical Handbook* by Jeff Mayo. Distance from Sun is mean distance.

[105] Synodic cycles of Mercury and Venus begin with their retrograde inferior conjunction.

[106] This phenomenon occurring in Solar Returns was also written about in Chapter Six.
[107] The Sun-Venus synodic cycle progressing to heliacal rising or setting also brings change.
[108] Jupiter is the author's IC ruler, suggesting that father and daughter have a long history.
[109] See the Bibliography for references to books interpreting the 360 degrees of the Zodiac.
[110] Rather appropriate for a soul with a triple conjunction in Sagittarius.
[111] I have observed Antiscia and Contrascia synastry conjunctions to the IC for this love.
[112] Using Porphyry house system. It trisects each quadrant into three equally-sized houses.
[113] Source: *The Rulership Book* by Rex E. Bills.
[114] These aspects also contribute to the feelings of loyalty inherent in such friendships.
[115] The author's mother passed away with the transit South Node in Scorpio conjunct his natal Saturn within 30' of arc.